DATE DUE

AP 15 '96			
MY 15 '07			
JY 28 '97			
SE 30 '98			
WD 16 '05			

DEMCO 38-296

Mechanics of
Sound Recording

MECHANICS OF SOUND RECORDING

Tony Zaza

PRENTICE HALL
Englewood Cliffs, New Jersey 07632

Library of Congress Cataloging-in-Publication Data

Zaza, Tony [date]
    Mechanics of sound recording / Anthony James Zaza.
      p. cm.
    Includes bibliographical references and index.
    ISBN   0-13-567660-6
    1. Sound—Recording and reproducing.   I. Title.
TK7881.4.Z39 1991   90-45899
  621.389'dc20   CIP

Acquisitions editor: George Kuredjian
Editorial/production supervision: Fred Dahl
Cover design: Karen Salzbach
Prepress buyer: Mary McCartney
Manufacturing buyer: Susan Brunke

This book can be made available to businesses and
organizations at a special discount when ordered in
large quantities. For more information contact:

    Prentice-Hall, Inc.
    Special Sales and Markets
    College Division
    Englewood Cliffs, N.J. 07632

© 1991 by Tony Zaza
A Simon & Schuster Company
Englewood Cliffs, New Jersey 07632

Printed in the United States of America
10 9 8 7 6 5 4 3 2 1

0-13-567660-6

Prentice-Hall International (UK) Limited, *London*
Prentice-Hall of Australia Pty. Limited, *Sydney*
Prentice-Hall Canada Inc., *Toronto*
Prentice-Hall Hispanoamericana, S.A., *Mexico*
Prentice-Hall of India Private Limited, *New Delhi*
Prentice-Hall of Japan, Inc., *Tokyo*
Simon & Schuster Asia Pte. Ltd., *Singapore*
Editora Prentice-Hall do Brasil, Ltda., *Rio de Janeiro*

for **Tatiana**
the sweetest sound

CONTENTS

PREFACE

Sound is significant. It is more than accompaniment. The sound track has a storytelling function. Learning how the audience may be affected by aural imagery requires an understanding of the entire sound recording and playback process. Creative options come often out of technical limitations as well as technical developments. Technology influences aural and musical inspiration. For creative and financial reasons, study of the recording process is well worth the effort.

Mechanics of Sound Recording was conceived as a very practical and systematic guide to the entire sound recording and reproduction process, using the model of motion picture and television production. The text is organized as a series of chapters dealing with a series of ideal engineering "black boxes." Sound data enters each box and leaves it modified in some way. The goal of the text is to give a thorough understanding of the positive and negative effects of this process as it relates to film, video, and audio-visual production. Realization of the limits of the process leads to creative choices of technical options.

Dialogue, music, and sound effects are the basic narrative elements the reader will learn to record, modify, and combine. The voice is considered as one of several important tools of the trade. Charts, graphs, tables, and check-lists clarify matters.

Each chapter discusses one element in the recording/reproduction chain, and it may stand alone as a reference for other communication arts media production processes, such as multi-image audio-visual presentation. The language is nontechnical where possible, save for clearly defined basic definitions. The information is up-to-date and accessible to both professionals and amateurs interested in a thorough overview of process and technique.

The overall perspective of the text is to outline the limitations and primary aspects of each element in the process, while stressing the creative manipulation of sound elements. A necessary link is drawn between technology and creativity. Clarity, fidelity, and communication are the fundamentals goals of the recording/reproduction methodology. The text outlines for the writer/ director/producer how technology affects the storytelling function of the sound track. Microphone placement, for instance, is discussed as an important step in the development of an aesthetic of sound recording. The chapter on budget shows clearly how technology influences creativity where the dollars available influence choices. The playback chapter discusses the ways audience may be influenced by the sound experience.

Significant technical how-to sections deal with wireless microphones, portable recorders, choice of microphones, the narrative function of editing and mixing, and the computer-based production options. Of singular import is the thorough examination of location recording for fiction and nonfiction programs.

TONY ZAZA

Mechanics of
Sound Recording

THE SOUND RECORDING PROCESS

After some historical notes, the "black box analogy" is presented—an approach to sound recording as an "information system" that can be broken down into separate elements for study. Also discussed are the basic requirements, principles, and measurement of sound.

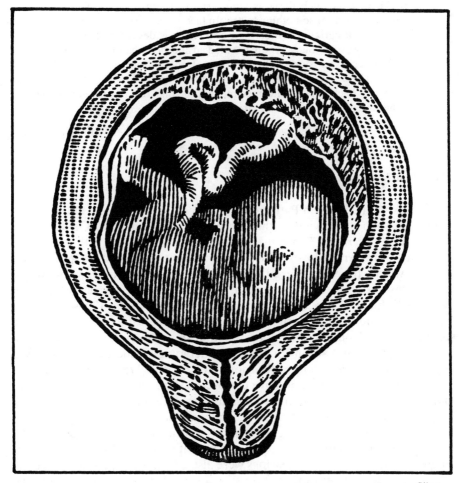

Silence

If there were complete rest and immobility there would be complete silence. And if there were silence and nothing moved, nothing would be heard.

—Attributed to Euclid, *Sectio Canonis*, Introduction

There is no such thing as empty space or empty time. There is always something to hear or something to see. In fact, try as we might to make a silence, we cannot. For certain engineering purposes, it is desirable to have as silent a situation as possible. Such a room is called an anechoic chamber, its walls made of special materials, a room without echoes. I entered one at Harvard University . . . and heard two sounds, one a high and one a low. When I described them to the engineer in charge, he informed me that the high one was my nervous system and the low one was my blood circulation.

—John Cage, *Silence*

Historical Notes

The Greek mathematician Pythagoras (sixth century B.C.) studied the origins of musical sounds, arriving at the concept of pitch. In 1638, Galileo in his *Discourses Concerning Two New Sciences*, associated pitch with vibrational frequency and asserted the existence of "sympathetic vibrations or resonance"; in other words, the vibrations of one body can produce similar vibrations in another distant body. Joseph Sauveur (1653–1716) first suggested the name "acoustics" for the science of sound. Three scientists of the 1700s, Bernouli, D'alembert, and Euler experimented with mathematical techniques for measuring motion. Hooke's 1676 determination *ut tensio sic vis*, regarding the connected stress and strain for bodies undergoing elastic deformation, was applied to sound by Euler and Bernouli in 1744 and 1751, respectively.

Pythagoras is reputed to have discovered, by trial and error, the mathematical ratio of sounds that are consonant with each other. He attached equal weight to strings and judged their consonances by ear. He varied the procedure, doubling and halving the lengths of reeds and using other proportions. He poured cyathi (one pint liquid) into fixed weight vessels and struck them. The lengths and thicknesses of the strings were also examined to provide tests of his measurements. Further work on acoustics was done primarily by theoreticians until the time of Rayleigh who established a synthesis of the experimental and theoretical approach that still applies. Despite the early discoveries of the physicists of antiquity, little has been added to our understanding of the propagation of sound and its perception; we are left with the conclusion that the history of acoustics is a neglected subject.

The Black Box Analogy

Each element of the sound recording process can be considered as part of an overall system of ideal engineering "black boxes." We shall examine the general functions and limitations of each of these boxes, acting on the assumption that problems in the recording process stem from an inability to anticipate the limitations of the system. Inasmuch as the final result will never be as good as the original sound, the goal is therefore to preserve as much of the quality of the original signal as possible. All of the "black boxes" in the process simply alter, modify, or disguise deficiencies in the original recording. (See Figure 1-1.)

An ideal "black box" takes the input signal and performs its function in a *linear* manner. For example, if it is a tape recorder, the output should be exactly

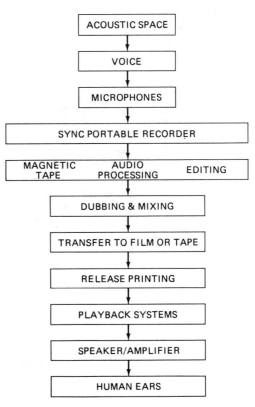

Figure 1-1 Audio flow through a series of black boxes. Every box has some effect on the signal.

the same as the input. A waveform obtained from a microphone should match the acoustic waveform fed into it. An amplifier should amplify the signal by the same amount at every frequency. If you apply this criterion to the visual portion of filmmaking, you might very well feel that the camera and film are very much *nonlinear* black boxes. Sound demands a higher degree of efficiency in each process. (Since automated sound processes involve computer-assisted technology, the processing of sound information may be understood as a simple flow chart. [See Table 1-1.])

The Basic Requirement: Silence

The great paradox of sound recording is that, for communicative purposes, it requires silence. What is silence and how does the audio designer detect it?

Physically, sound is energy in the region of the electromagnetic spectrum whose wavelengths have the capacity to excite the sensation of hearing. Try as we might, we can find neither a space free of it nor a duration that is empty of it. We discover, instead, quiet spaces where quiet means "calm"or very little "movement or activity"; it characterizes a place free of noise. Noise, however,is defined by quite subjective criteria: It is anything you do not wish to hear. Discriminating between silence and noise is a critical sensitivity for the audio designer. In fact, silence is a building block upon which an entire palette of sound coloration must be built. Silence for the technician is simply the absence of noise.

According to philosopher/scientist George Berkeley, our knowledge of anything is merely our sensation of it and the ideas derived from these sensations. Sound is the sensation experienced through the faculty of hearing, and there is, to the trained ear, a marked difference between the silence in an empty ballroom and the silence at midnight on a lonely road.

TABLE 1-1. Information processing.

Input:	Classification—Coding
	Recording–Collecting
Control:	Sorting—Sequencing
	Calculating—Interpreting
Storage:	Summarizing—Compressing
	Memorizing—Feeding back
Function:	Imagination—Manipulation
Output:	Communicating—Transporting
	Numerical
	Alphabetic
	Symbolic
	Chemical
	Electrical
	Biological

Keeping a mental notebook of sound facts through observation is the primary way the audio designer creates an inventory of sense memories for the imagination to reprocess into sound ideas. Although there was nothing in nature to recommend itself as the sound of the engines of the Starship Enterprise, recollections of the *class* of sounds in nature that engines make are the starting point for poetic license.

Observation means *listening*. What are we trying to hear? Generally, we hear only what we want to hear. God has endowed the ear and the psyche with elaborate mechanisms that discriminate against and often filter out unwanted sound. The process is so spectacular and mysterious we often think that "we are hearing things." Attention span plays an important role in sensitivity, but conditioning oneself to hear *all* the noises in a given space is a slow process, often maddening. You have "arrived" as a soundman when you can no longer find a suitably quiet recording space!

It helps to understand how sound propagates, as well as its physical properties—frequency (pitch) and amplitude in relation to duration. Inasmuch as these basic properties help define the nature of a specific sound, being able to spot them enables you to deftly recreate them.

Principles of Sound

Frequency (Pitch)

Frequency is periodic motion or vibration measured in cycles per second (hertz). Any sort of motion—in this case of air particles—that repeats itself in equal intervals of time is *periodic*. If the motion is back and forth over the same path, it is called *vibratory*. A *vibration* is one trip back and forth. The period of the motion T is the time required for one vibration. The frequency of the motion f is the number of vibrations per unit of time and therefore the reciprocal of the period:

$$T = \frac{1}{f}$$

Musical tones are qualified according to pitch, but vibrating bodies generate, besides their fundamental frequency, *overtones* or *harmonics*. These are higher partial tones that define the "timbre" of a sound often referred to as brilliance, edginess, coloration and that give rise to design terms such as the "fullness" and "plasticity" of sound impressions. Recognition of these distinctive traits is part of the craft of the audio designer.

Musical instruments cover a range of 10 octaves. The *spectrum*, that is, the range between the lowest and the highest tone to be heard, stored, reproduced or transmitted is called the *bandwidth*.

Together with the low tone harmonics, the *transients*, or changes in time, define the nature of the sound source or instrument.

Amplitude (Intensity)

Amplitude is displacement from a middle position, measured as sound energy crossing a square meter (decibel). The amplitude of the motion is the maximum displacement from its equilibrium position at any instant. Commonly thought of in terms of "loudness," it is a very relative indication of the magnitude, strength, or dimension of the stimulating agent. For the sound designer the size of an object or space may be aurally created with an understanding of the allusions drawn from amplitude. It is an average rate at which sound energy is transmitted. Ideal propagation of sound energy in waveform exhibits intensity proportional to the square of the sound pressure, but in most recording situations this will not hold true. Direction of the flow must be specified.

Phase (Harmonics)

Phase is the coincidence of wave energies. Two motions may have the same frequency and the same amplitude but differ in phase. A series of frequencies may be multiples of a fundamental frequency produced by the resonances of air in a sound propagation system.

Audible Spectrum

The sound recording process, as a system for conveying information to the listener, relies upon a person's hearing ability. The average accepted range of human hearing is defined as an audible spectrum between 20 and 20,000 Hz, but this is not true for all age groups. Newborn babies are able to sense frequencies between 20 and 20,000 Hz, but a person's upper limit of sensitivity falls by 2,000 Hz with each decade of life. By the age of 30-something we are fortunate to have a range of 200 to 12,000 Hz in the big cities. Some of the loss is due to health and diet, factors that can adversely affect the oxygen content and circulation of the blood. Smoking, for instance, greatly numbs the senses. The quantity of oxygen-bearing hemoglobin in the area of the tympanum and spiral cochlea seems to directly affect the ear's range of sensitivity. Standing in front of speakers in a rock club or riding subways will hasten the process of desensitization. Coupled with an estimated 1-db rise in noise level per year in cities like New York and Chicago, and you have some idea of the limitations the audio designer must overcome.

Since the fundamental tones determine the perceived tone pitch, the overtones and formants determine the typical sound color (timbre) of the instrument, sound source, or voice. Pitch is often thought of as a subjective perception; in fact, perfect pitch is the gift of birth which degenerates in time, thus accounting for discrepancies in perception, likes and dislikes. The designer must take into account the limits of the average audience. (See Figure 1-2.)

Formants arise from resonance formation of sound sources and are marked by tone ranges of high intensity. Older people tend not to discriminate overtones since they hear less of the high end (frequencies between 10,000 and 15,000 Hz). Playback quality in movie theatres has been increasing as surveys

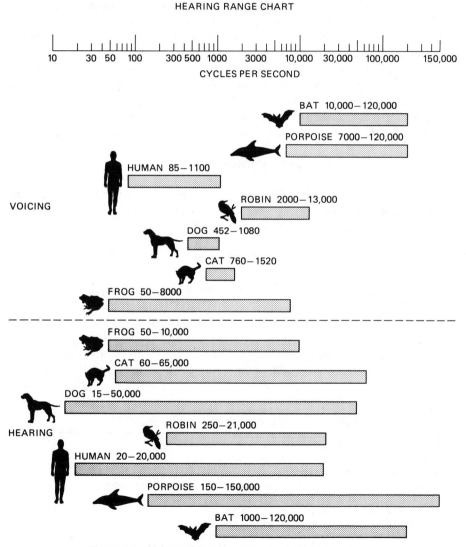

Figure 1-2   Voice and hearing range chart for various fauna.

show audiences are younger. Improved sound quality, unfortunately, may go unperceived by a large population of senior citizens whose audible spectrum has been reduced to 50–9,000 Hz.

Dynamic Range

The span of volume in a musical rendition between fortissimo (high) and pianissimo (very soft) is a qualification of loudness. The perception of loudness is subject to severe conditioning by the environment. Everything would seem loud to Bantu tribespeople when transported to the city. In contradistinction, silence may be deafening to the heavy metal rocker from the city sent to rest in the country. His ears are so used to high sound pressure levels that his ears will seek an immediate balance with lack of pressure.

Trying to record the dynamic range of a sound source for the sake of "reality" is not always possible due to the limits of some microphones to accept the range of pressures. Extremely high sound pressure levels often distort, while excessively low SPLs often are lost in hum and noise. Microphones, we shall see later, are chosen according to their ability to handle certain SPLs.

Sound Pressure Level (SPL)

Sound pressure level (SPL) is measured in decibels (dB). The minimum audible difference in sound level is about 3 dB. (See Table 1-2.) (Differences in intensity in dB are calculated as 10 $\log_{10}$.)

Propagation

Sound travels spherically out from the sound source equally in all directions in free space with a velocity of nearly 330 m/s until reflected, refracted, or absorbed. A sound gets weaker as distance from the source increases. The intensity of the sound is inversely proportional to the square of the distance from the source (inverse square law). The rule holds true in enclosed and open spaces close to the source. In reality, sound waves tend to reflect, mix, or

TABLE 1-2. Rules of thumb for sound pressure levels.

- A tenfold increase in intensity (Power) = 10 dB.
- Doubling the audible intensity is equivalent to a rise of 3 dB.
- The speed of sound in air = 770 mi/hr.
- The velocity of sound in the open is influenced by temperature more than pressure.
  At 21°C, speed is 344 m/s (1,100 ft/s).
  At 50°C, speed is 360 m/s (42 ft/s faster).
- 13,000 Hz = 1 in, and 30 Hz = 36 ft.

superimpose, that is, cancel each other out by arriving in phase with another wave of equal amplitude. In addition to the fact that sound travels faster in warm air, wind also affects the direction of travel of sound, refracting waves up or down.

Reverberation

In an enclosed space, sound waves are repeatedly reflected back and forth by the boundary planes. This reflection, called *reverberation*, may be measured in time from the source to the listener. In the immediate proximity of the sound source, the direct sound emitted is more intense than the sound reflected back by the walls and corners. As we get farther away from the source, intermixing of the direct and reflected sounds takes place, and the space appears uniformly filled with sound. The point at which the direct sound and reverberation are in balance is called the *Hallradius*. A microphone placed within the radius emphasizes the direct waves; when placed outside the radius, it exhibits greater intensities for reflected waves.

The size of the radius may be controlled by altering the size of the space, the surfaces of the space, the contents of the room, the kind of microphone used, and the angle at which it is placed.

Reflection

If the sound wavelength is smaller than the dimensions of a given surface, *reflection* of the waveform takes place. The angle of incidence equals the angle of reflection.

Refraction

Sound speed is proportional to the density of the propagating medium. If a wave moves from one medium to another of differing density (such as from air to water), the wave may travel slower or bend in a new direction.

Diffraction

Sound travels infinitely unless impeded by an obstacle. Waves longer than the size of the obstacle tend to react as if unimpeded, but smaller waveforms (higher frequencies) will be diffracted or reflected back. Lower frequencies cause most of the problems of noise leakage, for instance, in recording, since they are larger than most reflecting objects. Nevertheless, almost any object—the microphone, a camera, actors—is likely to bounce back specific frequencies smaller than their width. This accounts for the loss of high frequency response.

Measuring Sound

Sound is light energy moving at a slower speed than that of light. All vibrating matter produces sound. Its movement is charted as a path of compressions and refractions of air or another medium. The air itself does not move, only the disturbance of the air. This disturbance is what creates the sensation of sound.

The disturbance—sound pressure—is measured in *decibels* (dB). The maximum possible sound pressure results from 100% modulation of the atmosphere; this quantity is 194 dB.

When two sound waves have the same interval in a cycle—that is, when they are moving in the same direction with the same relative displacement—they are said to be *in phase*. In this case, the pressures are the same, the resulting pressure will be twice that of each wave, and the sound pressure level will increase 6 dB. A loudspeaker near a person's ear reproduces the impinging noise with a 180° time lag, thus generating about the listener a zone of silence.

The Decibel

To state how loud a sound is in absolute terms, you refer to the pressure of the atmosphere at the seashore, expressed in dynes per square centimeter. Atmospheric pressure at the seashore is 10^6 microbars, or 14.70 lb/in^2. The sound pressure at the *threshold* of hearing, the faintest sound that can excite the eardrum in healthy humans is 0.0002 microbars or dynes/cm^2.

The wide range of amplitudes makes expressing the power in absolute terms unwieldy.

A solution is to express the power of a sound in terms of its being "so many times" louder than a standard. This standard is 0.0002 dynes/cm^2, the pressure of one atmosphere at the surface.

In logarithmic notation, 100 can be expressed as 10, 100,000 as 10_2. The log to the base 10 of 100 is 2. Consider the following formula:

$$\text{A Bel} = \log \frac{e}{e_{st}} = \frac{\text{Energy}}{\text{Reference energy}}$$

$$\text{A Decibel} = 10 \log \frac{e}{e}$$

But power is proportional to energy squared:

$$\text{Decibel} = 20 \log \frac{P}{P_{st}} = \frac{\text{Power}}{0.0002 \text{ dynes/cm}^2}$$

The decibel is therefore an indication of *relative* power. "Decibel" really means that the power level of a signal is related to the power 0.0002 dynes/cm^2. Whenever a number is given, it means "so much louder than another sound." (See Table 1-3.)

TABLE 1-3. Sound level chart of noise levels in dB for various sources.

Sound	Decibel Level (dB)	Number of Times the Threshold
Faintest sound	−5	
Threshold of hearing	0	1
Normal breathing	10	10*
Whisper	20	100
Studio background	25	
Empty theatre	30	1,000
Your home	50	100,000
Department store	60	1,000,000
Speech	70	10,000,000
Factory	75	
Subway	100	10,000,000,000
Jet engine	120	1,000,000,000,000
Close machine gun	130	10,000,000,000,000
Threshold of pain	140	

* Times as loud as 0 dB.

ACOUSTIC SPACE AND ITS CONTENTS

How do you determine the quality of a recording space? An explanation of how sound propagates precedes a practical description of the basic laws of acoustic engineering. The "naturalness" of sound is discussed in terms of how viewers can be influenced by sound (psychoacoustical factors). Some ideas are shared about planning and modifying a space for better recording—reverberation time, sources of noise, a troubleshooting inventory.

Acoustic space.

Previously sound had emanated from a single point of view in accordance with the bias of visual culture with its fixed point of view.

—Marshall McLuhan

Now they [the mathematicians] observed in the first place that there cannot be sound without the striking of bodies against one another . . .

—Archytas, from Porphyrius (third century A.D.) in his commentary on Ptolemy's *Harmonics* quoting a no longer extant work

Propagation of Sound

Most theoreticians already agreed that at least some activity of the air was involved when Aristotle first emphasized the actual motion of the air as it applies to sound propagation. Atomic theory revivalists von Guericke (1602–1686) and Gassendi (1592–1655) ascribe sound to the emission of fine, invisible particles. Kircher, in 1650, also declared that air was not necessary for sound, although his bell-in-vacuum experiment must have been bogus. For in 1660, Robert Boyle repeated the experiment and discovered that sound was indeed dependent on a *medium* for its transmission.

In 1635, Gassendi measured sound at 1,473 Paris feet (32.48 cm) per second, noting that velocity was independent of pitch. Borelli and Viviani, in 1656, determined that wind was a factor and got 350 m/s. In 1740, Branconi showed that temperature was also a factor. The Academy of Sciences in Paris made the first accurate measurement in 1738 for the speed of sound at 0°C, arriving at a quantity of 332 m/s.

Newton had begun to develop a "wave" theory of sound in 1687 stating that air moved in accordance with his law of the oscillating pendulum. Later, Laplace discovered that, in view of the rapidity of motion, compressions and rarefactions follow the *adiabetic* law whereby changes in temperature lead to higher values of elasticity, equaling the product of the pressure and the ratio *y* of the two specific heats of the air.

Our modern assessment defines *sound* as wave movement of the air audible to the human ear! For the experience to occur, there must be an acoustic medium. Will a bell placed in a vacuum ring? No. Airborne sound propagates from the sound source spherically with a velocity of nearly 330 m/s. The ratio of this sound pressure as a function of distance can be represented as 1/Distance as pressure falls. This is valid for propagation without reflection in a free space.

In an enclosure, such factors as *eigentone* (the resonance caused by the presence of parallel walls), *reverberation* (the echo caused by the reflection of sound out of phase from the original signal), as well as others contribute to the degeneration of the pure propagation.

An ideal space would have a characteristic close to outdoors, or a so-called *dead acoustic*, with little or no reflection of sound, little or no loss introduced by the recording system. The ideal room appears to be in the configuration of a pyramid; no two sides face each other or reflect to each other. (See Figure 2-1.)

In recording, therefore, the signal that reaches the *transducer*, or energy-converting system (microphone), is composed of direct and indirect sound from many sources. Trying to reduce or eliminate this indirect signal is the work of the sound recordist. Controlling the ratio of the wanted to unwanted signals (signal to noise ratio) accomplishes this.

Basic Acoustic Properties

Sound is vibration in gaseous, liquid, or solid medium, manifesting itself as pressure fluctuations in the medium. It is characterized by the instantaneous amplitudes of the pressure fluctuations (see Figure 2-2), as well as by their frequencies and phase relationships.

Here are some rules of thumb:

- At any point, the sound pressure is the sum of all pressures due to all waves passing through that point.
- Sound intensity is a measure of energy passing through a unit area per second.
- The power of a sound source is the total energy radiated in all directions.
- Normal speaking level 18 in directly in front of the mouth is 76 dB.

Inverse Square Law

If sound radiation is taking place in a free field (outdoors) with no reflections, we can consider the mouth as an ideal sound source radiating sound in all directions. The intensity I of this signal at a distance r is given by the sound power W emitted by the source, divided by the surface area of the sphere with radius r:

$$I = \frac{W}{r^2}$$

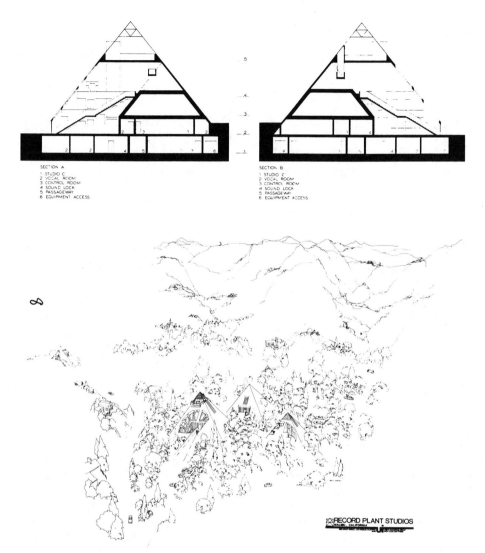

SECTION A
1 STUDIO C
2 VOCAL ROOM
3 CONTROL ROOM
4 SOUND LOCK
5 PASSAGEWAY
6 EQUIPMENT ACCESS

SECTION B
1 STUDIO C
2 VOCAL ROOM
3 CONTROL ROOM
4 SOUND LOCK
5 PASSAGEWAY
6 EQUIPMENT ACCESS

RECORD PLANT STUDIOS
MALIBU, CALIFORNIA

Figure 2-1 Interior (top) and exterior of Record Plant Studios: a pyramid solution to the problem of ideal recording space. No two surfaces reflect toward each other: variable acoustics, maximum room. (Courtesy Urban Innovations Group.)

At a sufficient distance r from the source (in the far field), the intensity I is also proportional to the square of the sound pressure p, whereby p is proportional to I/r. This relationship is called the *inverse square law*. This law can be applied by means of two guidelines:

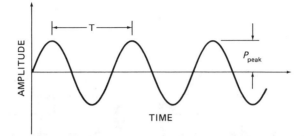

Figure 2-2   Sinusoid, the most simple pure tone.

- Sound decreases by 6 dB for every *doubling* of the distance to the microphone.
- Sound increases by 6 dB for every *halving* of the distance to the microphone.

(At normal distances, the losses due to absorption by the air itself plays a negligible role.) If the observer moves twice the distance away from the source, the sound level will decrease by ¼ of the original level. This means a decrease of 6 dB. Outdoors, there is little problem of sound arriving at the microphone.

Free Field and Reverberant Field

A space in which the boundaries exert a negligible influence on the sound field is deemed a *free field*. It lacks any physical object that might disturb, reflect, or diffract the waveform. This condition can be found outdoors above the ground and indoors where walls are lined with sound-absorbing materials. The inverse square obtains in the free field: For every doubling of the distance from the sound source, the sound pressure level drops 6 dB.

A *reverberant*, or *diffuse*, field is a space in which reflection causes uniform sound distribution over the entire space. (See Figure 2-3.) Hard, reflective surfaces placed nonparallel to each other prevent standing waves and preserve homogeneity of the diffuse field. Your living room is a hybrid of these two extremes—free and diffuse—and is therefore a *semireverberant* room.

Frequency Distribution of Sound

All sound signals are essentially a combination of sine waves constituting a *signal frequency spectrum*. A *pure tone* (a single sine wave) is represented as a line in this spectrum while any periodic or quasiperiodic signal is given by a number of discrete sine waves in the frequency spectrum. (See Figure 2-4.)

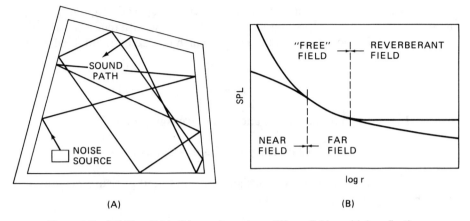

Figure 2-3 (A) Free field; (b) reverberant, or diffuse, field; multiple reflections.

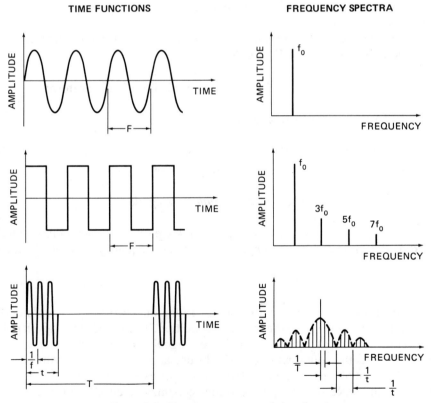

Figure 2-4 Frequency spectra and time functions.

Noise signals are defined by infinitely closely spaced frequency components. The spectrum is represented as *spectral density*, with the commonly used quantity of PSD (power spectral density), which can be mathematically signified as:

$$W(f) = B \overset{\text{lim}}{\to} 0 \qquad T \overset{\text{lim}}{\to} \infty \frac{1}{BT} \int_0^T P_B^2(t, f)\, dt$$

where B is the signal bandwidth and T the averaging time.

Sound Pressure Level and Magnitude

The most commonly used designation for sound pressure magnitude is *root mean square* (RMS), defined as:

$$P_{RMS} = \sqrt{\frac{1}{T} \int_0^T Tp^2(t)\, dt}$$

The sound pressure level in decibel (dB) is defined as 20 times the logarithm of the ratio of the sound magnitude P_{RMS} to the reference magnitude $P_{0\,RMS}$, which equals 20 P.

The relationship between these magnitude quantities is often used to characterize a signal (see Figure 2-5):

$$\text{Form factor } F_1 = \frac{P_{RMS}}{P_{av}} = 1.11 \text{ for pure sinusoidal waveforms}$$

Keep the following relationships in mind:

- 1 atmosphere = 1,103 bar = 760 mm Hg = 1,013 × 10⁵ Pa = 194 dB
- 1 Pa = 1 N/m² = 10 μbar = 10 dynes/cm² = 94 dB

The Speed of Sound Propagation

Propagation occurs at speed c, the characteristic for the medium, which thereby determines the wavelength λ for a given frequency from the formula:

$$\lambda = cT \frac{-c}{f}$$

Indoors. The problem of sound radiation becomes trickier indoors because we no longer have the free field condition. The sound at any given point is a combination of direct and reflected signals. If the room is a normal environment, the sound will be fairly diffuse at any particular position. This ideal situation of random reflected sound comprises what we generally perceive as "natural" since it corresponds to the recognizable aural sense memory of similar spaces.

When this random state is not attainable, a condition known as *standing*

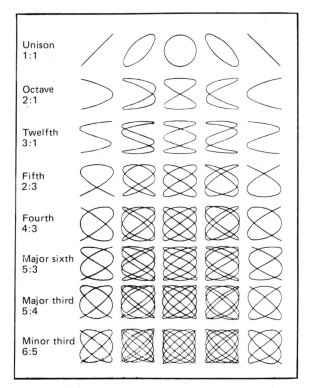

Figure 2-5   Pure sine waves in relation to musical chords.

waves occurs. In this state some frequency component in the signal has the same wavelength as a dimension of the room (or a multiple of it). The entire room can then act as a resonator, producing a sense that something is just not "right."

Large enclosures.   The amount of sound reflected from the walls of an enclosure is a direct function of the absorption of the walls' surface material. One way of describing this quality of absorption is to use the acoustical term *absorption coefficient*, which is merely the ratio of energy absorbed to the incident energy. It ranges from 0.01 for marble to 0.99 for fibreglass wedges found in an anechoic chamber. (See Table 2-1.) To arrive at the total absorption of the room, multiply the surface area of each of its surfaces by the relevant coefficient and add them all together.

The *reverberant time* of the room can be calculated as follows:

$$\text{Reverberant time} = \frac{\text{Volume of room}}{s_1 + s_2 + s_3 + s_4}$$

where S = a surface area in the room.

There is much debate over appropriate reverberation times for particular

TABLE 2-1. A selection of various absorption coefficients.

Material or Product	Frequency (Hz)								
	62	88	125	250	500	1k	2k	4k	8k
Brick wall	.02	—	.02	.02	.03	.04	.05	.07	.10
Celotex building board (¹/₂ in unpainted)	.04	—	.06	.10	.15	.21	.26	.26	.29
¹/₈ in hardboard on 1 in battens	.30	—	.32	.43	.12	.07	.07	.11	.18
¹/₂ in wood panelling on 1 in battens	.33	—	.31	.33	.14	.10	.10	.12	.15
Average woolcord carpet with underfelt	.02	—	.04	.13	.36	.60	.69	.62	.52
Average haircord carpet with underfelt	.05	—	.13	.17	.24	.29	.30	.30	.37
Wilton carpet with underfelt	.04	—	.08	.22	.51	.64	.69	.71	.70
Curtains: Velour draped	.05	—	.06	.31	.44	.80	.75	.65	.60
Lightweight over 2 in air space	.00	—	.04	.10	.20	.50	.60	.50	.40
Heavyweight over 2 in air space	.00	—	.06	.16	.30	.55	.65	.65	.65
Full Concert Hall audience with Orchestra	.39	—	.54	.66	.78	.85	.83	.75	.71
Membrane Absorbers: (typical figures) High-density mineral wool backing 12 in air space	.81	1.15	.87	.47	.30	.15	.15	.15	.15
Porous Absorbers: 0.5% perforated front 6 in air space	.60	.95	.77	.52	.38	.22	.18	.17	.15
25.0% perforated front 6 in air space	.40	.80	1.10	1.05	1.00	.98	.95	.80	.60
Wire-mesh front 6 in air space	.40	.80	1.10	1.05	1.00	.98	.98	.97	.95
Typical "Acoustic" Tile on 1 in air space	.10	—	.14	.52	.52	.61	.61	.65	.65

Note: The above results are from single samples of materials and absorbers, and on occasion are higher than unity due to diffraction at edges of samples. Where quantities of materials or absorbers are used in large unbroken areas lower absorption values will result.

activities. Generally, a quiet sound recording booth has a time of less than one second (or beat). Any room over three seconds has an echo effect. A brief but surprisingly accurate test for reverberation time is to clap your hands once in an empty room and listen carefully for its echo counting the seconds thus: 1,001, 1,002, 1,003, etc. You learn to recognize the point of reflection from the din of the cracking sound of the clap as it decays producing a softer residual.

    While the surface area and its reflectiveness determine the reverberation of the space, the presence or absence of actors, audience, or large objects affects the subjective perception of echo time. The absorption of a surface is stated in terms of a unit called a *Sabin*, which is equal to a surface area of 1 ft^2 having an absorption coefficient of 1.00. As previously stated, the total absorption value in Sabins is sum of each value of each surface area. Remember, however, that absorption coefficients vary with the frequency of the incident sound waves. The standard test frequency is 500 Hz. The test reference for speech intelligibility (the standard) is 2,000 Hz. The range of acceptable reverberation times for rooms with primary functions may vary with the size of the audience.

Naturalness

Reverberant time affects two primary concerns of the sound recordist, intelligibility and naturalness. Natural sound for film and television work has come to be associated with "realism." Strictly speaking, then, in terms of traditional Hollywood studio techniques, realism means preserving straight match continuity. Although the "natural" sound of a given space, such as a classroom, may be an easily attainable effect to record, this sound element may or may not fit into the specific "realism" of the film, or into the series of shots into which it is meant to blend. *Blending*, or the seamless flow of images and sound, is only one possible directorial approach to the problem of narrative or storytelling.

The necessity to match shots within a scene aurally and to preserve a specific logic visually in space and time often precludes the use of "natural" sound. For instance, a room may be "hard" or "soft"; that is, echoes abound or it's a dead space. In the context of the immediately preceding shot, such as a kitchen adjacent to a bedroom, the naturally hard sound of the kitchen would break the seamless continuity when matched to the naturally softer sound of the bedroom. Although this is reality, it may destroy screen reality since the break in sound level and *texture* would be noticeable, potentially distracting, and often perceived as noise.

Planning Acoustical Spaces

The choice and size of a room depend on the wavelength of the lowest frequency to be recorded or transmitted. The most useful recording space is one with *angular* walls to scatter the sound and to prevent standing waves. This approaches the outdoor free field effect—no reflected sound. The ideal space, however, is seldom found in location shoots. The space must therefore be treated with acoustic materials and modifications.

In any given room, normal reflection patterns can be created by alternating soft and hard surfaces on all six areas (the four walls, ceiling, and floor). If the space seems too dead, hard surfaces must be introduced. If the space is too live, absorbing materials must be introduced. (Any absorbing material can act as *soundproofing*.) If the space should have a neutral, average ambiance, a combination of absorbing, reflecting, and diffusing materials must be used. When time and money are at a minimum, ingenuity rules.

Here are some examples of hard and soft materials:

- *Absorbers*: carpets, draperies, furniture, tile, people.
- *Reflectors*: windows, mirrors, panels, plaster board, doors.
- *Diffusers*: egg cartons, geometric forms of corrugated board, screens.

Note that adjustable soundproofing is best since conditions from shoot to shoot may vary.

Some other points to keep in mind are:

- Since most studios require hard floors for camera movement, the ceiling must be almost totally absorptive.
- Each of a series of alternating soft and hard surfaces must be set opposite its opposite.
- All modifications must take into account the position of the microphone.
- Sound damping is often the only treatment a given room needs. One must learn to listen for certain ambient noise the microphone can pick up like:
  —Air vent rumble.
  —Air conditioner vibration.
  —Flushing or running water in concealed pipes.
  —Floor rumble.
  —Electrical (AC hum) noise from fluorescent lights.

3

SPEECH

For sound to be intelligible, recording must compensate for the deficiencies and peculiarities of the sound source. You are given sample voice tests and guidelines for the evaluation of voice from a directorial point of view. The description of harmonic composition of the vocal sound helps you to evaluate and control actors. Enunciation exercises are also provided.

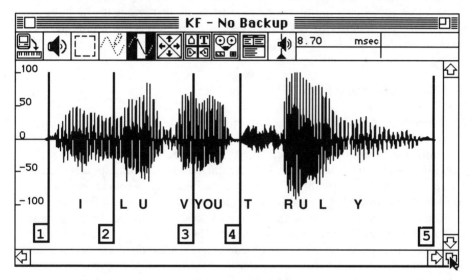

Nondestructive editing. On Digidesign's Sound Tools System, to say "I love you truly" play from 1 to 5. To say "I truly love you," play from 1 to 2; from 4 to 5; and from 2 to 4.

According to Dr. Karen McComb of Cambridge University, England, an experiment on red deer proved that the recorded roars of a stag are enough to bring a doe into heat. Is there a more convincing testament to the power of sound, and particularly to the vocal resonators in nature, to stimulate a response?

The Need for Intelligibility

Minute differences in the quality of the spoken word—timbre, duration, intensity, growth, and decay of the word pattern—can reduce intelligibility and therefore the effect of the spoken word. According to Michael Rettinger, in *Acoustic Design and Noise Control* (Chemical), understanding speech requires the recognition of consonants. To improve intelligibility of speech in a room, a comfortable hearing level must be determined; echo, delayed reflections, and standing waves must also be controlled, and noise eliminated. Rettinger goes on to set the conditions necessary for intelligibility in an enclosed space, indicating that the *signal response characteristic*—a factor of enunciation and fidelity of reproduction through an acoustic system—is a primary concern. The sensitivity of a microphone or of the ear, for instance, depends on *signal level*—the capacity of an individual to increase vocal pressure relative to changes in distance.

Noise can *mask* syllables, with high frequencies tending to produce greater masking. Overloading, poor amplification, and excessive reverberation cause distortion of the signal through any sound reinforcement system between source and audience. Understanding the effects of reverberation helps you to control intelligibility.

Most speech, with an average power level of 65 dB at a distance of 3 ft from the source, requires sound reinforcement in enclosed spaces. Rettinger reveals the paradox that, although 95% of the acoustic power of long-time speech lies in the low frequencies below 1,000 Hz, intelligibility is greatly dependent on the higher components. The ANSI (American National Standards Institute) publishes an Articulation Index, which helps to determine the perception level (under test conditions) of a distinct signal.

Speech

Speech is fundamentally an "overlaid" function, that is, it is the secondary reason for breathing. Human vocalization is something that seems to have come as an afterthought. The equipment used for speaking is really designed for breathing and eating. The lungs are the source of the energy (air). As we prepare to speak, air is drawn into the lungs. Prior to the first syllable the muscles contract in short strokes sending pulses of air through the larynx (windpipe). It has been shown that these pulses coincide with syllables.

The larynx sits on top of the windpipe and the muscles of the larynx form the glottis out of the vocal folds. It takes the shape of a V aperture. During quiet breathing, these muscles are relaxed. To make a sound, these muscles contract, building up pressure until the vocal folds are forced briefly apart. A puff of air escapes. This process is repeated perhaps 100 or 200 times per second creating a sound that is the beginning of the voice—*phonation*.

Sophisticated communication, however, requires a little more in the way of variation than just a simple burst or grunt at 150 cycles per second. A steady note doesn't tell us much. Fortunately, this tone may be modified in several ways:

- Rate of puffs (pitch): To increase the rate, increase the tension in the cords or the subglottal pressure. Either method will increase pitch, but the English language doesn't use this method.
- Size of puffs (intensity): Only subglottal pressure is increased.
- Richness or complexity: The shape and size of the throat and other cavities are altered.
- *Phonation* occurs with the involuntary process of passing the air from the lungs through the trachea and over the vocal cords, setting up vibratory impulses in the mouth.
- *Amplification* occurs through the resonance activity of the oral cavity and sinuses (explained in the next section of this chapter). Nasal tone is caused by the blockage of air into the mouth by a soft palate or nasal vellum.

Acoustics of Speech

Wave motion.   The particles of air at the mouth are put into motion. The energy is passed on to the next molecule. Each particle does not travel very far. The motion of the particle is sinusoidal in nature, that is, it vibrates around its rest position. (See Figure 3-1.) The particle can be said to be vibrating at a specific frequency (in the figure the frequency is 2 Hz). The *wavelength* is the distance from peak to peak. The *amplitude* is the height of the wave or the intensity of the motion.

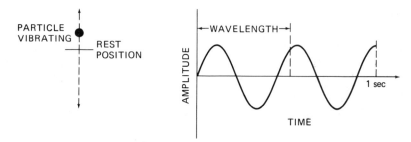

Figure 3-1   Graph of particle in motion.

Resonance

The physical property of resonance is the prime mover in creating speech variations, and it is defined as the reinforcing or prolonging of sound by reflection or synchronous vibration. As an analogy, we can make a pendulum (which has a natural period of vibration determined by its size) swing even higher than it might by hitting it with an impulse of energy that has the same frequency as the natural period of the pendulum. A different frequency would not reinforce the swing (no positive change), and it might even stop the swing completely!

The same principle applies to sound in a cavity. If we introduce acoustical energy in the frequency range that corresponds to the cavity's (or room's) natural period—determined by its dimensions—the energy can build up while reflecting from walls and meet itself in step. Note that the frequencies near the resonant frequency are reinforced, while the nonresonant ones are attenuated.

Vocal Resonators

As a series of impulses, phonation is a periodic force containing a fundamental frequency and multiples of the fundamental, or **harmonics**. When this acoustical pulse train is introduced into a cavity (nose, throat, mouth), the natural resonant frequency of the cavity may be excited by one of these harmonics from the vocal train. The harmonics near the natural resonant characteristics of the cavity are greatly reinforced and those that are not near are diminished. (These cavities are considered to be highly *damped*, that is, when the pulses cease, the sound dies out quickly.)

You can change the resonant frequencies of your mouth, for example, by putting your hand over it. When the shape of these cavities is changed—in terms of either volume or aperture—the natural period of resonance and therefore the sound change.

While the mouth and throat are quite variable, the nasal cavity is the least important since its shape cannot be changed. The nasal cavity can be taken out of the vocal circuit only by moving the *vellum* in the roof of the mouth. (English speakers with a *lazy vellum* are noticeable by the pronounced nasal quality imparted to the voice.)

Harmonic Composition of Vocal Sound

The vocal sound from the larynx is a train of pulses, as shown in Figure 3-2. It can be shown that this periodic waveform is a combination of a family of sine waves, the fundamental tone having the same frequency as the pulse train and carrying most of the energy. (See Figure 3-3.) In addition to this fundamental, harmonics (or overtones) are present at higher frequencies that are multiples of the fundamental. A graphic representation of the different frequencies with their energy contents is shown in Figure 3-4.

If we were to graph the *frequency response* of the vocal tract (mouth and throat), we would find that only certain frequencies are passed through it, some

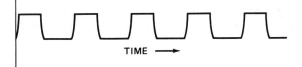

TIME ⟶

Figure 3-2 The train of pulses in the vocal sound.

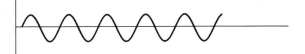

Figure 3-3 The fundamental tone.

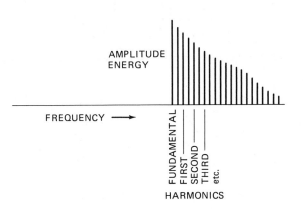

Figure 3-4 Harmonics (overtones) at varying frequencies.

greatly attenuated, some considerably amplified by the resonance of both cavities. (See Figure 3-5.) These two formant areas are where resonance occurs. They are different for each sound, moved up or down the frequency range by changes in the shape of the throat or mouth or by the opening and closing of various apertures. If we were to pass the family of frequencies through this acoustic system, we would end up with a family of frequencies that were shaped by being passed through this system. The two graphs are superimposed in Figure 3-6.

So remember that formants depend only on the *shape* of the vocal cavities, and the fundamental frequency depends on the construction of the vocal cords in the larynx. *Changing the formant frequencies has nothing to do with the pitch of the voice.* A tenor and a bass could have the same formants for a similar sound, but, since their fundamentals are different, they would sound quite different. Therefore, we can say that average human speech is composed of a multitude of frequencies. If we consider a random sample average of many voices, the energy distribution looks something like the graph shown in Figure 3-7. *The greatest amount of energy lies between 20 and 4,000 Hz, but the* articulation *and* definition *of the voice are in the higher frequencies.*

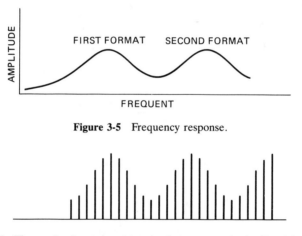

Figure 3-5   Frequency response.

Figure 3-6   The result of superimposing the formants on the family of frequencies.

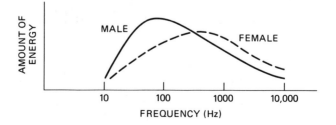

Figure 3-7   A random average sample of voices (energy distribution).

Articulation

The director who understands how the voice apparatus functions can control the emphasis and intonation of an actor's "performed" lines of dialogue. Speech is made intelligible through *articulation*, or adjustment of the vocal cavities. Five basic formants are possible:

1. *Plosive*: Complete stoppage of the sound path, producing the "P" and "B" sounds.
2. *Fricative*: A narrow slit is opened, creating the "th" and "sh" sounds.
3. *Lateral*: The middle line of the mouth is stopped, producing the "L" resonance.
4. *Trill*: The uvula vibrates or "rolls," creating "R" resonance.
5. *Vowel*: The vocal path is relatively unobstructed, producing pure tones.

Enunciation Exercises

To fully examine the roll of your own vocal apparatus in forming speech trains, exaggerate the use of the lips without uttering a sound and have others try to guess what you are saying. Try this alone in front of a mirror. For articulation, the following tongue twisters make excellent practice in sensing the formative elements at work. The entire exercise should be read without errors within 60 sec:

1. Amos Ames, the amiable astronaut, aided in an aerial enterprise at the age of eighty-eight.
2. Some shun sunshine. Do you shun sunshine?
3. Fine white wine vinegar with veal.
4. Bring a bit of buttered brown bran bread.
5. Geese cackle, cattle clow, crows caw, cocks crow.
6. Eight gray geese in a green field grazing.
7. Six thick thistle sticks.
8. Lucy likes light literature.
9. A big black bug bit a big black bear.
10. Peter Prangle, the prickly, prangly pear picker, picked three pecks of prickly prangly pears from the prickly prangly pear trees on the pleasant prairies.
11. Theopholus Thistle, the successful thistle sifter, in sifting a sieveful of unsifted thistles, thrust three thousand thistles through the thick of his thumb. Now, if Theopholus Thistle, the successful thistle sifter in sifting a sieveful of unsifted thistles, thrust three thousand thistles through the thick of his thumb, see that thou, in sifting a sieveful of unsifted thistles

thrust not three thousand thistles through the thick of thy thumb. Success to the successful thistle sifter.

Vocalization Exercises

Of all sounds, the voice is the most sophisticated. With diligent training and practice, the vocalist is capable of simulating an extremely wide range of sounds.

The first step in voice production is breathing—so important that improper breathing is the primary cause of vocal problems. The flat, pancake-like diaphragm sits under the lungs. As you inhale, it flattens out creating the *sea of respiration* and providing power for voice projection.

Deep breathing fills up the neglected backside of the lungs, providing pressure, which may be controlled, and deep resonance and stability of intonation. The untrained vocalist may expand that air but continue to speak using only the residual air trapped at the top of the lungs. Although to the ear the level loss may sound negligible, in most recording situations the microphone will pick up a more severe drop in level. The frequency span will change giving a "throaty" tonality leading to raspiness and loss of intelligibility. Lack of air pressure from the nasal passages produces a flat tonality to the voice.

Mums and nuns exercise. To eliminate nasal vellum, take a deep breath, "think" the sound down more into the face, relax the jaw, put head over knees, and say "na-na-na." With the same breath, "think" the sound down into the mouth and lips, saying "ooooooo, aaaah." A jaw that is tight from nervousness prevents you from getting air into the resonating cavity of the mouth. Deep breathing will slow down the heart rate to start relaxation. Raise the chin up into the air, open the mouth wide, and repeat the exercise several times until the actor or narrator "loosens up."

Stage fright. Stage fright can be eliminated by means of breathing and vocalization techniques. Stage fright or nervousness causes various reactions in the body: shortness of breath, trembling, dry mouth, pounding heart, blushing, cold sweat, chills, nausea, labored breathing, insufficient and/or shallow breathing. Physical rigidity is also quite often the direct result of fear. Any attempt to correct these reactions by bracing the muscles causes more tension and loss of freedom.

Here are some tips on overcoming nervousness:

1. Regular, deep, slow diaphragmatic breathing lessens the symptoms of nervousness.
2. Stage fright also happens because of fear of a poor performance. Be fully prepared. Have your presentation or music memorized!
3. You cannot sell anyone anything if you are not convinced of it yourself.

4. "An optimistic 'I CAN' attitude is basic to success."—Van Christy. Be confident in your ability and talent.

5. Avoid frenzied attention to last-minute details before a performance. Talk yourself into remaining calm and unruffled. Maintain an attitude of preparation on the big day.

6. Stage "anticipation" is desirable. Caruso said, "The artist who boasts he is never nervous is not an artist; he is a liar or a fool!"

7. Another cause of stage fright is lack of experience. Perform in front of the public often.

8. Have humility, but do not apologize constantly for your mistakes.

9. As you step out on stage, feel as if you are a hostess inviting your audience to your home for supper. Graciously make them welcome and offer your talent to them.

10. When you devote your entire attention to communicating to your audience, the perception of fear falls into the realm of less attention. Your fear is not so great.

11. Practice meditation or relaxation techniques before a performance. Your body, mind, and memory will be fresh to react to the artistic message if they are not clouded with agitated thoughts of fear and failure.

If you are a musician or vocalist:

1. Think through every single piece of music; run over it in your mind, the day before the scheduled performance. Then you can switch to "automatic pilot" during the actual performance.

2. Learn music early! Then you will be confident that everything at your end will go well. Don't leave this area to chance.

3. Practice sessions the week before the performance should be as long and as frequent as in your normal practice schedule. You may want to perform the entire recital in a run-through rehearsal each day for a week before the performance.

4. On the day of the big recital or performance, warm up your voice lightly. Do some physical exercises; eat two to four hours before the performance.

5. Long, animated conversations tire the voice. Rest, relax, read a book, do needlepoint before a performance.

Vocal imaging. Dialogue is generally considered to take precedence over all other elements in the sound mix. However, it is only partially necessary to determine how dialogue will flow and combine with other elements in the early stages. The mix is where the final balance is achieved.

The ability to use the human voice as an instrument for vocal imaging—

creating sounds for narrative—depends on training in the following mechanical processes:

- Pitch control.
- Focusing the vocal center.
- Inflections or the vocal mirroring of speech patterns.
- Modulate monotones.
- Tummy breathing.
- Jaw placement.

Vocal accent, the primary method for creating narrative emphasis, is created through appropriate diction, pronunciation, rhythm, and intonation.

Inflection.   A change in emphasis and/or inflection (pitch or tone) produces interesting, albeit humorous, results:

It's all **over** my friend.
It's all over my **friend.**
You do something to **me.**
You do something to me?
What is this crazy thing called, love?
What is this crazy thing called **love**?

Voice-Over Production

Understandably, care in direction is required to produce effective narration and voice-over tracks for film and television applications. This section details the physical properties of the human voice and the requirements for articulation. The significant element in the actual recording is the director's ability to elicit the proper attitude from the speaker. *Attitude* is the performer's realization of the tonal aspects of the script, the unusual nuances of speech, in addition to pacing and delivery. The implications of the words must be communicated through diction and erudition.

To this end, the director must certify that the performer understands the intentions of the script and the nature of the audience. There is always room for interpretation, so opinions should be solicited but final judgement/evaluation is the domain of the director.

Voice-over and narration are budgeted as a line item priced according to the Screen Actors Guild minimum, which for an industrial (nontheatrical) hour is $261. Since additional time is always needed, a half-hour add-on is $76 and callbacks for revisions are $142/hour.

Prior to the recording session, someone must check the script for errors and omissions, abbreviations, acronyms, calculations, and especially pronunciation and intonation cues. The session coordinator, often the assistant director, should make certain the performer is comfortable and has something to drink and something with which to write during the takes.

The audio engineer should be recording each take in consecutive numerical coded order, annotating bad takes and placing a head and tail beep to demarcate takes for high-speed rewind and counting.

The choice of microphone is the single most important technical element in the process. (See Chapters 4 and 5.) The placement also determines, to an extent, the tone of the recording as much as the mike pattern. Authoritative (aggressive) presence is achieved with close-miking; more conversational, relaxed vocalization is achieved at a 2- to 3-ft distance, depending on the kind of mike chosen. The engineer must maintain a consistent level and listen for clothing noise and noise from other sources.

New technologies have been developed to synthesize voice. These vocal emulators use an element to generate voice-like sounds at different octave ranges. (See the octave explanation in the next section.) TASCAM's Vocalizer (see Figure 3-8), for instance, can be connected to a recorder via MIDI interface and programmed to create a voice line. The audio designer composes a rendition using a set of parameters, which might include voice guide scales, pitch-to-MIDI converter, or external sources like a musical instrument, the human voice, and pots and pans! Essentially, the Vocalizer creates a rhythmic, song-like track that marries to music and effects. It is one of a new generation of tools whose impact is just beginning to affect the way sound is manipulated.

Figure 3-8 The Breakaway Vocalizer, a voice-generating music box that processes human voice via its mouthpiece and/or musical instrument inputs into multitimbral, octave-jumping "singspiel." The device interfaces with most PC-based workstations.

Octave.   In his general discussion of musical and unmusical sound in his *Theory of Sound*, Baron John Rayleigh recognized that the ear is capable of discerning more than 1,000 different gradations of pitch. He described a model for this chromatic scale in which he defines the *octave* as the double of a given frequency. This ratio gives rise to the following proportions:

2-1 = octave
3-1 = twelfth (octave + fifth)
4-1 = double octave
5-1 = double octave + major third
3-2 = fifth
5-4 = major third
4-3 = fourth
8-5 = minor sixth
6-5 = minor third
5-3 = major sixth

A certain kind of note that the ear cannot resolve is called a *tone*, that is, a note is made up of tones with the pitch of the note being the gravest of its tones. Harmonic overtones of a note modify the character of the note but are independent of pitch. Rayleigh arranged a system of tones thusly:

$$Do = 1 \quad = c \qquad Fa = 4/3 = f \qquad Ti = 15/8 = b$$

$$Re = 9/8 = d \qquad Sol = 3/2 = g \qquad Do = 2 \quad = c$$

$$Mi = 5/4 = e \qquad La = 5/3 = a$$

4

MICROPHONES: TYPES, PATTERNS, SPECIFICATIONS

Following definitions of the basic types of microphones—dynamic, condenser, pressure, pressure gradient, etc.—patterns and specifications are explained. Both these areas play a large role in how microphones are selected and used (the subject of the next chapter).

Dynamic Versus Condenser Microphones

Sound is a pressure wave traveling outward from its source into space; at any given moment and point in space, the sound is defined by the pressure variation taking place. A *microphone* is a transducer that converts acoustical energy into electrical energy. In a *cardioid* microphone, for example, delayed sound waves are allowed to reach the backside of the diaphragm of a pressure gradient transducer. This microphone is said to be *unidirectional*, that is, it accepts sound from only one direction. (See Figure 4-1.)

Microphones operate on a number of principles:

Principle	Structure	Example
Resistance control	Carbon	Telephone
Piezoelectric	Ceramic/crystal	Hydrophone
Electromagnetic	Magnet	Hearing aid
Electrodynamic	Moving coil (dynamic)	"Dynamic" mic
Electrostatic	Capacitor	"Condenser" mic

Of these types of microphones, the last two—moving coil (or dynamic) and capacitor—are used primarily for film, video, and audio recording (both in the studio and on location). We will therefore confine our discussion to them. (See Figure 4-2.) In the *dynamic* microphone, the coil follows diaphragm movement, generating an electric voltage in the coil. This voltage can be directly picked up and taken by a connecting lead to the mixer or to the tape recorder. *Condenser*

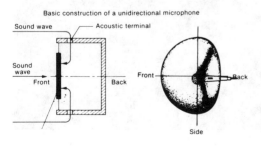

Figure 4-1 Basic construction of a "unidirectional" cardioid microphone.

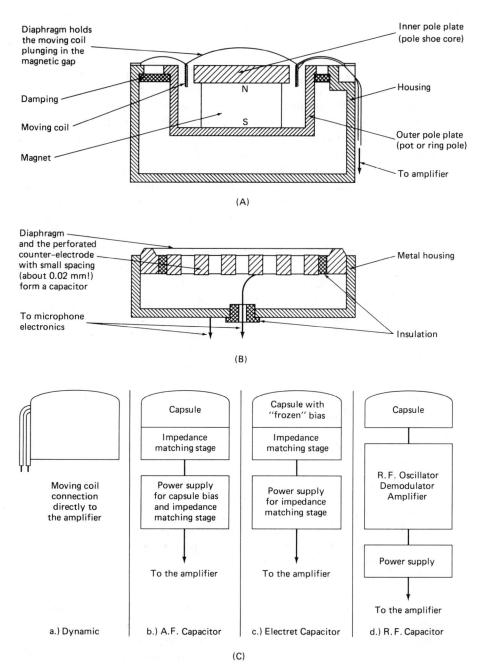

Diaphragm holds
the moving coil
plunging in the
magnetic gap

Inner pole plate
(pole shoe core)

Damping

Housing

Moving coil

Magnet

N

S

Outer pole plate
(pot or ring pole)

To amplifier

(A)

Diaphragm
and the perforated
counter-electrode
with small spacing
(about 0.02 mm!)
form a capacitor

Metal housing

To microphone
electronics

Insulation

(B)

Moving coil
connection
directly to
the amplifier

Capsule

Impedance
matching stage

Power supply
for capsule bias
and impedance
matching stage

To the amplifier

Capsule with
"frozen" bias

Impedance
matching stage

Power supply
for impedance
matching stage

To the amplifier

Capsule

R. F. Oscillator
Demodulator
Amplifier

Power supply

To the amplifier

a.) Dynamic   b.) A.F. Capacitor   c.) Electret Capacitor   d.) R. F. Capacitor

(C)

Figure 4-2   (A) Moving coil microphone; (B) condenser microphone; (C) block diagrams of
various transducer principles.

(or capacitor) microphones operate in different ways, depending on their construction:

- *AF capacitor:* A very light, tightly stretched metal electrode (often plastic foil covered by vaporized metal) is placed in front of a counterelectrode of metal or metalized ceramic; the electrodes form a capacitor. The capacitance of this condenser varies as the light electrode vibrates.

    This variation of capacitance is used in the DC-capacitor microphone to generate an alternating voltage in the following way: The capacitor is charged by high resistance from a polarizing voltage source to a constant charge, which lingers across the capacitor and varies with the sound pressure fluctuations. These voltage variations, because of the high resistance source, must pass first through an impedance-matching stage before traveling to the recorder.

- *Electret capacitor:* In this variation of the AF type, the polarizing voltage is "frozen" in the capacitor, making the external polarizing voltage unnecessary and reducing the cost.

- *RF capacitor:* No polarizing voltage is applied. Instead, the capacitor is used as a frequency-determining capacitance in a discriminator-tuned circuit, to which a radio frequency (usually 8 MHz) is assigned. The capacitance variations cause the audio frequency signal from this circuit to be activated and delivered to the capsule.

Both dynamic (moving-coil) and condenser microphones convert acoustical energy into electrical energy.

Step 1: Acoustic energy (alternating air pressure) strikes the diaphragm of the microphone.

Step 2: As the diaphragm vibrates in accordance with the difference in pressure between its front and rear sides, acoustic energy becomes mechanical energy.

Step 3: The mechanical energy (vibration) of the diaphragm is converted into electrical energy (alternating current), in accordance with the intensity and frequency of the sound pressure.

From a comparison of the characteristics of condenser and dynamic microphones (refer to Figures 4-2 and 4-3), it is apparent that condenser-type mics are inherently more accurate. The diaphragm of a dynamic microphone is attached to a coil of wire at its center and supported at its edge. This coil converts mechanical to electrical energy. The coil adds to the mass of the vibrating diaphragm, and the greater the mass of a moving object, the more the object resists a change in motion. Response is therefore less faithful to changes in pressure than a condenser microphone's response.

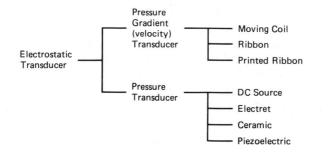

Figure 4-3 Types of microphones.

Here are some other pros and cons of the two types of microphones:

- The higher mass of the dynamic system creates resonance problems. All objects possess one or more resonances. The larger the mass, the greater the resonance. In a microphone, the output increases sharply at the resonant frequency of the diaphragm.
- Ideally, the resonant frequency should be well above 15 kHz to avoid an audibly *peaked* output. Only the finest condenser and ultrafine dynamics exhibit resonance-free response, that is, "natural" quality.
- Some dynamics exhibit *feedback* at high volume levels at its resonant frequency.
- A condenser microphone's diaphragm produces less *harmonic distortion* and *intermodulation distortion* at a wider range of frequencies.
- The condenser diaphragm is less sensitive to mechanical vibrations transmitted through stands and its own casing.
- Condenser microphones generally have a higher output level; so they exhibit a better *signal-to-noise ratio*, even when used with less than ideal preamplifiers.
- Dynamic microphones are more sturdy and supply their own power (preamplification). Condenser types are more delicate and require the use of battery-pack preamplifiers or input preamps at the recorder.

The *directivity coefficient* (DI) facilitates comparisons among microphones. This coefficient states the relationship between the power output of a nondirectional microphone and a directional type of equal sensitivity in a diffuse sound field. For example, an ideal cardioid microphone has a DI of 3. Since the intensity of sound decreases as the square of the distance, it follows that the cardioid may be used at a distance of 3, which is 1.7 times farther back than the nondirectional microphone with the same amount of background ambiance.

Which Type to Use?

How a microphone is built is often the reason for its selection for certain applications. The first condensers, for instance, were too delicate for field work. The size of the magnet and the material used for the diaphragm have a direct relationship to sensitivity as well as handling ease.

Here are some structural considerations in choosing microphones:

- The ability to reinforce studio acoustics.
- The ability to isolate sound sources, so that they can be processed separately.
- Discrimination against unwanted noise.
- Sensitivity to handling, wind pressure.
- Shape, size, weight, cost.
- Impedance (discussed in a later section).

Types of Microphones

Sound recording microphones operate on two basic principles (see Figure 4-3): pressure and pressure gradient.

Pressure

The transducer (or "element") exposes only the front side of the diaphragm, which is activated directly by the sound pressure independent of the direction of sound incidence. Ideally, it is *omnidirectional,* no front or back emphasis, but rather a uniform circular sensitivity. (See Figure 4-6.) This type of mike is also called *carbon, crystal, dynamic, electrostrictive, moving coil, condenser.*

Pressure Gradient

The diaphragm is moved by the resulting force of the pressure difference at the front and at the back of the diaphragm. Sound data reaches both sides of the diaphragm. Sound arriving from the side is rejected. The pattern or sensitivity in space is ideally *bidirectional,* and the field pattern is that of a figure-eight. It is sensitive only in front and back. (See Figure 4-7.) This type of mike is also called *velocity, ribbon, figure-eight.*

Pressure gradient transducers come in three forms (refer to Figure 4-4):

1. *Moving coil:* The diaphragm is normally formed of plastic with a wound coil resting within a magnetic field. As the diaphragm vibrates due to

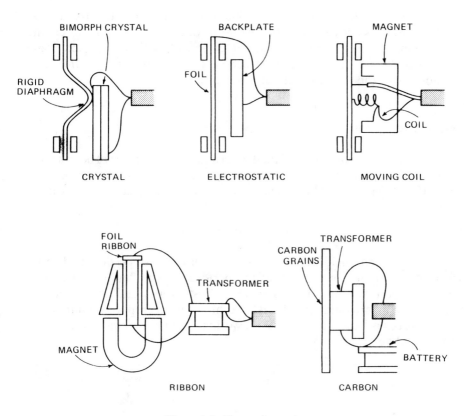

Figure 4-4 Types of transducers.

sound pressure changes, the coil is moved through the magnetic field, inducing a voltage across the coil.

2. *Ribbon:* A belt-shaped aluminum foil diaphragm is corrugated to allow uniform vibration over a broad frequency range. When the sound wave excites the diaphragm, which acts as a conductor within the magnetic field, a voltage is developed across it. The ribbon is very fragile; if exposed to wind it will stretch out of shape. Symmetrical construction of the ribbon and a very large magnet provide equal acoustical impedance at the front and rear of the diaphragm, creating a bidirectional pattern. Attaching a sealed labyrinth to the rear creates an omni pattern. If an acoustic port (small hole) is introduced in this labyrinth allowing a velocity component, the pattern becomes unidirectional.

3. *Printed ribbon:* A diaphragm is sandwiched between two concentric ring magnets, whose magnetic flux flows from north to south poles in the direction of the radial axis. A single-piece diaphragm coil assembly con-

sists of a plastic film with an aluminum spiral ribbon coil on its surface. Sound waves arrive at the diaphragm through the inner and outer ring openings, as well as through the center hole of the inner magnet. Some versions are of a tougher construction; the ribbon forms a permanent bond with the stable plastic film based diaphragm.

Microphone Patterns

In practice, microphones are classified according to their angles of acceptance, or *patterns,* as opposed to their generic powering functions, dynamic or condenser. (See Figure 4-5.) The principal patterns and their characteristics are as follows:

Omnidirectional

Exists as hand-held but often as small "lavalier"-type designed to be concealed by pinning or clipping to the performer. The "minis" have been acoustically adjusted to compensate for "chest" tones and should not be utilized as a standard omnidirectional hand-held type microphone. Omnidirectional microphones have an equidistant working radius of sound sensitivity of about 5 ft. (See Figure 4-6.)

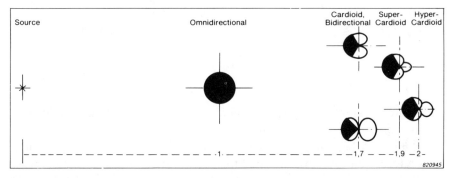

Figure 4-5   Microphone patterns; a cardioid can be placed at 1.7 times the source to omni distance for equal pick-up.

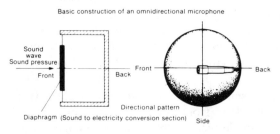

Figure 4-6a   Construction of omnidirectional.

Figure 4-6b   Omnidirectional pattern.

Bidirectional

A *bidirectional* microphone suppresses sound from the sides while being sensitive in front and back. Its figure-eight pattern generally has a working range of from 5 to 15 ft front-to-back. (See Figure 4-7.)

Cardioid (Unidirectional)

A hybrid, heart-shaped pattern of sensitivity is formed by combining bi- and omnidirectional types. The configuration is termed "unidirectional," having a pear-shaped pattern of frequency sensitivity from the head to a range of nearly 25 ft.

The cardioid offers greater working distance with the same amount of "room tone" in the pickup pattern as the omni. Proper angling offers better *isolation* of unwanted noise while controlling balance. However, they are not uniformly responsive at high and low frequencies, producing a marked coloration of *off-axis* sound and reverberation background. By comparison, the omni has very little isolation but gives full coverage especially when used from above. (See Figure 4-8.)

Supercardioid

A *supercardioid*, a class of unidirectional microphone, is extremely sensitive in one narrow direction with great isolation of noise at the sides. Nicknamed called the "shotgun," it uses an interference tube (15–18 inches long), which permits extremely high rejection at 90° off axis. Beamwidth is a function of frequency, the pattern becoming more narrow with increasing frequencies. However, if on-axis response is flat, the sound produced by a shotgun in a reverberant room will be "tubby" since very little high frequency information is being gathered. (See Figure 4-9.) The pattern includes maximum

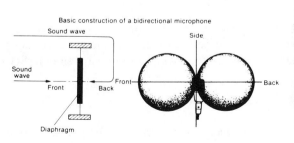

Figure 4-7a Construction of bidirectional.

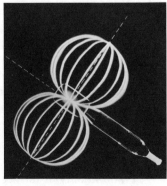

Figure 4-7b Bidirectional pattern.

Figure 4-8   Cardioid pattern.

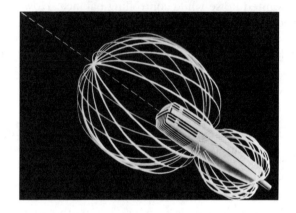

Figure 4-9   Supercardioid "shotgun" pattern.

rejection at 125° off-axis. It has more gain before feedback when used with a speaker system and the greatest difference between front and back hemisphere pickups (8.7 dB down at side).

Hypercardioid

The *hypercardioid* pattern has maximum rejection at 110° off-axis. It is the tightest pattern with the greatest rejection of distant sounds and room reverberation. It has the most gain-before-feedback (12 dB down at sides). (See Figure 4-10.)

Hemispherical

Found only in surface-mounted microphones (such as the pressure zone system), the *hemispherical* is an omni pattern cut in half by the surface that the element is mounted on.

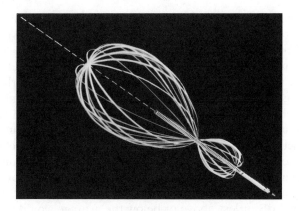

Figure 4-10   Hypercardioid pattern.

Half-supercardioid

The supercardioid pattern is halved by the surface mount of a pressure zone mike.

Phase Coherent Cardioid

This boundary microphone has unidirectional characteristics.

Microphone Specifications

Frequency Response

Frequency response is the relative reaction of a system to changes in frequency (pitch) in cycles per second. Often this covers the audible spectrum. It is a measure of the receptivity of the microphone to each frequency in the range 20 Hz to 20,000 Hz at a given test amplitude. If all microphones were completely linear devices, the graph of their ideal *frequency responses* would show all frequencies transduced alike. (See Figure 4-11.)

An extremely high-quality microphone might be specified as deviating no more than $+/-1.5$ dB from the nominal response over much of its range.

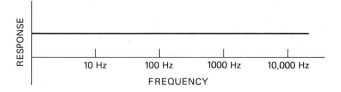

Figure 4-11   The ideal frequency response curve.

Frequency response determines the overall character of a microphone's sound. A response range of 100–10,000 Hz is good enough for many music recordings. For proper intelligibility of speech, a range of 250–7500 Hz should suffice. Finding a system that will handle both, as well as effects occurring outside these ranges, is a problem in film and television work.

The range and shape of the response must be selected to meet the needs of a specific application. Most microphones that are tailored to control specific acoustic conditions either make up for acoustic problems or provide a desired effect. In practice, only a small number of microphones are practical on location since mixing of many systems introduces matching discontinuities. Graphed ratings note each model's maximum deviations in decibels above and below its average frequency response; the smaller the deviation, the *flatter* the response. Deviations of 3 dB or less above or below the average would be close to a flat response, signifying the capability of recording a wide range of music. However, in many instances bass must be exaggerated over treble or voice boosted and treble enriched; a flat response would not be helpful. Some systems, then, would be chosen for their emphasis or lack of emphasis on certain ranges as well as angles.

Microphones, however, are inferior to the human ear in discriminating between direct and reverberant sound. Reverb is bass heavy, while high frequencies are more rapidly absorbed than lower. As a result, variations in overall working distances affect most response curves, especially those of directional microphones. The output of directional microphones is proportional to the difference in pressure at the front and rear of its diaphragm, and this pressure difference becomes very large at low frequencies when the element is close to the sound source. The response specs of a given system, then, are valid only for an ideal situation. *Response will be different for most microphones according to the direction from which the sound comes.* For example, a directional microphone with flat response will exhibit "muddiness" when placed far back in a large space.

Sensitivity

Sensitivity is the electrical output of a microphone produced at a given sound pressure level. *Open circuit sensitivity* is the output voltage produced (in decibels relative to 1 V) into an open circuit load at a SPL of 74 dB (1 μBar). *Power level* is the output power produced (in decibels relative to 1 mW) into a load matching the microphone impedance at an SPL of 94 dB. In general terms, sensitivity is the strength of a microphone's electrical output for a given input of sound. This is helpful to know when matching several systems for multiple miking. Balance can be achieved without complex logistical planning.

The measure of sensitivity is also an indication of efficiency. A classical dynamic may have a sensitivity of 0.2 mV/μBar from 200-Ω internal impedance. A model giving 0.25 is considered sensitive, and one with 0.1 is unsuitable for the recording of low frequencies.

Condenser microphones always have a preamplifier in the casing; otherwise their high impedance would not allow the signal to be transmitted along a cable. It is difficult to produce a very low-noise preamp capable of receiving without overloading a signal given by a condenser element placed in a strong acoustical field.

Coloration

A moving coil dynamic uses resonances to render its frequency response flat. When the signal appears suddenly, it takes time to move; when the signal disappears suddenly, the resonator continues to produce a signal. The result is that the *transient signal* (a percussive sound) is colored by the inherent resonances of the microphone. This explains differences noted by the ear between systems of identical characteristics. Coloration, then, is composed of internal noise produced by the mic as well as externally induced harmonics of the primary signal.

In general, condenser systems use resonators only in the high frequency area where coloration has little effect. Fidelity is excellent. Ribbon systems can color low frequencies, often giving a "rich" tonality to a flat voice. Some dynamics color even greater ranges, but they can also improve voice and filter out imperfections naturally. Coloration is also a function of the kinds of materials used to construct the mic.

Signal-to-Noise Ratio

In microphones, internal background noise is a function of electron movement or thermal activity. This thermal noise is a fixed characteristic of a system and adds to the overall noise output.

Bass Rolloff Starting Point

The *bass rolloff starting point* is the position at which every system loses its response to low frequencies (generally around 100 Hz). Unidirectional systems roll off at higher points to avoid emphasizing bass under certain conditions. They also tend to lose their directivity at low frequencies; in large spaces, units may pick up unwanted bass reverb from all directions. However, if you are trying to accentuate the flavor of a grand organ, try an omni or uni with flat bass response (no rolloff above 30 Hz).

Effectiveness

The measure of directivity in unidirectional microphones is called *effectiveness*. How well a system can pick up sound from the front while ignoring side and back sound depends in part on how weakly or strongly it discriminates against *each* frequency at each point. This can be graphed as a *polar pattern*. At frequencies up to 5,000 Hz, omni microphones are usually sensitive to sound from all directions, but at higher frequencies they become less sensitive to side and rear signals.

Dynamic Range

Dynamic range is the difference between the level of the highest sound pressure a system can accept and the system's internal signal to noise or ambient noise level. The lower limits of dynamic range average 20 to 40 dB. The upper limit for some of the very best systems is 120 dB, but this capability itself may be a source of distortion when the microphone is used at close ranges. In general, dynamic systems are able to better withstand extreme SPLs without input overloading.

Most film and TV application problems may be solved with the use of cardioids and supercardioids. When used in the same position as a normal and less sensitive cardioid in high noise levels, the shotgun-produced voice level remains constant, while secondary signals are deemphasized.

Placing the shotgun twice the distance from a given source obtains the same ratio between secondary and direct sound as with conventional microphones with cardioid characteristics. The great rejection trait makes the "off-mike" condition more noticeable. This means isolation is severe. A person 2 ft to the side of a Sennheiser 816's prime sound source target would be so far off-mike as to be inaudible. Working range can be up to 100 ft.

Off-Axis

Often the microphone is placed as close as possible to the sound source in long shots and as far away as possible in the close-ups to avoid *tip-up* and severe discontinuity of *presence*. In practice the microphone is rarely moved more than 3 ft from its close-up to its long position from rest. Furthermore, the microphone distance to the actor's mouth during movement must remain constant, or a level loss will occur. Altering the angle of axis toward 180° to the source means:

- A direct drop in volume but not a drop in secondary signals or noise.
- Falling off of high frequencies.
- Capture of unwanted ambient reflections.

Here is how the various types of microphones behave:

- *Omnidirectionals* do not exhibit off-mike or off-axis problems, but the level of background noise captured is generally high.

- *Bidirectional* microphones are susceptible to rumble but are good for two-shot coverage of two speakers.
- *Cardioids* have narrow acceptance patterns but less room for handling and movement error, working well on mounts.
- *Ribbon* and *bidirectional condenser* microphones can be damaged by use in high sound levels (air displacements). Explosions are best recorded by dynamic or electret condenser omnidirectional types.
- *Velocity* (which implies speed and direction) or *unidirectional* microphones have loose diaphragms sensitive to waves striking perpendicular to the surface in front and behind, but they are deaf to the sides. The direction of a wave does not effect pressure except at high frequencies.

Popping and Clipping

Since the microphone is designed to change mechanical energy into electrical energy, any form of vibration is detected by the system and heard on the track. Vibrations can be mechanically passed up the mike cable to the microphone itself. Since the microphone is eventually delivering the electrical signal, other problems must come into consideration. Interference from poor shielding, fluorescent lamps, and other electromagnetic systems can induce noise. (Interference is discussed in the next chapter.)

Air can have motion without being considered sound. Wind, the pressure of which on the diaphragm of a microphone causes *popping* sounds, is a serious problem on location. *Clipping* is caused by high-velocity wind or high-level sounds that overload the system, producing, in effect, silence.

Fortunately, the particle velocity of the wind is much higher than human speech, so a screen can be placed over the microphone to stop the high-speed energy, but not the vocal energy. Many microphones have a built-in windscreen. With some of the sensitive RF condenser types, a foam screen is often recommended even for indoor shoots to reduce the tendency of the plosives (Bs and Ps) to cause popping sounds, and to reduce the "swishing" sound of quick microphone movement. (See Figure 4-12.)

Immunity to wind noise is a design feature of many microphones. Some have a double metal casing to lessen both wind and handling noise. Others incorporate a double mesh external and internal screen. However, if the position of the microphone relative to wind direction cannot be changed, a shock mount/windscreen system must be used.

Figure 4-12 Shotgun mike with windscreen. (Source: Neumann.)

In a typical setup, the microphone is secured in a vibration-absorbing cradle (shock mount) made of lexan and rubberized support struts. The entire assemblage is slipped inside a zeppelin-style windscreen. The position of the microphone with respect to the inner surfaces is critical in maintaining full frequency response. The mount positions are therefore not arbitrary, but have been acoustically calculated to create a neutral acoustic space within the windscreen capsule. In this way, wind noise is suppressed (by as much as 20 dB), while all other characteristics of the system are unaffected. (See Figure 4-13.)

Physical Options

Many microphones provide special features integral to the construction of the system.

- *On/off switch:* This feature allows for instant cutoff of high-level input, or simply saving power when power is provided by a battery.
- *Bass rolloff filters:* A built-in switch drops out bass energy at a rate of 3 to 6 dB per octave, starting at about 200–400 Hz while deemphasizing bass response. This is used, for instance, when an omni microphone is used in a long hall with strong bass reverb, or when using a unidirectional system that tends to pick up bass reaching it from behind.
- *XLR cable connector:* This sturdy three-pin cable connection provides positive locking, tight fit, and superior noise reduction in handling. The DIN standard connectors tend to be more troublesome. Adaptors tend to loosen and cause intermittent line dropouts if not taped securely.

Figure 4-13 Breech-loaded zeppelin-style Lexan windscreen with shock mount for 816 shotgun. (Source: Litewave.)

- *Attenuator:* A built-in switch lowers output level by 10 dB, helping to reduce the chance of overload in uncontrolled situations such as crowd scenes.
- *Black matte:* Many microphones can now be supplied in a dull black matte finish, which eliminates reflections of light that could bounce into the camera lens. This also aids in concealing wireless and other mini-mikes, which must be placed on performers or objects in the field of view.

Other Specifications

Here are some additional *electromechanical specifications for microphones*:

- *Directional characteristics:* The variation in response for different angles of sound incidence for a given microphone.
- *Directivity coefficient:* A comparative term indicating the power output of a nondirectional mike in relation to a directional one of equal sensitivity in a diffuse sound field. An ideal cardioid microphone has a direct current of 3. Since the intensity of sound decreases as the square of the distance, it follows that the cardioid may be used at a distance of 1.7 times farther than a nondirectional microphone with the same amount of disturbing ambient noise obtained.
- *Directivity:* A rejection figure, stated in decibels, indicating the attenuation of sound from an angle relative to the zero position. For supercardioids, the angle of best rejection is at 235°, for a cardioid at 180°.
- *Effective output level:* This sensitivity rating is the ratio, in decibels, of the power available from the mike relative to 0.001 W at a sound pressure level of 10 dynes/cm^2.
- *Equivalent noise:* In a completely silent room, a transducer still generates some residual noise. This noise can be measured, and it is figured by relating a microphone's sensitivity to the threshold value of hearing, 2×10^{-4} µBar. A more common method is stating the signal to noise ratio.
- *Polar pattern:* The directional pickup in space displayed as a graph of sensitivity in decibels versus angle of sound incidence.
- *EIA sensitivity:* Called *Gm rating*, an open circuit sensitivity rating of −65 dB re 1 V/µBar is a high sensitivity. Medium sensitivity is −75 dB, −85 dB, a low sensitivity.
- *Impedance:* The *nominal load impedance* indicates the optimum matching load that utilizes the microphone's characteristics to the fullest extent. Impedance is a combination of DC resistance, inductance, and capacitance, which act as resistances in AC circuits. An *inductive impedance* increases with frequency; a *capacitative impedance* decreases with frequency. Both introduce a phase change.

- *Matching:* Insuring, via transformers, that the impedances presented by a load are equal to the internal impedance of the generator to avoid loss of power, which causes poor signal to noise ratios.
- *Inductance:* The resistance of a coil of wire to rapidly fluctuating alternating currents. The field built up by the current resists any change in the rate of flow of the current, and this resistance increases with frequency.

5

MICROPHONES:
USE AND SELECTION

The section on selecting microphones for an application includes a discussion of booms, long-distance mikes, shotguns, lavaliers, hand-helds, and special-purpose instruments. Included is a lengthy section just on pressure zone microphones (PZMs). The selection and use of all these types of mikes are then explained.

Of the many types of microphones, which is the best suited to any given on-location application? The answer to that question depends greatly on your experience, know-how, and imagination. Yet it is neither practical nor possible for you to field-test the hundreds of microphones offered for professional use. So the experience of others must be called on to limit the field. As a result, you will find only two or three basic microphones available get the job done.

For example, Sennheiser and Neumann provide the most widely trusted and used cardioid condenser location and studio microphones. They are equally expensive and sensitive, allowing for very little user error. In combination with some very inexpensive and relatively less sensitive ElectroVoice and AKG systems, the Sennheiser MKH 70, Neumann KMR 82i, and Schoeps MK41 are basic tools of the trade. What matters is how they are used.

In this chapter, we will give you the basic guidelines and tips you need to make the best selection. (See Tables 5-1 and 5-2.)

In practice, 3 rules of thumb apply:

1. The cost of a microphone tends to be a clear indication of its accuracy.
2. The impedance of the recording system limits the choice of microphones.
3. The subject dictates the choice of microphone pattern, because subject implies source parameters.

Selecting the Proper Microphone for the Application

Boom, Long-Distance "Shotgun," and Other Rangefinder Microphones

Extremely directional hypercardioid microphones isolate wanted sounds from background, or separate background from foreground while focusing attention and "naturalizing" multiple sound sources. Not only is background eliminated, but "panning" the microphone can create startling spatial effects. RF condenser types are best suited for exterior location use, while the more delicate electret condensers behave better indoors where wind cannot foil their clarity. The considerations are expense, power supply requirements and sensitivity to shock and wind. (See Table 5-1 and Figure 5-1.)

TABLE 5-1 How to choose the right microphone

Intended Use	Limitations	Options
1. Close miking	Seen in shot, popping	Hand-held omni or mini pin
2. Distant miking	Placement, movement, level	Cardioid
3. Noisy location	Natural sound	Hypercardioid
4. Feedback problem	Mounting, coverage	Cardioid
5. Proximity effect desirable	Seen in shot, matching	Pinned mini omni
6. Pinned on actor	Rustling, bass boost	Mini uni electret
7. Suspended on boom	Range, coverage	Supercardioid
8. Multiple sources	Isolation, movement	Omni or multiple mike setup

TABLE 5-2 Physical characteristics of various microphones by class

Class	Perks and Limitations
Omni dynamic	Widest, smooth response in average space but takes in everything. Minis can hide.
Omni condenser	
Bi dynamic	Full, rich resonant character for voice but emphasizes front to back equally.
Bi condenser	
Cardioid dynamic	Isolates environmental noise sensitive to handling
Cardioid condenser	
Supercardioid dynamic	Extends working range, but with increased directionality.
Supercardioid condenser	
Hypercardioid condenser	Extremely narrow field; bass boost when close. If careless, overloads.
Hypercardioid dynamic	

Schoeps microphones are pressure gradient condensers that are impervious to interior sound reflections affecting the acoustic clarity of Sennheiser and Neumann shotguns. In confined spaces with hard walls, traditional choices tend to exhibit increased boominess and echo. Furthermore, as the sound source moves increasingly off-axis, only the audio level is affected (it drops); coloration or alteration of frequency response, which occurs with other condensers, is not a factor with Schoeps. A special swivel mount allows the Schoeps MK 41 capsule to be flush-mounted on the wall or ceiling without problem.

Lavalier or Miniature "Clip-On" Microphones

The first generation of compact lapel-type omnidirectional microphones were hung around the neck, mostly dynamic, and metallic. Electret condenser

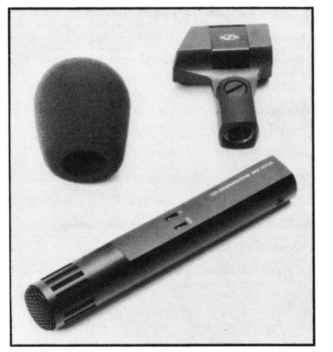

Figure 5-1 (A) AKG CK8 mid-range shotgun; (B) swivel mount. (Source: AKG.)

technology gave rise to lexan heads smaller than a thumbnail, quietly invisible and noise-free while matching the sensitivity of "hot" condenser directional mikes. Their primary use is as wireless microphones, but as hardwire mikes they require battery packs and must be handled with care. (See Table 5-2 and Figure 5-2.)

Lavaliers are designed to emphasize the voice while deemphasizing background. Consequently, they tend to favor the dominant sound source in a given space. Concealment is the primary reason to use them in the first place. Most systems are omnidirectional, but unidirectional versions are available that suppress feedback in live performance situations where PA systems impact the acoustics of the space.

Used both as hardwire microphones as well as wireless, the newer generation of mini-mikes are less susceptible to handling and clothing noise. Tram and Sonotrim capsules are especially well matched for use with the Neumann and Sennheiser RF condenser shotguns. Their audio mixes smoothly with production tracks from shotguns. Most of the mini-mikes currently in use are seen in Figure 5-2.

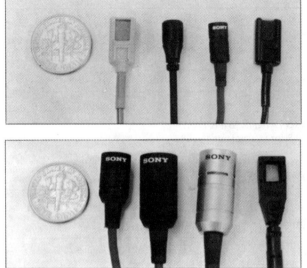

Shown from left to right:

Tram TR-50

Sennheiser MKE 2

Sony ECM-77

Sonotrim STR

Shown from left to right:

Sony ECM-44

Sony ECM-55

Sony ECM-66

Crown GLM 100

Figure 5-2   An array of lavalier mikes.

Hand-Held, Desk, or Stand-Mounted Directional Microphones

The basic midrange cardioid RF condenser is the studio workhorse. In the street, the cardioid dynamic takes the punishment required for an everyday interview microphone which may be hand-held or mounted on a short (3-ft) fishpole for ENG/EFP production. These mikes do not perform well beyond 5 ft, at which point only wireless systems or shotguns will get the job done. Handling noise is the primary consideration. Shure and Electro-Voice have solved this problem well, but Beyer has some wonderfully sounding ribbon cardioids that make every voice special. (See Tables 5-3, 5-4, and 5-5, and Figures 5-3 and 5-4.)

TABLE 5-3   Shotgun types

Sennheiser	816, 416TU (ME-80 Capsule), MKH 70, MKH 40
Neumann	KMR82i, KMR 8li, RSM 190i Stereo
Beyer	MC 737PV, MC736PV
AKG	C451EB/CK-9 (Capsules), CK 8
Schoeps	MK 41 (Capsules), MK8
Shure	SM 89
EV	RE45 N/D (dynamic)
Sony	ECM 672, C-48, C-76
Audio Technica	AT815

TABLE 5-4 Mini-Mikes

TRAM TR-50PS
ISOMAX III, TVH (Hypercardioid)
SONOTRIM Mini STR
Sennheiser MKE 2
Schoeps MK 2
Beyer MCE 5
Sony ECM 50PS, ECM 44, ECM 66, ECM 77
AKG C567E
EV RE 94, CO85, CO90 (RE85 Dynamic, 649B Dyn)
Shure SM 83, SM 11 CN, SM98 for instruments
Coherent Mini Mic
FRAP (for instrument clip-on)
CROWN GL Series GLM 100

TABLE 5-5a Directional hand-helds

Electro Voice	RE15, RE16, RE-11, RE-10 (Dynamics)
Shure	SM 62, SM 63L, SM 82, SM 87
Neumann (switchable)	KM 881, KMS 84
Sennheiser	ME 40 Capsule, 406, 106, MD 21
Beyer	M 58, M 69, M88
AKG	DS 95, C100s, D-190E, C451-CK1,4,5 caps
Schoeps	MK 4, CMC34, CMH 34
Sony	C37p, ECM56f
Audio Technica	AT811, ATM31, ATM21 AT813

TABLE 5-5b Omnidirectional hand-helds

Beyer	M101
EV	CO15p, Do540, Do56, RE50, RE55, 635A
Shure	SM60, S72G, SM76
Neumann	KM83
Schoeps	MK3 CMH 32U

Wireless Transmitter/Receiver Systems

Each of the suppliers in Table 5-6 offers a system with advantages and disadvantages, and each requires the use of a top-quality omnidirectional mini mike. The systems are listed in order of the author's preference based on their overall flexibility and versatility under many different exterior and interior conditions: the ability to operate quietly and efficiently AC or DC, near heavy RF (such as in Las Vegas), under studio conditions and on location, in many configurations (for instance, piggybacked for ENG camera attachment), and so on. (See Figure 5-5.)

Figure 5-3   Electro-Voice RE15 dynamic cardioid. (Source: Electro-Voice)

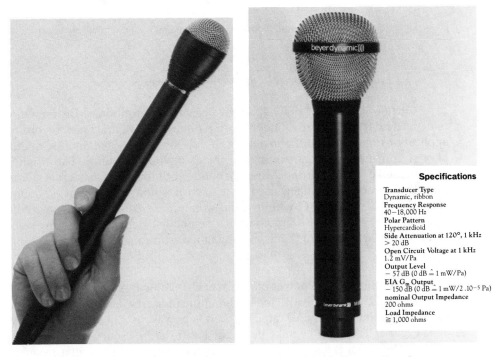

Specifications

Transducer Type
Dynamic, ribbon
Frequency Response
40–18,000 Hz
Polar Pattern
Hypercardioid
Side Attenuation at 120°, 1 kHz
> 20 dB
Open Circuit Voltage at 1 kHz
1.2 mV/Pa
Output Level
− 57 dB (0 dB ≙ 1 mW/Pa)
EIA G$_m$ Output
− 150 dB (0 dB ≙ 1 mW/2 .10⁻⁵ Pa)
nominal Output Impedance
200 ohms
Load Impedance
≧ 1,000 ohms

Figure 5-4   Beyer dynamic ribbon hypercardioid hand-held. (Source: Beyer)

TABLE 5-6 Suppliers of wireless transmitter/receiver systems

1. Micron	5. Nady
2. Swintek	6. Coherent
3. Sony	7. Audio
4. Vega	8. Sennheiser

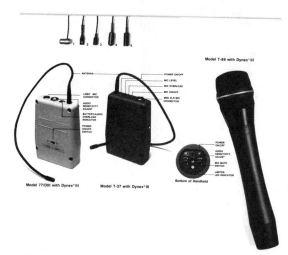

Figure 5-5 Vega T-89 hand-held wireless with optional lavaliers. (Source: Vega)

Special Purpose Microphones

Certain situations call for specially designed microphones. Instrumentation and field testing, stereo, underwater, parabolic and digital music recording applications have stirred the invention of new systems. Some antique microphones still have applications in the era of digital recording. The original dynamic mike used with the Auricon sound-on-film camera has great noise-cancelling properties. When used in a fixed position, it cuts out *all* sound beyond a 3-ft radius. RCA built some wonderfully sounding ribbon studio microphones, which give a "radio drama" embellishment to almost any voice and added rich resonance that is missing in most untrained voices. (See Table 5-7.)

Sony miniature electret condensers. These mikes are exceptionally small and lightweight, constructed of aluminum in narrow head configurations. Since most mikes are 1 in or larger (a 7,500-cps wave is 2 in long), *diffraction* must occur. The larger the mike head, the lower the frequency where bending occurs. The effect is less sensitivity at particular angles at particular frequencies. (See Table 5-8 and Figures 5-9 and 5-10.)

TABLE 5-7   Special purpose microphones

Shure	Sm10A intercom head-mounted dynamic; SM90 surface-mounted
Neumann	U87 multi-pattern studio condenser, TLM170
Fostex	M11RP printed ribbon studio
Schoeps	BLM3 boundary mike
AKG	D-112 Cardioid dynamic handles SPL to 168 dB; D-330 Black
Sony	C-48 multipolar studio condenser
Micron	TX503 hand-held transmitter/microphone
Neumann	RSM 190i stereo zoom shotgun (MS stereo)
Fostex	M22RP printed ribbon stereo (MS)
AKG	C-422 multipattern stereo studio mike
Schoeps	ORTF Stereo MSTC-34 spaced pair; CMTS 301U coincident stereo
Dan Gibson	Parabolic stereo microphone system
Bruel and Kjaar	Hydrophone
Calrec Soundfield	CM4050 Mono/Stereo ambisonic full field remote control
Crown PZM microphones	2½ lexan triple boundary for camera isolation, SASS stereo

TABLE 5-8   Electret condenser microphones

ECM 50	Smallest head, omnidirectional lapel-type condenser.
ECM 16	Lightweight economical version of the 50, whose response matches single system Super 8 sound cameras and cassette recorders.
ECM 19B	Cardioid pattern, hand-held.
ECM 99	One-point stereo condenser, dual cardioid.
ECM 150	Subminiature condenser desktop mike on telescoping mount.

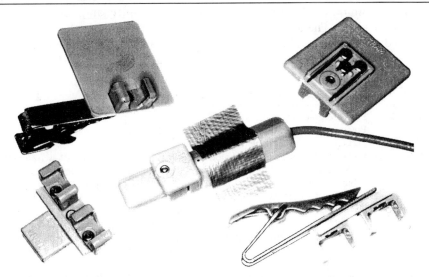

Figure 5-6   The TRAM TR-50PS class of mini-mike is an omnidirectional that matches the high gain of studio condensors. Clips for various kinds of mounts are also shown.

Figure 5-7 KMR-81i midrange RF condenser shotgun, one of the most widely used location systems. (Source: Neumann)

The sound at the head of the microphone is a complex combination of:

- The direct sound from a voice.
- Sound reflected from surfaces.
- Background noise (ambient noise).

Neumann transistor condenser microphones. A switch below the mike head allows you to choose the patterns. The directional characteristics are cardioid, bidirectional, and omnidirectional. This microphone reproduces low frequencies equally in all patterns. Capsule membranes are evaporated gold on polyester film. The axis of maximum sensitivity is at right angles to the body. (See Table 5-9 and Figure 5-7.)

Sennheiser series of condenser microphones. Electret condenser microphones from Sennheiser operate according to the audio frequency condenser mike principle. A bias voltage of more than 100 V is "frozen" into the diaphragm permanently. This constant charge is in the form of an alternating current when the diaphragm is moved by the pressure of sound waves. An FET in the mike amplifies the generated electrical signal and changes the impedance to a lower value. The audio output may now be processed in the same way as with a dynamic mike. The flexible diaphragm is made of metalized plastic foil with a permanent electrostatic charge. (See Tables 5-10 and 5-11.)

TABLE 5-9 Transistor condenser microphones

KM 86	Pressure gradient, warm sound
KM 88	Pressure gradient miniature, has nickel diaphragm.
KM 83	Pressure, interchangeable capsules, warm sound
U 87	Pressure gradient, response below 30 Hz is rolled off to prevent low frequency blocking. This rolloff may be switched to 200 Hz to allow compensation for bass tip-up common to all directional mikes at close range. For studio applications with high sound pressure levels.
U 47	Pressure gradient cardioid, dual membrane.
SM 69	Pressure gradient, stereo upper element rotates 270°. No phase differences (arrival time). 9 switchable patterns independent of each other. Can use MS/XY intensity stereo technique and monophonic recording with two different patterns.
KMA	Most lavaliers close on body produce unusual sound pressure characteristics above 1,000 Hz. The KMA compensates for the phenomenon.

TABLE 5-10   AC condenser microphones

ME 80	Directional tube shotgun, pressure gradient interference.
ME 40	Supercardioid directional, pressure gradient.
ME 20	Omnidirectional, pressure transducer.
K 30	Battery pack and impedance balance transducer.

TABLE 5-11   RF condenser microphones

MKH 70	Hypercardioid.
MKH 816	Ultradirectional tube shotgun.
MZA 6-2	Battery pack.
MZA 15-U	Battery pack with xlr plug.
QPM 3-5	Internal Nagra preamp for use without battery.
MKH 416	Supercardioid pressure gradient, interference.
MKH 436	Cardioid.
MKH 126	Omnidirectional lavalier type.
MKH 106	Omnidirectional.
MKH	Series with designation 6 are phantom powered.

RF condenser microphones do not use a DC bias voltage. Instead, the condenser element is part of a tuned RF circuit, operating at 8 MHz. This frequency is generated inside the microphone by a crystal-controlled oscillator. The low element impedance at the high frequency and the oscillator are the secrets behind the unique high signal to noise ratio of RF condenser mikes.

Extremely directional microphones allow users to isolate sound sources creating naturalistic separation and focus of attention. Background is eliminated, the working range is extended but mikes must be used very precisely on axis to avoid severe off-mike characteristics. The RF condenser types appear best suited for most exterior applications. The modular electret condenser types offer economy and versatility indoors. Sennheiser's ME 80 and ME 88, the AKG CK8, and the Bruel & Kjaer systems are typically recommended (See Table 5-12, and Figures 5-8 and 5-9.)

Stereo microphones.   The movement to two-track location recording has complicated the arena for microphone choices. In one sense, two identical mikes of any class, shape, or ilk can be mounted and positioned to obtain some

TABLE 5-12   Bruel & Kjaer microphones

4011	Prepolarized cardioid condenser.
4012	Cardioid with 2 channel power (130 V), handles 168 dB.
4003	Low noise omnidirectional condenser.
4004	High-intensity omnidirectional condenser. A-B stereo set (2 4003s plus power supply)

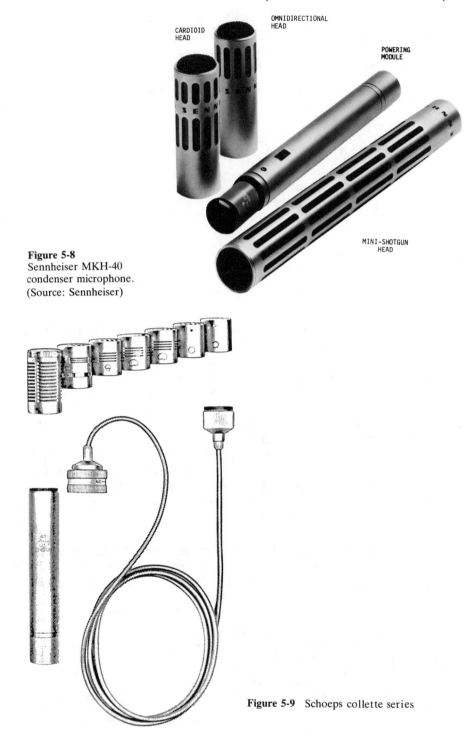

Figure 5-8
Sennheiser MKH-40
condenser microphone.
(Source: Sennheiser)

Figure 5-9 Schoeps collette series

semblance of separation for two-track recording. An alternate system utilizes twin capsules in one mike casing. Several techniques have evolved for enhancing the separation of stereo audio materials in the field. Some specific mikes that lend themselves to voice rather than to traditional music recording are herein presented.

The Schoeps stereo twin microphone mounting system employs two matched Collete series capsules mounted 170 mm apart at an angle of 110° (the ORTF stereo principle). Outdoors, the capsules can be mounted in the Rycote "ball gags."

Sennheiser recommends their spaced-pair mounting of two MKH 40 condensers. Nearly every manufacturer has a proprietary version of the stereo microphonics system. In practice, however, mounting and the nature of the sound source dictate the choice. See the section on stereo recording.

The performance of twin mounted microphones depends on the types used. The response curves of omnis are independent of sound direction while the internal impedance is constant. Much less affected by wind their light diaphragms float but sudden bursts can shock velocity-type omnis. (See Figure 5-10.) Directional mikes function well only if they are away from objects that can disturb the acoustic field; the obstacle disturbs the pressure less than the velocity. The supercardioid shotgun combines the output of pressure device (omni) and the output of a velocity device (bi) into a double-element transducer. The output of the omni is not proportional to the angle of incidence, while the output of the ribbon is proportional.

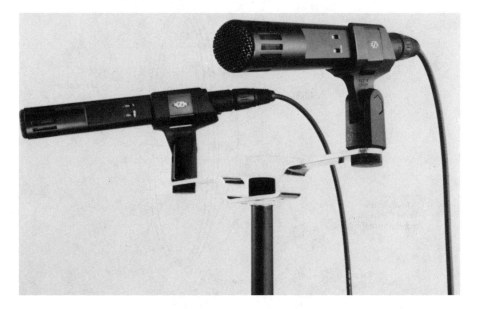

Figure 5-10   Sennheiser MKH-40 condensers in a stereo mounting. (Source: Sennheiser)

Parabolic microphones.   A conical reflector gathers sound from the direction in which it is pointed and directs it to a mike mounted at a focal point in the reflector. The system employs an omnidirectional mike and a highly directional reflector. Parabolics reject all off-axis waves, and accept signals only at the focal point but cover the entire reflective surface. The system is aimed by hand or from a tripod until a usable signal is obtained. Its response is 300–15 kHz; impedance, 150–600 Ω. With a working range of 100 ft to $3/4$ mi, effective range depends on:

- Strength of the signal.
- Atmospheric conditions.
- Extraneous noise.
- Frequency (it is more sensitive to high frequencies).

Disadvantages:

- Difficult to monitor.
- Subject to wind interference.
- The shield is subject to scratching and warp, magnifies sunlight, and can damage mike elements.
- Subject to resonance frequencies due to shape and construction.

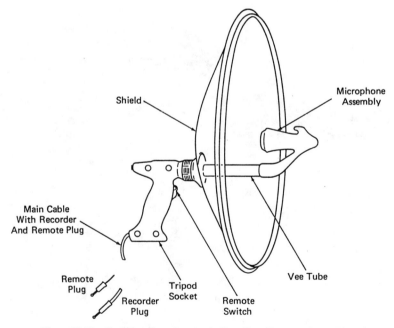

Figure 5-11   Construction of a parabolic mike. (Source: Dan Gibson)

Underwater sound measurements.   For underwater recording, the microphone must (see Figure 5-12):

- Be corrosion-free and waterproof.
- Withstand high pressure ranges without reducing sensitivity.
- Have good shielding (such as neoprene rubber, which has an acoustic impedance similar to that of water).
- Be as free as possible of self-induced noise.
- Drive very long transmission cables and therefore have high internal capacitance.

Bruel & Kjaer make the standard underwater mike, the Hydrophone, which is an omnidirectional piezoelectric transducer with a sensitivity range of 1 Hz to 100 kHz. (The propagation of sound underwater for any frequency is four times greater than in air; diffraction becomes a problem only at very high frequencies.) The piezoelectric principle is reversible in that it allows for the transmission, as well as reception, of sound waves.

TABLE 5-13   "Antique" microphones still in use

RCA 77DX	Cardioid ribbon—polydirectional studio mike
RCA BK-5	Cardioid ribbon—uniaxial, corrugated ribbon
RCA Bk-12	Subminiature dynamic, nondirectional
RCA Bk-14	Dynamic omni cartridge type 20-20 kHz
Shure 720B	Crystal (1938)
Shure 703S	Crystal (1936)
Shure 33N	Carbon (1932)
Shure 40D	Condenser (1935)
Shure 556B	Dynamic (1938)

Pressure Zone Microphones® (PZMs)

At one time life was simple. Because microphones could not get the job done on location, most of the sound for motion pictures was recorded in the studio and then "*dubbed*" editorially to match the visuals. Improvements in wireless technology brought recording back out into real space. In the 1980s, a new system of microphones, employing a simple principle of coherent sound wave reception, has opened up new options for the audio designer.

Of the special purpose class of microphones, the Pressure Zone Microphone® employs a mini electret condenser head mounted face down next to a sound-reflecting plate or boundary, where direct and reflected sounds combine effectively in phase over the entire audible range. It provides, as if by magic, excellent clarity, smooth frequency response, great fidelity, and virtually no off-axis coloration.

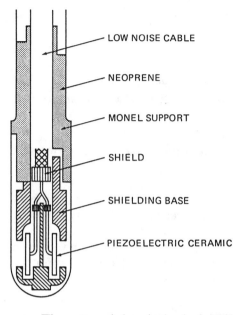

LOW NOISE CABLE

NEOPRENE

MONEL SUPPORT

SHIELD

SHIELDING BASE

PIEZOELECTRIC CERAMIC

Figure 5-12   Construction of the Hydrophone.

The pattern is hemispherical, 180° up from the center of the capsule while affording great operating range. There is no phase interference between direct and reflected sound, but rather a 6-dB increase in sensitivity due to the coherent addition of direct and reflected signals. Reverberation is reduced by 3 dB over conventional omnidirectional microphones. Signal to noise ratio is high due to the 6-dB increase in acoustic sensitivity and the low internal noise.

In theory, when a microphone is placed near a reflective surface, reflective sound is delayed relative to the direct signal. With the microphone diaphragm oriented parallel with the boundary and just above it, the direct and reflected sound arrive simultaneously at the slit between the element and the boundary. This Pressure Recording Process™, invented by Ed Long and Ron Wickersham, lead to the development by Ken Wahrenbrock of the PZM® system. The *pressure zone* is the region next to the plate where direct and reflected waves add in phase at all audio frequencies.

There may be a slight phase shift but its effect on frequency response is outside the range of audibility. The distance at which the element is placed from the plate is extremely critical and determines the extent of high frequency response. (See Figure 5-13.) Within a few millimeters of a large surface, direct and reflected waves add coherently because, close to the surface, the air particles are still in phase as they accelerate after being brought to a stop by the boundary. This creates a pressure field right at the surface of the boundary. A pressure field exhibits uniform pressure everywhere. A pressure-calibrated electret, when flush-mounted, has a flat response. Because of the undamped resonance of its diaphragm, the element has a pronounced rise at high frequencies when used in a free field.

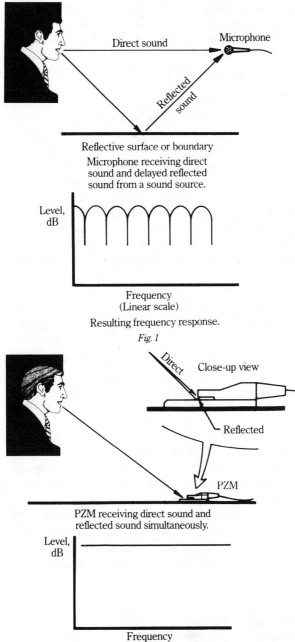

Figure 5-13 Direct and reflected sounds with the PZM®. (Source: Crown International)

When a Pressure Response Microphone® is placed in a cavity (pressure sound field), the response becomes uniform with frequency. When flush-mounted, it exhibits no high frequency peak. In the PZM® system, no signal can ever arrive on-axis but can enter only at the sides of the opening, thereby maintaining a flat response for all angles of incidence in the hemisphere surrounding it.

The system is relatively new, and experimentation has provided a rich inventory of applications. Various baffling arrangements have been used to control directional and coloration characteristics. For instance, placing some foam behind the capsule can make it more directional at high frequencies. Pantyhose pulled over a darning hoop and clamped by the outer ring of the hoop makes a fine windscreen. The plate can be mounted virtually anywhere, even on a fishpole with remarkable results. Since the system has excellent rejection at high frequencies behind the plate if the plate is raised, it can be placed vertically in front of a moving camera (that is, at the edge of a dolly) while rejecting high frequency camera noise in the moving shot.

The advantages in using the PZM® system include its:

- Capacity to be hidden on-camera since it does not look like a microphone.
- Phase-cancelling effects for fidelity.
- Coverage and long range (one plate can cover an auditorium if mounted properly).
- Wide pickup pattern, precluding the use of multiple miking setups.
- Small diaphragm mass, which eliminates most noise from rubbing or touching the element when used as a lavalier or wireless microphone.

Ideal Placement

To find the ideal position for a Pressure Zone Microphone®, "walk" the mike. With one ear closed, walk through the recording space and find the position from which the rehearsed dialogue or sound to be recorded is subjectively best to your ears. Drop the PZM® at that position! The PZM® may be used very close up since it does not exhibit proximity effect. High-level percussive sources can be miked with great fidelity and no overload. Furthermore, the microphone is virtually invisible since it does not look like a microphone. The PZM® does not exhibit comb-filter effects. (See Figure 5-14.)

Figure 5-14 Pressure Zone Microphone®

The Realities of the PZM®

According to Robert Herrold of Audio Technica, many myths have developed about surface-mounted microphones, some of which may be dispelled through practice.

- The 6-dB sensitivity increase of PZMs is a function of the boundary size and angle of incidence of the impinging sound.
- To maintain the 6-dB rise, the angle should be between 30° and 60°, oriented in the direction of the sound source.
- There is no sensitivity increase for very low angles (0–5°), except when the microphone is on a wall or floor.
- It would take a boundary size of 8 ft on edge to get a sensitivity increase down to 100 Hz, 16 ft down to 50 Hz.
- To efficiently attenuate sound at 100 Hz, the boundary surface must be greater than 16 ft on a side.
- The actual polar response of omni and uniboundary microphones on a small boundary is not truly hemispherical or hemicardioid unless the angle of incidence is within the 30°–60° range. In Figure 5-15, note that a 90° *spherical angle* equals a 90° angle created by the intersection of two surfaces like a floor and wall. A 45° *spherical segment* equals the intersection of three surfaces.

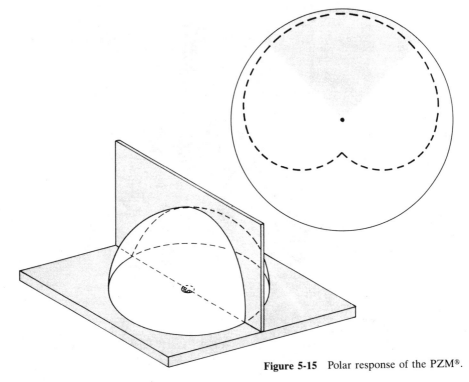

Figure 5-15 Polar response of the PZM®.

- The microphone can pick up random incident sound, which often adds some coloration.

Application Techniques

Here are some of the basic applications for studio and location recording. (The PZM® works only on phantom power; it no longer requires interfaces.)

Special hard-to-mike situations

- Mount a PCC-160 directional boundary mike on the camera dolly facing the action, and track the sound right along with the action. The result is full rejection of camera noise. (See Figure 5-16.)
- In tight spaces (such as under the dashboard of an auto, airplane fuselage, barrel, tunnel, and so on), hide a PZM 6FS to pick up all the action.
- Conceal a PZM 6R with light textiles on a table to pick up intimate conversations without distortion.
- Use the PZM as a wireless fishpole mike to assure full coverage of wide, cluttered shots.

Figure 5-16 A PZM mounted on the front of a dolly will effectively isolate camera noise from behind. A 2½-angled lucite panel will exhibit 90% cancellation of camera vibration and noise. Room with hard walls may reflect some secondary signals into the pattern.

- In recording situations with loud sounds (150-dB SPL) and sudden movement, like a fight scene outside a storefront, place one or two PZM®s on the surface to get full coverage without overload and off-axis coloration.
- A PZM® on a 4 × 4-ft panel suspended over an audience or crowd ends "muddy" pickup of voices, applause, and other sounds. (See Figure 5-17.)
- For interviews, place a GLM-100ENG on the interviewer facing the subject, thereby eliminating the "mike-in-the-face" syndrome.
- An orchestra, marching band, jazz ensemble, pipe organ, or other large sound source is typically recorded using four versions:
  —*A single bipolar panel for near-coincident stereo*: The closer the panel is to the source, the wider the stereo spread created by the intensity or

Figure 5-17 A PZM® suspended over a group.

Bipolar PZM (Stereo plate)
edge view

Figure 5-18 PZM®s mounted back-to-back for near-coincident stereo.

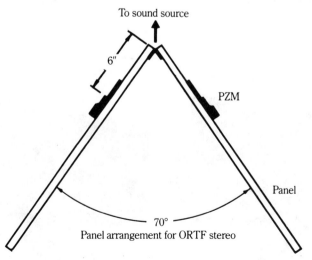

Figure 5-19 Two cardioids mounted at an angle.

level differences between channels and by the time differences between channels.

Mount two PZM®s back-to-back on opposite sides of the panel. (See Figure 5-18.) Aim the edge at the center of the source 5 to 20 ft behind the conductor, 14 ft high. The farther from the source, the greater the pickup of reverberation. Try the bipolar on the floor, on the edge, with the PZM® elements at the junction of floor and the vertical panel.

—*Near-coincident stereo (ORTF, NOS) ORTF*: Use two cardioids angled 110° and spaced 7 in apart horizontally. (See Figure 5-19.) For the NOS, set the angle at 90° and the spacing at 12 in. Two PZM®s are mounted 6 in from the edge of two 2-ft-square panels linked to form a V whose apex is pointed toward the sound source. The angle of panels is about 70°. Vary the angle to change the stereo spread. The imaging is sharp and accurate.

—*Spaced-pair stereo*: Use two panel-mounted PZM®s set 6–10 ft apart, 14 ft high, 5–20 ft from the first row of players/actors. Wider placement broadens the stereo spread. An inconspicuous live concert setup is to place two PZM®s 4–10 feet apart on the floor, 10–15 ft from the source. A center fill mike is sometimes needed. A PZM® may be mounted on a 4 × 4-ft panel or on the wall in front and the back of a large hall, or on other space like an airplane hanger.

—*Sports coverage*: A PZM® pyramid aimed at the field clearly picks up quarterbacks' signals. (See Figure 5-20.) Suspend a 2 × 2-ft panel with two back-to-back PZM®s over the center of a basketball court for full stereo coverage. For ball and foot noises plus crowd reaction, place PZM®s on the floor just outside the boundary at center court in tennis. During interviews, try a clip-on. (See Figure 5-21.)

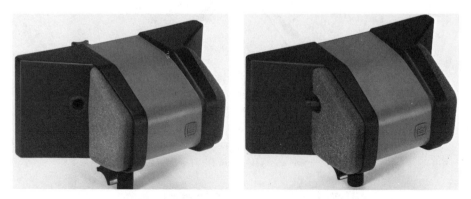

Figure 5-20   The stereo PZM™.

Figure 5-21   PZM® clip-on omni.

Microphones for Recording Music

In practice, nearly every conceivable kind of microphone has been tried at one time or another in the recording of music, vocals, chorus, and the like. The film industry even had its own proprietary design in use on the sound stages of MGM for decades until they (Church microphones) were stolen in the 1970s, never again to be seen.

Instruments may be miked individually or with one studio-grade microphone from above in the center of the scoring stage. Instruments may have the element actually secured on it (a pick-up mike) or suspended on a stand or boom. Stands tend to amplify floor vibrations, which may or may not help the overall sound. Music industry pros are not always interested in fidelity. Embellishment and modification of the source (because of its deficiencies) is often the modus operandi. Choice of the mike is dictated by the quality and quantity of instrumentation, orchestration, and vocalization. A chorus is the most difficult to mike for fidelity. An organ recital presents the most severe ranges of intensity and nuanced chordal movements. Wireless and PZM systems have begun to solve some old problems. (See Figures 5-22 and 5-23.)

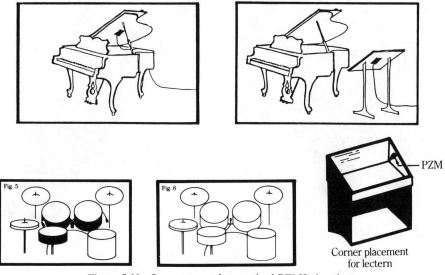

Figure 5-22   Some set-ups for standard PZM® situations.

Figure 5-23 A PZM GL series lavalier can be mounted on the surface of the guitar near the sound propagation portal.

Application Notes for PZMs

Some characteristics to remember about PZM®s are as follows:

- The bipolar PZM® and V panels track the motion of moving sound sources more accurately than a spaced pair of microphones.
- If the PZM® element is mounted in a corner, the direct sound is boosted 18 dB, while reverberant sound is boosted by only 9 dB. Distant sources sound closer and clearer than they do with a conventional omnidirectional microphone.
- Low mass and high damping of the PZM® diaphragm make it relatively insensitive to mechanical vibrations, such as table and floor thumps or

Figure 5-24 The AKG C414 B-ULS is a studio-grade condenser with four patterns that anticipate the near perfect response required for digital recording in the music studio. (Source: AKG)

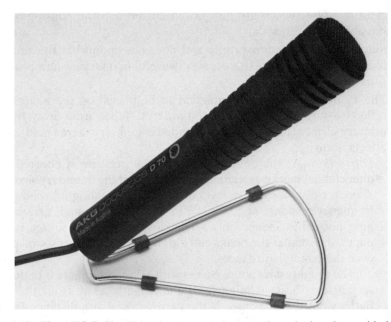

Figure 5-25 The AKG D-70 ME is a low-cost stand-mounted vocal microphone with dynamic proximity effect to boost weak bass vocals. (Source: AKG)

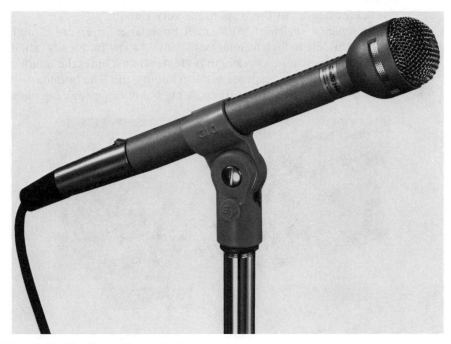

Figure 5-26 The Electro-Voice RE 10 is an economy rugged dynamic omnidirectional for hand held music and vocals. (Source: Electro-Voice)

clothing noise, which are not picked up through the housing but only possibly through the air.

• Since the PZM® is low profile and does not "point" at the subject, it reduces "mike fright." It is especially useful in interview and courtroom situations.

• The PZM® was originally intended to be placed on the nearest large reflective surface (the *primary boundary*). When used away from the primary surface (for instance, suspended in mid-air in a free field), several effects occur:

—*Diffraction*: At the boundary surface the pressure is boosted at frequencies having a wavelength on the order of the boundary size. A 1-ft diameter disc boosts the level at 1,000 Hz, creating a broad peak in frequency response at 1,000 Hz. (This holds for sounds arriving at or near normal incidence only.) The closer the sound source is to the panel, the smaller the peaks and dips because the direct sound prevails over the edge disturbances.

The roughest response occurs with a disc; the square is better and a rectangle is best. Aiming the panel slightly away from the source flattens out the response. If the panel is used at a distance from the source, reverberant sound reflections from the room surfaces approach the panel from all directions with a net smoother response. With the bipolar PZM®, none of the direct sound approaches the panel at normal incidence; so the response is very smooth!

—*Low-frequency shelving*: With small boundaries, pressure doubling occurs at middle to high frequencies, creating a low-frequency "shelf." At frequencies whose wavelength is greater than 6 times the boundary width, the frequency response is down about 6 dB. The boundary acts as a low-frequency shelving filter. A big boundary means big bass; a

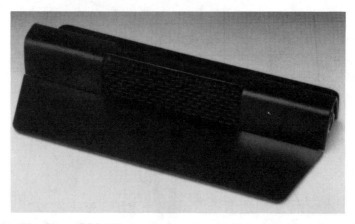

Figure 5-27 The Crown PCC 160 phase coherent cardioid is an excellent floor mike where feedback is a problem in recording a live concert. (Source: Crown)

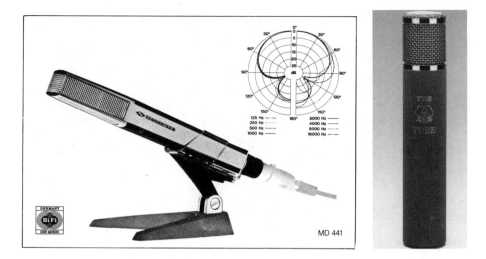

Figure 5-28   The Sennheiser MD 441 (A) and the AKG "TUBE" (B) are traditional studio microphones that enhance vocal and handle high SPL, giving smooth, well-rounded "colored" renditions of the musical event. (Sources: Sennheiser & AKG)

Figure 5-29   Two stand-mounted Bruel & Kjaer 4004s cover the percussion possibilities of live performance. (Source: Bruel & Kjaer)

Figure 5-30   In Las Vegas where there is more RF per cubic foot than anywhere else on earth , very few wireless systems work free of interference. Nevertheless, wireless hand held systems are the choice to isolate vocals from background.

small boundary, small bass. The flattest low-frequency response occurs when the PZM® is floor- or wall-mounted. The closer the sound source is to the panel, the flatter the low-frequency response. (This is not the same as proximity effect.)

—*Increased directivity*: The bigger the boundary, the lower the frequencies that are rejected from the rear, since sounds approaching the system from the mike side are picked up more strongly than from the side or rear.

The polar pattern created by diffraction is omnidirectional at low frequencies smaller than the dimension (D) of the panel: $F = 188/D$.

The pattern becomes hypercardioid and supercardioid at mid to high frequencies. At the highest frequencies, it is hemispherical.

Powering Functions

Microphones may be powered in several ways, and they are usually marked accordingly:

- *"T" powering* requires 10–12 V, which usually comes from a DC battery "A + B" powering same. A red dot on the barrel indicates 10–12 V European polarity rewired to match the Nagra.
- *Phantom powering* is a power supply system in which the current flows from the positive supply terminal, via the electrical center of the two modulation leads, to the microphone. The system requires 48 V; an alternate version is a $+12, -12$-V option. It has two equal resistors at the

modulation terminals, with the return through the cable shield. Any interference in the microphone output caused by noise superimposed on the powering voltage is thereby reduced by the common mode of rejection, which for Sennheiser and Neumann systems exceeds 80 dB. There is no difference of potential between the two modulation leads. Microphone outlets equipped with phantom powering accept the outputs of dynamic, ribbon, and any tube-equipped condenser systems without the need to turn off the power supply voltage. Very long cables may be used because of the high audio level output, but the amplifier input may have to be padded down to avoid overloading.

- A *dynamic moving coil* microphone generates its own power.
- *Preamps* are built-in transformers found in Nagra and other professional recorders that allow for switching to all modes, including dynamic. Universal preamps provide switching to + 12, − 12, 48 V. Newer preamps are labeled "Qpau, Qpu-T." Older models are QPM 3-5 and QPSE 200 XOYO, for Sennheiser microphones.

Red-Dotting

A microphone may take the (DC) power it requires from one of several sources:

- A regulated 12-V battery pack attached to the microphone or placed in-line between the system and the recorder.
- A cable amplifier (KAT-II cable), which takes 12-V power from the Nagra recorder via the accessory socket to the microphone.
- A mixer with 12-V battery-powered transformer inputs.
- Phantom powering (as described), 12 V or 48 V.
- Preamplifier modules mounted inside the Nagra, which are switchable from 12 V to 48 V.

Some Nagra recorders have reversed polarity wiring at the microphone inputs (XLR 3-pin inputs). Since this causes signal cancellation, either the Nagra or the microphone must be rewired. Switching polarity on microphones is called *red-dotting* because a small red dot is placed on the base of the barrel to signify compatibility with the European polarity. The battery pack can be rewired with phase-reversing pigtail microphone cables, or you can use a switchable microphone. In any event, the soundperson won't always know if all microphones are of the correct polarity until they are plugged into the machine that is actually used. (See Figure 5-31.)

Resistor pads are also used to match impedances. Resistors consume power, always causing a greater loss than that of the transformer. The pads, however, may be used in either *balanced* or *unbalanced* circuits. "L" pads are

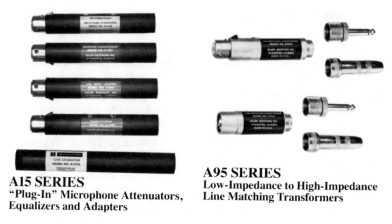

A15 SERIES
"Plug-In" Microphone Attenuators,
Equalizers and Adapters

A95 SERIES
Low-Impedance to High-Impedance
Line Matching Transformers

Figure 5-31   Phase-reversing accessories and preamps. (Source: Shure)

for unbalanced lines, "U" is for balanced lines. The pad maintains direct connection between the two circuits and can't balance out noise as well as a transformer, which is capable of complete isolation.

When microphone manufacturers change their designs, they often change the powering designations and polarity of their systems. The problem consists of deciphering whether the given microphone is a two-wire or three-wire system (unbalanced or balanced), "red-dotted" (polarized) or not, dynamic supplying its own current, or condenser requiring external batteries, and high or low impedance. Finding all this out can be exasperating. Proper marking and identification are a matter of experience and discipline.

Phasing

The motion picture industry has only recently standardized the cable connector configuration to Canon XLR 3 pin type connectors. Some existing standards for phasing outside the film industry indicate that the correct phasing for microphones is such that an increase in pressure on the diaphragm produces a positive charge on pin 1 of the European DIN connector and on pin 2 of the US XLR-3 connector. For early Nagra III and IVs, phase-reversal battery packs or cables should be used to correct microphones supplied with incorrect polarity.

Sound Problems

Impedance

The winding or magnetic coil of a microphone has a characteristic known as impedance. In professional systems, it is of low magnitude (600 Ω or less). For a microphone to match the tape machine electrically, the impedance of the recorder input should be the same or close to the output impedance of the microphone. If these are identical then:

- The power transfer is maximum.
- The frequency response should be flat.

Otherwise, the signal is distorted, diminished, or lost. The reason has to do with the fact that the microphone diaphragm physically vibrates when sound hits it. When the sound intensity reaches a certain level, the diaphragm can move no farther back and forth. This condition of *nonlinearity* results in a "clipping" of the waveform. (See Figure 5-32.) This condition of imbalance flattens the peaks of the wave.

Overload creates the same condition but in voice recording, normal dynamics seldom exceed 60 dB. Most production microphones can handle a full shout at a reasonable distance without overloading. For explosions, jet planes, subways, and excessive wind gusts or storms, special systems must be used. Proper placement also insures against distortion and overload.

Balancing and Matching

To operate properly and to distribute the audio signal efficiently and in a linear fashion, a microphone system must have its input and output impedances matched correctly. An audio unit is designed to deliver a given *signal level* into a prescribed *load impedance* only if it has the correct signal level at its input terminals. Potential mismatches can occur around a single unit, that is, input and output load impedances may be incorrect. (See Figure 5-33.) The results can be any of the following:

- Signal levels that are too high or too low.
- Noise or distortion introduced into the system.
- Bandpass affected due to reactive elements in the mismatch point reacting to high audio frequencies differently than to low ones.

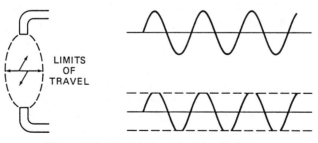

Figure 5-32   Limits of travel of the diaphragm.

INTERCONNECTION DIAGRAMS
FOR MKH CONDENSER MICROPHONES

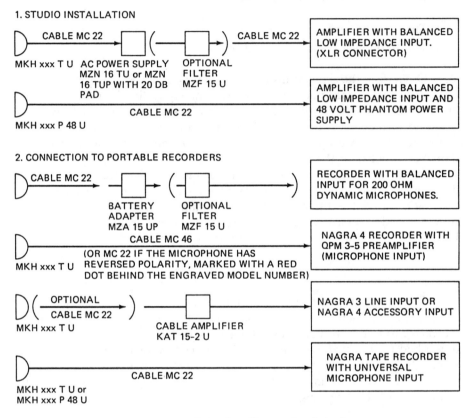

Figure 5-33 Balancing. (Source: Sennheiser)

Transformers are used to match impedances. Besides "transforming" the impedances of the circuits, the signal voltages are also transformed to different values. There can be a one-to-one voltage transfer, or a step-up or step-down voltage action according to the impedance selected. A well-designed transformer has an *insertion loss* of about 0.5 dB across the bandpass.

Diffraction

The very presence of the microphone causes some problems. When obstacles are placed in the path of a sound wave, they cause the wavefront to bend a bit. *Diffraction* is the bending of sound waves. If the dimensions of the obstacle are much less than the wavelength of the sound, there is little diffraction. If the frontal dimension of the microphone is of the same order as the wavefront, diffraction will take place. The wavelength of a 7,500-Hz signal is 2 in, and that of a 15,000-Hz signal is 1 in. Since microphones are generally 1 in or larger, diffraction must occur. The larger the head, the lower the frequency where it starts to occur. Even the mini tie-clip lavalier cannot avoid the problem.

The ideal microphone is therefore a point in space. (See Figure 5-34.) The graph in Figure 5-36 indicates that this microphone tends to be less omnidirectional as the frequency increases; this diffraction therefore causes a loss response at high frequencies when the speaker is at an angle other than 0°. On the upside, if the speaker's voice has high frequency energy (sibilant), the microphone can be tilted at an oblique angle so that the sound source is *off-axis* or *off-mike* causing the high frequency response failure. (See Figure 5-35.)

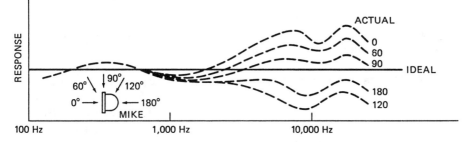

Figure 5-34   Diffraction in a typical omni microphone.

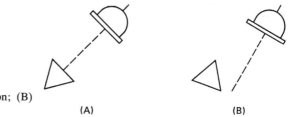

Figure 5-35   (A) Normal position; (B) off-mike position.   (A)   (B)

Proximity Effect

Any microphone having a ribbon element in it (bidirectional) has problems in the low frequency region. Ribbon mikes cannot be used close to the source since the low frequency response of the ribbon is accentuated when the distance between source and microphone is less than a wavelength. Due to the extremely low resonance frequency of the ribbon, rumble is easily introduced when the microphone is suspended on a boom. Any microphone operating on the velocity principle (cardioid, hypercardioid, bi, poly) tends to be "boomy" when used close to the actor. (See Figure 5-36.)

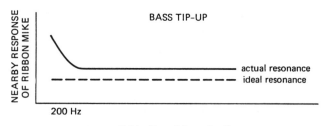

Figure 5-36 Bass "tip-up" effect.

Audio Cable Problems

A grossly overlooked source of noise problems is the basic garden-variety microphone cable. It's stepped on, bent, twisted, pulled, cut, nicked. Its connected terminals are often allowed to loosen, lose screws, jingle, tangle, and generally go haywire just when you thought it was safe to record. When troubleshooting for problems, always *check the cable first*. Even if it was fine during the last take, a connector may break at any time. (See Figure 5-37.)

SCR noise. Power line frequency can become contaminated by a rich harmonic spectrum generated by saturated power transformers, by fluorescent lights' ballasts, and, most drastically, by the clipped waveforms emitted by lighting dimmers' SCRs (silicon controlled rectifiers). The magnetic fields radiated by these sources cut across the conductors of a microphone cable and induce voltage that is heard as hum or buzz at high frequencies. Twisting the inner conductors minimizes this electromagnetic susceptibility.

Electrostatic hum. The power line and microphone cable act as two plates of a capacitor causing the AC voltage to be electrostatically coupled into the cable, which is heard as hum. The higher the impedance of the mike circuit, the greater the induced noise voltage. A grounded, electrically conductive screen around the cable (the shield) offers a low-resistance path to ground-shunting electrostatic hum. Fully wrapped aluminum tape offers 100% protection. Braided shields offer greater flexibility on the job and provide nearly 97% rejection.

TABLE 5-14 Physical characteristics of basic elements

Conductor carries the signal, uses solid or stranded wire of various gauges. Solid wire is cheaper and requires less room, but tends to break with flexing.

Insulation isolates conductors. Thermoplastic materials require less thickness, are tougher. Thermosetting (rubber, neoprene) is more flexible.

Shielding is any defense against interference.

Jacketing protects inner elements. Thermoplastic is lighter, cheaper, water-resistant. Thermosetting is limp, lies flat, has better low-temperature characteristics.

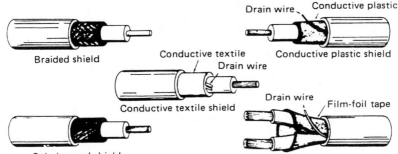

Braided shield · Conductive textile · Drain wire · Conductive plastic · Conductive plastic shield · Conductive textile shield · Drain wire · Film-foil tape · Spiral-served shield · Polyester film-aluminum foil shield

Notes

- Solder connections carefully. Poor soldering may cause hum pickup.

- Be sure to connect each wire as shown below. If the hot and cold sides are reversed, the output will be out of phase with correctly connected microphones.

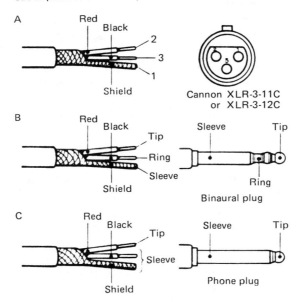

Figure 5-37 Various types of shields.

Ground loops.   Common mode noise is caused by electrical potential differences (ground loops), created when the cable shield is connected to a ground on both ends between equipment. This happens because additional ground paths are created in parallel with the hard-wired AC power line grounds. Noise may come across as hum, radio interference, or ultrahigh-frequency internal equipment oscillation. "Floating" lines, where none of the center conductors are grounded, or "balanced" lines, where a transformer center tape is grounded, avoid such problems. Often cutting the shield at the mixer/recorder end of the microphone cable helps.

Crosstalk.   Leakage occurs when signals enter adjacent channels of a multichannel cable, either by capacitive coupling or electromagnetic induction. Canare Cables with shielding of each channel prevent static coupling. To reduce the possibility of magnetic induction, different pitch twisting of each adjacent channel prevents the alignment of magnetic fields, thus minimizing inductive coupling.

Handling noise.   Sharply bending, vibrating, or twisting a cable can cause the spacing to change between conductors and between the shields. This changes the capacitance coupling between conductors, thereby generating noise. Handling noise is minimized by using "packed" cable, which holds its dimensions and resists stretching.

Low-level noise.   During quiet periods, a microphone generates extremely low-level signals, which make some cable susceptible to EMI (electromagnetic interference). Temperature changes, flexing and mechanical vibration can contribute to the capacitance changes that produce hum.

Microphone Placement

Because of its basic configuration, the cardioid microphone turns out to be best suited for the rigors of film, video, and AV work. It diffracts sound, but its angle of acceptance coincides with the camera's *angle of interest*. It is subject to bass tip-up but is insensitive to the major portion of extraneous noise that usually comes from the rear—set noise and camera noise.

Microphone placement determines the noise level in the recording. While noise (that is, anything you do not want to hear) may not have been objectionable on the set, it may be very obtrusive on the tape. This prime consideration makes for new believers—(to paraphrase scripture) they shall hear the inaudible.

Several psychoacoustic factors make the elimination of noise essential. The playback level in the theatre is usually higher than recording levels. Average noise levels on the track tend to be quite distracting in projection. In the live recording situation, the listener detects noise in "stereo" (two ears), and the brain localizes it and often disregards it. In projection, it is heard monophonically and can mask speech. If sound cannot be obtained without noise present, the problem may be reduced by establishing an identity for the noise.

The Ideal Position

Regardless of the situation or the type of equipment used, a couple of rules of thumb apply:

- The microphone should be as close to the subject as the shot size allows. The edge of the frame dictates the minimum distance. (See Figure 5-38.)
- The normal microphone position is *above and in front* of the source. Imagine a 2-ft cube in space, with the human head in one corner and the microphone in the diagonally opposite corner. This is the optimum position for best *fidelity* of voice, since it creates an acoustic space ratio of 1 : 1 (voice box versus spatial pattern of sensitivity of a given cardioid microphone). (See Figure 5-39.) The placement of the microphone at an angle of about 45° to the plane of the sound source maximizes efficiency and isolation.

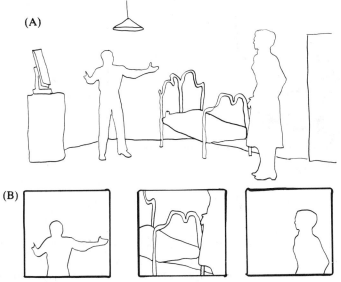

Figure 5-38 (a) The scene; (b) individual frames, details of the master should match aurally in terms of background, clarity, S/N level, perspective. When a scene is composed in separation—when an establishing shot is broken down into its narrative details—the parts appear closer, more integrated than in the whole (long take). Separation is a primary editorial function with the role of bringing people or things emotionally and physically closer, by cutting to details of the primary shot, than they would otherwise appear in one master shot. The aural imaging, however, will determine how "seamless" the edited sequence will appear. It is not inevitable, however, that sound should be subordinate any more than it should be in a less complex array in which the *density of detail* is of a lesser degree. The challenge to the audio designer in this sequence is to make something more of it within the limits of, and with reference to, what came before and what will come after the sequence in question. Convention ruled that the same mike be used in each shot and moved no more than twice the initial mike-to-subject distance in any direction from the closest position in the central shot of the sequence. The director must decide on the intimacy or detachment, with the resultant change in recording technique.

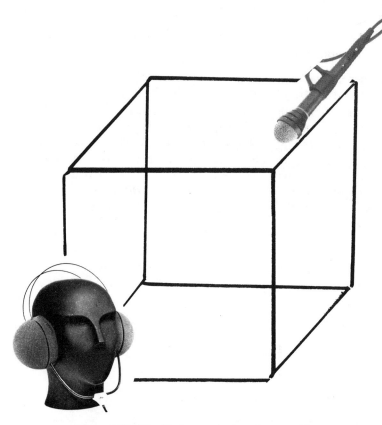

Figure 5-39   The ideal normal microphone position.

The human head may be used as the basis for the proportional distancing of a microphone in a sequence with differing shot sizes and movements.

The ideal placement of the mike offsets the problems associated with the three elements of the sound reaching the microphone in complex combinations:

1. The direct signal from the source.
2. The reflected signals from proximate surfaces.
3. The background noise, rumble, air pressure.

With the microphone angled toward the mouth, the source of the direct signal, the actor's chest blocks front reflections while absorbing back reflections and ambient noise. The microphone element is away from the floor and ceiling, two obvious sources of reflected noise. It is pointing away from the camera, making it unlikely to pick up its intermittent clicking. The suggested working distance is 2 ft.

As the shot changes, the recordist should use multiples of the basic original set-up, that is, moving the microphone twice the distance while holding it at 45°. If the inverse square law holds, the mixer can control level changes. Clearly, the recordist can avoid severe drops or peaks in level, as well as off-mike errors due to movement of camera or actor within the shot, by moving incrementally, doubling or halving the distance. These changes cue the tape recorder operator (mixer) to raise or lower the *gain* by 3 dB. This is the most basic way of insuring sound continuity—a 3–5-dB range from master to close-up in a scene (if that is the goal).

Some directors allow an actor's voice to drop out as he or she moves away from the camera, as if to capture a perceptual reality. In *Citizen Kane,* as the subject moves away from the observer, the voice diminishes. In practice, the realities of the screen often dictate the necessity for no break in *literal* continuity; that is, the audio level remains continuous regardless of the position of the source, thus creating a fundamental screen illusion whose philosophical implications are beyond this text. Figure 5-40 offers a selection of typical location set-ups with placement solutions. This basic set-up works for most microphones. It is not meant to be rigid, but provides a geometric method for controlling the recording situation.

Deciding how much to move the microphone is a craft, but it can often be reduced to a multiple choice guess. In moving shots, for example, the more narrow the pattern of the microphone, the more exacting and limited the movement of the microphone, since even the slightest errors may cause severe off-axis effects.

You would *expect* the vocal perspective to be slightly altered in the move from a close-up to a medium or long shot. Structurally, however, the track does not have to correspond physically and literally to the proximate image. Each image or event fact has a life of its own, but in the strict notion of Hollywood straight-match continuity and synchronous sound "lip sync" recording, the quality of the sound from the shot in Figure 5-39(A) should match that of the shots in Figure 5-39(B) without a break, a seamless marriage. Yet if, in the first shot, we move the microphone as drastically out of the stated proportion as the camera moves, the change can create an awkward condition, a kind of space/time warp. In the second series, if we raise the gain for the direct signal, so that it "sounds" realistic, the secondary reflected signal may be too loud.

This matching is a subjective judgment of relative spacial coordinates of foreground and background. In practice, the *space seen* has a *presence* or background tone, which is immediately perceived and which defines all successive shots in that space. Although directorially, a close-up must of necessity "sound" close up and a long shot must have a sound that reinforces the viewers' sense of "distance," there is great conjecture as to what constitutes actual presence. How does one "hear" a small or close space in relation to a large or long space?

(*Text continued on page 99*)

Figure 5-40   Microphone placement for various types of compositions, with movement.

Tracking shot has soundperson running in unison with subject across the axis of the shot to capture footsteps, breathing, grunts, and any dialogue during the dash. Sense of wind brushing past windscreen may be useful, but care is necessary to keep the "shotgun" on axis and at the uniform 10–12 ft from subject throughout the shot.

Subject is being filmed from overhead hanging camera as she peers over balcony. Subjective (POV) shot is miked with midrange cardioid from behind for environmental sounds only.

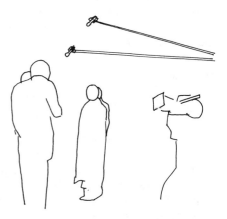

Both foreground and background couples need to be covered. A pair of matched midrange cardioids are staggered overhead from the camera position to preserve the perspective.

Exterior two-shot on steps taken from below. A cardioid with a small windpop screen maintains the intimacy of the shot.

Figure 5-40 (cont.)

Group exterior. Coverage is necessary of severeal speakers taken over-the-shoulder of the principal subject. A shotgun hypercardioid in a windscreen is angled from 10 ft to "grab" individuals.

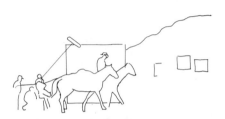

Exterior subject moving away from camera. A hypercardioid 5 ft from camera position allows natural fade while pickup of hooves is maintained.

From behind reflector (note shadow) on angle 10 ft from crawing subject during a dusty scuffle with gunshots. Low-angle shot allows close miking.

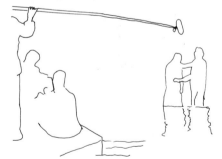

Water both absorbs and reflects sound. Quiet exterior subject requires sensitive overhead pickup of all nuances of water ambiance without emphasizing splashing. Shotgun in windscreen and windsock 6 ft above subject.

Subject moves quickly toward camera as camera trucks backward. A tricky trajectory and movement require a boom to maintain average subject-to-mike distance without intruding into the movement. Midrange hypercardioid is kept on-axis while avoiding clunking noise from all that moving gear.

Figure 5-40 (cont.)

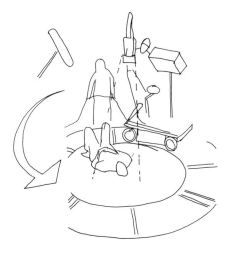

Most 360° shots require directional miking from above, dipping into the "envelope" surrounding the apparent camera angle. No movement of the mike is necessary until the camera reaches the semicircle.

Exterior walking-talking shot requires exacting mike-to-subject distancing via hypercardioid that rejects background noise while keeping pace with camera movement.

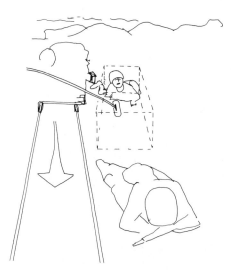

Noisy exterior battle sequence with subject crawling in the rubble. Subject and mike move forward. Camera is taking a profile, low-angle, close-up shot. Mike is within 5 ft.

Mike position is stationary, but boom sways left as couple converse and move camera left to right across axis. Midrange hypercardioid, kept on-axis from above, allows natural fade. Shot is rather wide and might call for a wireless set-up.

Figure 5-40 (cont.)

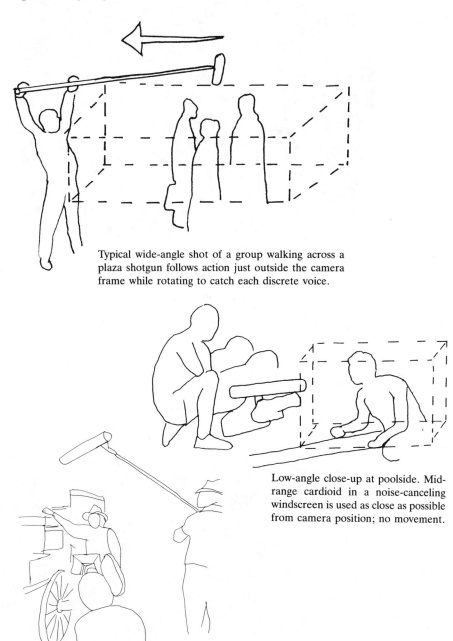

Typical wide-angle shot of a group walking across a plaza shotgun follows action just outside the camera frame while rotating to catch each discrete voice.

Low-angle close-up at poolside. Mid-range cardioid in a noise-canceling windscreen is used as close as possible from camera position; no movement.

Typical exit/entrance of "vehicle" and single speaker. Shotgun in screen taken from above camera as it tilts up. Boom remains stationary as group moves out of frame.

Figure 5-41 (Godard's *LaChinoise;* source: New Yorker Films)

Typical two-shot, interior; a directional microphone placed underneath close to the frame line and angled toward female will preserve intimacy, reduce discrepancy in intensity of female to male voice. Bernardo Bertolucci's Before the Revolution (1962) aurally invoking the 1960's state-of-mind.

Even the fake "studio" exterior of Jean-Luc Godard's Weekend (1967), requires isolating directionality of the "shotgun" microphone set at 45 degrees to these subjects from above one foot of head room. The result is less background interference. Weekend questioned the authenticity of live vs pre-recorded sound in a fictionalized docudrama.

Figure 5-41 (cont.)

The spacial orientation suggests at least two emotional planes. Ambiance from an omnidirectional mike may be used to "build" qualities of silence. Here, the room is the subject in Two or Three Things I Know About Her, Godard, 1966.

The interplay of foreground to background audio can be assured with separate miking of moving foreground from above with a directional cardioid and background with a bi or omnidirectional mike. The two-track technique requires more care but achieves greater separation. Bertolucci's The Spider Strategem (1970).

Figure 5-41 (cont.)

Emotional moments often come across as ludicrous when the shot is dubbed. Should the director attempt to capture the natural ambiance of the moment or synthesize it? Timing, reactions, and intense, brief aural nuances are tough to lay-in. Try a mid-range cardioid (Senn 416) for close-miking underneath. What is the truth of the shot? See Michaelangelo Antonioni's Story of a Love Affair (1950).

This is the tail-end of an action shot requiring a very mobile fishpole cardioid set to follow action and still get down in close for this low-angle medium quiet interior of Patrick Swayze and Jennifer Grey in Vestron's Dirty Dancing (1987).

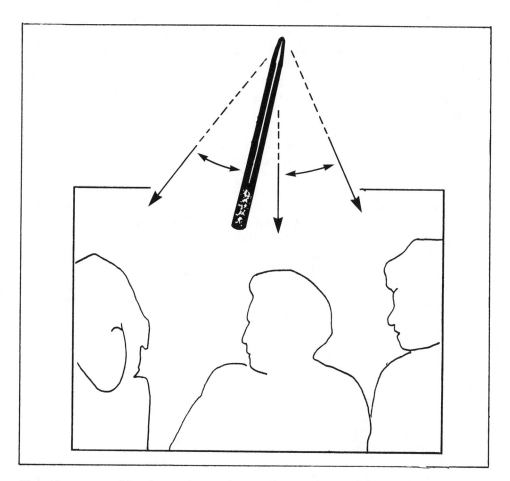

Three-shots are rare. Often they require separate wireless mikes on each subject to insure complete coverage especially when there is movement. Otherwise a very dexterous boomman must cover from above with a standard cardioid.

Life gets simpler, however. In practice, the microphone movement is never as gross a change as the camera movement. The same proportion is maintained as a multiple of the original cube. If the initial set-up takes into account the successive shots in the sequence (this is why the sound designer must study the script), the microphone seldom moves more than 3 ft in any direction. All the boom person has to do is maintain the same ratio of microphone to performer distance and angle. Understanding the trajectory and microphone angle of acceptance is critical. The boom handler must be comfortable and move with subtlety from *one* spot. If the movement is very complex, multiple microphones in fixed positions may be used for full coverage, or a wireless microphone may be placed on the actor(s) in combination with overhead full-field coverage.

See Figure 5-41 for "intimate" examples. Each of the shots in that figure present situations with multiple solutions. However, one microphone set-up will ultimately produce better sound clarity as well as the appropriate spatial effect. The two-shot on the dance room floor could be handled frontally from the camera position at eye level with an omni or from above with a unidirectional. What if anything needs to be isolated?

The *mirror image shot* had no movement, so talent could be pinned with an omni lavalier or miked from directly above with a studio-grade omni condenser or dynamic. Godard reportedly used the interview-style hand-held cardioid from the side. A sense of intimacy must be preserved. Miking from below with a dynamic cardioid, you avoid excessive clothing noise. From farther back and under, the directional isolates the sounds of affection. From above, perspective is enhanced and reflections absorbed by bedclothes (Figure 5-41).

A tough moving *tango shot* with classical framing requires either the sensitive movement of the shotgun on a boom from above or the fixed overhead coverage of a studio-grade Neumann omnidirectional wide-field mike.

Multiple voices are best miked individually with the mounted mini-mike lavalier, but careful overhead boomwork with a midrange shotgun would be ideal.

Booms and Fishpoles

Mounting systems consists of two elements:

- A suspension system, which absorbs vibration while holding the microphone in position allowing for variable angling.
- A vertical support, which allows for the placement of the microphone above the action and pointed down a sound source, generally an actor's mouth.

Suppression of mechanical noise during microphone movement and handling is of primary concern for the recordist. After the microphone is secured in

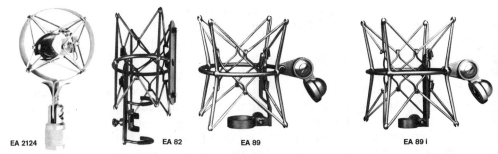

EA 2124   EA 82   EA 89   EA 89 i

Figure 5-42 Cradle mount is a typical stationary studio rig suitable for omni and cardioid coverage of groups or three or more characters in standing or seated positions.

the suspension cradle (see Figure 5-42), the microphone cable is looped to prevent its slapping against or stressing the connector and/or suspension pole. The cable is then taped securely every 2 ft to the pole to avoid clunking against the hollow rod. Some poles allow the cable to run through the center.

The work of the boom handler, who is essential to the best sound quality possible, is a true craft. Stand and podium mounting should be avoided since vibrations are conducted from the floor up through both objects into the microphone. Also, typical of most hanger-type boom mounts is the inability to remotely alter the angle of acceptance of the microphone. A geared elbow *cueing device* allows for rotational orientation simply by twisting the pole against the weight of the microphone. This action must be done quietly and quickly to avoid going off-axis during complex moving shots. *Boom shadow,* caused when the pole moves under an overhead or side light, is another

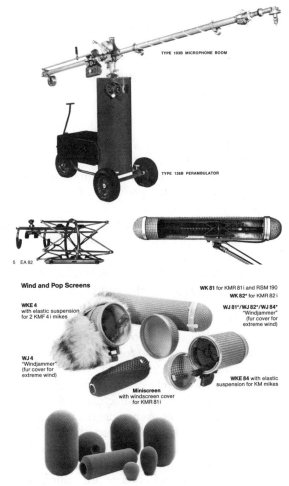

Figure 5-43 (A) The Mole-Richardson Perambulator-style Boom was the primary studio rig often brought out onto location because of its reach and precision. It was costly and somewhat inconvenient.

problem which must be avoided by proper placement and use of a boom or fishpole with a cueing head. Rehearsal for the timing of these small, intricate movements is often a luxury.

Aerodynamically stable windscreens or the "zeppelin" types afford further protection against both mechanical and wind noise in the studio and outdoors. Designer Les Drever has spent a decade refining the art of suspension systems for professional shotgun and cardioid microphones used on location. A rubber-damped double cantilever suspension on lexan mounts, attached to an adjustable working angle grip, allows for hand-held and boom operation. Up to 25 dB of wind noise can be suppressed by the mesh windscreen on the short end, and 16 dB on the long end with very little effect on frequency response. (See Figure 5-43.)

Wireless Microphones

Radio, or "wireless," microphone systems are composed of three elements:

- The microphone (usually an omnidirectional electret condenser).
- A receiver.
- A transmitter.

While the system is not without its inherent problems, it nevertheless frees the recordist from problems of placement and field coverage. If understood and used properly, radio microphones have the capacity to solve a multitude of recording problems, for two reasons:

- Since the microphone is pinned to the sound source, it is already operating within its ideal position as close as possible to the source.
- Since it is not tied to a recorder, it is infinitely mobile and therefore never off-axis or subject to the normal limitations associated with camera angle and size of shot. The subject is always "on," in theory.

Wireless microphone technology is primarily responsible for the movement back to location recording, formerly a hazardous venture at best. Prior to the mid-1970s, the sound for most Hollywood films was recorded in the studio under controlled conditions and "dubbed" seamlessly over the visuals. A great deal of effort went into creating the sense of live, exterior atmospheric sound achieved through the manufacture and manipulation of hundreds of elements of sound information. Achieving the spontaneity and authenticity of live sound, however, was costly and time-consuming. With wireless technology, we again have the luxury of recording on location. Because the microphone no longer presents constraints, the framing, scale of the shot, camera movement, and general compositional choices are unlimited. For example, recording usable sound on location for long shots was always difficult. Since the wireless mike is proximate and hidden in the shot, and since drastic movement is possible, the action genre film has flourished in the two decades following the introduction of hybrid wireless technology.

Placement of the wireless elements. The lavalier-style "mini" omnidirectional *microphone* element has been redesigned by some manufacturers to be easily concealed under clothing, either taped directly to skin or planted in any available place. (See Figure 5-44.) The metallic capsule configuration of the early Sony ECM 50 series yielded to the smaller, flat mini rectangular lexan (plastic) head of the TRAM TR-50 which may be taped, pinned, clipped, or buried. The idea is to plant the head *face up,* as close as possible to the mouth and angled obliquely *up and out.*

The *transmitter,* a radio frequency device cabled to the microphone, has a thin, pliable cable and antenna. Small enough to be hidden in a pocket or under clothing, it is most easily mounted on the performer via a cotton pouch and belt worn under the costume. It should be placed where it will be jostled the least (small of the back, back pocket, against rib cage, vest pocket, and so on). The transmitter is preset and left alone once it is secured to the body.

The *receiver* may consist of one or more individual receiver units and/or antennas. It is mounted directly at the recording station, generally into a mixer if more than one system is being used or directly into the balanced microphone input of the Nagra if in solo operation. The ideal position for the receiving antenna is as close as possible to the transmitting antenna, but not closer than 18 in from any large metal object or near reflective surfaces. Raising the

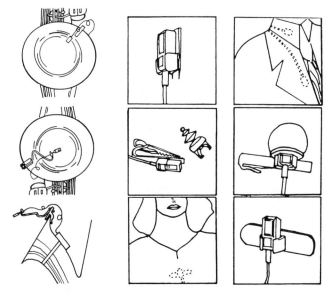

Figure 5-44 The wireless microphone and various mounting options (pin, tac, tape, clip).

The *transmitter,* a radio frequency device cabled to the microphone, has a thin, pliable cable and antenna. Small enough to be hidden in a pocket or under clothing, it is most easily mounted on the performer via a cotton pouch and belt worn under the costume. It should be placed where it will be jostled the least (small of the back, back pocket, against rib cage, vest pocket, and so on). The transmitter is preset and left alone once it is secured to the body.

The *receiver* may consist of one or more individual receiver units and/or antennas. It is mounted directly at the recording station, generally into a mixer if more than one system is being used or directly into the balanced microphone input of the Nagra if in solo operation. The ideal position for the receiving antenna is as close as possible to the transmitting antenna, but not closer than 18 in from any large metal object or near reflective surfaces. Raising the receiver above the recording area normally reduces interference from props, equipment, and people! To check for signal loss and blind spots, always *walk* the transmitter through the location set and adjust the antenna to eliminate dropout areas.

TABLE 5-14   Wireless microphone field practice tips

- Typically, location shoots call for at least four sets of radio microphones, that is, one plus three backups with different frequencies in case of location interference.
- Bring along at least four sets of spare batteries, and test them *in* the system with a meter before leaving for the location shoot.
- Although using the same brand of wireless is recommended, often a certain make and model does not work under specific circumstances while another will.
- Diversity systems utilize multiple antenna set-ups to avoid dropouts, but clipping can occur when two people share the same microphone on diversity. The reason is that the system switches between signals, automatically selecting the best signal at any given moment.
- In long "walk-and-talk" shots, a wireless boom may be required since obstacles may be in the trajectory of the movement.
- Bigger YAGI-type unidirectional antennas help eliminate interference from commercial broadcast and military antennae.
- New buildings generally have greater RF absorption than older structures.
- Older (illegal) low-power transmissions have less chance of interference and usually overpower paging systems and harbor patrol systems.
- Every microphone must be tested at each location.
- The microphone line must *never* cross the antenna line. Both should be kept as taut as possible.
- Since you can rotate the antenna with a nondiversity system, direction is not critical. Transmitter and receiver antennas must be kept parallel to each other.
- When wiring up a performer, try to keep the microphone as close to the neck or mouth and the antenna as far from the body as possible, since body water absorbs RF. Surgical tubing around the antenna provides insulation from perspiration. Undershirts provide further isolation and a taping surface.
- 3M Micropore Action Tape facilitates fixing to skin (especially for chorus girls on whom it's a trick to conceal a microphone and transmitter). Dry the skin with an alcohol prep then apply the tape. Velcro-lined pockets and belts can be sewn into a costume to hold the system.

TABLE 5-14   (continued)

- The thickness of clothing and how it reacts with the electret determines how to bind the lavalier to the actor. Anchor the microphone in a way that a loop is left and some slack can be available when the actor moves or stretches. Rehearsal is a luxury but it's the only way to determine cable noise. Forming a small induction loop by tying a knot toward the head of the microphone tends to make the system less sensitive to rustle and cable-induced noise.
- Sweaters are porous and let the most sound through. Either apply tape outward to the cloth and facing away from the body, or sandwich the microphone between two triangles of tape.
- Ankle-level transmitter placement seems to work well with snow or wet ground, which reflects the signal.
- For standing shots, placement in the small of the back is convenient; for sitting, side hip or frontal placement avoids crushing the cabling.
- For movement, running a flexible antenna around the waist allows for fluid movement, running, and complex action.
- Rubber bands effectively bind the tips of antennas and microphones, stretching with movement or taking up the slack with bending.
- Have performers remove keys or coins from their pockets and take off metallic chains on the costumes.
- Insure the performer's privacy by making certain the unit is turned off between takes or by notifying them that they are live while off-camera. Actors should not be encouraged to turn off the transmitter without notifying the crew.
- High temperatures tend to ruin almost all electret condenser elements.

Antenna length is critical and depends on frequency. Best performance is obtained with the transmitting antenna as high as possible on the performer. Run the antenna wire in the opposite direction to the microphone cable or instrument cable. The audio cable forms a ground; so position it as far away as possible from the antenna for maximum power output.

The receiver's working range is generally *line of sight;* that is, with good ground plane, reception should occur from any point that the recordist can see from his/her station. In practice, the working distance tends to be within 100 ft where the nature of the activity prohibits use of conventional miking. In many cases, however, the working range is subject to interference from spurious radio waveforms, free magnetic fields, and other wireless systems. Since wireless microphone systems are often used in multiple miking set-ups, each has its own assigned operating frequency. The frequencies are not arbitrary, but rather are assigned by the FCC for specific regions. With luck, the chosen frequencies are not too close to existing frequencies already in use on or near the location by other commercial systems and stations.

The lower the level setting of the transmitter, the greater the signal to noise level of the recording. Extremely high levels tend to reduce the dynamic range for voice renditions. (The standard level for voice at the transmitter is -2 to -4 dB on the VU meter.) The optimum gain control depends on the:

- Sensitivity of the microphone.
- Intensity of the voice.
- Distance between microphone and mouth.

Transmitter and receiver antennas should be of the same length and style (whip, wire, coaxial, or stub).

Set-up for recording.   The transmitter, once securely fastened to an object or performer, should be set and tested, never before. The reason is that body characteristics, mounting peculiarities, and the microphone position determine the overall quality of the signal being recorded. The transmitter is turned on first. In most systems a red indicator lamp (LED) goes on and stays on as long as there is no interference. Level adjustments are made with prenotched settings that the manufacturer has designed into the transmitter.

The receiver generally has a gain control, which should be left at its median position unless the shot or situation requires great amplification. All of the future level adjustments should be done at the recorder. Unless a serious problem occurs (generally an actor speaks too softly, requiring the transmitter level to be adjusted), it is best not to attempt drastic alterations in the settings made at the receiver and recorder/mixer. Generally a meter reading of greater than -15 dB VU indicates a usable signal. (See Figure 5-45.)

A few of the several innovative, clever methods for placing or mounting mini microphones are listed in Table 5-15.

Principle of operation.   Most wireless microphone systems operate in the VHF (very high frequency) high band where there is less electrical noise and less interference from business band radio than is commonly found at lower frequencies. One characteristic of VHF radio waves is their tendency to travel outward in straight lines from the transmitting antenna. When a receiving antenna is placed within the range of the transmitted signal, with no nearby objects to interfere, only one ray reaches the antenna. The intensity of this ray varies in accordance with the inverse square law. If the distance between the two antennas doubles, the signal power drops to one-fourth of its original signal, but audio level is not dependent on the separation of transmitter and receiver. Understanding this aids the recordists in balancing levels during extended moving shots where displacement means serious level drops.

Absorption problems.   Plants, animals, and even performers can absorb radio waves. Depending on the angle, the absolute signal level, and the nature of the object, a small increase in noise level or a complete *dropout* of the signal may occur. To overcome the possibility of this happening at any time during the shot, *diversity antenna systems* are utilized. Two receivers with antennas are spaced at different angles, thereby making it unlikely that rays to both antenna would be absorbed at the same time. The receiver with the stronger signal at any one moment is selected by a combiner.

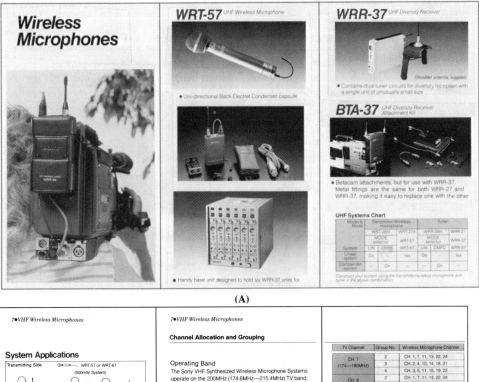

(A)

7●VHF Wireless Microphones

System Applications

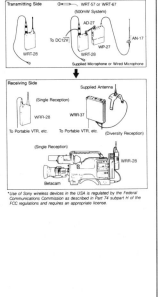

Use of Sony wireless devices in the USA is regulated by the Federal Communications Commission as described in Part 74 subpart H of the FCC regulations and requires an appropriate license.

7●VHF Wireless Microphones

Channel Allocation and Grouping

Operating Band
The Sony VHF Synthesized Wireless Microphone Systems operate on the 200MHz (174.6MHz—215.4MHz) TV band, which corresponds to TV channels 7 through 13 in the USA.

Channel Allocation
Each of the 7 available TV channels is divided into 24 wireless microphone channels with a separation of 200kHz, giving a total of 168 potentially usable channels. By virtue of PLL synthesized tuning, the WRR-410 tuner and WRR-420 diversity tuner allow pushbutton selection of any of these channels, whereas the WRT-410 microphone and WRT-420 transmitter are designed for operation on 48 channels, covering all 168 channels with 4 models.

TV Channel	CH. 7 & 8	CH. 9 & 10	CH. 11 & 12	CH. 12 & 13
Microphone	WRT-410-7	WRT-410-9	WRT-410-11	WRT-410-12
Transmitter	WRT-420-7	WRT-420-9	WRT-420-11	WRT-420-12
Tuner	WRR-410			
Diversity Tuner	WRR-420			

Channel Groups
The 24 wireless microphone channels in each TV channel are grouped and preset for ease and simplicity of multi-channel operation.

Group 1 (Full Access Channel Group): Operation on any of the 24 wireless microphone channels is possible, except those used locally for TV broadcast. However, taking into account the possibility of interference caused by the harmonics of the local oscillator of the tuners, it is recommended that, for safety's sake, Group 1 not be used in places where one of the other groups can be used.

Groups 2—4 (Individual TV Channel Groups): Each group consists of 6 wireless microphone channels specially selected for simultaneous operation without intermodulation distortion. In addition, if the chosen channels are subjected to interference from the surrounding TV stations, it is possible to switch to either of the other two groups or any other TV channel.

TV Channel	Group No.	Wireless Microphone Channel
CH. 7 (174—180MHz)	2	CH. 1, 7, 11, 13, 22, 24
	3	CH. 2, 4, 10, 14, 18, 21
	4	CH. 3, 5, 11, 15, 19, 22
CH. 8 (180—186MHz)	2	CH. 1, 7, 11, 13, 22, 24
	3	CH. 2, 4, 10, 14, 18, 21
	4	CH. 1, 3, 6, 14, 18, 24
CH. 9 (186—192MHz)	2	CH. 3, 5, 9, 15, 20, 23
	3	CH. 3, 6, 11, 17, 19, 23
	4	CH. 1, 8, 10, 13, 21, 24
CH. 10 (192—198MHz)	2	CH. 3, 5, 9, 15, 20, 23
	3	CH. 3, 6, 11, 17, 19, 23
	4	CH. 2, 5, 10, 16, 20, 22
CH. 11 (198—204MHz)	2	CH. 2, 4, 10, 14, 18, 21
	3	CH. 1, 5, 7, 13, 16, 24
	4	CH. 2, 7, 14, 16, 20, 23
CH. 12 (204—210MHz)	2	CH. 2, 4, 10, 14, 18, 21
	3	CH. 1, 5, 7, 13, 16, 24
	4	CH. 4, 7, 11, 15, 21, 23
CH. 13 (210—216MHz)	2	CH. 1, 7, 11, 17, 19, 22
	3	CH. 2, 4, 8, 12, 15, 22
	4	CH. 3, 5, 11, 15, 19, 22

Group 5 (Odd TV Channel Group): This group operates in the odd-numbered TV channels 7, 9, 11 and 13 for simultaneous operation of up to 13 channels.

TV Channel	Wireless Microphone Channel
CH. 7	CH. 1, 7, 11, 13, 22, 24
CH. 9	CH. 1, 9, 23
CH. 11	CH. 14, 19
CH. 13	CH. 3, 23

Group 6 (Even TV Channel Group): This group operates in the even-numbered TV channels 8, 10 and 12 for simultaneous operation of 11 channels in all.

TV Channel	Wireless Microphone Channel
CH. 8	CH. 1, 7, 11, 13, 22, 24
CH. 10	CH. 1, 9, 23
CH. 12	CH. 14, 19

With these unique channel allocation and grouping plans, the Sony VHF Synthesized Wireless Microphone Systems meet the critical professional requirements of easy setup and use anywhere, effective utilization of the limited frequency band, and reliable multi-channel operation without intermodulation interference.

(B)

Figure 5-45 (A) Microphone configuration may be hand-held or "tie-tac" style. This typical kit includes mounting pack for transmitter, stackable receivers, dual tuner circuits for deversity reception, a shoulder antenna, metal fittings for Betacom. (B) Channel allocation and grouping for Sony wireless systems. (Source: Sony)

TABLE 5-15a   Wireless microphone checklist

1. Examine coaxial (rubberized flexible) cables for breaks that cause dropouts.
2. Fresh, fully charged batteries. Weak or cheap batteries cause a guaranteed RF loss.
3. Never touch antennas when in operation.
4. Use the *squelch* adjustment for internal muting.
5. Remember: Signal to noise level varies inversely with the transmission distance.
6. Antennas must be vertical at all times.
7. Phasing and drift problems require dual diversity antenna systems.
8. Knotting the thin electret microphone cable eliminates clothing noise.
9. Camera noise may be lessened using a DBS class *noise gate* built into some systems.
10. Range is line of sight, with good ground plane. Standing water absorbs RF.
11. An auto ignition is a source of interference.
12. The signal travels in straight lines in all directions upward from ground parallel.

TABLE 5-15b   Trade hints for radio microphone mounting

Felt Squares: 3 × 3-in swatches can be wrapped around the microphone and matched to a performer's clothing color. They block wind but sacrifice frequencies over 12 kHz.

Thumb: The microphone is mounted on a performer's thumb while he or she is holding a cup of coffee, to hide the element from the lens's field of view.

Clipboard: Tape the mini or PZM GL head to a clipboard resting on a desk or being held.

Purse: Tape the element onto the side of a purse being held.

Eyeglasses: Set the element inside the temple piece of the glasses.

Collar: Hide the element in the shirt or blouse collar.

Ace: Use a skin color ACE bandage to conceal the element.

Reflection problems.   Most wireless microphones are not operated in free, unobstructed space. Practically all surfaces have some effect on the propagation of VHF radio waves; metallic surfaces and even wood or concrete act as reflectors. The signal reaching the receiving antenna is generally a composite of direct and reflected radio waves. Essentially an oscillating electromagnetic wave, the VHF signal can experience either an increase or decrease of intensity depending on how direct and reflected signals combine (addition or subtraction). A difference between the two paths of half a wavelength (36 on VHF channels) results in completely out-of-phase conditions at the receiver. Signal level deviations of this nature are called *multipath* cancellation.

If the two waves are of equal strength, they totally cancel each other out, producing a *dropout.* Generally the dropout condition can be restored to normal signal level by changing the position of the transmitter, but this solution is impractical for the performer. Alternatively, orientating the antenna or receiver a few inches, or employing diversity receiving multiantenna set-ups, is easier. *Space diversity* systems employ circuits that select audio from the receiver with the strongest signal at any given moment. *Polarization diversity* uses two receiving antennas that are rotated to different polarizations. A vertically polarized antenna can be nulled out by a horizontally polarized receiver antenna. (Bear in mind that even antennas of identical polarization may have problems with reflected signals—for instance, if a performer bends over while the mike is transmitting polarization changes.)

Blocking problems.	Directional wireless microphones run into several types of positioning problems:

- If the boom person is not careful, the tracking can move into a *null* (created when the mike's pattern of sensitivity falls outside the sound source field) and lose the signal entirely.
- Transmitters used near each other (such as in a group conversation), whose frequencies are too close, may block each other out. They *beat* against each other, and the receivers cannot discriminate between them. If the frequencies are, for instance, 5 kHz apart, a 5-kHz buzz is likely.
- Nothing else in the vicinity must transmit on the wireless's frequencies; so each region must be checked for TV station and police usage.
- A stationary video camera with an attached wireless (like the "piggyback" system in Figure 5-46) is fine, but when the camera operator moves, the antenna position changes, sometimes drastically, giving rise to a new set of problems. The shot must be auditioned to avoid dropouts.

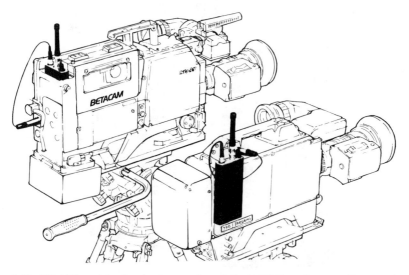

Figure 5-46	Hitchhiker-style piggyback mounting of wireless DC receiver on a Betacom is now standard practice. Any system can be adapted, but Swintek was the first using their Mark QDC VHF receiver units. (Source: Swintek)

Field problems

The bottom line in audio production is *saving time*—specifically, avoiding the need for costly looping and retakes. Here are some troubleshooting and trouble-prevention tips.

- *Radio interference:* VHF (high-band, 150- to 216-MHz) wireless mikes are not susceptible to CB and FM radio interference. Economy (low-band, 30- to 50-MHz) wireless systems can pick up CB calls. Tunable systems in the commercial (88- to 108-MHz FM) band often drift and are overwhelmed by commercial stations. (See Figure 5-47 and Table 5-16.)

- *Popping:* An optional on-off switch for the microphone element is needed because turning off a transmitter causes a "pop." The receiver seeks and locks onto the strongest signal it detects; if a transmitter is turned off, FM interference is more likely. With the transmitter on, either use the mike switch or lower the receiver gain until ready for next shot.

Figure 5-47 The Micron Channel 1 and 2 tunable wireless system. Micron Pocket Transmitters, 115db S/N, control panel shows click-stop level adjustment, LED indicator, and secure Lemo pin linkage. (Source: Micron)

TABLE 5-16   Sources of RF interference of wireless systems

Horse saddles	Spray with silicones, baby powder.
Auto interiors	Remove rattling objects, check glove compartment, rear-view mirror, trunk. Spark plug suppressors reduce idling noise.
Light mounts	Diffusion materials mounted in front of car-mounted lights tend to flap up in the wind.
Fluorescent lights	AC hum from vibratory nature of this source creates noise, including the pulse-like movement of electricity being turned on and off.
Dollies	Manual and hydraulic movements, dry wheels squeaking seats, boom clutch, and flapping cables are problems to eliminate in rehearsal.
Metal objects	Whenever two metal objects touch, they can generate static—neck chains, bracelets, springs in a bed or car seat, and so on. The transmitter must be either removed from the vicinity of these sources or taped down.
Camera	Some cameras exhibit RF noise. Make a test run.

- *Antennas:* Their selection and placement are crucial for maximizing transmission distances. Half-wire dipole antennas give a 3-dB boost in effective radiated power over most 18-in quarterwave flexible wire antenna. This doubling of transmission power is ordinarily achieved at the expense of cutting battery life in half. Orienting the antennas horizontally tends to eliminate commercial FM or mobile business radios, whose radiation is vertical. To avoid TV station interference, which is from horizontally radiated signals, set the wireless's antennas vertically.

- *Diversity system "talk":* Stacking diversity antenna systems vertically, with the receivers next to the audio console, may cause *talk,* that is, locally radiated oscillator radio signals interfering with each other. Distance them 2 ft apart.

- *Waist-level options for moving shots:* The standard mounting method is to start the antenna at waist level and then run it up the back and over the shoulder (parallel with the receiver's vertical antenna). An option is to start in the armpit or crotch and run it down the arm or leg. A rubber band is fastened to the free end, with a safety pin to allow for flexibility.

- *Static:* This is caused on stages by electric motor brushes, SCRs from dimmer boards, and unsuppressed engine ignitions from the street—all of which enter via the AC power lines. DC powering of the antenna diversity boxes ends the danger.

- *Multipath cancellation:* Structural steel, metal surfaces, and other metallic objects cause waveform reflections, which reach the receiver out of phase with the primary wave, cancelling it. This null, or dropout, can occur regardless of the transmitter/receiver distance. Short-range dropouts are much "snappier." Mylar set dressing acts like metal, as do crowds and storms. Some scenery is made with papermaché over chicken wire.

2 a

2 c

2 e

2 d

Figure 5-48 Alternate wireless antenna placements.

The wire screening acts as an excellent radio reflector and antenna. "Weaving" one dipole antenna into the chickenwire kills the dropouts.

- *Hidden metal:* Concrete floors have "ground planes" caused by the encased steel mesh. Walls may contain sheet metal heating ducts or steel girders. Diversity is needed where reflective surfaces exist. To avoid two falling into the same null spot, keep all antennas at a minimum of 18 in away from all metal and at least 8 ft apart.

- *Computer interference:* Most computers have microprocessor clock frequencies, ranging from 2 to 8 MHz, rich in harmonics, that cause buzz in wireless reception.

Band	Interference
40 MHz	Every 3.7 m
400 MHz	Every 30 cm, VHF and TV
900 MHz	Every 16 cm, UHF

Keep away from computers.

- *Dead points:* Each frequency band has dead points, but VHF signals are subject to fewer of them. Wireless transmission reliability can be improved as power is increased to gain higher field strength even at dead points. Table 5-17 compares field strength to distance. In addition to how the microphone is held or positioned, the distance between the mike and the speaker's body affects field strength.

- *Buzz tone versus dropout:* Signal to noise ratios and dynamic range specifications are meaningless if not related to the *available RF* of the wireless receiver, which is affected by the distance from the transmitter to receiver, sensitivity, and other factors. The loss of RF while passing through a dropout zone creates a noise like a buzz. A buzz tone is a noise

TABLE 5-17 Field strength as a function of distance

Frequency Band	Distance	20 cm Away from Body	Attached to Body	20 cm Away from the Back of Body	Attached to the Back of Body
VHF Band	100 m	57 dB/m	−5 dB	−5 dB	−9 dB
40.68 MHz	50 m	68 dB/m	−5 dB	−5 dB	−8 dB
UHF Band	100 m	65 dB/m	−5 dB	−9 dB	−17 dB
488 MHz	50 m	76 dB/m	−5 dB	−11 dB	−16 dB
UHF Band	100 m	67 dB/m	+5 dB	−14 dB	−6.5 dB
948 MHz	50 m	75 dB/m	+1 dB	−9 dB	−15 dB

that is generated by an external source, that is, an intrusion on the audio from switches, arc lights, ignition, anything generating a "plasma effect." Antenna system tricks do not stop buzz tones. A noise gate (like the dB-s compander system by Swintek) should help.

When a buzz tone is present, there is a peak in the general noise, which intrudes on the low-level audio signal. If the threshold of the low-level audio is raised 25%, the intrusion is lessened. The top and bottom of the full audio spectrum is compressed 50%, raising the threshold of the low-level audio far above the average noise level. Less noise gets into the transmitter. When the signal is re-expanded in the receiver, a level loss occurs but the buzz tone is eliminated. Level is raised in post-transfer stages. Consequently room ambience is also controlled, especially where camera or motor noise intrudes. When using a noise gate, set the audio level by controlling the input sensitivity of the microphone into the transmitter; that is, vary the power input, not the audio "pot" control. Thus, the threshold of the noise gate is set to eliminate background noise.

For example, two characters are speaking while sitting at the edge of a fountain. Both actors are pinned with wireless, and the transmitter level is set for the level of the fountain noise. The fountain is "gated" completely out so that there is no noise at all. A regular Sennheiser 415 is adjusted to barely pick up the sound of water going back into the fountain. The threshold of the transmitter is adjusted to the fountain noise. Using the combination of the wireless noise-gated on dialogue and the hard wire 415 for the fountain, this shot was actually made in one take.

TABLE 5-18   Uses and abuses of wireless microphones

Avoid using . . .

- Wireless microphones to solve complex movement problems when good boom work and coordination provides a crisper and more effective signal in a given space.
- Microphone in heavy traffic or heavy RF areas, such as New York City, airports, major highways, parking lots, and the like.
- A wireless alone without the subtle blending of a conventional *cover* microphone, which provides the environmental integrity that the omnidirectional short-range electret isolates.
- Wireless systems with clothing made from synthetics, polyesters, plastics, taffetas, and hard fiber garments, which conduct and generate noise, as well as making taping difficult. Double-sided tape helps to hold down the ruffles and pleated decorations.

Consider using . . .

- One of the new generation directional lavalier systems whose electret capsules produce greater rejection of unwanted reflected noise and feedback from studio and extraterrestrial interference.
- The lavalier microphone mounted lower on the body in scenes that do not involve over-the-shoulder speech. This offers natural rejection of breathing and chest cavity noise sources. If two people are facing each other, each microphone picks up the other person's dialogue.
- One microphone with its gain control wide open to record only room background to take the "edge" off the relatively isolated sound from pinned microphones. This creates a greater blend of environmental to speech signals with a wireless system.
- The second track of a stereo recorder provides the ambiance and transition sound elements, to be used later to cover jumps in level at edit cuts.
- One very directional condenser (a shotgun) mixed with the wireless electret set-up for a more natural presence in a shot or scene. One technique is the Nakamichi Three Point System. (See chapter on stereo.)

TABLE 5-19   Selected inventory of microphone accessories by manufacturer

Electro Voice

Shock Mount 307	Adapts any microphone with $3/4$-in diameter cylindrical shank for boom or stand use. Accommodates windscreen.
Attenuator 380	For use in mike line, reduces signal by 10 dB but does not affect response. Prevents overloading of electronics with extremely high-level sound input.
Cutoff Filter 513a	A low-frequency cutoff filter for use with low-impedance mikes. Eliminates unwanted noise and reverberation components below 100 Hz.
Transformer 503	In-line transformer for matching low-impedance mikes to high-impedance amplifier circuits.

Beyer

Stereo Rail ZMS 1	Rail for mounting two mikes for stereo recording.
Shock Mount EA 24	Suspension unit with elastic mount for mikes with shaft diameters from $25/32$-in to $1^{1}/_{16}$ in.

Neumann

Phantom 48VDC	Portable AC power supply for two mikes.
Hanger MNV 87	Auditorium cable hanger for all mikes allows for simple suspension over rails and overhead bars.

Shure

Phase Reverser A15PR	Reverses the phase of a balanced line without modification of equipment.
Low Pass Filter	Provides a low-frequency pass and high cutoff to reduce high-frequency noises equalizer.
Presence Adapter	Adds brilliance and "presence" to vocals or instruments in broadcast applications.
Response Shaper	Provides sibilance filtering in recording. Flattens response in mikes exhibiting a rising characteristic in the 6-kHz region. Provides a 4-dB dip in response at 6 kHz.

Atlas

BS-36W Professional	Mobile Boom Stand—Grip-action clutch with integral air suspension system counterbalances boom weight and swivel joint at mike mount.
Gooseneck	A flexible shaft attachable to any stand.

AKG

PADS	10- or 20-dB pad attenuator inserted at base of mike.
Swivel	For insertion between capsule and mike preamplifier, permitting angling of capsule by $+/-90°$.

Sennheiser

Cable Amplifier KAT 15-2	Allows direct connection of condenser mike to Nagra line input. A switchable low-frequency cutoff filter is built in.
Mike Pre-amp VV 200 T	Raises the output level of dynamic mikes to that of RF condenser. Gain is 20 dB. Power to amplifier is supplied via the audio cable.

TABLE 5-19 (continued)

Battery Adapter MZA 15U MZA 15	Supplies power to condenser mikes. Can be connected any-where in the line. Uses nine mercury cells, 60-hr life. Test LED lights up when XLRs are connected.
Roll-off Filter	Inserted between power supply and mike cable amplifier input. Low frequency is 6 dB at 50 Hz and 15 dB at 25 Hz. *When* used with dynamic mikes, rolloff is at 200 Hz.
Shock Mount MZS 805	Adjustable heavy duty antivibration boom mount with mess screen.
Telescope Boom MZS 802	Allows for mounting electret condenser mikes on Super 8 cameras for single system sound recording.

TABLE 5-20 Special condenser microphone accessories by Sennheiser

Battery Adapter MZA 6-2	Connected to the mike (Teuchel) at any point. Uses nine mercury cells, lasting 60 hr. Must be disconnected to avoid discharge.
Battery Adapter MZA 15-U	This has Cannon XLR connectors, when plugged into each other pack tests itself through built-in diode (LED).
Power Unit MZN 5-1	For two mikes, connects to 220/110 V supplies. Can be set at any point along mike cable.
Transistor KAT 15-2	Can be used for symmetrical low-impedance dynamic mikes, to line and accessory inputs, a cable preamp with a switchable footfall filter.
Roll-Off Filter MZF 15	Set between supply voltage source and amplifier input. Teuchel connectors roll off at 100 Hz.
Connecting Cable KA 1	Triple conductor screened cable fitted with 3-pin connectors.
Cable Transformer TM 514N	Connects low-impedance mikes to high-impedance input mike end: 5-m shielded cable, recorder end 0.4-m shielded cable, and 3-pin XLR transformation ratio of 1:16.

TABLE 5-21 Connectors (refer to pages 120–121)

Figure	Common Connector Name	Manufacturer(s)	Typical Application and Remarks
1	XLR-3 male line connector	Amphenol Cannon Switchcraft Others	Microphone cable, Eclair NPR sync-pulse
2	XLR-3 female line connector	Amphenol Cannon Switchcraft Others	Microphone cable, adapters
3	XLR-3 female body connector	Amphenol Cannon Switchcraft Others	Microphone connection on recording equipment, Eclair NPR sync-pulse. Also available as "L" connector (not illustrated)
4	XLR-3 male "L" body connector	Amphenol Cannon Switchcraft Others	Microphone connection on recording equipment (reversed) such as Nagra III, Auricon MA-11. Also available as straight connector (not illustrated)
5	Teuchel 3 pin male line connector	Teuchel	European microphones, Sennheiser, Neumann, etc.
6	Teuchel 3 pin female line connector	Tuchel	European microphones, Sennheiser, Neumann, etc.
7	10 pin male bayonet	Amphenol Kings	CP-16/A mixer connection
8	Tuchel 4 pin male line connector	Tuchel	Nagra IV and 4.2 sync-pulse input
9	XLR-4 female line connector	Amphenol Cannon Switchcraft	Eclair NPR power cables, connection at camera
10	XLR-4 female body connector	Amphenol Cannon Switchcraft	Eclair batteries, Anton/Bauer batteries f/Eclair
11	2 pin MS connector, (military style)	Amphenol	30 volt battery power lights. Also available with other pin arrangements as specialty connectors on Photosonics cameras, etc.
12	UHF coaxial connector	Amphenol Kings	Wireless receiver antennas, video monitors

TABLE 5-21 (continued)

Figure	Common Connector Name	Manufacturer(s)	Typical Application and Remarks
13	3 pin female locking connector	Jaeger Kings	Cinema Products CRA-6 motor, Panavision zoom controls
14	Lemo 6 pin male/female connector	Lemo	Arriflex 16-BL remote on/off switch connector on handgrip.
15	4 pin male, light shield connector	Amphenol	Movieola sound head connectors. Also used for adapters.
16	BNC male connector	Kings	Beaulieu sync-pulse generator, many T.V. applications.

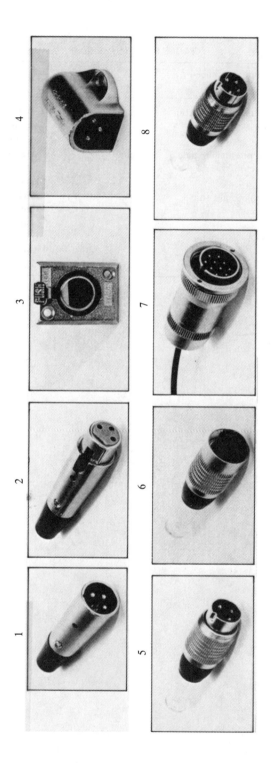

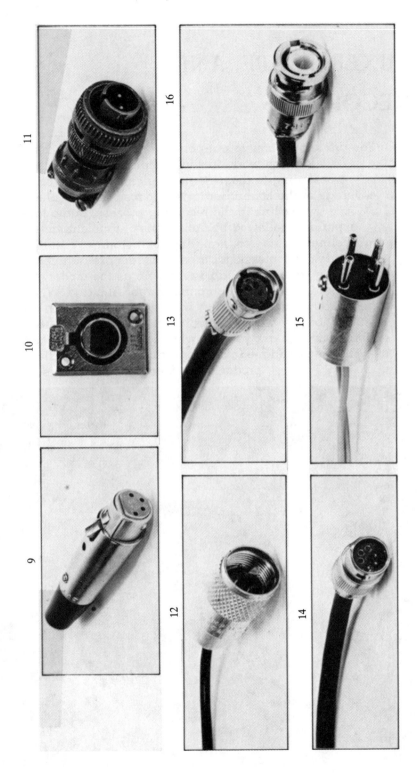

MIXERS, TAPE, AND RECORDERS

You are shown how to put portable microphone mixers to use in location work, including details on such techniques as crossfading to disguise noise elements while obtaining full coverage of the sound in a given space. The manufacture of the weak link in the recording process, audio tape, is then explained, followed by definitions of tape characteristics and guidelines for its use, handling, and storage. Finally, the main features of professional tape recorders are outlined, using the Nagra series of portable recorders as the model. Attention is paid to sound synchronization for film and TV. You should become thoroughly familiar with recorder operation and able to set up for any type of recording situation. Toward that end, the approach is to ask yourself what can go wrong at each point in the electromagnetic and tape transport. The basic Hollywood production procedure is followed step by step.

Mixers

In its simplest, most practical form, a *mixer* is a junction box that relays and combines multiple microphone inputs into one microphone input to the recorder. Sophisticated advances in wireless microphone technology may have shifted the work of the recordist back out into the streets, but reliance on wireless systems often creates a dependence on multiple microphone set-ups. As always, the role of the microphone mixer is critical to obtaining a clean, usable production track. Balancing and cross-fading are the chief techniques in using the mixing console properly.

Passive Versus Active Mixers

Like any other black box system, the mixer may introduce unwanted noise. Although many commercial systems have filter networks for equalization and attenuation of the incoming signal, a passive box may turn out to be better than an active one in location work. Trying to control the spectral quality of the signal, while also balancing and fading, is often too much to ask during the rigors of a location take. The postproduction process offers greater time and control. Once information is clipped at the production track stage, it cannot be put back in.

Active mixers have the capacity to boost the incoming signal. This may be helpful in some situations, but it also tends to boost the noise level in the master track because the signal is not "cleaned up" in the recorder. Portable mixers, which may be operated from DC battery power or powered from the recorder, are often the source of noise problems. It is better to use multiple microphone connections directly into the recorder (Nagra allows for three direct inputs controllable by the mike and line pots) than to misuse the mixer as a simple junction box for multiple microphone setups. When possible, take the time needed to find a coverage problem solution that reduces the number of microphones used. Otherwise, it is imperative that proper mixer fading and crossfading technique be utilized.

Of the available location mixers, the most compact and easy to use are:

- The original Nagra BM mixer. (See Figure 6-1.)
- The Sela 2880.
- The PICO AD145 mixer.

Figure 6-1   The Nagra BM mixer. (Source: Nagra.)

(The latter two are for the Nagra). For ENG work:

- The Shure FP-31.
- The Coherent MX80.
- The Audio-Technica AT4462 Stereo Field Production Mixer.

Desirable Features

When selecting a mixer, look for several features. Perhaps the most important practical feature is to always have graded pan pots (faders), so that you can repeat settings exactly. It is very time-consuming to "get back" settings you have already obtained and somehow lost. Marking the point with a marker or tape is messy, unreliable, and annoying, but the only other option. Noise-free faders (pots) are preferable. Other things to bear in mind are:

- Rental units tend to be dirty with grit at the pots; so check this before leaving a rental house.
- A sensitive monitoring jack output and phase-reversing switches at the inputs are important working features to accommodate those last-minute emergency mikes with the wrong wiring.
- Three-pin Cannon XLR inputs are mandatory.
- Metering systems tend to be inaccurate distractions. (See Figure 6-2.) Better to trust the recorder meter and monitor output.

Lower-Level Versus High-Level Mixing

In *low-level mixing,* each source is fed directly to an associated fader without preamplification. *High-level mixing* with a preamplifier gives a better signal to noise ratio at the input to the fader and permits the use of constant impedance faders. However, you must assume that the electronics of the box do not add appreciable noise.

A *constant impedance fader* (potentiometer) presents the same resistance to signals from all sounds whether it is open or closed. It therefore introduces a greater loss into the circuit when partly open than does a simple fader, and a

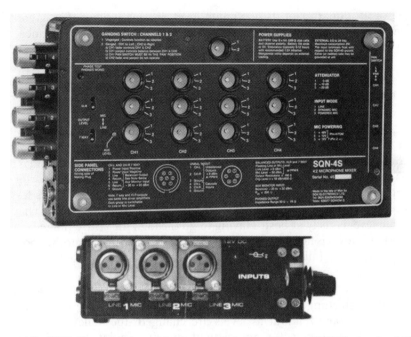

Figure 6-2   SQN-4S stereo mixer with base panel presets. (Source: SQN Electronics, Ltd.)

preamp is required. The operation of one fader does not affect the apparent output of any other source, as happens in the mixer with simple faders.

A *logarithmic fader* has a constant ratio of gain or loss between successive *studs* or equal degrees of turn.

Cross-Fading

The technical quality of the track is therefore a function of the reaction time and ear of the mixer, as well as the sensitivity of the console. The quicker the transition, the less control afforded to the mixer. Additive noise can be caused by having all input faders open regardless of whether something is "on-mike." To overcome the problem, the mixer operator may elect to rehearse and preset each input at a quarter of the master gain control level, if all are similar

TABLE 6-1   Basic specs of pro mixer/microphone connections

- Microphone inputs accept low-impedance microphones or other low-level sources.
- Line inputs accept high-impedance, high-level sources, such as tape recorders, tuners, or amplifiers.
- Line outputs may be phone jack or phone jacks. Inputs should be balanced 3-pin XLR connectors, but are often Din 3-pin phono or mini jacks.
- Many mixers have semifixed resistors corresponding to the output channels; level adjustments may be made manually.

levels, or at a quarter of its maximum level, if each input differs greatly. By leaving the volume control the nonspeaking actor on (set, for instance, 6 dB down from full level), you have accomplished two things:

- Added negligible noise.
- Made the cross-fade easy to execute.

As the sound source changes position, one control is faded down while the other is faded up, and so on for three or more inputs if you have the dexterity! Since the physical manipulation of the fader may also induce noise (and is heard if done poorly) the more discreet the movement, the better. The quarter-level compromise between the full movement from top to bottom offers less of a chance for error. Even with practice, moving on the *anticipation* of a change in dialogue level is risky at best. Having to go through the entire range (scale) of gain to 0 dB down is not easy to time while raising the gain on another pot to the *exact* position for full modulation. Many mixers opt for a fixed compromise position and never move the faders during a shot.

While creating exacting, full modulation perspective within a given shot can produce startling sound, another risk is trusting too fully in the standard VU meter average readout as levels are changed, the belief being that the average is close to the actual intensity at any given point. Since the meter is always slower to react than your eye/hand coordination, there is an inherent accuracy limitation in any cross-fading. The Nagra *modulometer,* a very accurate peak-reading meter, should be used as the primary mixer monitoring guide, since it also reflects what is actually coming into the machine at the record head. Set the Nagra Line Level gain at 0 dB, and then control the input with the mixer master gain control to obtain an averaged (0 dB to +2 dB) signal.

Note: Mixer level is always first adjusted at the mixer. Gain control during recording is more precise at the Nagra, but should be left alone. Monitoring on the Nagra is set in "direct" earphone selector switch, so that the operator hears the signal after mixing but before amplification in the recorder.

Relative levels. As a general rule for the simultaneous mixing of speech with music on location or in the studio, some consideration must be given to the *listeners' preference* as well as to the requirements of the medium.

- Speech occurring after music requires 4–6 dB lower level of recording.
- Music occurring after speech requires 2–3 dB increase in level.

These rules of thumb are by no means standard, but they speak to the fact that, as far as the mixer is concerned, the transition between two different kinds of sound must be anticipated. The transition should not only be unnoticeable (through crossfading), but, as a matter of intelligibility, must also reach the preferred listening level gradually. That level is a function of loudness, the actual intensity of the live signal, and, again, listener's preference. The predominant obsession of the hi-fi industry dictates a much greater transition to a higher level for music than required for conventional playback in the theatre. Both the mixing studio and the exhibitor take into account the regional and temporal preferences of audiences and make adjustments year-to-year.

Some films require specific adjustments of relative levels and interpretations of listeners' preferences. For instance, musicals require higher levels to reproduce the dynamic range of full orchestras, and dubbed foreign films call for more balanced levels for intelligibility in the U.S.

Tape

Although magnetic recording theory was known in the 19th century, the physics of tape manufacturing were not sufficiently refined until the late 1930s.

Components

Magnetic tapes are constructed of three primary ingredients:

- The *backing,* onto which the oxide is coated, is a flexible, durable plastic substrate.
- The *binder,* or "glue" in layman terms, is the adhesive that holds the oxide and other material important to proper tape function to the backing.
- The *oxide* powder, which is dispersed in the binder, serves as the magnetic memory onto which the signal is impressed.

Each primary element is designed so that the ingredients are compatible and meet product requirements.

Backing. This is the material that supports the oxide and isolates tape layers. In the past, it has been made of wire, paper, acetate, and early ester-based materials. In modern audio recording tapes, the backing is usually a plastic material called *polyester.* In certain applications, where using relatively thin polyester is necessary, the backing material is stretched to increase its mechanical durability; in this case, the backing is said to be *tensilized.*

All polyester backings have superior mechanical properties compared to the paper or acetate materials used in older magnetic tapes. First, polyester resists breakage better than paper or acetate, especially if the later has damaged or nicked edges. Second, polyester does not absorb water and swell, rendering recordings useless in many cases, as do acetate and paper. Generally, polyester is mechanically more stable than acetate or paper.

The polyester backing is supplied in the form of roughly 2-ft-wide rolls called *jumbos*. These jumbos are quality checked for tensile strength, smoothness, and freedom from physical distortion. These tests assure a dependable, quality backing material for in-plant processes and reliable finished product.

Binder.   The material that adheres the oxide to the backing is called *binder*. Binders are composed of many ingredients, all chosen specifically to insure proper performance in the intended applications. One important element of the binder is the lubricant which, because it is added and mixed throughout the binder, will not wear off the surface. Instead, as the tape wears, lubricant remains in the binder; it is not a thin coating layer on the tape surface that can wear off with use. The binder with the oxide powder and solvent chemical form a liquid solution called the *dispersion*.

Oxide.   Manufacturing starts with producing iron oxide from iron scale (or rust). Because the scale is nonmagnetic, it undergoes several processes to produce a usable magnetic oxide. The first step is the addition of a base, which causes a yellow slurry to form. The yellow slurry is then washed, filtered, and dried in a rotary kiln where the temperature and humidity are controlled. This process yields alpha ferric oxide, which is still nonmagnetic. Next, the alpha ferric oxide undergoes a reduction process to produce a black material, and then oxygen is added, creating a brown gamma ferric oxide. After quality control testing at the oxide plant, the oxide is shipped to one of the tape manufacturing plants.

Manufacturing

The manufacturing of magnetic tape starts with the testing of the limpy magnetic oxide and its dispersal in the binder in a ball mill, which is a large rotating drum with steel balls inside. The speed and time of the milling are carefully controlled until the oxide agglomerates disperse uniformly throughout the binder. Speed, temperature, and time cycles in the milling are critical because overmilling results in fractured oxide particles impairing performance, and too little milling results in incomplete mixing yielding a rough dispersion and a poor rough coating. The process is electronically monitored, and frequent samples are taken to insure a uniform, quality dispersion for coating.

After milling, the dispersion (a mixture of solvents, oxide, and binder) is pumped into holding tanks for temporary storage before it is filtered and routed to the proper coater. The coating process is where three primary tape ingredients meet to become a finished tape product. The backing in jumbo rolls is fed through the coater at a precisely controlled speed, and the dispersion is pumped into a trough where the coating rollers transfer the dispersion to the backing in an accurate quantity so that the coating thickness and smoothness are uniform.

At this time, when the dispersion is wet, the "web" passes between two magnets to align the oxide particles to improve magnetic output. After this orientation, the web travels through the drying ovens to drive off the solvents and cure the binder. The dry cured web is then wound onto cylinders to form jumbos.

If the tape needs no further special processing, it is inspected for compliance to established specifications. All material that fails to pass specification is junked. The material is then sent to the slitter, a device that cuts the tape into proper widths. If special processing is to be performed to produce premium tapes, the jumbos are routed to a machine that polishes the tape's surface.

The surface treater that polishes the tape is essentially an arrangement of rollers through which the tape passes and the oxide coating is compacted to form a more uniform and smooth surface. This improvement in the surface quality increases output at high frequencies, especially in cassette tapes operating at $1^{7}/_{8}$ ips, and reduces the variation in output due to irregularities in the oxide coating.

A sample of the surface-treated jumbo is then electrically tested to check for adequate sensitivity at low and high frequencies. If the jumbo passes quality control testing, it is sent to the slitter.

The slitter is a set of rotating knives that cut the jumbo into specified widths, such as 0.150 in for cassette tape. (See Figure 6-3.) As the tape is slit, it is wound onto hubs or reels. Hubs of cassette tape are stored until the tape is to be wound into a C-O, which is an assembled cassette shell with only a leader.

After the tape is wound into the C-O, several quality control tests are performed, such as mechanical torque and play mode to insure product integrity. If the finished cassettes pass these tests, they are labeled and packaged for shipment to the branch. Eight-track and reel tape is tested in ways relevant to each format; these products are then packaged and placed in plant warehouses for distribution.

Emulsions and Bases

Consistency of the emulsion (or coating) is very important, particularly with the Nagra, which allows for multiple bias adjustments to accommodate many fine low-noise emulsions. Scotch 808 and 809 are the current standards. AGFA PEM 468 is a popular mastering emulsion, and AMPEX makes some competitive versions. Whatever is chosen must be used throughout.

Magnetic film (16-, 35-, and 70-mm widths) is available in *fullcoat* (that is, completely coated widths) or in *stripecoat* (with coats down the sides, center, or both). Super 8-mm fullcoat is also made for specialized sync sound reel-to-reel recording.

The location of the magnetic flux, which constitutes the actual sound track, differs with each format. (See Figure 6-4.)

The positions and widths of magnetic and optical tracks have varied over the years. Figure 6-5 illustrates the more common formats. The oxide and track

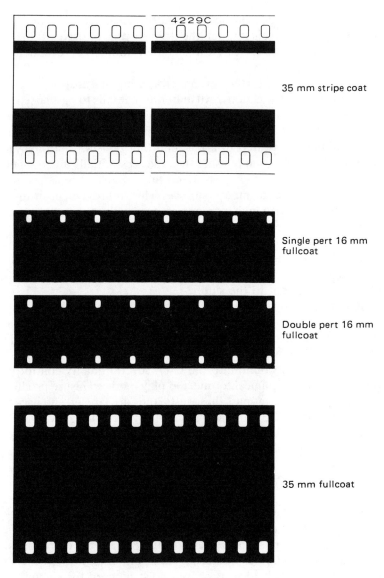

Figure 6-3   Magnetic tape widths.

positions differ widely. Figure 6-6 shows the configuration for the Type M video format. Dropout occurs where oxide has been loosened or abrazed off the tape. Limiting the number of dropouts per centimeter of tape (or per unit of time) is a primary quality control measure. Tensile strength is also of primary importance since videotape is used under great stretch and stress over the recording heads of typical tape decks.

Regardless of the quality of the emulsion, fidelity and signal to noise ratio

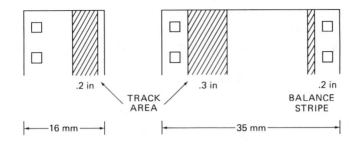

Figure 6-4 The location of the sound track on magnetic film.

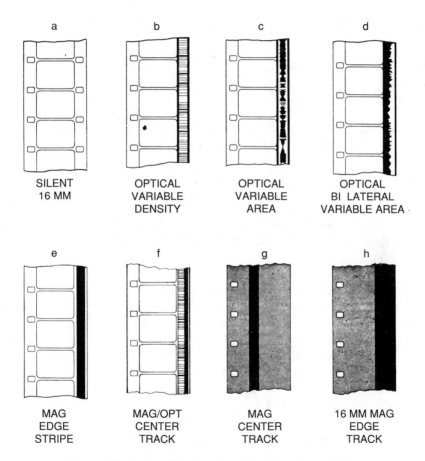

Figure 6-5 The location of oxide and track positions of film.

are also fixed by the precision of the slit in the magnetic head. Dust and debris clog the slit and limit fidelity. (See Figure 6-7.)

Quarter-inch reel-to-reel recording tape is available in three thicknesses: 0.5 mil, 1 mil, 1.5 mil. As the base becomes thicker, it is considered to be stronger, more stable, and less likely to exhibit print-through. The standard thickness is 0.5 mil.

The base is either acetate or polyestar (mylar):

Base Material	Advantage	Disadvantage
Acetate	Breaks cleanly	Very sensitive to temperature and humidity
Mylar	Quite stable	Will stretch
Tensilized mylar	Less tendency to stretch	Costs more
Estar	Will not break	Can damage transport

Limitations

Marshall McLuhan noted that the medium is the message. When audiotape is the medium, the message may be in danger. No magnetic medium is a safe format for storage. All are subject to the same electromagnetic hazards that can cause accidental erasure. As a magnetic medium, audiotape has built-in limitations that cannot be easily overcome, subject as it is to severe physical stresses. The backing tends to stretch, curl, and eventually break. The process of prestretching (tensilizing) the tape does little to insure stability.

Storage of magnetic tape is therefore a conditional hazard, which can be minimized by:

- Bearing in mind that some tape transports are "soft" and some "hard," in terms of the pressure exerted as the tape is pulled across the heads.
- Keeping the tape away from magnetic fields, such as those given off by electrical generators, microphones, headsets, loudspeakers, refrigerators, and the like.
- Store tape at 60–70°F and 40–60% humidity.

The storage capacity of floppy disks may be very high, but CD-ROM and

TABLE 6-2 Components of recorders to clean

Capstan and pinch roller.
Tape guides.
Reel flanges and hubs.
Erase head.
Reel motor turntables.

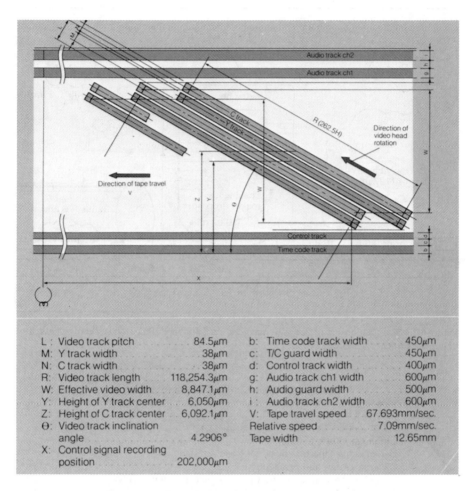

L : Video track pitch	84.5μm	b: Time code track width	450μm
M: Y track width	38μm	c: T/C guard width	450μm
N: C track width	38μm	d: Control track width	400μm
R: Video track length	118,254.3μm	g: Audio track ch1 width	600μm
W: Effective video width	8,847.1μm	h: Audio guard width	500μm
Y: Height of Y track center	6,050μm	i : Audio track ch2 width	600μm
Z: Height of C track center	6,092.1μm	V: Tape travel speed	67.693mm/sec.
Θ: Video track inclination		Relative speed	7.09mm/sec.
angle	4.2906°	Tape width	12.65mm
X: Control signal recording			
position	202,000μm		

Figure 6-6 Type M video format. (Source: Panasonic.)

other optical methods are proving to be the best suited and most reliable storage formats for audio and video.

Also, despite precautions during its manufacture, irregularities in the physical quality of the magnetic tape occur. A dust particle entering the process at any point, once embedded in the magnetic "soup," leaves a nonmagnetic spot. The needle-shaped particles (0.3 to 1.0 microns in length) tend to fall out of the matrix in time. Slitting tolerations, the quality of the materials and chemicals, and the level of control of the entire process all conspire to degrade the performance capabilities of even the best-rated tapes. If there is truly a weak link in the sound recording chain, it is in tape manufacturing. (See Figure 6-7.)

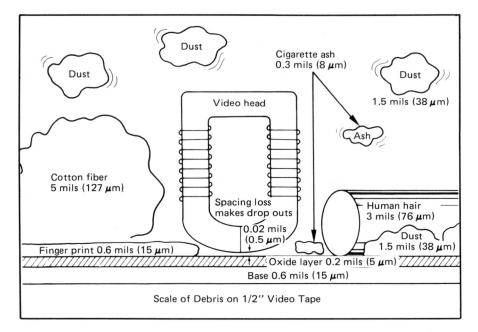

Figure 6-7 Size relationship of debris to magnetic head and tape. Precision and narrowness of slit determines fidelity. (Source: TEAC.)

TABLE 6-3   Tape handling do's and dont's

Cut off wrinkled leader ends.
Fix or discard any reel with a bent flange.
Check for "lipping" or poor packing.
Use masking tape that does not leave a residue.
Clean machines and heads often.
Don't lay reels on top of transports or near magnetic fields.
Store vertically.
Avoid food, liquids, smoke, ashes, and tape "goo" on reels and tape.
Climatize tape for a few hours before use.
Avoid finger oils on emulsions.
Don't store near heat.
Work in a cool, dry space.
Use carbon dioxide (CO_2) in case of fire near tape.
Always wind six turns.
Rewind tape if cinching occurs until a uniform layering is achieved.
Use Freon TF as a cleaning solvent or isopropyl alcohol.
Never clean rubber pinch rollers with anything but alcohol.
Carry the reel by the hub.
Clean dust off empty reels before use.

Tape Characteristics

Bias.   Tape is inherently a *nonlinear* medium; that is, you do not obtain exactly what you put in. By mixing a very high-frequency *bias* signal with the audio waveform, however, the recording process can be made more linear. The bias signal is at least five times as great as the highest audio frequency, to avoid any intentional interaction with the primary signal. The injected signal varies for differently coded tapes. Each tape has an optimum bias amount for proper recording on that particular emulsion with specific recorders. If the signal is biased improperly:

- There is some distortion of the signal.
- The noise (hiss) level increases.

Clipping and the dynamic range.   Every recording medium has an *inherent noise level,* usually on the molecular level, which determines the level of the lowest amount of energy that can be recorded. An analogy is the grain structure in photographic film stock. Therefore, the background noise in the tape medium sets the limit for the most quiet sound that can be recorded. When the recorded sound is no longer louder than the background noise, the lower limit of the medium has been reached. The point beyond which the tape can no longer accept the signal is the *overload point.* At this point of saturation, distortion, or *clipping,* occurs.

In the area between these limits, defined as the *dynamic range,* we can record with reasonable efficiency. For tapes in current use, the dynamic range is of the order of 50–60 dB, comparable to the dynamic ranges of microphones and the human voice. In recording, it is often necessary to compress the dynamic range to preserve linearity. (See Figure 6-8.)

Preemphasis.   A noise reduction of the tape emulsion is achieved through saturated recording of high frequencies (above 20 kHz). When the high frequencies are increased (or *preemphasized),* the signal is flat. An increase in the recording current does not produce an increase in the recorded signal. As an audio processing technique, a black box is used to redistribute the energy at specific frequencies to produce spectral balance in the signal. The signal to noise ratio is improved. Speech and music have the greater portion of their energy (intensity) in the middle and low ranges.

Print-through.   Because the tape is wound on itself and the tape is storing tiny magnetic fields, print-through may occur, in which each layer alters the layer above it. On a tape with normal level recording, you can detect the print-through by listening. It should be no higher than 50 dB below the full level

TABLE 6-4a   Magnetic tape properties

- *Intrinsic coercivity* is equivalent to the ultimate field intensity required to reduce intrinsic induction from saturation to zero.

- *Remanence (retentivity)* is the induced flux remaining in a film 0.5-in wide after a longitudinally applied field is reduced in intensity from 1,000 to 0 oesteds.

- *Peak bias* is the high-frequency AC signal added to an input signal during recording in order to produce maximum long wavelength output upon playback. It varies for different emulsions.

- *Maximum undistorted output* is the measure of the 1,000-Hz output level capability of a film relative to a DIN reference level of 32 mM/mm.

- *Distortion level* is the value, in decibels, of third-order harmonic distortion of the reference level at 1,000 Hz.

- *Uniformity* is tested by visually noting variations on a standard VU meter as the film is simultaneously recorded with a 1,000 Hz at its peak bias.

- *Weighted noise level,* also called *bias* or *zero-signal noise level,* is a tape property obtained through the comparison of the weighted noise of a given tape with a lab standard. Weighting reflects the low-level hearing characteristic of the average human ear.

TABLE 6-4b   Mechanical defects of magnetic tape

- Improper slitting in manufacture, causing weave during transport.

- Imperfections in the coating process, causing dropouts, where the signal disappears or wavers.

- Improper winding (spoked appearance).

- Improper bias (high noise level on tape).

- Too thick for the type of recording transport, resulting in abrasion.

- Too thin, resulting in stretching and print-through.

on the tape. If the tape is saturated (recorded into distortion areas), the print-through can be as high as 25 dB below full level.

Print-through increases with temperature, the duration of storage, and the thinness of base material.

Recorders

The Recording Process

In the microphone, acoustic energy is converted to an electromagnetic waveform, which can be stored on audiotape. (See Figure 6-9.) The tape emulsion can be considered as a field of tiny magnets scattered about in random order when not magnetized. (See Figure 6-10.) Passing the tape over the recording head, in which the electromagnetic field is changing, lines up the magnets so that a record of the field is made. (See Figure 6-11.) The record of the electromagnetic energy on the tape might relate to the waveform itself as

Compression of Dynamic Range for Tape Recording

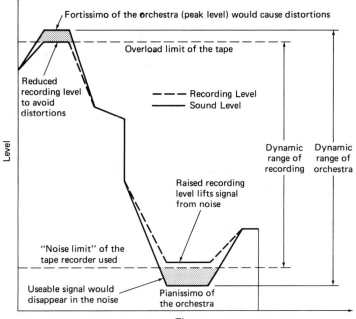

Time

(A)

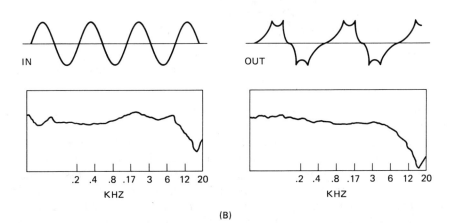

(B)

Figure 6-8 An oscilloscope comparison of the frequency responses of two different brands of cassette tape, recorded on the same machine, indicates how tape can determine high-frequency limits. At the left in (B), the highs are slightly peaked and enhanced. At the right, they are considerably reduced or attenuated. (Source: Sennheiser)

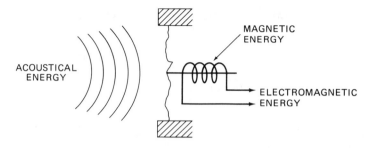

Figure 6-9 Acoustical energy is translated into magnetic, then electrical energy.

Figure 6-10 Unmagnetized and magnetized tape particles.

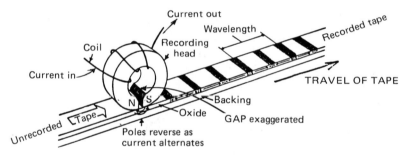

Figure 6-11 The record head—a magnet whose sensitivity is a function of the precision of the gap.

shown in Figure 6-12. Once the record is made, it can be stored and played back later.

The basic configurations of capstan and sprocket drive recording/playback head system are shown in Figure 6-13. For either type of drive, the tape transport must be able to pull the tape at a constant velocity across the heads.

In friction (or capstan drive) recorders, slippage can occur, causing *wow and flutter,* which is noise caused by the poor contact between tape and head. Sophisticated capstan-drive systems have their motors regulated by a crystal oscillator and use a sync pulse generator to deposit "electronic sprocket holes" on the tape as a reference of the recorder speed at any given moment. If any speed anomalies occur during recording, the sync pulse aids in the speed-correction process at playback, thus reconstructing a constant-speed track.

Most 16-, 35-, and 70-mm film recorders are sprocket-driven, with a combination of synchronous and torque motors. The tape is held in place by a

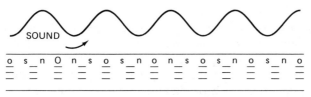

MAGNETIC FIELD ON TAPE

Figure 6-12   Magnetic field on tape is a print of the waveform.

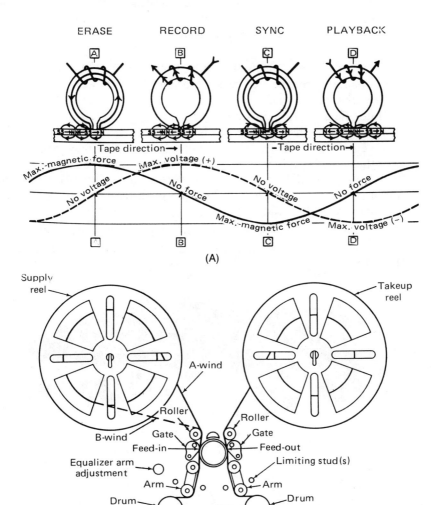

(A)

(B)

Figure 6-13   The basic configuration of (A) head position and (B) a sprocket drive system.

sprocket wheel engaging the sprocket holes in the tape (actually film), thereby maintaining constant pressure across the record head. This pressure, however, introduces other problems, such as *picking* at the sprocket hole as the teeth engage, the possibility of slippage and tape being slit by the sprocket wheel, and problems associated with inaccurate *pitch* (the distance between sprocket holes) due to dry, stretched, or cheaply manufactured stock.

Professional recorders have a *head nest,* consisting of four heads: erase, record, sync, and playback. (See Figure 6-14.) The highest frequency that can be recorded is limited by the precision and size of the gap of the recording head.

Any of these heads can create problems in the recording stage.

What can go wrong at the record head?

- Poor contact between head and tape, causing wow and flutter.
- A permanently magnetized head, causing hiss and due to:
  —Defective bias signal.
  —Motor fields setting up stray field.
  —Disconnecting head while bias is turned on.
  Noise can be increased 6 dB. If a prerecorded tape is played and passes over the record head, high frequencies are "worn off." The magnetized head causes a sound like rushing water. If head is in the playback mode and it goes away when the tape is lifted from the head, the problem is definitely with the head, not the tape.
- High-frequency response suffers as the gap on the head wears larger.
- Dirt, smoke, or emulsion particles on the head can fill the gap and cause dropouts.

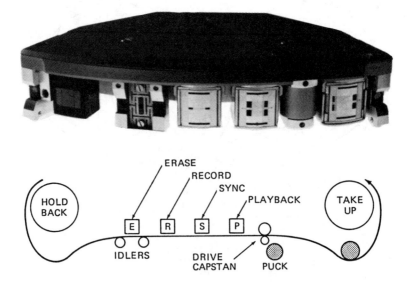

Figure 6-14   Head nest and capstan drive transport; friction holds the tape in place.

- *Azimuth error,* or the angular deviation between the axis of the sound head slit and the imaginary right angle to the direction of the tape transport, causes waveform distortion.
- *Flutter and wow,* or the deviation of frequency resulting from irregular motion in the recording transport, caused by deformation of the recording medium (tape, disc, film). Flutter occurring at random rates is called *drift.*

What can go wrong at the playback head?

- Everything that can go wrong with the record head.
- The shield on the playback head, which protects it from stray magnetic fields, is out of adjustment, creating an excessive amount of hiss or *AC hum.* This is not on the tape.
- Poor amplifier design, defective components, and overloading, resulting in signal distortion.
- Poor microphone placement, allowing too much energy into the transducer circuit, causing overloading. Controlling high-level volume must take into account the limits of the amplifier.

What can go wrong with the sync signal?

- Not there, not present on the tape.
- Undermodulated, so that it cannot be read or *resolved.*
- Too strong—overloading the tape, bleeding into adjacent audio, and causing buzz.
- Defective waveform.
- Out of alignment due to sync head azimuth error.

The recorders used for film, television, and audio/visual sync applications are generally DC-powered portable location recorders. In the early days of sound, the recorders were all sprocket-driven, AC-powered, large, and cumbersome, and they required some kind of bulky voltage inverter to operate on location. Currently in practice are small capstan-driven modular 0.25-in-tape reel-to-reel recorders, which allow for greater recording time, in a smaller package, at lower stock costs. Sprocket recorders generally use magnetic film of 16-, 35-, or 8-mm widths.

The recorders now in use as standard operating formats in film and video field operations include the following:

Nagra T-Audio TC is an analog reel-to-reel ¼-in tape recorder suitable for double-system video editing applications, computer-assisted sound sweetening, pilot transfer, and OB-van installation for remote field recording. The TC function refers to SMPTE time code synchronization features (center track timecode). (See Figure 6-15.)

Figure 6-15   Nagra T Audio TC. (Source: Nagra.)

Time code and audio are recorded on separate heads and a microprocessor automatically shifts the time code into phase during both record and playback to compensate for the difference/distance between heads. A separate center track head allows for the "stripping" of a tape that contains audio information. High-speed time code readers allow shuttle speeds up to 60 times the nominal speed during locator and synchronizer transfer functions.

Three independent channels are keyboard-controlled. The system locks to a master machine like a VTR for postproduction and automated editing. The addition of the accessory TA-BOX next to an editor allows the operator to select the control of two recorders and to select between audio recording on the VTR or on the T-Audio.

The Nagra Digital (see Figure 6-16) offers 3 hours of uninterrupted 4-track digital audio recording on standard ¼-in 7-in reels. Original recording can be made at 18-bit resolution assuring good headroom and security on location against excessive level rises. The rotary head format allows expanded sample wordlength of 20 bits with 4 bits per sample of auxillary data capacity. The Nagra D has a standard longitudinal time code track. Channels available include 4 digital, 1 analog (PWM) cue track, 1 time code track, and 1 control track.

The Stellavox Stelladat portable R-DAT recorder uses the time code standard developed by NHK with schronization via AES/EBU, word sync, or video sync. Recording can be made at 44.1 or 48 kHz and is compatible with all

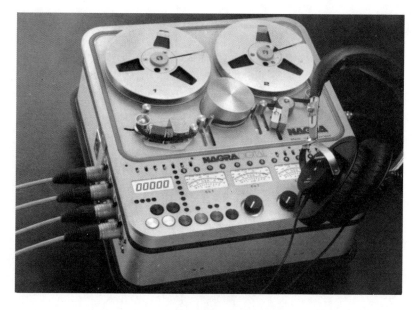

Figure 6-16   Nagra Digital recorder. (Source: Nagra.)

other R-DAT recordings made on other R-DAT machines. An electroluminescent matrix panel displays all data needed during recording (see Figure 6-17):

Level monitoring.
Time counter and time code frame.
Recording frequency.
Battery life.
Number of digital errors.
Preemphasis selection.

The Stelladat climate control design allows for use in rugged terrain, high altitudes, areas of severe humidity, or outside temperatures far below freezing. The Stelladat uses the same kind of controls in the same locations as an analog recorder. Completely modular and interchangeable design options accept all possible input/output connectors including XLR, Lemo, RCA, and Tuchel. Time code options include AES/EBU, SDIF2, and SPDIF digital inputs.

Nagra IV S-TC is the basic stereo Nagra outfitted with time code options and a control keyboard for video and motion picture field applications. Each key of the outboard has three modes: direct, shifted, and numeric. The direct functions are marked in black in the upper portion of the keys, accessed by pressing the key while Nagra is in Direct mode. Shifted keys are red marked below the key and accessed by pressing when Nagra is in Shifted mode. Black

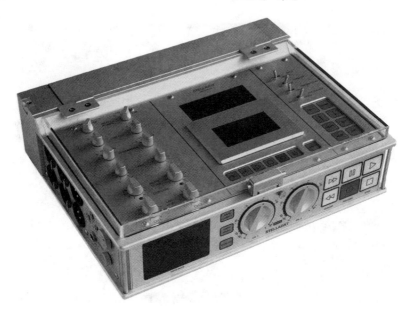

Figure 6-17   Stellavox sync sound recorder. (*Source:* Crosscountry Film Video, N.J.)

mark numeric functions are accessed by pressing same when Nagra is in Numeric mode. (See Figure 6-18.)

FIELD USES OF TIME CODE AND THE NAGRA IVS-TC

- *To record double-system sound with picture shot on film at 24 or 25 fps to be edited and released on film,* use Aaton or Arriflex time-coded cameras with a Nagra IVS-TC or Nagra with an external electronic slate. European standard Steenbeck or KEM flatbed editors may be able to read the code, but as yet a totally automated system in film is not ready.

- *To record double-system sound with picture shot on film at 24 or 25 fps to be edited on videotape and released on film,* Burbank Studios has a 24-fps video editing system, but they are rare. Editing must be done in 30-fps videotape. The film negative is conformed to the edited videotape. (See Table 6-5 for comprehensive options.)

Noise

Like all other elements in the sound processing chain, tape recorders add noise to the useful signal. Some of the chief classes are:

- *Background noise:* Recording and playback amplifiers can add to the hiss from the tape oxide, which is present even if no signal has been recorded.
- *Modulation noise:* If tape is not transported in a perfectly regular manner, wow, flutter, and tape vibration noise is induced at high frequencies,

(*Text continued on page 150.*)

Figure 6-18 Nagra IV S-TC. (Source: Nagra.)

TABLE 6-5 Field uses of time code and the Nagra IVS-TC

RECORDING DOUBLE SYSTEM SOUND WITH PICTURE SHOT ON FILM AT 24 OR 25 F.P.S. TO BE EDITED AND RELEASED ON FILM. This is still the most common way of doing things, though editing on videotape is being done as an alternative on some jobs because of the lack of film time code equipment. At present there are not a great many cameras available that record time code on film, and far fewer "smart" editing machines that can read this code and automatically search the sound magstripe for matching time code, in order to sync dailies without the help of a human editor. But full automation of this onerous task is coming, and in the meantime, it behooves the mixer to become familiar with 24 or 25 F.P.S. time code systems. It is also incumbent on him or her to educate the producers and directors they work with to the benefits of using time code, and to develop a sense of trust in them. Otherwise, in the future you will wind up in the ludicrous situation of shooting with a time code camera and NAGRA but *still* using a conventional clapstick with scene and take numbers "just in case."

On the other hand, do not overlook the shortcomings of time code, and do not promote it for those jobs where it is unsuitable. For the immediate future, you have only two options for film time code systems, using either one of the few time code cameras, or a non-time code camera and an electronic slate.

In either case, the NAGRA IVS-TC's internal time code switch must be set to 24 or 25 F.P.S., and some means provided for coordinating the sound and picture time codes.

RECORDING DOUBLE SYSTEM SOUND WITH PICTURE SHOT ON FILM AT 24 F.P.S. TO BE EDITED ON VIDEOTAPE AND RELEASED ON FILM. The necessity of editing a 24 F.P.S. film in 30 F.P.S. videotape adds many complications, not the least of which involve time code. The edited videotape will be used for release, whereas here the film negative will be conformed to the edited videotape, and then prints will be struck from it. As far as the production sound recording is concerned, the procedures are identical.

TABLE 6-5 (continued)

RECORDING DOUBLE SYSTEM SOUND WITH PICTURE SHOT ON FILM AT 24 OR 30 F.P.S. TO BE EDITED AND RELEASED ON VIDEOTAPE, such as outside film segments for tape shows or filmed TV series. In this case, the film will be converted to videotape on a RANK-CINTEL or BOSCH machine.

Now the question is: "To what time code standard should the NAGRA be set for this application?"

For the answer, consider that the film camera has a crystal-controlled motor that will run at exactly 24 or 30 F.P.S. when exposing the negative, but the RANK-CINTEL or BOSCH will run that negative at exactly 23.976 or 29.97 F.P.S. when making the transfer to video at 29.97 F.P.S. (The 23.976 F.P.S. comes from 24 F.P.S. times the ratio of the TV sync frequency, 59.94, to 60. This is 0.1% slow, and the same ratio as 29.97 to 30.) Thus, regardless of whether the camera is running at 24 or 30 F.P.S., if 30 F.P.S. time code is used when recording the sound, when the audio is transferred to videotape at 29.97 F.P.S., it will be slow by exactly the same 0.1% as the picture, and stay in perfect sync.

The AATON/PANAVISION system is the exception to this rule. It will only function if both the camera and recorder are set to the same frame rate, so for use with a 24 F.P.S. camera the NAGRA must be set to 24 F.P.S. time code. Be sure to mark the sound report accordingly. Transfer houses that can handle AATON time code will have a 23.976 F.P.S. reference to produce the required 0.1% slowdown.

While the frames of film shot at 30 F.P.S. will have a one-to-one correspondence with the frames of the video transfer, film shot at 24 F.P.S. requires a further manipulation in the conversion to video at 30 F.P.S. (It's actually 29.97, but easier to discuss in terms of 30.)

There are two basic systems. The first was developed to show film on live television, but also is found on some videotapes. While it is used primarily with positive prints, it is described here in terms of a negative with double system sound both to compare it to the second system, and in case you ever have to work with it.

In the first method, every fourth film frame is printed twice, producing two identical video frames. In the course of one second, the 24 original film frames will generate an additional 6 frames, giving a total of 30 video frames. To the viewer's eye there is nothing amiss, since the film's *average* speed is still 24 F.P.S., even though it is actually speeding up and slowing down alternately. (3 frames at 30 F.P.S., 1 frame at 15 F.P.S., 3 frames at 30 F.P.S., 1 frame at 15 F.P.S., etc.) Remember that even though the film camera is shooting at 24 F.P.S., the NAGRA must still be set at 30 F.P.S. The audio time code frames won't line up with the original film frames, but after the conversion they will match the video frames exactly. (See Figure 6-19.)

The second method, called the "3:2 pulldown," is used in the current film-to-tape transfer process. To understand this method, you must first know that each video frame is actually composed of two superimposed "fields." The first field consists of all the odd-numbered scan lines, and is interlaced with the second field, which consists of all the even-numbered ones. For a frame rate of 30 F.P.S. the field rate is 60 F.P.S. (fields per second). When the video image originally comes from a video source (like a video camera), the same image is scanned twice to produce both fields for a given frame. In the 3:2 pulldown transfer, however, the first film frame is scanned by the first two video fields, the second film frame is scanned by the next *three* video fields, the third film frame is scanned by the next two video fields, the fourth film frame is scanned by the next three video fields, and so on, alternating every other film frame. The result is that half the film frames will generate two video fields, and the other half will generate three. The average of 2.5 fields/frame times the 24 F.P.S. film rate gives 60 F.P.S., which is the required field rate for 30 F.P.S. video.

TABLE 6-5 (continued)

This splitting of film frames between two video frames does mean that scenes with rapid motion or splices between scenes may produce certain video frames that appear blurred when seen in freeze frame, but this is usually not too noticeable when viewed at normal speed. The relationship between film and videotape frames when using this method is an alternating pattern of three video frames with both fields taken from the same film frame, followed by two video frames with their fields taken from different film frames. Like the first method, the film's *average* speed is still 24 F.P.S., although it is speeding up and slowing down alternately. (1 frame at 30 F.P.S., 1 frame at 20 F.P.S., 1 frame at 30 F.P.S., 1 frame at 20 F.P.S. etc.) Again, the 30 F.P.S. audio time code frames won't line up with the original film frames, but they will match the time code frames in the video transfer. (See Figure 6.19.)

There is something else to be aware of: the 0.1% reduction in speed between the original filming and the video playback. The very slight slowing down of the actions in the image will be undetectable, and the corresponding lowering of pitch in the sound will go unnoticed in dialog, but musicians with perfect pitch may hear music as fractionally off-key.

RECORDING DOUBLE SYSTEM SOUND WITH PICTURE TO BE SHOT ON FILM AT 25 F.P.S. TO BE EDITED ON VIDEOTAPE AND RELEASED ON FILM OR VIDEO-TAPE is incredibly simple when the single EBU time code standard is compared to the multiple SMPTE time codes. Both film and videotape run at the same frame rate (25 F.P.S.) and the same speed, there being *no* 0.1% slowdown as in SMPTE 29.97 F.P.S. time code.

Thus the NAGRA is *always* set to the 25 F.P.S. time code standard, no matter what is being done—recording, playback, film, tape—all are treated exactly the same.

RECORDING DOUBLE SYSTEM SOUND WITH VIDEO PLAYBACK IN USE. Some shots involve a television set on camera, showing a pre-recorded scene played back on videotape. Three systems are currently in use.

1. A special 24 F.P.S. video system which can work with or without time code. Without time code, and one film camera in use, the camera is set to crystal-controlled 24 F.P.S., and the NAGRA uses regular 60 Hz crystal sync. Multiple film cameras must be driven by the video machine, and it will supply a special 60 Hz sync signal to the NAGRA in lieu of the crystal. When time code is in use, the NAGRA should be set to 24 F.P.S. internal time code, or it can be fed time code from the video.

2. A modified standard 29.97 F.P.S. video system which always uses time code. The camera must run at crystal-controlled 29.97 F.P.S., or be driven by the video machine. The NAGRA should be set to 29.97 F.P.S. *non-Drop Frame* internal time code, or it can be fed time code from the video.

3. An ordinary videocassette system without time code can be used when the quality of the television picture is of no concern. Whatever audio time code standard was used for the rest of the production should be used here.

SYNC AUDIO PLAYBACK WITH PICTURE TO BE SHOT ON FILM AT 24 OR 30 F.P.S. AND CONVERTED TO VIDEOTAPE can also benefit from the use of time code, both to simplify editing, and to minimize the number of generations of audio required.

This method, as used in music videos, starts with the studio audio multi-track master, which can have audio program on all but two of the available tracks. Time code will be recorded on the last track, and the next to last track will be left blank because of cross talk in the head stack. (It may be possible to put 60 Hz sync on that track for other purposes, but it is not needed for time code.)

Next a scratch mix is made for playback. This can be stereo, or mono if a click track is wanted on the second channel. This mix is recorded on a time code stereo ma-

TABLE 6-5 (continued)

chine, with the time code in the center track. Since this mix will only be used for play-back, its quality doesn't matter. It is even possible to make various mixes, say one with the vocal up for use when filming the lead singer, and others featuring different instrument solos. Because the time code will be identical at the same point in the song, any mix will sync up with every other one.

It is important, when making these scratch mixes, that *the multi-track master tape be resolved to the time code* on it, in addition to transferring the time code to the ¼ inch tape. If the master is not resolved, then the playback NAGRA will have to resolve variations in the master tape as well as the ¼ inch, and while the NAGRA resolver can do this more than well enough to maintain visual lip-sync accuracy, the momentary changes in speed required, though inaudible, may be enough to upset some time code devices further along the line. In addition to the ¼ inch track for playback, some transfer labs will make all the necessary tapes at the same time, including a 1 inch videotape audio only with the final mix to be used as a master for the release track, and a ¾ inch videotape audio only to be used in editing.

The 0.1% lowering of pitch mentioned in a previous section can be avoided by *cross-standard resolving*. Recording studios use 29.97 F.P.S. time code as standard, so if the playback NAGRA is set to 30 F.P.S., and *resolved* to that speed, then the music will be played back 0.1% fast while filming and thus the 0.1% slowdown during transfer to video will be cancelled out, and the videotape will sync up exactly with the multi-track master. The final mixdown for the release track can now be made directly from the edited video, without any intervening generations.

Resolving as described above requires a NAGRA IVS-TC, a QSLS resolver, and an ARPC or QSIP interface.

In addition to resolving the playback tape, it will be necessary to establish an initial sync point, and several methods are available.

The old-fashioned way uses a second NAGRA set to record with an open mike on the set. The film camera is rolled, slated with a clapstick, and then the playback is started. In editing, the release music track will be matched by ear to the scratch track recording of the playback. If this second NAGRA is a time code unit, it must be set to 30 F.P.S. too. If a 60 Hz crystal sync machine is used, its tape must be resolved and transferred to sprocketed magstock, which will then have to be synced up to the picture negative before it is transferred to video.

A much more elegant method is to feed the time code from the audio playback tape to an electronic slate, or to a video monitor with a character generator, and film that at the head of each take. Still another possibility, if a time code camera is being used, is to feed it the playback audio time code continuously.

SYNC AUDIO PLAYBACK WITH PICTURE TO BE SHOT ON FILM AT 25 F.P.S. AND CONVERTED TO VIDEOTAPE is also very simple in the EBU system. All that is needed is a resolving set-up that can play the tape at the same speed as it was recorded. There is again no 0.1% speed change to compensate for. Resolving, and establishing an initial sync point are done as in the previous section.

RECORDING DOUBLE SYSTEM SOUND WITH PICTURE SHOT ON VIDEOTAPE is much simpler than the preceding processes, but has one extremely important caveat. *Unlike* the methods using a film camera and then transferring to videotape, where the time code used could come from a generator in the recorder, or one in the camera, or a separate master generator, in video recording the time code *must* come from the video recorder, and the NAGRA time code standard used *must* match the video's exactly; if the video time code is 29.97 Drop Frame then the audio must be 29.97 Drop Frame too. Ditto for EBU 25 F.P.S. time code.

TABLE 6-5 (continued)

The reason for this is that the video time code contains information that the audio time code does not, particularly in regard to color field and frame alignment. This data is absolutely necessary for synchronization with video time code. When done properly, this method allows the audio transfer machine to locate the sound on the ¼ inch tape by time code and automatically sync up and transfer the sound to the videotape without much human supervision.

There *are* two procedures for using time code in video recording in which time code *generated by the audio recorder* is either sent to one of the video recorder's *audio* tracks, or entered as user bits in the video time code. Since the audio time code is not synchronized to the video frame edge, it must be passed through a regenerator controlled by the video clock to match its timing to that of the user bits in the video time code. The video operator should do this as a matter of course, but it never hurts to check. Neither of these methods aligns the sound track to the video picture with frame line accuracy, but they do provide for a means of syncing up picture and sound. They should also be kept in mind both as an emergency procedure if there is a failure in the system of sending the video time code to the audio recorder, or for use in some types of documentary work where the time code must use a radio link, with its inherent signal dropout problems. Repeated loss of video time code recorded on the audio tape will make the automated syncing impossible, and also will prevent the audio track from being resolved properly. With continuous audio time code on the audio tape, however, it can be resolved, and then synced up to the videotape at some point where the audio time code was received and recorded on it.

SYNC AUDIO PLAYBACK WITH PICTURE SHOT ON VIDEOTAPE is also simple in that there are no 0.1% speed changes involved. The caveat here is that the audio playback tape must be resolved to *exactly* the *same* standard it was recorded at, *regardless* of what standard the video recorder is using. This follows from the fact that the videotape always runs in "real time"; whatever speed it is recorded at, it will play back at the same speed. (Always? Well almost always. There may be a rare exception, but it is of no concern here.) Thus the audio tape must run in real time too.

If the NAGRA is to be used to self-resolve, with a QSLS and ARPC or QSIP, the internal time code switch must be correctly set to the playback tape's standard. Hopefully the tape will be properly marked, as there is no easy way to identify some time code standards uniquely from the time code signal on the tape itself, using only the NAGRA. (There is one indication—without a QSV speed varier the QSLS will not resolve a 24 or 25 F.P.S. time code if the NAGRA is set to 29.97 or 30 F.P.S., or vice versa. It will resolve a 24 F.P.S. time code to 25 F.P.S., or a 30 F.P.S. time code to 29.97 F.P.S. as indeed it is intended to, and the 0.1% difference will not be readily apparent on the QSLS's phase meter.) Otherwise you will have to use the NAGRA's "TC SEARCH" function to attempt to determine the tape's time code standard. Play a section of the tape and note the HH MM of the recorded time code. Rewind and search for HH MM 00 24—if you don't find it, the tape is 24 F.P.S. If you do, search for HH MM 00 25—if you don't find it, the tape is 25 F.P.S. If you do, search for HH MM 00 01 (but don't use a zero for the minute's unit position)—if you don't find it, the tape could be either 29.97 or 30 F.P.S. Drop Frame. If you do, the tape could be either 29.97 or 30 F.P.S. non-Drop Frame. (Unfortunately, the IVS-TC cannot read time code if you were to try to advance the tape by hand slowly enough to watch the frame count increase one at a time.)

Source: Courtesy of Jim Tanenbaum, CAS, and Manfred Klemme, extracted from their guide, *Using Time Code in the Reel World* (1987).

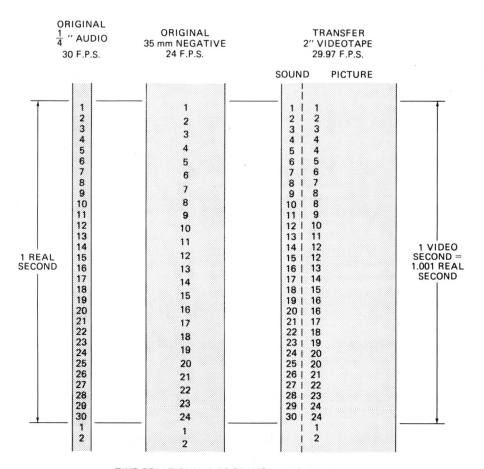

TIME RELATIONSHIP OF FRAMES IN DOUBLED 4TH
FRAME TRANSFER OF FILM WITH DOUBLE SYSTEM
SOUND TO NON-DROP FRAME VIDEOTAPE

Figure 6-19 Time relationships of frames. (A) 3:2 pulldown transfer of film with double-system sound to non-drop frame videotape. (B) doubled 4th frame transfer of film with double-system sound to non-drop frame videotape. (Source: Tanenbaum-Klemme)

making the recording sound "dirty." Pressure pads on the heads and a lack of filters increase the probability of modulation noise. Irregularities in the tape and tape edges, in conjunction with imperfect magnetic layers on the tape, may cause amplitude modulation noise due to amplitude fluctuations.

- *Asperity,* or dropout noise, is caused by dirt, scratches, and particle pollution of the magnetic oxide, as particles lift the tape off the head. Methods for reducing dropout noise include:
  —Cleaning the tape before it reaches the record head.

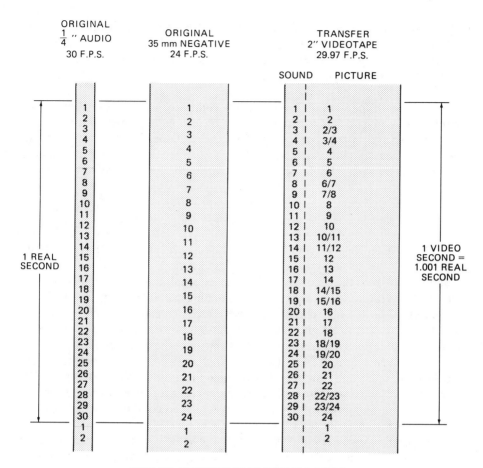

TIME RELATIONSHIP OF FRAMES IN 3:2 PULL-
DOWN TRANSFER OF FILM WITH DOUBLE SYSTEM
SOUND TO NON-DROP FRAME VIDEOTAPE

Figure 6-19B

—Increasing the specific pressure of tape on the head, thereby pressing
  particles back into the emulsion.
—Overbiasing the tape (which works only in Europe with matte-backed
  tape).

- *Head magnetization noise:* DC current produces a DC signal across the
  heads; although inaudible, it causes an audible modulation noise. Unless
  well shielded, the heads are subject to magnetization and to the earth's
  magnetic field when the recorder is used in a vertical position. A magnetized head records a DC signal. As long as the tape is normally transported, only the modulation noise is heard during playback; when the

tape is accelerated from stop to normal running speed, a pop can be heard. It marks the differential of the recording of the DC signal with respect to the accelerated time. The effect can be used to check if the record head is demagnetized.

Record a tape with all level controls counterclockwise and listen to the simultaneous playback. Stop the tape by lifting off the pinch wheel rubber roller, and then restart it. No pop should occur. If it does (0.24 s after release of the pinch wheel, the interval being the time the tape takes for passing from the recording head to the playback head at 7.5 ips), the head needs to be demagnetized.

Sync Signal

Prior to the introduction and widespread acceptance of SMPTE/EBU Time Code, the basic sync reference was a tone pulse (plus and minus), generated either in the recorder or from an external source (a sync generator). The electrical reference is a 60-Hz pulse matching the 60-Hz frequency hum of a regulated AC power line. The sync pulse is merely a record of the camera motor speed, like a voice print magnetically recorded on the upper edge of 0.25-in audiotape. It defines the constancy or regularity of the camera motor, which is supposed to be running at 24 fps (frames per second). The pulse does not create synchronous operation, nor does it insure that the motor runs "up-to-speed." It *is* used as a playback reference, revealing any discrepancy of more than 5% between camera and recorder speed as an off-speed condition requiring to be *resolved* during the transfer to an editing medium.

A simple flow chart illustrates the basic setup for synchronous transfer from a 1/4-in reel-to-reel Nagra to a 24-fps sprocket-driven recorder (see Figure 6-20). Both the interfaced resolver and the sprocket recorder are locked to the AC line. The Nagra may be run on battery (DC) or AC.

Transfer from a multitrack recorder to a videotape recorder using a synchronizer that locks both into a SMPTE time code reference is diagrammed in Figure 6-21.

Several multitrack machines may be linked for mixing by use of a basic audio synchronizer that also uses the SMPTE time code as a basic reference in addition to a given manufacturer's proprietary sync pulse system, such as the TEAC/TASCAM Simulsync.

Historically speaking, several sync pulse systems evolved after the initial interlock system, which employed a camera with an AC sync motor and a recorder with an AC sync motor both plugged into the same AC line source. This guaranteed that both machines ran at the same speed. Other sync set-ups included a recorder with a built-in synchronizer running on AC and a camera with an AC motor; and the predominant news gathering fully DC battery powered Nagra with built-in synchronizer linked to a camera driven by a DC

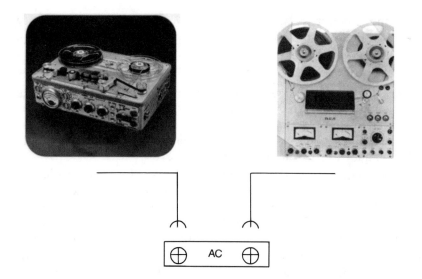

Figure 6-20 Basic transfer from capstan $^1/_4$-in tape to sprocket-driven $^{16}/_{35}$-mm mag fullcoat.

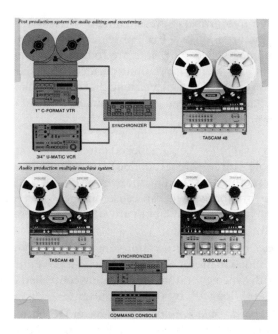

Figure 6-21 (Top) Transfer from multitrack recorder to videotape recorder through a synchronizer. (Bottom) Linkage of several multitrack machines for mixing.

constant speed motor (regulated) by cable. With the introduction of crystal oscillators in both camera and recorder, the necessity for the cable was later eliminated.

Historically, several systems were in use:

- *Fairchild Pic Sync System:* Used mostly in fixed studio applications. Relies on a 14,000-Hz carrier modulated by 60-Hz (camera-driven by an AC sync motor). The system, though not very flexible, was used as the predominant mode of "recording to playback" (the Hollywood Studio Technique) for the musicals of the 1930s.

- *Rangertone:* Colonel Ranger built one of the earliest sync recorders. This system places the sync signal in the center of the audio track at a 5° angle, so that it is not picked up by the playback head. However, if it is too strong an audible hum is apparent. Furthermore, strong bass energy in the audio track looks like the sync signal and interferes with the transfer process.

- *Pilotone and neopilotone:* The universal standard. Two offset pulse trains are recorded by separate heads and picked up by separate heads. The audio head scans the whole area. Since the two signals (sync pulses) are out of phase by 180°, no audible sound is detected.

Camera drive systems. Several camera drive systems have been in use in the motion picture industry. Each provides a method to achieve a fairly constant 24-fps running speed, but none are foolproof. Time code, likewise, does not insure that all systems are running perfectly. But the code is an exact "time" map of the position of any given frame that can be linked with any other sound frame automatically. The single predominant cause of sync problems is with irregular power sources:

- *Synchronous AC motor:* You are locked into AC line voltage via standard electrical cable (three-wire grounded), providing, in theory, constant voltage and exactly 24 fps running speed. However, a voltage drop of more than 20%, as in a brownout, can cause off-speed conditions. Since the recorder must also be run AC, both are affected in the same way and run synchronously.

- *Constant speed motor:* This runs approximately 24 fps powered by battery (DC). This induction motor can run off-speed if power drops. It is usually combined with sync generators for governor-controlled operation whose fluctuations are "logged" by the sync pulse.

- *DC variable speed "wild" motor:* This runs on DC battery, and its speed can vary from 2 to 600 fps. It can be made to run at 24 fps by speed-tuning via a tachometer or with a crystal battery AC/DC inverter or sync generator link.

- *Crystal-controlled constant speed motor:* A DC motor is locked into 24-fps operation by a crystal-controlled feedback circuit, which steps voltage up or down to maintain sync operation, up to a finite correctable point per thousand frames. The recorder must also be crystal-controlled.

- Multiduty and "interlock" motor: This DC servo-driven or AC sync motor is used in the dubbing studio to control banks of high-speed recording and playback machines, which can be interlocked through their motors on one shaft and a coded signal. A distribution network delivers exact 60-Hz 120-V AC current to all machines at the same time; all motors rotate in sync at 24 fps. Some systems have an AC/DC converter, which allows the use of a low-noise DC servo drive motor. The projector used in the studio is also interlocked to this system.

The Transfer Paradox

In the case of a slow camera, speed up the sound! By speeding up the sound, you make it run frame for frame with the actual camera footage. A correction of 4% (one frame per second) is not noticeable in the projected picture. If the entire film is projected at 24 fps but shot at 25 fps (the European standard), the effect is passable. Intercutting 24 and 25 fps may be bothersome since the overall reference for voices change.

However, a slight *pitch shift* is detectable in the sound track of 4% at 24 fps. However, it doesn't matter if the recorder is off-speed. Pitch shift is very subjective, quality of sound arising out of frequency. It may be measured as the frequency of a pure tone having a specified loudness level which seems to the average normal ear to occupy the same position in a musical scale. Speed changes of 5–6% can be acceptable depending on what is being intercut with it.

Absolute pitch is a gift very few people possess. If an entire film were off 8%, no one might be the wiser. But if the recorder is running off-speed, a whole chain of negative events occurs with the audio signal, which cannot easily be repaired without spending much time and money. In this case, the signal would be altered, not just running slower than sync.

THE FORMAL LOCATION
RECORDING PROCESS

Many things can be done during the location shoot to make all
the steps thereafter much easier and the overall quality of the
finished product much higher. First, you are shown the basic
sync sound recording procedure, including tips on start marks
and take identification. Also explained are perspective miking,
continuity, and room tone. What should be brought along on a
location shoot? The answer to that question is found in the
section on the basic location recording package. Finally,
intercom systems and multitrack recording systems are
described.

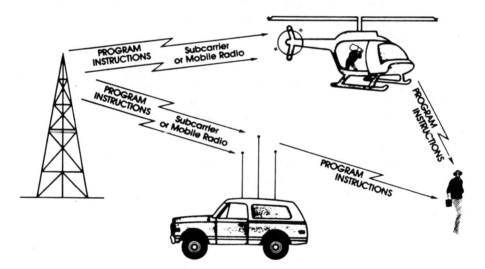

Basic Sync Sound Recording Procedure

1. Secure all cables and check connectors for damage, broken pins, and grounds. Most portable reel-to-reel and cassette recorders are not grounded. Check the location for faulty two-wire ungrounded appliances or other electrical units that can be a hazard if the recorder accidently comes in contact with metal surfaces.

2. Batteries have a limited shelf life, yet battery life is critical to optimum recording efficiency. Check the voltage in the recorder with a drain: Average and peak level must be at maximum. In the Nagra, 12 Duracell size D batteries should run the system for 24 hours continuously or for the greater part of a five-day work week. NICADs are not recommended. They are costly, suffer from memory effects of poor charging, and cannot be shipped inside the recorder by air. There is also the danger of accidently reversing polarity since the terminals are not always clearly coded.

3. Degauss and clean all magnetic heads gently with denatured alcohol to remove all traces of emulsion from the gaps. Acetone is the most efficient solvent. Oxide has a habit of jumping up from the case between the tape and the heads, causing noise.

4. After threading the tape, run up at least 10 ft of head leader, which tends to get damaged or stretched during recording. Deposit a 1,000-Hz beep tone as a head reference, deposit a verbal slate by indicating: roll number, date, location, recording speed, and sound take number. Write the identical information on the tape box and on the recording log sheet. Sound take numbers run continuously regardless of scene changes.

5. Check the internal noise level of the recorder by listening with all faders down and the function switch in "test" position. The headphone switch should be in "Direct" for the test. Hot environments tend to increase transistor noise. Running AC through the ATN induces some AC hum, which is heard but generally not recorded, although leaks are not uncommon.

6. Run a test for *speed* and *power*. The Nagra has an indicator that comes on if the crystal oscillator is functioning and the system is up to speed in test or record position. The Nagra is also equipped with a shorting plug, which should remain inset to the 4-pin pilot input (XTALN) receptacle on the right side of the case. If conventional cable sync is being used, turn on the recorder, turn on the camera and, look for the pilot flag to go up (a white geneva cross). Listen for the

TABLE 7-1   Location recording checklist

1. Check the grounds in each location in a room, especially in kitchens. Beware of standing water on floors in an old home with two-wire ungrounded appliances. It's possible to accidently touch metal to metal over a wet surface and arc a Nagra or your hair. Use a voltmeter; some homes are still D.C.

2. Check that all systems are low impedance since long cable runs are likely.

3. Use balanced 3-pin XLR inputs that go to ground at the mixer. These cancel static hum or spurious radiation in the area that cables can pick up.

4. When matching impedances from microphones, it's fine to go from low to high but not vice versa. Line loss occurs due to the mismatch, or harmonic distortion is latent.

5. All cables should be shielded and of a heavy gauge to withstand abuse on location— stepping, tugging, bending, dolly runs.

6. Identify, label, list, and insure all equipment. Try a color code system. Take along a cable continuity tester and selectively number microphones with matching cables for quick changes.

7. Anticipate phase problems with microphones, take along reversing adapters for last-minute nonred-dotted microphones.

8. Check batteries with a load drain. Take along double spares and AC power adapters, transformers, or inverters. Never use small appliance kit adapters, they can't handle the drain.

---

beep tone from the camera when it is turned on. If the beep tone stays on, the camera is running off-speed. The speed power indicator should be "on" continuously unless there is belt slippage or power fluctuations.

7. Try to set the recording level between 74 dB and 84 dB on the microphone potentiometer dial, to peak no more than +2 dB on the modulometer on the top scale. Unlike a VU meter, which gives the average of volumes, the modulometer gives a peak reading. *It is the opinion of the author that it is better to overrecord than undermodulate.* Overcompensation at least provides a strong signal with all the low-frequency information preserved, while high frequencies (which tend to be lost in post-production) are fully audible. All high-level information that might distort due to a high record level is bound to be lost in later stages. However, one cannot put back what is lost or omitted in the original recording. Under-recording guarantees higher noise levels in the recording and the loss of intelligibility, necessitating more work in post-production.

The normal recording level for the Nagra is 0 dB. The peak reading modulometer makes it easier to maintain full modulation since it measures rapid crest values. VU meters sluggishly register at midpoint of +/− 10 dB from the actual magnitude.

Riding the gain is not recommended because it is difficult to catch rapid changes. Rehearsal should give you some idea of an estimated average midpoint setting.

8. Make a brief test recording, rewind, and play it back. Set line gain control to 0 dB. Set volume control to maximum. Turn down all micropots. If

the signal is linear, the modulometer should read 0 dB or the same as record level during playback while approximating the period swing of the needle during recording. Playback generally reads at a lower average level. Listen for background noise and rumble.

9. Changes in level in an attempt to ride the gain are more objectionable than the distortion or losses it attempts to avoid. Moving the microphone is a better idea.

10. Generally, it is not wise to filter during recording unless a persistent and repetitive mechanical noise (like a fan) can be lessened. Since you cannot easily predetermine the effect of the bandwidth attack of the built-in filters, it is likely that needed signal components will be inadvertently lost.

However, attenuation of low frequencies may improve clarity in voice recordings. Use a pad at the microphone to quiet down transistor noise and to reduce response to camera noise, since it can drop the overall level.

In recording linearly, the tape is loaded with signals that produce a modulation noise. These signals are eliminated at a later stage, but the noise tends to remain. The LF attenuator and HP filters can help. Use top-quality headsets to monitor effects (20-20,000 Hz).

11. Make a notation of the potentiometer level settings and recording speed on the log sheet.

12. Make certain reels are secure on the bobbin with thumb screw washers, so that the recorder may be carried upright without reel misalignment.

13. For fast forward, keep the pinch wheel level locked, set the toggle switch to fast forward, turn the principal function selector to loudspeaker playback.

14. For fast rewind, open the pinch wheel, set the toggle to rewind, and set PFS to playback.

15. For most recording applications, monitoring should be done in the "direct" tape position, which samples the signal before it is processed by the system. In "tape," the signal arrives from the playback head after processing with a slight delay.

16. The line level control augments the "mixer" and "accessory" inputs, which can accept microphones with adapters. A level of 0 dB on this pot approximates 74 dB on the microphone pot. A total of four sources may be connected to the Nagra without a mixer.

17. For highest fidelity, use 15-ips recording speed. However, this limits recording time. The Nagra can accept 7-in reels and 11-in reels with an adapter platen. Average fidelity for all sources of aural material (voice, music, effects) occurs at 7.5 ips, which approximates the 24-fps camera speed; 3.75 ips results in proper saturation and fidelity for voice without care for background.

18. The QSLI module in the Nagra automatically resolves each speed to the crystal reference and compensates for belt slippage, power losses, tape thickness, temperature, and mechanical drag losses. However, speed setting of the recorder is independent of camera speed.

19. When changing tape emulsions, check that the bias adjustment is properly set for the new characteristics of the tape. Tape hiss increases if the bias is incorrect.

20. The monitor speaker level control should be preset and left alone as a standard reference for all playback judgements of relative loudness from take to take, as well as for relative noise levels.

21. Sound takes are numbered consecutively regardless of shot or sequence:

Scene 1, take 1, sound 1
Scene 1, take 2, sound 2
Scene 2, take 1, sound 3
Scene 2, take 2, sound 4 (NG)

---

22. Adjust the line level to midrange when a mixer is used. Mixer master gain control suffices for level changes. Leave the Nagra setting at its low-noise, full-modulation position as determined by tests through the mixer when hooked up. Resets for specific microphones used alone would not be made at the line pot.

23. Use the limiter only on high levels (such as a jet plane) if likely to occur at any time during the recording.

24. Noise is cumulative. When not in use, set mixer microphones at half level to reduce average noise ratios.

25. Simultaneously, the recordist must monitor level and noise, watch microphone positions (for boom shadows, etc.), anticipate movement and drastic level changes (such as gunshots), but the director must delegate authority. It is responsibility of the recordist to call a cut if there is a serious problem with audio.

26. Every shot must have a recorded sync reference tone or time code. If it is missed at the start, it must be added at the end. Acceptable references include: electronic slate, hand slate, autoclapper from camera, flashlight beep tone generator, time code.

Start Marks and Take Identification

Here is the procedure for a take:

- Be sure the following information is inscribed on the board: scene, take, roll, sound, director, date, location. Alternatively, you can simply use time code. Some cameras employ an electronic clapper, which is a miniature quartz lamp at the gate that generates a beep tone when flashed upon turn-on of the camera motor. Commands are always given after the clapper goes on. Options include external time code slates. (See Figure 7-1.)

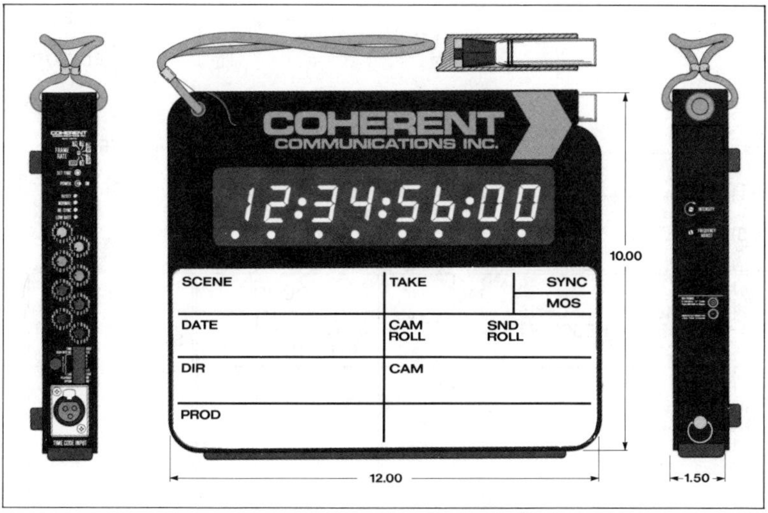

Figure 7-1 A time code slate. (*Source:* Coherent Communications, Inc.)

Production No. ____________ Date: ____________

Title: ____________ Roll No. ____________

Mixer: ____________ Sheet No. ______ of ______

Boom: ____________ Location: ____________

Head Tone ______ dBM SYNC ☐ WILD ☐

PRINT CIRCLED TAKES ONLY

Scene No.	Take	Roll	Notes	Scene No.	Take	Roll

Figure 7-2 Sound log note form.

| FILM | SOUND |

☐ FILE

☐ EDITOR

REPORT

☐ PRODUCER

TITLE _____   DATE _____

LOCATION _____   PAGE _____

EMULSION _____ MAG. _____ CAMERA _____

ROLL NUMBER	SCENE NUMBER	SCENE DESCRIPTION	TAKE	SOUND			FOOTAGE		SEE SPECIAL NOTE
				Sync Roll	Wild Roll	Mos	START	END	

SPECIAL NOTES (Continue on back of page)

Figure 7-3 Sound log. Various formats are dictated by project and lab.

- Always turn on the sound recorder first, then the camera.
- Wait for the speed/power indicator, then perform the slate.
- Turn off recorder last; this allows for room tone footage and tail slate, if required.
- Deposit room tone at the end of each new location. Use the normal setting for the level in the previous takes; then record the silent ambiance

of the space. This material is used in post-production for balancing and matching.

Calling the Take

The director's slating procedure should take no longer than 20 seconds if everyone is paying attention and there are no technical foul-ups (see appendix for Nagra Manual and recording practicum):

Call	Response
"Quiet on the set"	Silence.
"Sound"	Recordist: "Speed" (after flag is up).
"Camera"	Operator: "Rolling" (after sync verification).
If no sync flag comes up on the Nagra, soundperson calls cut here!	
"Scene One"	Focus on slate.
"Take One"	
"Sound One"	
"Clack" (of board)	Clap, clack, or slate must be seen in shot.
"Action"	Remove board, allow 3–4 s run-up for actors to "breathe."
"Cut"	Camera turns off first, then sound.

Perspective Miking

Techniques for preserving sound perspective in film production recordings follow the general rules for preserving straight match continuity.

The camera is the eye of the audience, performer, and director. If the performer is some distance from the camera, the dialogue logically sounds farther away than someone in the foreground next to the camera. In preserving this relationship, the environmental sounds around the action become important clues in establishing the aural viewpoint, auditory "style," and sonic mood. A distance reference is implied from the ratio of background to vocal relationships within the shot. Level discrimination tends to indicate that what the audience sees is what it hears.

Some recordists equate *mood* with perspective. Microphone placement and level adjustment provide control of the foreground to background ratio which, in straight match continuity, should mirror the position of speakers in the shot.

The choice of microphone determines accuracy. Sound mixer Jim Webb cites one example: "He wanted me to use the Sennheiser 415, and although I've used the mike when the situation warranted, I still prefer the 815. In a scene with Geraldine Chaplin where she drives up in a car, gets out, walks toward the camera, stops about head-to-toe in the frame, lights a cigarette with a stick match and flicks the match away. On the first take with the 415, [I] got the car door slam, the match strike, the traffic noise, and that's about it. On the second take with the 815, we got the door, her footsteps, the match strike, the flare when it exploded, her drag on the cigarette, the crackling of the tobacco as it lit, and when she flicked the match, I followed it down and got the "plink" when it hit the pavement. It wasn't anything special as an effects shot, but it sounded wonderful."

"You find dead spots," says Jim McLaughlin. "With a Panaflex X camera running in a pretty dead room you can hear the camera motor, and I fish with the 815 and find the spot where the sound is the least prominent, and that's the angle I gun for on that take."

"Most of the camera noise," adds Webb, "comes out of the lens opening of the [camera] blimp, hits a wall or whatever and comes back into the mike; so you've got to be able to find the null where, for whatever acoustic reason, the noise is less present, and you've got to be able to find that hole in the few seconds between the camera rolling and the start of the dialogue."

"You may be in a situation," explained McLaughlin, "where one actor is standing against a wall and a second actor is sitting with a window behind him. When the editor makes his cuts back and forth from close-up to close-up, you don't want the soundtrack to go from nice and quiet against the wall to suddenly cars and trucks outside the window, so you find a happy medium in the master shot and use the same angle in the close-ups."

Changes in ambiance from shot to shot may be disconcerting for the audience. In straight match continuity, it is better to stay with a less than desirable microphone angle for an entire series of shots than to correct the angle midway for better level or coverage, according to Webb and McLaughlin.

Using wireless and lavalier mini mikes often eliminates room ambiance. *Backmiking* is the utilization of a second more directional microphone mixed with the lapel mikes to achieve full room mood (perspective). "It's an attempt to put a little air into the track," explains Webb.

The stereo Nagra allows for compensation in voice recording where "some actors, like Robert DeNiro, work very soft and close." Without chest resonance, lavaliers have a tough time with timbre and dynamics. Coverage by a lavalier in combination with a shotgun allows you to achieve full resonance.

Close-ups.   You would expect the voice perspective to be slightly altered in the move from close-up to long shot. This literal approximation, however, serves no specific narrative function other than to conceal the structural shift in real space. The relationship of foreground to background, nevertheless, does not change in relation to the shot size. A shift in shot size, however, indicates a change in emphasis. What, then, is the true role of synchronous sound in this case?

The camera is panning as a group of three people converse in a room. Suppose we want to obtain the *natural* sound of diminishing voices as they move away (a Doppler analogy):

- The microphone could be held in a stationary position and there is no effort to compensate for level loss by riding the gain. The moment-to-moment microphone-to-subject distance changes, and the change in angular position or trajectory might cause severe under-recording of the passage. As this group moves, their conversation would then become inaudible.
- Riding the gain with a stationary microphone has the effect of altering the background-foreground ratio until the background dominates the scene.
- If the microphone is moved along with the action but the level is left in a set position, while the mike-to-subject distance remains approximately constant, all is audible but movement is not implied.
- If the performers are pinned with wireless mini mikes, the voice level remains constant but the background relationships are constantly altered along the trajectory of the shot, implying both movement and the *natural* voice rendition.

In practice, the microphone should seldom be moved more than 3–4 ft in any direction to preserve perspective; otherwise, background noise increases. Three primary elements may then be controlled:

- Level changes from shot to shot and within the shot.
- Echo or acoustic changes.
- Level of background noise.

Questions and Answers on Perspective Miking

Q: Does a shift in shot size imply a shift in aural space? Should the close-up sound more intimate than a medium shot?

A: Any shift in real time or real space requires some narrative movement on the track.

Q: Should the size of the space dictate the choice of a microphone's pattern?

A: Since every omnidirectional microphone, for instance, has similar but differing range patterns, it is difficult to attempt sizing the microphone to the room acoustics. However, the choice of pattern is more a function of what noises need to be isolated or omitted. Spatial considerations are handled in the mix.

Q: What is the narrative difference between *static* and *directed* microphone placement?

A: A static microphone with subject moving yields spatial changes.

A static microphone with moving camera yields time ellipsis.

A moving microphone with moving subject or camera yields spatial continuity.

Omni, cardioid, and hypercardioid patterns have different effects at the same or differing microphone-to-subject distances, potentiometer settings (amplitude), and angles of incidence.

Q: To what extent does the quest for a strong, linear signal suitable for transfer while being intelligible affect the dramatic and narrative characteristics of dialogue?

A: An omni used close up enhances the resonant quality of vocals.

An omni used at a distance diminishes vocal sibilance but emphasizes background noise.

An omni at great distances acts more like a directional mike.

An omni at high levels tends to pick up more reflected sound. At low levels, the voice appears gruff.

Off-axis, the omni changes response only when positioned as a boundary mike (PZM) altering voice components.

Directional microphones used close up become bellowy but at a great distance begin to act like omnis.

The relationship of microphone pattern to a given sound source and its acoustic space parameters is influenced by all of the preceding factors, as well as by what bounces into the pattern due to unwanted reflections when a mike is not used at its optimum position. If it is given that a microphone has a flat response, level changes should not alter frequency response. In practice this tends not to be the case.

The mixer/recordist can do much experimentation in trying to answer basic practical questions:

- How full a space are we trying to create? Suggest?
- What reflective surfaces need elimination?
- What modifications to voice are needed for improvement?
- What comes before and after the shot in question?
- What is the tone of the dialogue and the mood of the sequence?

Microphones may be chosen like lenses. Consider their pattern as the field (shape) of acceptance of sound. Consider their frequency response as focus or emphasis. Consider the sensitivity as range or as aural depth of field.

Continuity

In straight match continuity three quality parameters are essential:

- Intelligibility of voice.
- A believable sense of scale.
- The appropriate spatial orientation.

Level and presence for a particular shot are defined by all the shots in the sequence. Figure 7-4 presents a sample sequence that demonstrates the contextural problems of aural space/time in perspective miking. In the straight match, there should be no perceptible change in the audience's "feeling" of presence from shot to shot regardless of shot size. A close-up sounds much like a medium shot and wider shots because *the implied space (size of room) is identical in each shot.* Only the dramatic focus is different.

Changing microphones from shot to shot alters the signal to noise ratio and therefore the audience's sense of screen space (the effective reverb time), regardless of whether levels are matched or imbalanced. But each of two identical close-up takes of a woman speaking at

- different levels with identical mikes,
- different levels with different mikes,
- the same levels with different mikes, and
- the same levels with same mikes

has a unique narrative relationship to the visual, along with an acceptable logic of its own. However, there is a range of acceptable and unacceptable vocal renditions for each pattern selected.

At one point in a soundperson's career, it becomes necessary to develop a sense memory inventory to verify subjectively the most "natural" sound of a given source: by recording with a microphone placed close, midrange, and distant at high and low amplitudes. Perform this with:

- Omni.
- Cardioid.
- Hypercardioid.
- One, then two microphones for a shot with three speakers.

Many situations seem to beg for the use of several microphones. This introduces new problems:

- Mike noise is cumulative—each mike adding a bit of internal noise to the track.
- If a mixer is used, more noise enters the chain.
- Microphones may go out of phase, causing cancellation of important aural data.

Shot #1: CU one speaker.

Shot #2. CU another's reaction over dialogue.

Shot #3: Two-shot, both speaking.

Shot #4: LS all seen at table speaking.

Shot #5: MS from table level.

Figure 7-4   Sample shot sequence. Each detail should match aurally in standard studio technique.

To emphasize certain characteristics of voice, choose microphones that exhibit flat or increased sensitivity to specific frequencies.

• The proximity effect boosts bass.

- Directionality isolates lows.
- Off-axis placement drops out highs.
- Filtering deemphasizes specific bands.
- Equalize in the transfer stage.
- Recompose in the mix.
- Re-record in post-production audio processing.

Room Tone

Any given space has a characteristic ambient noise level made up of spurious signals whose sources can be discovered and often controlled. Some sources include:

- Windows.
- Flourescent lighting.
- AC line noise from walls and poor grounding.
- Camera noise.
- Wind noise in air ducts or heating system.
- Telephone.
- Kitchen appliance compressor noise.
- Floor vibrations.
- Hard surface deflection.
- Cable and radio waves.

The Basic Location Recording Package

Knowing what to bring along on a location shoot is essential to your success and to the cost-effectiveness of the project. This chapter discusses and itemizes what you need.

The Location Shoot Checklist

The checklist in Table 7-2 itemizes and specifies the basic package. Of all the equipment to have along—and to have working—the recorder is obviously the most important.

Seldom is a backup recorder either budgeted or requested. The miniature sync stereo cassette recorders generally fill the bill. The Sony Pro TCDIV and the modified Marantz model 530 add the least noise in transfer from a cleanly recorded cassette.

The chief concern is fresh battery (DC) power. It is very difficult to test for and determine batter life prior to an actual test in the Nagra. (See Appendix O on Nagra operation.) Take at least three spare sets of batteries. Nicads will not provide any guarantee of better performance, but at least allow for the option of recharging, so remember to take the charger with a 110/220-V switch (PAR).

TABLE 7-2 Field production checklist

FULLY "LOADED" NAGRA:
- [ ] 2 microphone preamps
- [ ] QGX crystal oscillator
- [ ] QSLI self-resolver
- [ ] ATN AC power transformer
- [ ] Shorting plug
- [ ] Reel locks (take spares)
- [ ] 2 spare, empty 0.25-in reels
  Case

- [ ] Standard wood clapboard
- [ ] Digital beep/slate
- [ ] Case 0.25-in Scotch recording tape
- [ ] 3 sets D cells
- [ ] Beyer DT 48 headsets
- [ ] 3–6 input mixer and cable
- [ ] 2 sets wireless microphone systems
- [ ] Soundkart
- [ ] Wireless fishpole*
- [ ] Lavalier (mini) microphones*
- [ ] Windscreens
- [ ] Windsocks
- [ ] Shockmounts
- [ ] Cradles
- [ ] Coiled extension cables
- [ ] Monitor headphones
- [ ] Cable twists
- [ ] Mixer*
- [ ] Mixer cable
- [ ] Mixer batteries
- [ ] XLR reversing plugs
- [ ] Tool kit
- [ ] Masking tape
- [ ] Log and clipboard
- [ ] Clapboard
- [ ] Communication headsets
- [ ] Communications headset extension cables
- [ ] Walkie-talkies
- [ ] Earphone for talent talkback*

BOOM-PERSON KIT:
- [ ] 16-ft fishpole
- [ ] 5-ft fishpole
- [ ] Y connector and earphones
- [ ] Coiled cable extension (phones)
- [ ] 3–25-ft microphone cables
- [ ] Cueing device
- [ ] Tennis shoes
- [ ] Cable ties (lowell)

- [ ] Windscreen and shockmount for:
  Sennheiser 816 TU
  Sennheiser MKH 40
  Schoeps Collette
  Tr-50 PS mini microphone
  Electro Voice (hand-held) RE-11
- [ ] 3 9-V battery packs
- [ ] Polarity-reversing pigtail
- [ ] Optional intercom (walkie-talkie)
- [ ] Gaffer tape
- [ ] XLR adapter plugs
- [ ] Betascreen*
- [ ] Wireless pouches*
- [ ] Slate amplifier
- [ ] Digital slate
- [ ] Boom monitors
- [ ] Bullhorn
- [ ] Monitor speaker
- [ ] Noiseless stands
- [ ] Bushings and adapters
- [ ] Penlight
- [ ] 25-ft microphone cables
- [ ] Markers/pens
- [ ] Padded mike clamp for table
- [ ] Stereo mounting rail
- [ ] Elastic microphone suspension
- [ ] Pantyhose (windscreen)
- [ ] Blankets (sound treatment)
- [ ] Pistol grip mike holder
- [ ] Audio isolation transformer*
- [ ] Comtek wireless headsets*
- [ ] Wireless microphones*
- [ ] Fisher boom (compact)
- [ ] Video transmitter*
- [ ] Cueing device*

---

*See "Specialized Gear."

Stereo Equipment and Field Recording

The *Nagra IV-S with time code* is a 2-track sync recorder with a built-in SMPTE/EBU80 time code generator/record/playback system designed for low-noise, accurate recording for film and video applications. Time code is recorded longitudinally on a center track of the audio tape in the same manner as on the third or fourth track of the video recorder. The SMPTE/EBU 80 standard splits each second of time code into frames or time code words—24, 25, 29.97, or 30 frames depending on the video standard used. Each frame is made up of 80 bits of data having a 1 or 0 value (binary code). Shifts in the voltage of the signal (biphase modulation) create the bits. A 1 (one) is created when an additional shift occurs in the middle of the normal *bit period*, 0 (zero) when the signal shifts from one state to another. This allows for the forward or reverse reading of the code at fast or slow speeds.

Of the 80 bits of data, 48 are used as follows:

- 26 bits for time information (hours, minutes, seconds, and frames).
- 16 bits of synchronization definition for "end of frame" and "reading direction" follow.
- 2 unused bits for user data when required.
- 1 bit for indicating if the recording is in *drop-frame mode*.
- 3 flag bits, of which one defines the color framing and the two others the binary group interpretation.

The remaining 32 bits are user-free and are called *user bits*. They may be used for reel number, year, location, or other information.

The code is needed for automated editing as well as for more traditional functions, such as common sync with multiple recorders (video, audio, film) for dubbing or post-production processing.

Motion picture application

1. Camera and Nagra time code generators are set from a master clock to allow them to run independently. If no master clock is used, the code can be set from either machine. Ideally, production data may be entered into the user bits during recording sessions. This eliminates "slates," saving time and stock while allowing for the automated transfer of selected takes (which have been logged during recording) and automated syncing of dailies.

2. When using a time code Nagra in conjunction with a camera without time code, the Nagra time code generator is set at 0 or the time of day. The output of the generator feeds an *electronic slate* (a dumb slate), which is photographed at the start of each take.

As an option, the generator can feed a video character generator which displays the time code on a video monitor for photographing. In TV commercial work, the code and the visual may be displayed.

3. In a conventional non-time-code sync shoot, the time code from the stereo Nagra is resolved as a crystal sync signal.

4. In film production for a music video, the music is prerecorded in the studio with SMPTE time code, then mixed down to 0.25 in with time code center-track transfer. On location, the stereo Nagra is used to play back the audio while the sync camera films action set to the music. This is the updated version of the standard Hollywood studio technique used for the 1930s musicals (film to playback). AC sync motors are replaced by time code. The playback speed of the Nagra is locked by a simple resolver that strips the time code from the playback and matches it against a crystal oscillator reference. The Nagra the playback and matches it against a crystal oscillator reference. The Nagra playback time code is distributed to:

- The camera time code track.
- Electronic slates.
- Video monitors.

The code on the film is identical to the code on the original multitrack audiotape; a final mix-down can therefore be made directly from the multitrack master to the videotape or magnetic film with no intermediate generations.

Video applications

1. With single or multiple cameras, Nagra may be *jam synced* from a master generator, which also supplies SMPTE time code to the video recorders. Continuous jam sync from the master generator insures "frame cdge" accuracy. An audio feed can also be provided by the Nagra for the VTR as a *guide track* for use during editing.

2. When using a field video recorder with Nagra, a master clock synchronizes the Nagra and field VTR. Both operate independently, allowing for wireless stereo microphone use and distant location recording techniques without interference.

3. Suppose you are videotaping live action to synchronous playback using Nagra and VTR. Using the same multitrack transfer technique as for film, the Nagra can then play back audio as well as time code to the VTR. It is possible to use the VTR time code generator and insert the audio time code from the Nagra as the user bits. The master multitrack audio tape can be exactly synchronized with the field or studio video, and the final mix made directly to videotape master without another generation.

Optional Sync Sound Recorders

Cassette recorders. Several consumer cassette recorders have made a dent in the low-budget market. They include compact, portable recorders from

Sony, Phillips, Marantz, and Uher. (See Figure 7-5.) The recording format is the 1/8-in tape in fast-loading cassettes. The most recent addition to this inventory of mini-recorders is the Sony Walkman. Like the other systems, it may be modified for location use with the addition (from The Film Group) of a crystal sync oscillator.

The chief features to look for in cassette sound recorders are portability, compact size, low cost, and low-noise specs. However, microphone connections tend to be more troublesome if the recorder has not been modified with XLR inputs. Otherwise, the sync cassette fulfills all the requisites for average production and may be teamed with virtually any film or video camera. Resolving up to a suitable editing gauge, however, can only be done by a handful of labs (Alpha-cine, TVC, Duart). But you can obtain a resolver and do "home-made" transfers.

Stellavox SP/9.   While the Nagra pretty much dominates as a production recorder in the United States (see Appendix), in Europe, *Stellavox,* a

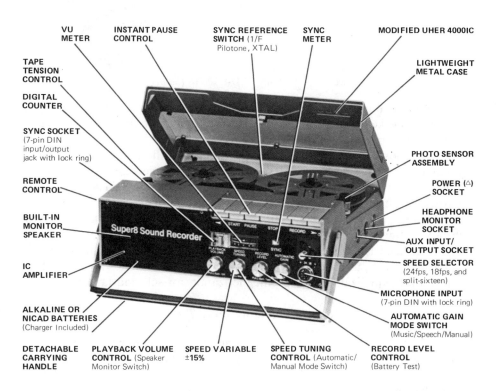

Figure 7-5   Portable recorders. (A) Super8 Sound Recorder (*Source:* Super 8 Sound, Inc.).

Figure 7-5   (B) Sony TCD-D10 Pro (*Source:* Sony).

system of equal prestige, has garnered the bulk of location work. (Scc Figure 7-6.) So it is likely that work outside of America will require some familiarity with this recorder.

The most interesting feature of the Stellavox is the simple interchange of mono and stereo recording modes. Preadjusted head nest assemblies plug in. The tape transport servo-drive motor has extremely low inertia and almost no gyroscopic effect on the capstan.

Three sync modes are available: Perfectone, Neo-Pilotone, and Synchrotone (time code).

The head assemblies available include: mono full-track, mono two-track, stereo half-track, and stereo quarter-track. These assemblies always include appropriate equalization and premagnetization for selected tape emulsions.

Super8 Sound Recorder Type IV

The recorder uses the full width of Super 8 fullcoat magnetic film, which has sprocket holes and accepts three sync references:

- Pilotone.
- Crystal.
- One-frame-per-second digital.

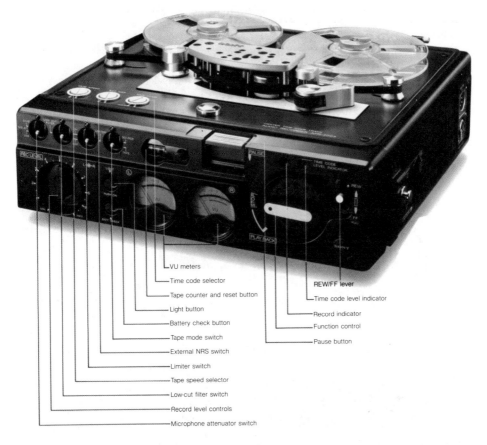

VU meters
Time code selector
Tape counter and reset button
Light button
Battery check button
Tape mode switch
External NRS switch
Limiter switch
Tape speed selector
Low-cut filter switch
Record level controls
Microphone attenuator switch

REW/FF lever
Time code level indicator
Record indicator
Function control
Pause button

Figure 7-5 (C) APR-2003 digital Audio Recorder (*Source:* Sony Pro Audio).

The recorder also acts as the basic studio recorder/editor transfer system. It is essentially a half-track mono recorder. The rate of the sprocket holes passing over the recording head is sensed photoelectrically by an LED and photo transistor. This rate is then compared to a sync reference from the camera, quartz crystal, AC line frequency, recorded sync pulse, and sync projector. Any change in the speed of the recorder generates an error signal that speeds up or slows down the unit. A sync meter gives visual monitoring of sync and allows for speed-tuning.

The sync meter and sync memory may be preset by locking the speed tuning knob in Auto, the sync reference switch to Pilotone and the ACpac to AC Line position. (The AC power pac contains the sync reference switches; it accepts low-level sync inputs and amplifies them to 1 V pilot.) Turn the speed-tuning knob until the needle stabilizes in the center. If it strays to the right, there's a loss of the master pulse; if it strays to the left, there's a loss of the slave pulse from the sprockets. (Always load the fullcoat magnetic film with the sprockets down).

TABLE 7-3 Location recording noise checkpoints

Interior:

- Intermittant rumble from camera drive mechanism and magazines. Tends to pass out through lens since glass transmits sound waves.
- Standing waves and other low-frequency rumbles occurring along the floor surfaces.
- AC hum from overhead fluorescent lighting fixtures.
- Induction from electrical cables on floor and sometimes in walls.
- Any reflected sound from cast, crew, and equipment.
- Background rumble through windows from passing trucks, buses, airplanes.
- Noise from recorder tape reels when the case is not closed.
- Broken mike cable grounds or damaged connectors produce noise when moved during a boom operation.
- Any noise outside the range of earphones.

Exterior:

- Airplanes.
- Wind.
- Horns.
- Ignitions.

Figure 7-6 Stellavox sp/9.

To preset the speed memory of Super8 Sound Recorder:

Connect the camera cable.

Set the sync reference to IF or Pilotone.

Pull out speed-tuning to Manual.

Turn on the camera.

Stabilize the speed-tuning meter needle.

Press in to Automatic.

When the camera stops, the recorder keeps running at the preset speed. The sync needle drops to the right since there is no longer a signal from the camera (unless both are crystal-operated). Upon starting the camera, both units are automatically set.

The recorders are essentially stereo two-track systems. Once modified for sync, however, they can be used only for mono recording.

ADVANTAGES:

Precise operating voltage.

Dolby noise reduction built-in.

Accepts metalized tape emulsions.

DC servo motor runs at $1^7/8$ ips.

DRAWBACKS:

Must be placed in *pause* mode for instant start.

Levels set with VU meter only.

Less rugged in field.

Communication Systems

It is often necessary for the recordist, boom person, director, actors, and others to talk during the shot and in a specific shot. Several methods of internal communication are possible:

1. Q-Aid (hearing aid-style) earplugs.
2. Walkie-talkies.
3. Wireless headsets.
4. Bullhorn (not discussed here).
5. Conventional headsets.

Q-Aid

The Q master is a tiny receiver that fits inside the ear. It:

- Cues actors on sound stages, in theatres, or on location.
- Allows a performer to sing or act to playback of prerecorded material without loudspeaker leakage.
- Gets instructions to stagehands or crew on quiet sets.
- Acts as a paging and intercom link for key personnel only.

- Feeds audio from a "blue" chromakey set to actors on a main set and the audio from the main set to the blue screen, so that dialogue is possible between actors hundreds of feet apart in different locales.
- Assists in TV commercial cueing and singing to playback.

The system works on the induction principle. A loop of wire is strung around the desired area of coverage and is connected to an audio amplifier. Voltage produced by the amp creates a magnetic field, which is picked up by the Q master and amplified.

Typical "Q" System Configurations

QT-1/QR-1 system

- One way, single transmitter, any number of receivers.
- One-way, multiple transmitters, any number of receivers, single frequency. Transmitters are operated in push-to-talk mode, with only one on at a time.
- One-way, multiple-frequency.

(Above systems can be grouped for simultaneous, independent operation on separate frequencies.) (See Figure 7-7.)

- Two-way, two-party. Full-duplex (continuous transmit while receiving), using two frequencies (preferably at least 18 MHz apart). For single-frequency operation, push-to-talk mode is required.
- Two-way, multiple-party, simplex.
- Two-way, multiple-party, half-duplex, two-frequency. One party can operate in continuous-transmit or push-to-talk mode. Other parties operate in push-to-talk mode only. First party hears all transmissions. Other parties hear only first party's transmission—not each other.

QX-1 system. The Model QX-1 wireless intercom master station expands the capabilities of a wired intercom system. It adds a party to a wired intercom system, without direct connection to that party. In effect, the QX-1 becomes a "station" on the wired system, with wireless communications to a walkaround party equipped with a QT-1 transmitter and a QR-1 receiver. Compatible interfaces are available for most popular types of wired intercom systems, such as RTS, Clear-Com, David Clark, and general-purpose four-wire types. In most cases, the QX-1 can be powered by the wired intercom system as well as by the wall-type power supply provided.

QX-2 system. The Model QX-2 wireless intercom master station allows up to six QT-1/QR-1 walk-around parties to communicate in a full-duplex

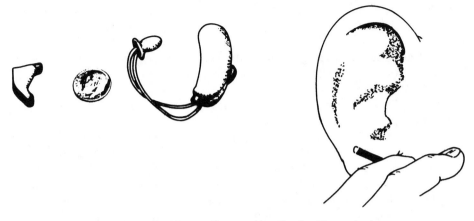

Figure 7-7   "Q" Master. (*Source:* Alan Gordon Enterprises)

(continuous-transmit while receiving), hand-free mode. All parties hear each other continuously. With an optional interface, the QX-2 becomes a "station" on a wired intercom system, allowing all wireless units to communicate with wired stations. Compatible interfaces are available for most popular types of wired intercom systems. The QX-2 contains one transmitter on a common frequency received by all walkaround parties, and between two and six receivers (depending on number of walkaround parties.)

Walkie-Talkie.   The Motorola Walkie-Talkie is a two-way portable FM radio available in VHF and UHF versions with three power levels, six battery sizes providing 6-W RF power in VHF, 5 W in UHF. It operates in dense adjacent RF traffic under great temperature ranges. Current models are free of *squelch tail,* the annoying burst of noise occurring at the end of each transmission. Battery life is typically 10–12 hr, but they cause problems as they drain. The basic range is nearly 5 mi; greater range is possible with *luggi-talkies* often used for ground-to-air communication at 10 to 90-W outputs, powered from a vehicle battery.

A Private Line (PL) option prevents interference from other units by means of a coded squelch allowing only the intended signal to trigger the receiver. The Private Line concept transmits as an inaudible portion of the signal. A radio not switched to PL hears every transmission on its frequency. The FCC has allocated specific bands for motion picture use: 173.225, 173.275, 173.325, 173.375. (See Table 7-4.)

Conventional headsets.   These are worn by the boom person, cabled down the pole, and linked via a Y connector to the mixer, which allows for monitoring of the signal as well as for communication from the recordist via a microphone element in the mixer console. Headset sensitivity must be

20–20,000 Hz, and they must be comfortable while providing isolation with standard ear puffs. (See Figure 7-8.)

Wireless (long-range) cue systems.   TV news gathering requires instruction and control when car, helicopter, and on-foot remote operations are in use. During live broadcasts, it is even more critical for adequate links to exist between director, crew, and station since conceptualization and editing are impossible.

A van-mounted receiver with a good quarter-wave antenna provides a greater receiving range than a portable wireless receiver worn on the body, because body-mounted antennas are never problem-free. A signal heard in the van is not always heard by the remote crew. It makes sense for instructions from a station to be sent first to the van for relay to the remote crew. (See Figure 7-9.) For example, a field reporter who is receiving IFB (or program alone) needs to know something about the audio quality of the program. Mobile and CB systems are designed to provide maximum intelligibility. This is obtained by restricting the audio bandwidth to 300–3,000 Hz and by using clipping to get the modulation percentage up. This is not broadcast-quality audio. Something in the range of 100 Hz–6 kHz audio response (program line) is required, and "broadcast quality is a mediocre standard.

Wireless systems can transmit continuously or in the push-to talk mode. For a one-way single transmitter, you can have any number of receivers. (See Figure 7-10.) Two-way, two-party continuous sets transmit while receiving

Figure 7-8   Sennheiser infrared headset. (*Source:* Audio Services Corp.)

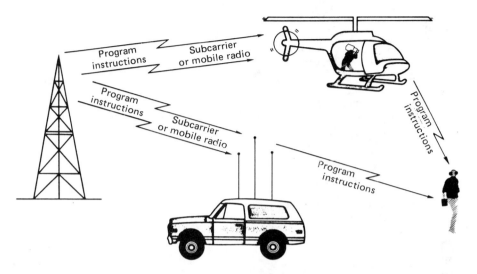

Figure 7-9   A wireless communication system.

(they are *full duplex),* using two frequencies at least 18 MHz apart. Two-way, multiple-party, half-duplex, one-party sets can operate in continuous-transmit or push-to-talk mode; others on the system operate in push-to-talk only and don't hear each other. A wireless intercom master station adds a party to a wired intercom without direct connection to that party or station. (See Figure 7-10.)

Multitrack

In 1941, Les Paul built the first electric guitar. Because there wasn't anyone to play rhythm for him during a period of self-imposed exile while seeking a new musical idiom, Paul laid the rhythm track himself, put it on a turntable, and played along with it. He then experimented with the addition of a bass track, one part on each disc, playing along with it to create a second disc, fostering the first sound on sound. Inspired by a friend, he tried putting a playback pickup behind the record head on his system, creating an echo delay. He used an Ampex for his tape sound-on-sound recording until 1952 when he urged Ampex to design a multiple track machine (like having eight tape machines together). A $13,000, 1,700-pound "multitrack" was born!

There is no secret to the basic multitrack technique. The decisions outlined in the sections on microphones and musical instruments are followed for each track recorded. In a basic 8-track machine, the first track is designated as a reference for all those that come after it. Once the tempo, or *click rate,* is determined for a program, it is inserted onto one track.

- *Overdubbing* is the process of adding discrete tracks against the tempo reference. The head design allows the operator to listen to the reference

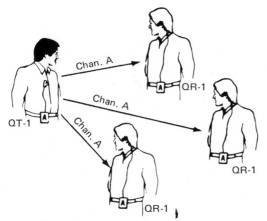

Transmitter can be on continuously
or in push-to-talk mode.

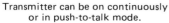

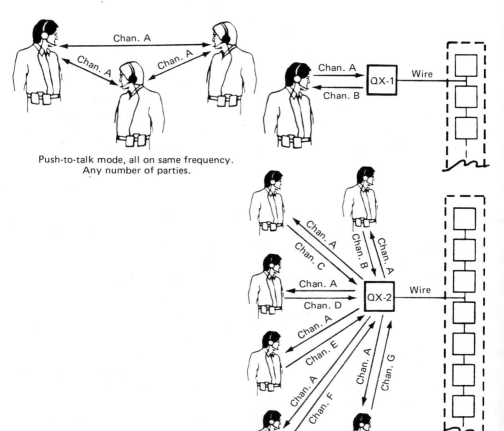

Push-to-talk mode, all on same frequency.
Any number of parties.

Wired
intercom
system

Figure 7-10 Push-to-talk mode. (*Source:* Swintek)

(A)

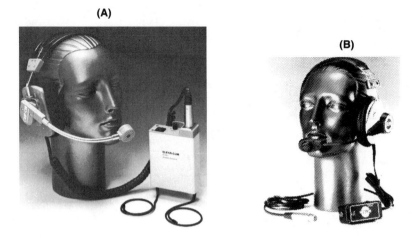

(B)

Figure 7-11   Wired intercom. (A) Wireless intercom; (B) infrared headset. (*Source:* A.G.E.)

TABLE 7-4   Operation of the Motorola HT600 Walkie-Talkie

1. Rotate the volume control a half-turn to clockwise to activate the radio.

2. A power-up alert tone is generated for a half-second and stays on if batteries need charging. If no tone is generated, the batteries should be changed.

3. Set the frequency switch to desired channel.

4. Listen for a transmission and adjust the volume to a comfortable level. If no transmission is heard, depress and hold the monitor button to unsquelch the radio, and adjust background noise to a comfortable level.

5. For a PL (private line) receive operation, place the mode switch in PL position, and the unit responds only to calls coded with the PL frequency. When a PL message is received, the LED goes on green.

6. To transmit, do not interrupt another user. Listen first for activity. When clear, press the push-to-talk switch on the side, and speak slowly 2 to 3 in from the voice grille. Then release the push-to-talk button. LED is on while transmitting. (See Figure 7-12.)

from the record head so that overdubbed inputs are in sync with the basic track.

- Track transfer, or *ping-ponging,* involves combining two or more tracks by rerecording them onto a vacant third track. A 4-track recorder (like the one first introduced by the Beatles) can be used to record up to 10 tracks with none of the tracks ping-ponged more than once. (See Figure 7-13.)

- *Punch-in,* or *insert, editing* is a technique used to record discrete sections of a track without rerecording the entire track. The punch-in feature is triggered by means of a footpedal control on multitrack recorders. (See (See Figure 7-14.)

QUICK REFERENCE CARD
ANTENNA AND BATTERY INSTALLATION

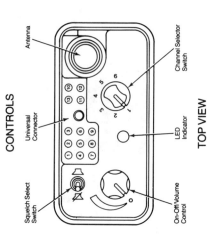

- Attach antenna to the radio by screwing it clockwise into the antenna bushing.

- Install battery by mating the notched end of the battery with the grooved base plate on the radio. Then slide the battery toward the battery latch until engaged.

- Remove battery by disengaging the battery latch (push and hold latch towards top of radio) and slide battery away from latch.

REMOVAL DIRECTION

INSERTION DIRECTION

BATTERY

BASE PLATE

BATTERY CONTACTS

BATTERY LATCH

CONTROLS

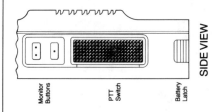

Squelch Select Switch

Universal Connector

Antenna

Channel Selector Switch

LED Indicator

On-Off/Volume Control

TOP VIEW

Monitor Buttons

PTT Switch

Battery Latch

SIDE VIEW

BASIC OPERATING PROCEDURE

TO RECEIVE:

1. Rotate volume control clockwise to turn radio on. Alert tone indicates that radio passes self test of microcomputer.

2. Set channel Selector to the desired channel.

3. For "Private-Line" (PL) squelch operation set the PL/Squelch toggle to the PL setting (🔔). LED will flash green if operating channel is busy.

4. For Carrier-Squelch operation set squelch select toggle to the Carrier-Squelch setting (P).

   (The squelch sensitivity is factory preset and can be adjusted by any computer-equipped Motorola Service Shop.

TO TRANSMIT:

1. Set Channel Selector Switch to desired channel.

2. Monitor the channel (press one of the monitor buttons if the radio is in PL operation mode).

3. When channel is clear press the PTT switch and speak slowly and clearly into the front speaker grille area. When finished transmitting release the PTT switch to receive.

ON TRANSMISSION:

LED will glow continuous red to indicate normal transmission. LED will flash RED to indicate low battery.

4. To turn the radio off rotate volume control fully counterclockwise.

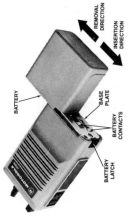

Figure 7-12 Quick reference operating procedure of Motorola Walkie-Talkie.

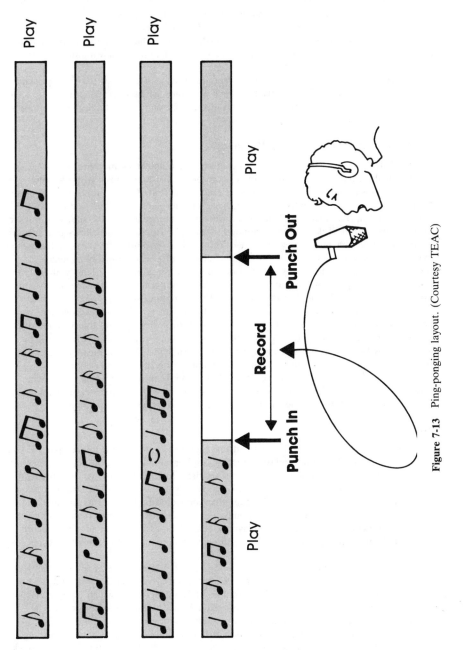

Figure 7-13 Ping-ponging layout. (Courtesy TEAC)

TABLE 7-5   What is multitrack?

As the name suggests it is multi- (or many) tracks. In the strict sense any tape that contains more tracks than the finished master can be called a multitrack tape. If, for instance, you were making a mono record and used a three-track machine the original three-track tape would be the multitrack original. When all the tracks had been recorded they would then be replayed by the multitrack recorder and mixed down onto a second (mono) machine to obtain the final master tape.

Today, of course, mono has been largely replaced by stereo but the same principles apply. Four, eight, sixteen or twenty-four-track machines are used to obtain a multitrack tape, then these are played back, mixed and re-recorded onto a two-track machine to obtain the stereo master.

What Are the Advantages of Using Multitrack?

Well, let's start with the problems of just using a half-track machine. In some cases it's the ideal format. If you simply wanted to record a solo piano piece with two microphones, there's nothing better and it's been used successfully for recording classical music for many years. For the creative musician, however, there are a number of drawbacks. It's basically an inflexible medium. Once you have committed something to tape, you're more or less stuck with it. Take Sound-on-Sound for example. In effect, this allows you to transfer one track you have previously recorded to the other remaining track. While this is taking place you can monitor the first track, play along with it and record both signals together onto track two. It's a great idea but there are three basic problems with it. One, if you repeat the process too many times, sooner or later you'll find that the hiss becomes objectionable. Two, the final product is mono (if at any time you replay both tracks together, you'll find one of them is out of sync with the other). Three, there's no margin for error. As you build up the sound, the levels need to be correct. If you find that the drums are too loud once you've gotten to the solo parts, the only way you can correct it is by erasing the whole thing and starting again. This doesn't, incidentally, mean you can't obtain good results—you can, but it takes a fair amount of skill and experience.

In comparison, multitrack recording offers several advantages while at the same time reduces some of the recording headaches associated with two-track, especially when recording more than one musician. The key to it all is what we call Simul-Sync.

What is Simul-Sync?

On a tape-recorder the Record and Playback heads are some distance apart. If you record something, the actual replay occurs a second or so later when the tape reaches the Playback head. Under normal circumstances this isn't a problem but if you wanted to record something and make a sound recording in sync with the first, you'd find it impossible. This is because the point on the tape that you would be listening to and the point where the recording was taking place would be different and therefore create a time lag. By building a combined Record and Playback head, it's possible to monitor and record at exactly the same point on the tape, hence the term Simultaneous Synchronization or Simul-Sync.

To illustrate a simple multitrack recording and the importance of Simul-Sync, let's take a typical line-up: Lead guitar/Vocals, Rhythm guitar, Bass and Drums, and see how a four-track recording fits together. The first thing to do is decide in which order everything will be recorded. Let's assume we want to make a basic rhythm track first, then afterwards, add the Lead guitar and Vocals on two different tracks.

The rhythm track would be no different than making a straight stereo recording with a mixer. The Bass, Drums and Rhythm guitar would be fed, via the mixer, to Tracks 1 and 2. When everybody felt the rhythm tracks were satisfactory the Lead guitar could be added. It is at this point that the Simul-Sync becomes vital.

TABLE 7-5 (continued)

Let's assume for the moment that we were using a machine without Simul-Sync. The lead guitarist would go into the studio to play his particular solo. Using headphones, he would listen to the rhythm track and wait for the point where the solo was due to begin. During this time everything he hears will be coming from the Playback head. The problem arises as soon as he begins to play. At the very moment he starts he will be listening to the section of tape immediately opposite the Playback head. The recording, however, will be taking place an inch or so away, opposite the Record head. No matter how close you put the Record and Playback heads there will always be a gap between them and this will cause a delay between any track that is being recorded and any others being played back at the same time.

While the recording is taking place, the Lead guitarist won't hear anything wrong but once all the tracks are played back together it will be obvious that the guitar is out of sync. The obvious solution is to record and monitor any previously recorded material at the same point on the tape. This is exactly what the Simul-Sync head does. Instead of using the normal Playback head, Tracks 1 and 2 (the rhythm tracks) are reproduced by the Simul-Sync head at precisely the same point on the tape where the new recording is being made. Once the Lead guitar has been correctly recorded onto Track 3, (you can't, incidentally, record and replay the same track at the same time, the Simul-Sync head gives you the choice of *either* recording or playing back) the Simul-Sync on Tracks 1 and 2 can be switched and normal playback used to check the signal on Tracks 1, 2 and 3. This time, the Lead guitar will be in perfect time with the rest of the backing. Exactly the same thing is done with the Vocals. This time Track 3 will be heard via the Sync head as well as Tracks 1 and 2 and the Vocals will be recorded on Track 4. When everybody is happy that they have the vocals right, the four tracks can be mixed down to stereo to create the final master.

With the two-track machine your final balance will be the one you achieve at the time of the recording. If a couple of days later the guitarist wants his solo to be louder or the vocalist thinks there should be more echo on his voice, there's nothing that can be done about it. On the other hand, with a multitrack recording there's no problem—it's just simply a question of remixing the master tape and incorporating the necessary improvements.

Besides the convenience for the musicians, multitrack recording offers benefits on the technical side. No longer do you have to hide the vocalist under the stairs in order to stop the sound of the drums or bass guitar feeding into the "vocal" microphone. With multitrack he can be recorded separately in complete isolation. With only three instruments on the rhythm track there's no reason why they can't be spread a little further apart in the room to keep separation. Another nice bonus is that you can re-use microphones. If you're just starting off and can only afford a couple of really good microphones, you'll at least be able to use them each time you record a fresh track. This will help to maintain a higher standard of recording especially when finances are tight. If you're careful with your choice of equipment, there's no reason why you can't get studio quality.

Courtesy of TEAC/Corp.

The multitrack recorder has become an integral part of the audio design lab and small studio recording systems. Linked to inputs such as a synthesizer, microphone, turntable, and computer music generator, and outlinked to a monitor and VTR, the multitrack functions (with a synchronizer and autolocator) as a complete recording and editing suite. (See Figure 7-15.)

Figure 7-14 Fostex 16-track multitrack recorder. (*Source:* Fostex)

Figure 7-15 The future is now. Midi-based 16-track recording studio with computer control.

TRANSFER

Loss of quality occurs at every stage of the process, and the electromagnetic transfer step is yet another point of potential loss. Yet, with care and understanding of the process, you can optimize quality. Before editing the sound track, you must convert it to an editing medium. Various kinds of transfers (from cassette, record, disc, reel-to-reel) are illustrated and a flow chart provided. Also explained are how time code helps and the requirements for editing in either film or video format.

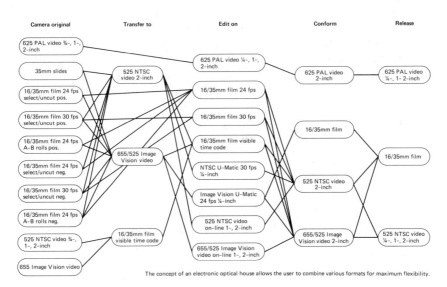

The concept of an electronic optical house allows the user to combine various formats for maximum flexibility.

Electronic optical transfer methods allow for the flexible combination of various formats.

Sound Transfer in the Film Chain

To edit sound by classical (cutting) methods, it is necessary to transfer from the ¼-in production track to a more efficient and practical format-sprocketed fullcoat magnetic film or economical stripe-coat magnetic film, which have the same dimensions as the picture. Sync is assured if the 60-Hz sync signal can be made to correspond to 24 fps, the projection rate of film. [See Figure 8-1(A).]

If the recordings were made under optimum conditions, all you need is a copy of the original. However, at this stage of the audio process it may be necessary to take corrective measures because of:

- Poor acoustics of the recording space.
- Imbalance between actor and background.
- Noise, camera clatter, AC hum.
- Poor recording technique.

Many corrections and enhancements are subjectively determined. It is apparent that in normal processing, the high frequencies suffer because of:

- Off-mike recording.
- Tape head losses.
- Playback head losses.
- Tape losses.

The transfer process attempts to use nonlinear devices to undo the results of nonlinearity in the original ¼-in master. Filters, equalizers, compressors, limiters, noise-reduction gates, flangers, phasers, and the like all act *selectively* on regions of the sound spectrum. (See Figure 8-1(B).) The 0.25-in master is transferred as the prerecorded pilot. One pulse is resolved driving the power amplifier of a synchronous fullcoat recorder. One such resolver is the Nagra SLO Sync Resolver and Speed Variateur. (See Figure 8-2.)

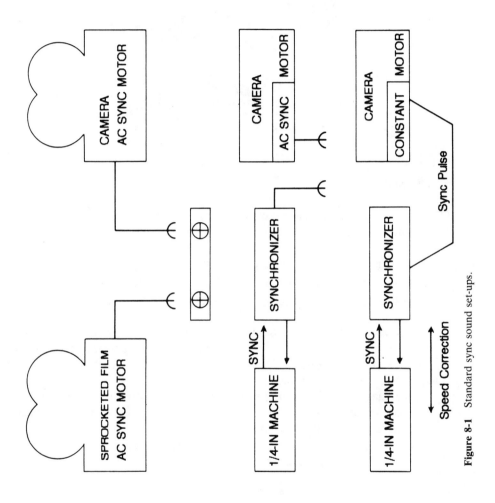

Figure 8-1 Standard sync sound set-ups.

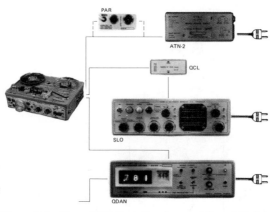

Figure 8-2   Nagra SLO Sync Resolver and Speed Variateur.

Transfer Process

The first attempt is to achieve overall equalization. Secondly, level standards are attained in reference to the requirements of the user:

- 0 dB is the overall standard for film.
- +8 dB is the broadcast standard.
- +4 dB is the reference for the music industry.

Television uses *audio following video* methods. Direct mastering leaves extra seconds that must be *time compressed* up to 14%. This *raises* the average audio level, increasing noise. Noise gates are therefore widely used. No other basic processing is attempted.

Transferring audio from widescreen formats requires *scamp* amplifiers, which pick up audio maintaining sync with the Rank Cinetel Topsy transfer system widely in use for film-to-video transfer.

Dolby-encoded material is decoded and separated, re-encoded, and "laid back" to the videotape master.

Nagra Settings for Transfer

The Nagra may be used as the master source machine for sync transfer to the next gauge. Playback level is set at the time of recording and logged. (See Figure 8-3.) The level at the line output is the same as when recorded if the "Tape/Direct" switch is in the "Tape" position. In "Direct," the line and playback volume must be used to adjust the level. This is the same level as that in the "Tape" position when the volume control is set to 0 dB. In "Direct," the microphone inputs are fed to the outputs.

Figure 8-3 Settings on the Nagra PFS switch.

The playback (loudspeaker) position controls the volume of the monitor and transfer module (QSLI). The amount of compensation can be read when the test meter is set to the "Synch," or SL, position. The "Pilot Playback" position indicates the strength of the sync signal (generally −2 dB).

Procedure for ¹/₄-in Transfer to Fullcoat

Here are the steps in transferring from ¹/₄-in to fullcoat:

- Connect the Nagra and fullcoat recorders to the same AC wall outlet. The ATN supplies power and a sync reference to the Nagra. The SLO resolver may also be used to supply power and a sync reference from the AC line. (See Figure 8-4.)
- Patch the Nagra to the fullcoat recorder, via a 2-pin line output cable, to the 600-Ω input of the fullcoat recorder.
- If you are using the SLO, preset the speed correction by auditioning the master ¹/₄-in tape and monitoring the readout (an ellipsoid display on oscilloscope). If the take is in sync, the ellipse is stabilized; if out of sync, it flips on its axis.
- Voice is recorded to pulse-coded ¹/₄-in magnetic tape.
- Only the good takes are transferred to fullcoat film.
- The edited fullcoat elements (dialogue, music, effects) are mixed to release format and to a pulse-coded 0.25-in protection master.
- Either the master mix is transferred to a high-contrast film stock and processed to become an optical sound track negative. *Or* the tracks are transferred discretely onto release prints with magnetic stripes: 4-track Dolby stereo or 6-track.
- The optical negative is a composite printed onto the picture stock. After development, this track is played back in the theatre.

TYPICAL TRANSFER CHANNEL

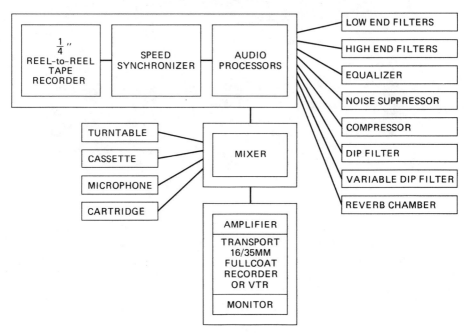

Figure 8-4 The transfer chain flow chart.

Make the corrections by manually riding the gain of the SLO until the ellipse is stabilized. After this rehearsal, make the actual transfer. Unless there are major deviations, one setting may be sufficient for the entire take and even the entire sound roll. The accessory Speed Variateur allows for a manual correction of an additional 7%. This mechanical method does not ensure perfect sync but has the advantage of visual monitoring. Log each take. (See Figure 8-5.)

- If the internal Nagra module (QSLI) is used, make the same matching of internal and external references. With the PFS switch in "Sync Playback" and the test switch in "Pilot Playback," observe the modulometer needle. If it is stable, a sync transfer may be made. If it fluctuates to the left or right during rehearsal, the take is off-speed and in all likelihood outside the limits of the automatic system.

- Having monitored, auditioned, and cued the sync, preset the resolver, and made log notes, you can proceed with matching modulometer level with the sync recorder's VU meter level. You are seeking a linear relationship between the deflection of the meter needles, averaging around 0 dB on both machines. The line potentiometer controls the output signal from the Nagra. The master gain control of the fullcoat recorder usually has a recommended preset position for normal transfers. Set the master gain

MGM STUDIOS   STUDIO TRANSFER & DUBBING LOG

ACCOUNT | SUB | PICTURE | SET   TITLE ____________ ____________ STAGE ____________   DATE ______

MATERIAL

BILL CODE	MATERIAL (TO BE) USED: INDICATE BY ☑		MATERIAL USAGE
	1/4 TRANS. HRS.	1/2 TRANS. HRS.	
920	35MM FULL COAT	☐	
921	35MM FULL COAT (CR. - RETURNED)	☐	
923	35MM SINGLE STRIPE	☐	
924	35MM SINGLE STRIPE MSNB – NEW BASE	☐	
926	35MM SINGLE STRIPE 3-M TYPE 336 – NEW BASE	☐	
930	16MM FULL COAT	☐	
950	35MM OPTICAL TRACK	☐	
951	35/32MM OPTICAL TRACK	☐	
952	35/32MM - DOUBLE RANK OPTICAL TRACK	☐	
		☐	

	TAPE REEL	3¾ IPS	7½ IPS	15 IPS
961	¼"	☐	☐	☐
962	¼" 7"	☐	☐	☐
963	¼" 10"	☐	☐	☐
970	¼" 10"	☐	☐	☐

	CASSETTES AND CARTRIDGES	
980	C-45 CASSETTE	☐
981	C-60 CASSETTE	☐
982	C-90 CASSETTE	☐
983	C-120 CASSETTE	☐
984	45 MIN. 8 TRK. CART.	☐
985	90 MIN. 8 TRK. CART.	☐

TRANSFER FOOTAGE

200 TRANS. OF SELECTED TAKES REGULAR HRS.	206 TRANSFER 3 TRACK TO 3 TRACK	210 STANDARD TRANS. REGULAR HRS.	220 TRANS. SEL. TKS. TO 16MM REGULAR HRS.	222 STD. TRANS. TO 16MM REGULAR HRS.	250 REPRINT TRANSFERS	255 OPTICAL TRANS. REGULAR HRS.	261 OPT. TRANS. TO 16MM REGULAR HRS.	CODE ____ DOUBLE TIME

BY ____________ EXT. ______

FOR ____________

ACCOUNT | SUB | PICTURE | SET   LO # ______ PO # ______

MGM®

MGM FORM 331C REV. 10-6-77

Figure 8-5 A transfer log. The format differs from lab to lab.

and leave it alone. Riding it always induces noise and can be heard during transitions of amplification. You can ride the line pot while transferring without problems.

- Make and audition a test recording of one take. You might hear noise, level drops, etc. Take notes and do a retake.
- The fullcoat recorder has a 10- to 20-sec start-up time to get to speed. So turn the fullcoat recorder on first, then the Nagra playback function switch. If time allows, it is safer to monitor each take rather than preset and hope that no mechanical problems occur during the transfer of an entire roll. However, if filtering or equalization is not being done, let the takes run through.

Every recorder motor has its own starting time characteristic as a function of design, film load, temperature, and cost. This means that, even if both motors are turned on exactly at the same moment, they may take different amounts of time to run up to speed, and one machine would have passed more footage than the other. The true sync reference point is therefore always a physical point from a clapboard, tone, or code.

- A high-fidelity speaker is essential for audition and monitoring. (See Figure 8-6.) Furthermore, playback levels should be set as high as you can stand them, since all the background "junk" is revealed if it is there, avoiding surprises later in the mix.
- The final transfer reel should represent a balanced representation of the original 0.25-in tape. When the choice occurs, it is better to lose low frequencies rather than highs during the transfer.
- To conserve mag stock, stop the fullcoat recorder first but allow it to run its cycle, slowing down to a stop, rather than "braking" to a halt. Part of the final words may be slurred.

Transfer of Records via Turntable

To make a clean, efficient transfer of records to magnetic tape, take the following precautions:

- The records must be spotless and unwarped, and they should be allowed to have sufficient time for the grooves to recoil after the initial audition before the actual transfer. When a stylus rides the groove (tracks), it deforms the vinyl. The groove must be allowed to reform before another play. However, when a click is heard during play, it signals some malformation. Resetting the tone arm pressure up to 4 gm and running the stylus over that point may repair the damage. Reset the pressure and replay to test it. (See Figure 8-7.)

(A)

(B)

Figure 8-6 Compact speaker-amplifier systems like (A) the Anchor 1000 and (B) the Kudelski DSM are adequate companions for playback of Nagra recorder field dialogue.

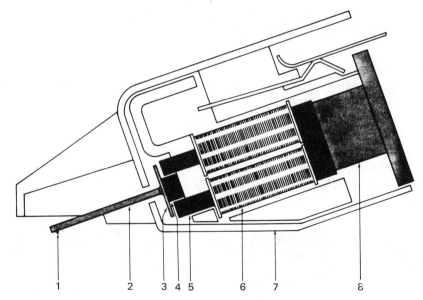

1. Naked elliptical diamond	5. Pole pieces (4)
2. Low mass aluminum cantilever	6. Induction coils (4)
3. Moving micro cross	7. Mu-metal screen
4. Block suspension	8. Hycomax magnet

Figure 8-7 The stylus.

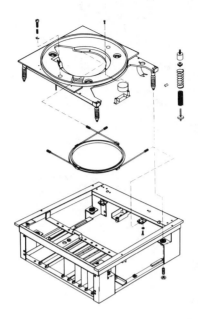

Figure 8-8   A professional turntable suspension system.

- The turntable should be manual, servo-drive, and belt-driven, with an isolated platter and precisely balanced tone arm. (See Figure 8-8.)
- Check the stylus force gauge and tone arm counterbalance for accurate tracking.
- The amplifier should be low-noise and isolated from inductance by means of a complete ground of all systems.
- The turntable should be insensitive to floor vibrations and acoustic feedback.

With regard to this last point, the NAB stereo standard calls for a *rumble level* in each channel at least 35 dB below 1 cm/s in the plane of modulation at

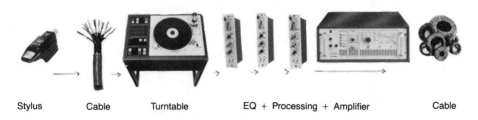

Stylus   Cable   Turntable   EQ + Processing + Amplifier   Cable

Figure 8-9   The trail of the audio signal.

100 Hz, with the ballistic traits of the meter specified and with playback equalization specified. The wow and flutter standard is $+/-0.3\%$ or 21 lines per minute drift on a standard 216-line strobe card.

The turntable represents a mini transfer channel each of whose components can add noise or distortion. As seen in Figure 8-9, the audio signal must travel from the stylus through cabling, filters and equalizers, amplifier through cabling to the next system in the chain. Each element is herewith discussed as appropriate.

Stylus. Effective *tip mass* is the most direct cause of groove deformation and distortion at high frequencies. Use mini cartridges to minimize system mass. A 1-mil stylus, tracking at 0.5 g, is safe for transfer,but it may not be the manufacturer's recommendation for "performance" characteristics.

All conditions are exaggerated by a worn stylus.

Pickup cartridge ratings. Vintage pressings call for different stylus cantilever standards, which should be adhered to for proper reproduction. Here are the appropriate ratings for tracking various types of records:

- For conventional phonographs, stereo.
- For early mono records, microgroove 25-μm tip radius.
- For early mono, standard groove 65-μm tip radius.

Amplifier. The chief problem is ground noise and an overloaded signal due to false manufacturer power ratings and impedance mismatching between amplifier and recorder. A 15-dB pad may be used to attenuate the signal before transfer.

If amplifier output is connected to a Nagra, the 3-conductor grounded and shielded cable terminates in a banana plug into the "Line Input" of the Nagra. The amplifier gain is set to midpoint. The line pot is the master gain control for the transfer.

Dirt, dust, scratches, and deformation from the first play transfer as noise from the record. Always use a new record.

Turntable. Minimize heat, tracking weight, and dust. Then perform a rehearsal and test recording to determine if the following are present:

- Induction noise.
- Speed fluctuations.
- Coloration from stylus design.
- "Hill and dale" effect resulting from the mechanical distortion of the vertical plane of the grooves.

- Slight distortions of the reproduced waveform due to pivoted tracking arms.
- "Pinch" effect caused by different actions of the cutter and replay styli (pronounced when a mono disk is played on stereo equipment; the spurious harmonics to main signal are out-of-phase).

Transfer from Sync Cassette to Nagra

Transfer of material recorded on a cassette recorder (1/8-in tape) is trouble-free if the cassette has been modified with a crystal control for its transport. The available sync cassettes (Sony TCD 5D Pro II [see Figure 8-10], Uher, Marantz PMD 350, and others) must utilize their own resolvers to transform the pulse code on the cassette 4th-track (NAB position) sync reference to a speed-controlling voltage.

Super 8 Sound, Inc. and the Film Group provide most of the gear necessary to outfit a simple transfer chain. The resolver should have little difficulty matching the 17/8-ips cassette speed to the Nagra's 71/2-ips recording speed. Since most of the top-quality cassettes have built-in Dolby or DBX noise-reduction systems, internal noise is usually minimal. However, the quality of the cassette tape emulsion matters more than any other element in the chain. The high-output metalized tapes may be rich in high frequency transients, which have to be filtered during the audio processing stage from Nagra to the editing medium.

All transfers are made onto another magnetic medium. The format (whose choice is essentially a budgetary consideration) differs with respect to the actual position and width of the recorded area; Figure 8-11 shows the more common configurations. Emerging media include compact disc and DAT. The

Figure 8-10   Sony sync cassette. (Source: Sony.)

TRACKING

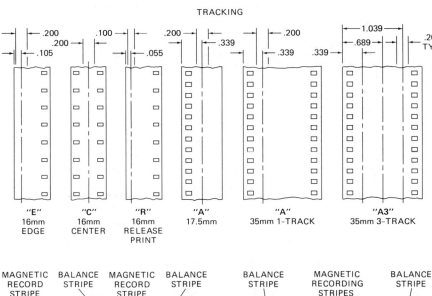

| "E" 16mm EDGE | "C" 16mm CENTER | "R" 16mm RELEASE PRINT | "A" 17.5mm | "A" 35mm 1-TRACK | "A3" 35mm 3-TRACK |

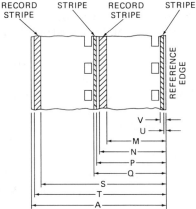

DRAFT USA STANDARD DIMENSIONS OF

Magnetic Striping of 16mm Motion-Picture Film Perforated Super 8, 2R-1667 (1-3)

1. Scope

This standard specifies the location and dimensions of recording stripes and balance stripes applied to 16mm motion-picture film with two rows of super 8 perforations in positions 1 and 3.

Dimensions	Inches	Millimeters
A	0.623 nom	15.95 nom
M	0.285 ↓ 0.002	7.24 ↓ 0.05
N	0.312 ↓ 0.002	7.92 ↓ 0.05
P	0.317 ↓ 0.003	8.05 ↓ 0.08
Q	0.329 ↓ 0.003	8.36 ↓ 0.08
S	0.599 ↓ 0.002	15.21 ↓ 0.05
T	0.626 ↓ 0.002	15.90 ↓ 0.05
U	0.003 ↓ 0.003	0.08 ↓ 0.08
V	0.015 ↓ 0.003	0.38 ↓ 0.08

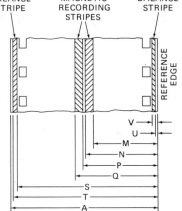

DRAFT USA STANDARD DIMENSIONS OF

Magnetic Striping of 16mm Motion-Picture Film Perforated Super 8, 2R-1667 (1-4)

1. Scope

This standard specifies the location and dimensions of the magnetic recording stripe and the balance stripes applied to 16mm motion-picture film with two rows of super 8 perforations in positions 1 and 4.

Dimensions	Inches	Millimeters
A	0.628 nom	15.95 nom
M	0.285 ↓ 0.002	7.24 ↓ 0.05
N	0.312 ↓ 0.002	7.92 ↓ 0.05
P*	0.316 ↓ 0.002	8.02 ↓ 0.05
Q	0.343 ↓ 0.002	8.71 ↓ 0.05
S	0.613 ↓ 0.003	15.57 ↓ 0.08
T	0.625 ↓ 0.003	15.85 ↓ 0.08
U	0.003 ↓ 0.003	0.08 ↓ 0.08
V	0.015 ↓ 0.003	0.38 ↓ 0.08

Figure 8-11 Tracking configurations of magnetic film.

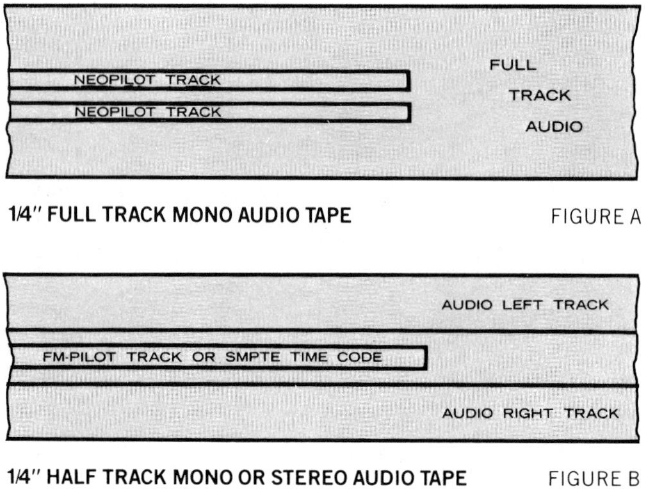

1/4" FULL TRACK MONO AUDIO TAPE   FIGURE A

1/4" HALF TRACK MONO OR STEREO AUDIO TAPE   FIGURE B

Figure 8-12   Various positions of the sync pulse.

universally common sync pulse type and position is the Neopilotone. Older types are pictured in Figure 8-12. Each type can be read and resolved only by its own system.

Figure 8-13 displays the difference in the striations of the magnetic oxide on tape in relation to the speed of recording. Note that the distance between data pulses increases with recording speed; fidelity and clarity also increase.

¹/₄-Inch Audio-to-Video Transfer

Completing all postproduction entirely in video requires the transfer of film and ¹/₄-in tape in sync to videotape. Syncing the ¹/₄-in tape occurs in the *telecine* at the time of picture transfer or later in the *audio layback* stage. With

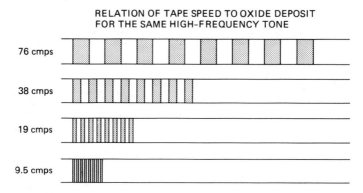

Figure 8-13   Relation of tape speed to oxide deposit for the same high-frequency zone.

the *unofficial* standard Aaton/Panavision Film Data Code (optically recorded on pix negative and magnetically on ¼-in) the Rank Cinetel Telecine transfer is automatic.

Here is how syncing is done in the layback stage using time code (see Figure 8-14):

- Transfer the original negative to 1-in master videotape.
- Make a ¾-in dub with matching time code, and use it as a video picture reference. An Otari MTR-90, converted for 1-in video, plays back audio only of the master 1-in. Record the ¼-in onto the Otari 1-in video master.
- A synchronizer, using time code, controls the transports of (1) the Otari with 1-in audio, (2) a ¾-in VCR with the ¾-in dub, and (3) a Nagra-T audio recorder.
- Transfer the original ¼-in audio simultaneously to 1-in and ¾-in masters.

If there is no time code, it can be added to the Pilotone mono original ½-in in the layback stage. This requires a stereo recorder for playback. The original Pilotone is *restriped* with time code. If the original is stereo without time code, the code can be added only by transferring to another generation of ¼-in.

An alternate system is to use the synchronizer to create pseudo time code numbers from the mono or stereo sync pulse of the original ¼-in to synchronize ¼-in audio to video. The audio- and videotapes are physically moved back and forth (as in conventional film editing) until sync is achieved.

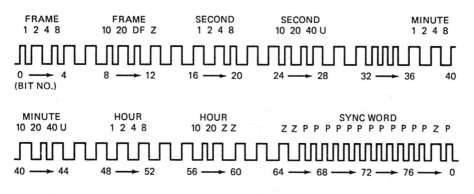

ILLUSTRATION SHOWS: 20 HOURS, 47 MINUTES, 58 SECONDS, 19 FRAMES
DF = DROP FRAME BIT, (USED FOR COLOR VIDEO ONLY)
P = PERMANENT ONE   U = UNASSIGNED BITS   Z = PERMANENT ZERO

SMPTE Time and Control Code

Figure 8-14   Syncing in layback using time code.

Aaton/Panavision Film Data Track

Film Data Track (FDT) is a way of coding individual frames of original camera
negative during the shooting by an optical device inside the camera. FDT is
exposed along the outside edge of the film and is both *computer-readable* and
human-readable.

- The *computer-readable* data track contains the following standard
  SMPTE format on every frame: hours, minutes, seconds, frames. It also
  includes one of the following six bits of machine-readable data paged over
  a number of frames: scene number, take number, roll number, date,
  production number, and camera number.
- The *human-readable* data track contains one or two digits of information
  on each frame in the following sequence:

  Sample (R 02 Tk 04 Sc 33 3C E 1 17P 54 86 07 14 09 12 36 s

  which corresponds to:

  Roll 2, Take 4, Scene 333C, Camera 117, Production 54, July 14, 1986, 9
  hours, 12 minutes, 36 seconds

  Frame zero is indicated by the "s."

Some Rank Cinetel Flying Spot Scanner transfer systems can read 16 and
35 negative and positive edge codes and use them to sync audio to picture while
serving as an interface between film and electronic postproduction (EPP).

Film Data Track, with an identical audio time code, can be transferred in
sync at either 24 or 30 fps to videotape. (See Figure 8-15.)

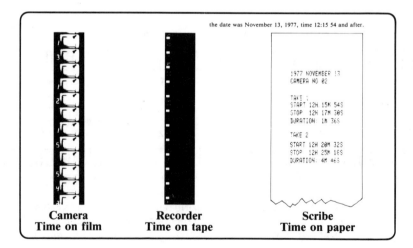

the date was November 13, 1977, time 12:15 54 and after.

1977 NOVEMBER 13
CAMERA NO 02

TAKE 1
START 12H 15M 54S
STOP 12H 17M 30S
DURATION 1M 36S

TAKE 2
START 12H 20M 32S
STOP 12H 25M 18S
DURATION 4M 46S

| Camera | Recorder | Scribe |
| Time on film | Time on tape | Time on paper |

Figure 8-15   Film Data Track coding of original camera negative frames.

Sync Fallacy

Generally speaking, synchronization is achieved by starting and stopping two machines whose motors are running at *approximately* the same rate per unit of time, with the luxury of marking the film and tape (or the videotape) with start and stop references. The references may be time code, beeps, hand claps, slateboards, flash frames. Projection and recording speeds, however, are arbitrary constants. Each system is constructed with varying degrees of precision, and reliability is subject to many variables, including human error. Perfect pitch is required to detect a voice track that is running more than 7 frames off the pace of 24 fps. Higher fidelity and higher resolution would be obtained at 48 fps and better still at 60 fps (Showscan).

It would be nice if the relationship between recorded sounds and images were identical to the actual one. If a camera is made to run at the same rate as the recorder, sooner or later the finished track and print may be made to *appear* as if they were happening at the same time. In fact, there is no such thing as synchronism. There is only the *simulation* of things occurring at the same time. (See Table 8-1.)

Television taxes the sensorium even less since its mosaic projections are low-definition, soft-contour transparencies that induce a trance-like sensual hypnosis enhanced only by aural definition.

Types of Sync Transfer

If the camera is running at 24 fps, 60 Hz (or pulses per second) are recorded per 7½-in of tape in 1 s. A *resolver*, or transfer synchronizer, counts the pulses coming off the tape and compares that number to the line frequency (60 Hz, or pulses per second, AC). If there are more or less than 60 pulses, the resolver slows down or speeds up the playback recorder to match frequencies as the audio signal is transferred by cable to the sprocketed sync recorder. The synchronizer automatically compensates for variations in camera speed by altering recording speed.

(There is a reason for the sync head's being located between the record and playback heads. If it were before the erase head, the pulse would be erased! If it were in front of the record head, the recording process would erase the

TABLE 8-1 Editorial methods for giving the appearance of sync

- Resort to using long shots where loss of lip sync is less noticeable.
- Use reaction shots as cutaways from speaker-listener asynchronism.
- Allow the sound to start first and end last when recording. Film the sound action after it begins and before it ends!
- Use voice-over narrative for "lost" sections.

pulse. If it came after the playback head, a defective signal could not be detected.)

The four types of sync transfer are:

1. *Self-resolving system*: The recorded sync pulse is matched to the AC line. The system adds or subtracts to the speed of the tape recorder so that the tape runs at the speed of the line frequency or $2\frac{1}{2}$ cycles per frame of picture.

2. *Power amplifier system*: The tape sync signal is amplified to a voltage/ power level capable of driving the synchronous motor of a film recorder in the studio.

3. *Strobe-light system*: The sync signal is amplified to a voltage level capable of triggering a strobe light. The light is directed at a stroboscopic disc on the film recorder's drive mechanism that is calibrated in the ratio of $2\frac{1}{2}$ flashes per frame of film. After both machines are running, they may be manually speed-tuned until the strobe disc appears stationary (as in the old Siemens interlock projector sound-on-sound recording system).

4. *Oscilloscope*: Hand-resolved matching is displayed on a cathode-ray tube and, as in process 1, manually locked into sync.

SLO Synchronizer

Before the advent of time code, sound synchronization in the transfer process was achieved via the Nagra SLO Synchronizer, which is designed to automatically modify the Nagra tape speed in playback. It matches a reference signal (AC line sync) to the sync signal on the tape. A cathode-ray oscilloscope displays the exact peak level readout horizontally (the reference signal) and vertically (the Pilotone signal).

A phase discriminator circuit compares the signals. The differences are translated into pseudo-DC signals, which control the speed of the Nagra motor. A locking range potentiometer allows the strength of the signal to be modified when large corrections (9%) are necessary due to camera wow and flutter.

Connected to the Nagra and power line, the recorder playback speed is automatically modified also. The transfer fullcoat sync recorded (16 mm/35 mm) runs on AC using the same line as Nagra and SLO.

Manually, the screen display is adjusted to maintain an ellipsoidal steady lissajous figure. A speed varieteur attachment further corrects up to 2.5%. A test rehearsal transfer is made to trace speed fluctuations on the studio tape, if any. Then the actual transfer is made using the "map" of corrections noted in the log during the rehearsal.

Picture and Sound Formats for Double-Band Projection

The *double-band*, or *interlock*, *projector* serves as an editing and preview tool in 16-mm work. It allows for sync playback of the separate magnetic track and picture to check edit sync and to get a feeling for whether the cut works on the screen in terms of its aural timing and perspective. These projectors can direct-record narration, voice-over, effects, or music on a magnetic striped print on the picture side or the magnetic film on the sound side. Furthermore, they allow for transfer from the optical soundtrack on the picture side to magnetic track on the sound side and the reverse, that is, from the mag sound side to the mag picture side. A 5-blade shutter and AC sync motor allow for telecine transfer. The variable speed function provides analysis of the edit points.

Interlock projectors were often used as a "poor man's sound studio" since virtually all post production functions could be accomplished with some creativity and dexterity. However, sound clarity was at best mediocre, that is, at the limits of 16-mm sound reproduction. Moreover, recording had to be perfect since a mistake meant recording the entire track all over again. Siemens and Sonorex projectors were edit room grade, while the Bauer P7 was studio grade with higher-intensity visuals and better audio clarity. Even in the brave new world of digital technology, a clever mind and talented hand can use the old interlock workhorse interfaced with quiet microphones, mixers, processors, and the whole range of audio design gear to create a finished first-generation master on a master positive or negative 16-mm original which will still provide the option for transfer to video.

AUDIO PROCESSING

An integral part of the transfer step, audio processing itself consists of a chain of "black boxes" used to modify, mask, or eliminate portions of the sound signal. By means of filters, equalization, noise suppressors, digital delay, and other band-manipulating systems, you can correct and/or embellish the sound track. Understanding what is lost in exhibition provides you with the basis for deciding what must be added or subtracted from the track in postproduction. Dolby noise reduction theory is presented, with emphasis on providing an inventory of audio enhancement techniques. The typical audio design lab is also described.

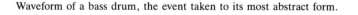

Waveform of a bass drum, the event taken to its most abstract form.

The primary goal of audio processing is to clean up or to create a new sound.

Unwanted alterations of the signal may occur at any point in the audio processing chain. The most serious are listed in Table 9-1.

The two basic forms of recorded material, analog and digital, provide the source material for audio processing. An *analog* recording consists of a continuously variable medium whose modulations are similar to the modulations of the original sound wave. A *digital* recording consists of a series of discrete values, each representing the amplitude of the sound wave at a given point in time and stored as a number in a computer memory. Fidelity is a function of how close together these points are (the *sampling rate*) and how many numbers there are to choose from when assigning values to each sample (the *byte size*).

Audio processing may take two forms: analysis or synthesis. The primary *analysis* functions are filtering, equalization, and noise reduction. The chief

TABLE 9-1 Kinds of distortion of the audio signal

Harmonic distortion	Acoustic change resulting from nonlinear relation between input and output channels at a given frequency.
Intermodulation distortion	Amplitude modification in which the *sum and difference* tones (harmonics of the original signal) are present in the recorded signal.
Amplitude distortion	Nonlinear relation of input- and output-induced harmonics as a function of voltage fluctuations or power consumption.
Dynamic distortion	Alteration of volume range of a program when it is transmitted.
Frequency discrimination	Exaggeration or diminuation of particular frequencies in relation to others, usually as a function of the resonance frequency of the system.
Phase distortion	Shifting of output voltage relative to input by an amount not proportional to frequencies present. Not detectable until it reaches a TV amplifier.
Scale distortion	Voice sounds too loud in the front seat of a theatre. The signal rendered higher or lower than is expected. Frequency distortion results since frequency response of the ear is different at different levels of volume.
Wow and flutter	Deviation of frequency resulting from irregular motion of tape in recording, duplication, or reproduction of a tone, or from deformation of the tape.
Drift	Flutter occurring at random rates.

synthesis functions are sampling, sequencing, syncing, and editing. Processing is part of the transfer/editing/mixing channel and can be understood as a series of black boxes selectively attacking the signal to modify, mask, or improve the track.

Analog Filters

Simple Filters

A *filter* is a network of resistors and condensers that allows for some frequencies to pass and others to be attenuated. The simplest form of filter, one resistor and one condenser, rolls off at a 6-dB octave above or below a given frequency. The nominal cutoff frequency is that at which the loss is 3 dB. This is a gentle filter compared to present-day sharp discriminating devices. (See Figure 9-1.)

- *Low-pass* filters pass all those below 800 Hz. They are used to eliminate frequencies below 60 Hz in voice recordings, reducing set rumble, wind noise and traffic contagion.
- *High-pass* filters pass all signals above 100–400 Hz. These reduce excessive tape hiss at 900 Hz and above, static, buzz, and some elements of voice sibilance.
- *Band-pass* filters pass only frequencies between two given values. These simulate effects and vocal changes, as in synthesizing a telephone or radio broadcast vocal from normal voice recordings.
- *Band-elimination* filters attenuate frequencies between two values. These filters are used to correct and dispel AC (60-Hz) hum caused by defective shields on mike cables, large fields near equipment, or fluorescent lights. Elimination of the fundamental (60 Hz) and the first two overtones (120 Hz, 180 Hz) is usually enough.

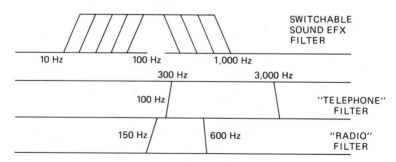

Figure 9-1 Filter graph.

There are three basic kinds of band elimination filters:

- *Dip filters* reject at three bands set at the frequencies of interest. Notice, in Figure 9-2, that the elimination of the hum takes the form of a sharp cut with gradual return. These bands are so narrow that it is virtually impossible to tell that they are there as far as the regular signal is concerned. They do not affect the total sound in any way except, of course, to remove the three unwanted frequencies.

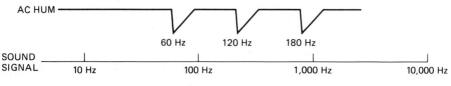

Figure 9-2 Dip filter graph.

- *Variable dip filters* remove any pure tone that might have found its way onto the track. They also remove camera noise, partially depending on the condition of pure tone varieties of the intermittent noise. If you analyze the camera noise and find that the frequency spectrum of its noise is as shown in Figure 9-3, then you can pass it through two dip filters operating at 74 and 1,285 Hz, thereby reducing the noise.

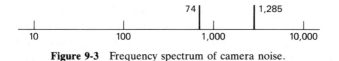

Figure 9-3 Frequency spectrum of camera noise.

- *Band rejection* filters can be adjusted to reduce a disturbing sibilance in the speaker's voice (the whistle effect of an excessive hiss on the "s" intonation) by reducing the excessive high-frequency energy.

Equalizers

Equalizers are more sophisticated filter networks that act on a larger segment of the frequency spectrum simultaneously and do not perform as drastically. In practice, the spectrum may be shaped in any way by the use of groups of equalizers. The only criterion is the *subjective improvement* of the voice and music. The voice can be equalized to make up for deficiencies with the following limits:

- A sharp filter removes sound that an equalizer cannot replace.
- Equalization through the addition of highs that have been lost through filtering or lost in recording raises the hiss level.

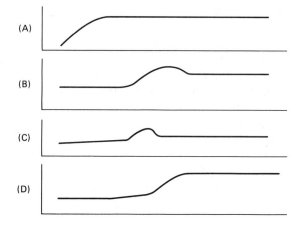

Figure 9-4 Equalizers (A) gradually roll off frequencies, (B) gently boost areas of the spectrum, (C) provide a "bump,"and (D) create a "shelving" action.

A sample combination of equalization and filtering for voice correction is shown in Figure 9-5.

Noise Suppressors

Good transfer channels employing "quiet" black box processing units introduce very little noise or nonlinearities except those inserted by equalizers. Nevertheless, every time the signal passes through a new system, both distortion and hiss level are increased. The transfer process aggravates this condition since amplification is generally linear. Overload, hiss, and other problems are magnified.

A device that acts as a gate to block unwanted background noise, while allowing the primary signal to pass, is called a *noise suppressor*. The primary requisite for its use is a *discernible difference* between signal and noise. (See Figure 9-6.) To operate, the gate needs a point at which you can set your "threshold." It then passes a signal above this point and stops a signal below it. The noise is present in the "treated" track under the dialogue but not between words. (See Figure 9-7.)

The "desirable" amount of suppression is a function of listening. The ideal noise suppressor—that is, one that would cut noise to zero—is undesirable; the change would be too drastic relative to "natural" environmental background sounds. Since you can hear the noise suppressor working, the threshold setting becomes a matter of compromise.

The actual noise suppressor shown in Figure 9-8 is also a *compressor*, which acts when no dialogue is occurring. In effect, the suppressor/compressor is a "squeezing" device; it takes the top 20 dB and presses them into only 10 dB.

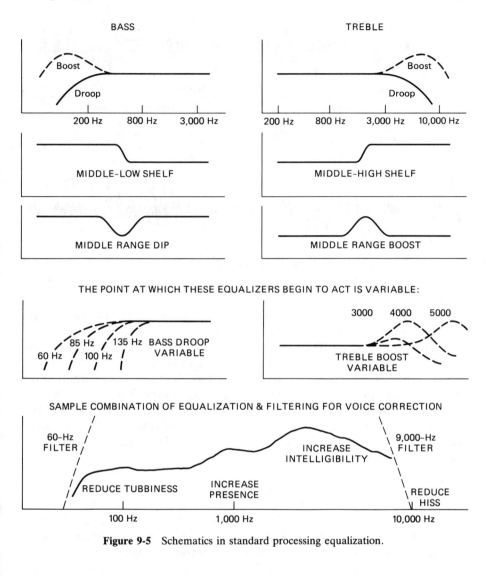

BASS

Boost
Droop

200 Hz   800 Hz   3,000 Hz

MIDDLE-LOW SHELF

MIDDLE RANGE DIP

TREBLE

Boost
Droop

200 Hz   800 Hz   3,000 Hz   10,000 Hz

MIDDLE-HIGH SHELF

MIDDLE RANGE BOOST

THE POINT AT WHICH THESE EQUALIZERS BEGIN TO ACT IS VARIABLE:

85 Hz   135 Hz   BASS DROOP
60 Hz   100 Hz   VARIABLE

3000   4000   5000

TREBLE BOOST
VARIABLE

SAMPLE COMBINATION OF EQUALIZATION & FILTERING FOR VOICE CORRECTION

60-Hz
FILTER

INCREASE
INTELLIGIBILITY

9,000-Hz
FILTER

REDUCE TUBBINESS

INCREASE
PRESENCE

REDUCE
HISS

100 Hz   1,000 Hz   10,000 Hz

Figure 9-5 Schematics in standard processing equalization.

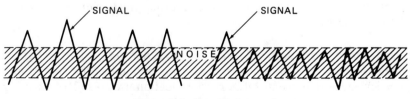

SIGNAL   SIGNAL

NOISE

Figure 9-6 Signal/noise graph.

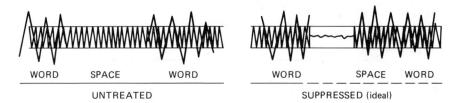

| WORD | SPACE | WORD | | WORD | SPACE | WORD |

UNTREATED   SUPPRESSED (ideal)

Figure 9-7   Ideal suppression compared to untreated signal.

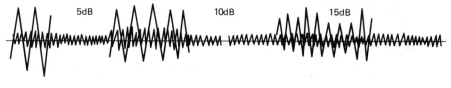

Figure 9-8   Actual noise suppressor.

It can be thought of as a "lifting"of the soft sounds or a "squeezing" of the loud sounds. *Only the dynamic range is changed.*

The compressor is used to even out peaks in a voice recording, since most people have a wider dynamic range vocally than is desirable for film work. Compression works without being too obvious. If the device is improperly balanced, one can hear the change in gain (thumping). The *auto-record* on some tape recorders is really a compressor. Also, if you raise the level of the program after compressing it, the background becomes louder. The 2-to-1 ratio is common in film work (4 into 2, 8 into 4, 16 into 8, depending on how much is needed).

De-Essers

The *de-esser* is a combination of a compressor and an equalizer. Since high frequencies tend to compress less than low ones, the result is an excess of sibilance in the track, which the de-esser effectively reduces.

The compressor is seldom used on dailies since there is no need to restrict the dynamic range at this point. It is better to *compress in the mix* where the video or film image can be used as a reference for subjective qualities of apparent distance, presence, pitch, etc. During voice-over recording, it is normal to compress.

DBX noise reduction.   The ear responds not to signal peaks but to the root mean square value of the signal, which is defined as the sum of all the frequencies/energies present. DBX noise reduction uses true RMS sensing to simulate human hearing response (the higher the compression ratio, the more severe the alteration of the signal). In reality, this type of system is a dynamic range expander; it allows the tape to accept almost twice the normal dynamic ratio. Residual tape noise is thus reduced, also lessening the problem of inherent cumulative tape noise in multitrack mixdowns.

In location practice the recordist usually attempts to "ride the gain,"that is, alter levels in anticipation of voice changes. At best you can only be close because shifting back and forth creates physical noise. The net result is a loss of either the highs or the lows in a given take. With a DBX or other noise reduction system at the recording channel, the peaks that the Nagra accepts are diminished to −10 dB. But there is a gain of 15 dB of "headroom" (with a 2-to-1 signal compression), for a total of 30 dB, which allows for the handling of the loudest shout without distortion. The signal-to-noise ratio at the −10 dB level is superior to a 0-dB level without noise reduction.

Upon playback, the DBX expands the signal back by 1 to 2. It allows the input signal to be reproduced exactly without added noise from the tape recording process, but no attempt is made to remove noise present in the original input signal. Consequently, the technique has become unfashionable as a location rental option for Nagra recorders.

You seem to hear the noise suppressor working because of the design function of the device. The attack time must be as short as possible, but the release time must be gradual enough so as not to act in the middle of the next word. (See Figure 9-9.) If the release time is short, the device seems to "pump" or "breathe." That is, you hear the action of the noise becoming louder and softer continuously.

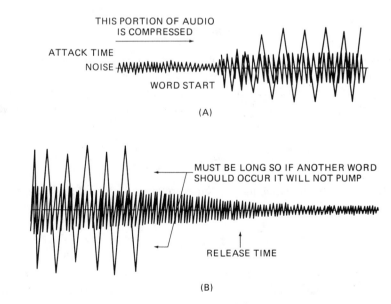

Figure 9-9 (A) Attack time; (B) release time.

This noise is actually heard to die down toward the end of each word. The transfer process therefore accomplishes two things:

1. Places selected sound takes onto a sprocketed or videotape editing medium.
2. Corrects deficiencies in the original recording.

Reverberation Units

Reverberation is the prolongation of sound waves by repeated reflection. A reflection longer than 1/20 s is called *echo*. Several versions of the old "echo chamber" are in use in addition to "digital delay" systems. (See Figure 9-11.) Magnetic recorder/reproducers can employ an array of several playback heads spaced at intervals along the tape transport to induce delay. A chamber enclosing long metal pipes laid in a straight line, or coiled with a loudspeaker unit at one end and a microphone at the other, induces delay. Echo chambers induce the delay by reflecting sound through the speaker against all hard wall enclosures. Another method involves the transmission of sound waves through a group of steel springs or liquid; vibrations are picked up from the sides of the tank.

Signal Processing Techniques

Compression

Compression is the reduction, or "holding" of, a signal within a given amplitude; this avoids overloading distortion in high-level dialogue and sound effects recording. Compressors have attack and release times whose precision is a measure of subjective quality. Compression ratios commonly used in film work are 30 to 10 (that is, an input of 30 dB goes out at 10 dB), 30 to 15, 20 to 10, etc.

De-Essing

When high frequencies have been compressed more than low frequencies, sibilance and hiss are reduced. This is the function of the *de-esser*.

Limiter

A type of compression, the *limiter* creates a ceiling of 1 to 3 dB during recording rather than holding down the peaks of dialogue in the accustomed ratios 30 to 10, etc.

Phaser

Serious distortion may occur due to cancellations when two or more microphones are used on the same channel and within 10 ft of each other. To *phase* the microphones, connect them to their respective preamplifiers and mixer inputs alongside each other. While someone speaks into them, set one pot at a normal level, note the level, and close the pot. Do this for each microphone. Then open them all. If they are out of phase, a drop in level occurs. Any system that reverses the electrical connections of one brings them all into phase.

Flanging

The creation of a series of harmonically related notches in the frequency response is called *flanging*. This was originally done by carefully manipulating two tape recorders that accepted and played back the same signal. One machine was slowed down manually by applying pressure on its supply reel; then the other was slowed down alternately to create a comb filter. Automated systems now in use tend to impart a musical quality to nonmusical sounds.

Expander

An *expander* is a form of automatic attenuator designed to help squeeze the infinite dynamic range of reality into the finite dynamic range of magnetic tape. Similar to a compressor or limiter, an expander alters variations in signal level between input and output. However, while compressors and limiters reduce the variations (5-dB variation in input level reduced to 1 dB in output), expanders "expand"them.

If a source creates sound with high points only 1 dB higher than the low points, the signal could get lost in tape hiss. A 1-to-3 expansion increases that 1-dB variation in input level to a 3-dB variation in output level, helping the signal to stand out from noise.

An expander can also be used as a noise gate. Since it has a compressor-like threshold of amplitude, the expander does not act on levels below that threshold. If a vocalist is being recorded with an expander in the system and suddenly stops singing, the audio input falls below the expander's operational threshold, and the remaining, nonexpanded ambient noise falls to an insignificant level. (See Figures 9-10 and 9-11.)

Analog Synthesizers

The prime example of the analog synthesizer is the Moog, which is made up of the following modules:

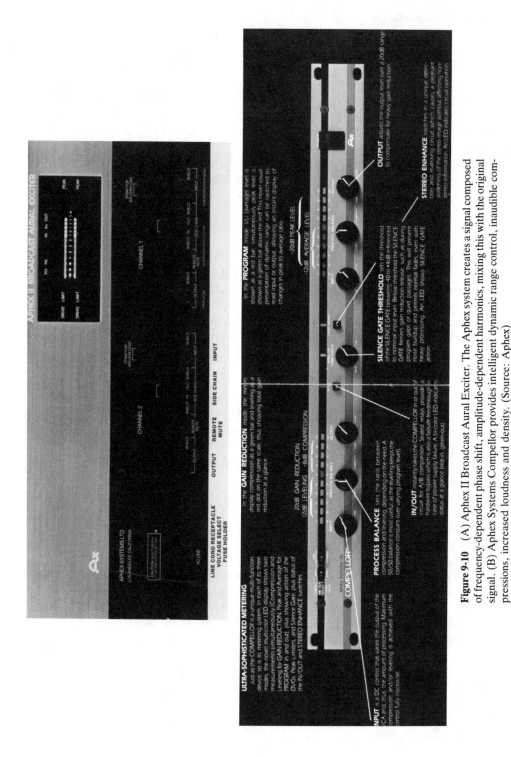

Figure 9-10 (A) Aphex II Broadcast Aural Exciter. The Aphex system creates a signal composed of frequency-dependent phase shift, amplitude-dependent harmonics, mixing this with the original signal. (B) Aphex Systems Compellor provides intelligent dynamic range control, inaudible compressions, increased loudness and density. (Source: Aphex)

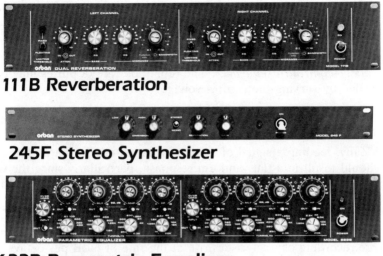

111B Reverberation

245F Stereo Synthesizer

622B Parametric Equalizer

Figure 9-11   Orban reverberation, synthesizer, and equalizer modules. (Source: Orban)

- *Oscillators*: The slow charge and rapid discharge of a capacitor in the oscillator generates a *sawtooth* waveform. Components of this complex soundwave are called *partials;* partials having small whole number ratios are *overtones*. While the sawtooth waveform contains both odd- and even-numbered harmonics, it can be modified into three other forms: (1) a *sine wave*, which contains the fundamental; (2) a *square wave*, with only odd-numbered harmonics; and (3) a *triangular wave*, also with only odd-numbered harmonics.

- *Mixers*: These may be *wet* (that is, powered), providing amplification and independent channel control, or *dry* (unpowered), with limited isolation and control.

- *Keyboard*: Pitch control is by means of a voltage-controlled oscillator, which provides scale, range, hold, and portamento parameters for each sound.

- *Voltage-controlled amplifier*: This provides envelope generation, when triggered from the keyboard.

- *Envelope generator*: Every key triggers two envelope generators, each having attack speed, attack height, decay time, and sustained level parameters.

- *Filters*: Fixed band-pass and variable voltage-controlled filters are used as *notch*-type filters. When they are turned up, the regeneration converts the voltage-controlled filter into a resonant filter similar to the acoustical formant filter. Resonance occurs at either the point of maximum amplification or minimum filtering.

- *Bode-Moog ring modulator*: This produces a tremolo effect when connected onto the amplitude modulator. Any sound may be transposed (up and down simultaneously) by modulation via a sine wave. Up is via *sum tones*, down is via *difference tones*.
- *Voltage-controlled sequencer*: The repetition rate of pulses may be controlled by varying the control voltage.

Need for Equalization

Ideally, feeding a signal of a constant amplitude into a mag recording head should result in a flat, uniform response, particularly since the voltage induced in the playback head is proportional to the rate of frequency change. A high-frequency signal produces a greater amplitude because it has more "magnets" and its "field" is changing faster than that of low frequencies.

Doubling the voltage produces a 6-dB increase in amplitude, and the magnetic recording characteristics rise at the rate of 6 dB per octave. If the frequency is raised one octave, or doubled, the output increases 6 dB. Output reaches a peak and tapers off, however, due to losses in the head from the gap and core *structures*.

Generally, high-frequency loss is corrected in the recording stage by boosting the level. No overloading takes place because sound generated by voice or instrument has less strength at high frequencies. (Tape overloads essentially at the same amplitude regardless of frequency.) Tape has no surface noise or modulation noise to add. It is therefore beneficial to put as strong a signal as possible on the tape regardless of frequency (without overloading at any frequency) to obtain the best signal-to-noise ratio. Thus little amplification is required in the playback or re-record stage.

Equalizing for low-frequency loss is usually done in playback (postequalization). Noise, however, is induced by reproduce amplifiers and some of the reduction can be done in *pre-equalization* during recording (but there is more power in the low frequencies). Multispeed systems utilize separate equalizer circuits at each speed. (See Figure 9-12.)

674A Equalizer

Figure 9-12 Orban 674A equalizer. A graphic equalizer allows the user to visually shape the frequency pattern with continuous control over center frequency, bandwidth, and amount of peak or clip. (Source: Orban)

Audio Design Lab

The basic concept behind an audio design laboratory is to take multiple input sources, pass them through a processing/orchestration stage, and arrive at aural image/fact inventories, which may then be stored for recall. Time code facilitates the process, but a simpler system may use any alphanumeric logging system with which the user is comfortable, as long as consistency is maintained throughout all stages relative to image references. The flow chart of a simple lab set-up is shown in Table 9-2, with other options in Table 9-3.

Here are some representative signal processors for audio design labs:

- *PQ-68 Notch Filter* (8-band): Ashly Audio's parametric equalizer can generate sharp curves to control feedback and resonances without audible side effects. Individual musical notes may be equalized if necessary. Very broad *shelving curves* may be generated to trim frequency extremes with no *ringing* or *ripple.*

- *SG-10 Sweep Graphic Equalizer* (5-band stereo): Furman Sound's unit combines graphic and parametric equalization, including input level controls, low cut filters, EQ in/bypass buttons.

- *Aural Exciter:* This system from Aphex works by generating additional program-related harmonic detail instead of trying to equalize what is no longer there. Offers any mixture of odd and even harmonics tone generated from 700 Hz to 7 kHz.

- *PA-88 Psychoacoustic Processor:* From Audio Logic, this processor uses 180° phase cancellation, narrow band delays, and indirect frequency pre-emphasis to create a side-chain interference signal, restoring the natural presence to the original signal.

TABLE 9-2   Audio design lab flow chart

Input Sources	Processing Orchestration	Storage
Audio cassette player	Multitrack recorder	Videotape
Manual turntable	Synchronizer	½″ AudioTape
Microphone	Synthesizer/keyboard	Audio disc
Audio disc player	Stereo two-track deck	Digital disc
Synthesizer	Mixer	Cassette
Reel-to-reel recorder	Stereo amplifier	Cartridge
16/35-mm mag recorder	Reverb/echo chamber	
Videotape player	Time compressor	
Cartridge player	Equalizer	
Projector (mag stripe)	Filter bay +	
	noise suppressor	
	monitor	
	speaker system	

- *Pitchtraq Programmable Pitch Transposer:* ADA unit produces all harmonizing effects within a 2-octave range, including harmony lines, octave shifts, synthesized textures, detuned chorusing, and harmonic alteration. An on-board computer allows full programming of 16 effects including sweeps, mix, regeneration, and pitch change.

- *H949 Harmonizer:* Eventide's digital effects system incorporates delay and pitch change capacity. Harmonizers can be used for "doubling" vocals, for delay equalization, and reverb/echo effects. Keyboard controls pitch change function in discrete musical steps.

- *FL 201 Instant Flanger:* With a PHASER CARD, this Eventide system uses differential delay to cause cancellations in the frequency spectrum of a signal. A "bounce" feature simulates tape motor "hunting."

- *2830 Omnipressor:* This special effects box combines a compressor, expander, noise gate, and limiter with dynamic reversal feature turning high-level input signals into lower signals than the corresponding low-level input signals. Musically, this reverses the attack-decay envelope and gives the effect of "talking backwards"when applied to a voice signal.

- *SP2016 Effects Processor/Reverb:* This unit from Eventide creates reverb effects including room and plate echo, Digiplex Echo (a digital version of multiple-head tape echo), dual robot voice effects, musical combs, chorus effects—dozens of multiple voices, each variable in time, amplitude, and space. Selective band delay, flanging, and phasing are also available.

- *Digital Tonmeister:* From Harmonia Mundi Acustica this system is a digital 6-parametric band equalizer/mixer, limiter/compressor, and send/return effects, with a dynamic range processor and level control.

- *902 De-esser Module:* DBX's "smart" de-essing operates independently of the input level with no threshold to set. The user may choose conventional broadband attenuation or attenuate only a portion of the high-frequency range. The sibilance reduction is controlled by as much as -20 dB.

TABLE 9-3   Other processing systems and their function

Processing Options	Function
Deltalab DL2 Acousticomputer	Clean digital repeats.
Digital Memory Module	
Maxon Analog Delay Flanger	Metallic quality and deep phasing sweep.
Lexicon Digital Reverb	Ambiance processor creates "rooms" and spaces.
Audio and Design Scamp Modules	Equalization, compression, expansion.
Deltalab Harmonic Computer	Pitch shifting.
Lexicon Audio Time Compressor	Acceleration, shift "small' to "large".
APT Holman Amps	Controlled equalization.
Eastern Acoustics MS50 Speakers	Exact stereo imaging.

- *2400 Stereo Audio Time Compressor/Expander:* This Lexicon unit reads SMPTE/EBU time code, ensuring that play time is controlled with long-term frame accuracy varying the amount of compression on a scene-by-scene basis. It corrects equalization errors inherent in off-speed playback. Compression or expansion entries can be made in the form of time code, play times, end times, pitch-shift ratios, speed-factor ratios, or percent playtime. With this processor, you can selectively eliminate discrete bits of audio program material from a given section per unit of time, for either time justification or program enhancement. (See Figure 9-13.)

- *Real-time spectrum analyser:* This equipment interfaces with a personal computer to create a third-octave real-time analyser with a data handling function by means of 31 filters that divide the audio spectrum from 2 Hz to 20 kHz into 31 one-third octave bands. Band amplitude and input levels are displayed on the computer CRT.

- *Differential load reactance compensator:* The Barcus Berry signal processor improves overall clarity via a high-speed dynamic gain control acting on program transients, adding brightness, enhancing presence, and eliminating frequency band masking. It is used essentially for loudspeaker reproduction when exacting monitoring and playback are essential, by monitoring and correcting speaker phase and amplitude coherence.

- *Vocoder:* The Talk-Box Vocoder (Sennheiser) makes it possible to separate the elements of speech from the airstream and substitute any audible signal for the air, thus allowing speech to be formed "around" a nearly

Lexicon Event Sequence

1:27:00	Leave titles at 1X to avoid VTR jitter		Compress boring dialog 20%		More boring dialog — Compress 20%		Compress 10% to increase excitement	
Original Play Time	5:00	15:00	20:00	10:00	15:00	5:00	15:00	2:00
Program Material	Titles	Action	Dialog	Fight Scene	Dialog	Action	Action	Credits

1:16:30		Compress 10% to increase excitement		Compress 5% to pick up pace		Don't compress or expand		Leave credits at 1X to avoid VTR jitter
New Play Time	5:00	13:30	16:00	9:30	12:00	5:00	13:30	2:00
Program Material	Titles	Action	Dialog	Fight Scene	Dialog	Action	Action	Credits

Figure 9-13 Lexicon Event Sequence: Groups of infinitely small intervals (in nanoseconds) are eliminated uniformely across the track segment, thereby shrinking it imperceptibly up to a point. This slicing of the digital pulse code appears to have psychological ramifications.

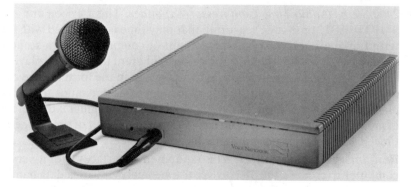

Figure 9-14   Voice Navigator.

infinite number of sounds. It uses 20 channels of band-pass filters on the voice input and the replacement output.

- *Vocalizer:* A voice-activated synthesizer acts as a pitch-to-MIDI converter that allows a vocalist to directly drive synthesizers and other devices equipped with a MIDI input. Monophonic parts may be directly sent to a sequencer or computer. If you can hum it, you can record it. The voice can drive up to 28 instruments. Prerecorded backgrounds (Smart-Songs™) allow for modification, transposing notes, rhythm change, and tempo alteration. Voice Guide corrects pitch so that vocal parts are in tune, and excites special effects like chorus, echo, and harmony.

- *Voice Navigator:* With Voicewaves MIDI applications software, which allows most MIDI commands to be programmed and recognized, the Voice Navigator offers complete voice control of the Macintosh computer. You can compose music while commanding your sequencer to stop, rewind, merge tracks, etc. without a mouse or keyboard. (See Figure 9-14.)

DUBBING

Dubbing and looping—the two basic techniques of re-recording dialogue in the studio—are explained, using sample dialogue logs and cue sheets. Automatic dialogue replacement (ADR) is compared with less sophisticated methods of postsynchronization. Described in detail are use of the foley stage for generating sound effects, the studio flow chart, and the procedures for directing and controlling a dubbing session.

The Universal Studios dubbing studio. (Courtesy Universal Studios)

If the recording process were perfect and its related techniques exacting, there would be no need to re-record lines of dialogue. In practice, however, the production track often is too noisy, has uncorrectable mistakes, or is dramatically poor. Although wireless and other locations techniques have greatly reduced the number of hours needed in the dubbing studio, directors still find it necessary to refine and improve certain key scenes. Quite often a performer is not available for a session, and the booking must be made very late in the postproduction process. Most SAG contracts call for a minimum required guarantee of re-recording time, since many actors tend to refuse to work in the studio dubbing lines after the production is over.

The Dubbing Flow Chart

The basic principle of dubbing lines is to make three closed loops of exactly the same length: (1) picture, (2) mag track, and (3) cue (often the production "scratch" track, used as reference), or music, track.

Refer to Figure 10-1. Similar sounds tend to be grouped into three tracks because few mixers can handle more than three tracks without loss of detail and accuracy. Dialogue from primary sources (location and studio) is broken down into its components—on-camera discourse, voice-over, vocalizations. It is then organized into:

a. *Three-track dialogue predub*: If there are many and complex effects, they too should be broken down into components.

b. *Effects pre-dub A, B,* and *C*: Music elements are separated into one master and/or multitrack music predubs.

Each of these clusters is mixed separately by different mixers. The result is a series of 4-track dubs for dialogue, music, and effects which have been corrected, balanced, blended, and otherwise made usable.

The audio designer, director, producer, or distributor has several release format options to which these three 4-track clusters may be combined:

c. Dolby stereo 2-track.

d. Dolby magnetic 6-track.

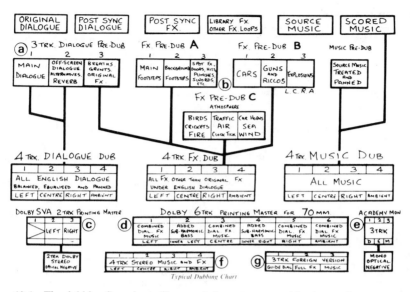

Figure 10-1   The dubbing flow chart. Classes of elements are combined onto discrete tracks for further blending.

e. Academy mono.

f. 4-track M and E for foreign prints, videocassette, and ancillary releases.

g. Foreign language version 3-track master.

See Table 10-1.

The Machine Room

The machine room is the electromechanical center of the dubbing/mixing studio. Its configuration has not changed since the advent of sound recording for film. Three pieces of equipment in the machine room are essential to the dubbing process:

- The *projector* continuously presents the scene to be rehearsed.
- The *reproducer* provides continuous playback of the cue track over speakers or headsets.
- The *recorder* is simultaneously switchable to record the "best" take of timed lip-sync dialogue.

Distributor.   The heart of the electromechanical system is a *distributor*, which takes the 220-V AC line and breaks it down into multiply grounded 120-

TABLE 10-1   A brief list of dubbing terms

Backing track	Prerecording of the accompaniment to a vocalist who then listens through headphones to a replay as he/she performs. The two signals are mixed to give the final rendition.
Back tracking	Preliminary recording done by the same performer and used as the accompaniment.
Cue	Signal to start.
Dubber	Recorder.
Dubbing	Postsynchronization of dialogue in the studio recorded in lip-sync to picture. Also incorrectly used, in place of "mixing," for the combining of music and effects tracks with voice.
Dubbing studio	Same as a mixing studio, but may have available a high-speed "rock-'n-roll" projector.
Dummy	Playback-only machine.
Loop	A form of re-recording dialogue that uses a 9-ft, continuously running loop of magnetic film, which provides a repeated sound structure, rhythm, or atmosphere. The actor listens to the pacing, intonation, and rhythm of the production dialogue track and tries to duplicate the recording. (No picture is needed.)
Mix	Blending and combining of many tracks (or microphones) into a smooth, continuous track.
Reproducer	A playback machine.
Recorder/dubber	A tape recorder using sprocketed magnetic film.

V (3-wire) AC lines, which are fed to all reproducers, recorders, and the projector. The distributor/generator is driven synchronous to the line frequency by an AC sync motor using an automatic start-stop system. In the studio, the distributor electrically interlocks all sprocket-driven machines. As one shaft turns one revolution, all others turn exactly one revolution.

Before the advent of computer-assisted interlock systems for film and video postproduction, the bridges between recorder/reproducers, projector and other machine room gear originated with one or more central distributors. The distributor is composed of a 220-V AC generator (an old-fashioned "dynamo"), which feeds current by virtue of its rotating shaft through voltage-controlled 110-V AC lines linked to each and every machine. All machine shafts rotate in unison with the distributor. The system insured perfect mechanical synchronization at 24 frames per second at 60 cycles per second AC line frequency.

Nowadays, each machine is equipped with either an AC sync selsyn motor or a DC servo-drive motor. Recent improvements include the use of DC-driven servo motors in the reproducers. The motors are free from AC hum, run from AC/DC inverter power units, and allow for computer-controlled interfaces.

With the high-speed capabilities of the more quiet servo-drive systems, for-ward/backward shuttle ("rock-'n-roll") is possible without slippage. The prime hazard is mag stock breaking in the transport. Autosensing brakes shut off the system when tension over the spindles occurs due to a film break. All functions may be controlled through the mixing console. (See Figure 10-2.)

Recorder. A master recorder may be single-, double-, or triple-tiered allowing for three fullcoat master tracks on one machine. The recorder is connected electrically to banks of *dummies* (that is, simple single-track play-back machines), each playing one sound element. (See Figure 10-3.) If the

Figure 10-2 High-speed DC servo-drive recorder/reproducer is the workhorse of the machine room. (Source: Magnatech)

Figure 10-3 A bank of dummies.

dummy can record, it is called a *dubber,* or record/reproducer. The machine room may have as many as 64 individual dummies. To save space, dubber transports are also available in double- or triple-reproduce versions. (See Figure 10-4.)

Projector.   Interlocked mechanically and electrically is a main projector whose shaft rotates in sync with every unit in the machine room (see Figure 10-5). Prior to 1975, it was a luxury to have a high-speed projector capable of up to 10 times normal (24-fps) speed. Dubber transport mechanisms were not sufficiently reliable at high speeds, and the costs were prohibitive for the handful of high-speed, high-intensity projectors. High-speed projection greatly reduces studio deadtime by allowing for instant rewind and replay. The same functions in realtime (24 fps in forward and reverse) is at best tedious and costly.

Mixer.   The mixing console controls all functions of the units in the machine room and the projector by push-button, but threadup is by hand. So a machine room operator is always on standby to check for breaks, torn sprockets, and the possibility of mag film jumping out of the transport sprocket drive.

The console can run all machines in unison or disengage selected units. For example, three dialogue tracks may be worked on, then held while work is

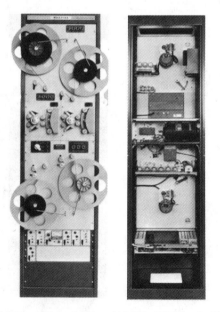

Figure 10-4   A triple-reproduce dubber: (A) front, (B) back. (Source: Westrex)

Figure 10-5 Main projector shaft. (Source: Kinotron)

done on another set of three tracks. Then all six may be run, and so on, as a master is built up from as many as 128 different source tracks. It is easy to understand that high-speed "rock-'n-roll" interlock projection saves enormous time and aggravation.

Source machines.   In addition to dummies and recorders, the machine room may have a series of *source machines*, which contain various formats of auditory material. Each is controlled as a single element and assigned a track position at the console, once the transfer to 16- or 35-mm full- or stripe-coat magnetic film takes place. Source units include ¼-in reel-to-reel tape recorders, stereo cassette recorders, cartridge decks, turntables, compact disc players, videotape players, and floppy disk sources from a personal computer or sound synthesizer.

Almost any nonstandard source, such as the sound stripe track from old Super 8 sound films, may be transferred using 60-Hz sync crystal resolvers to film and time-coded to tape. Each element ends up on an individual dummy for mixing. In this role, a dummy may be used as a looping machine. A loop of magnetic film of about 9 ft is made and threaded for a continuous playback during mixing. Generally, one effect, such as wind noise, runs on the loop. The mixer may "punch in" to the effect at any moment during the combining of tracks by using a fader assigned to the loop.

Machine Room Functions

A studio may have one machine room serving many functions (in addition to mixing) or a separate machine room for each function such as:

- Foley effects.
- Automatic dialogue replacement (ADR).
- Looping.
- Scoring.
- Narration recording.
- Video sweetening.

This fact, as well as high-speed projection, impacts the sound budget. All functions are generally billed at an hourly rate with mixing at 6- to 9-hr minimums and other functions at 2- to 4-hr minimums.

Foley Effects Recording

The foley room is lined with various choices of textured surfaces to duplicate the sound of different locations. A screen, a recorder, and an interlock projector (not necessarily high speed) are required. Foley artists (often editors) create sounds in sync (through trial and error) to the picture. Headsets are used to communicate with the recordists. Foley requires good timing and invention. (See Figure 10-6.)

Figure 10-6   Mix theatre. (Source: Lucasfilm, San Rafael, CA)

Automatic Dialogue Replacement (ADR)

In *automatic dialogue replacement,* the projector and recorder/reproducer act as a high-speed rock-'n-roll forward/reverse systems that automatically repeat the shot to be dubbed by live performers who watch the picture to lip-sync the dialogue in the studio.

1. A reel of cut work print is threaded on the projector.
2. A full roll of 35-mm magnetic film is threaded on the three-track recorder/reproducer.
3. The original sync dialogue (the production scratch track), if available, is placed on a reproducer (a dummy) and fed to headsets for reference to actors and director. A cue sheet is used for reference. (See Figure 10-7.) The following information is required on the cue sheet:
   • Names of characters.
   • Transcript of dialogue to be replaced.
   • Any overlapping dialogue and the lines over which they occur.
   • Start and stop footages and frame counts.
   • Date and production number, EQ data, speed, and production title.
4. Common start marks provide exact sync, with mechanical and electrical interlock assured by sync selsyn motors.
5. The sound mixer sets the programmer on the start and stop footages of the first line of dialogue to be replaced.
6. On a signal from the director, the process of playback, repeat, and record begins. A high-speed shuttle allows for rapid re-cue and retakes.
7. Recording is made on track 1 of the three-track stripe. If the playback button is not activated, the next take is recorded over an automatically erased first take, and the entire process is repeated for each line. The maximum reel length is 10 min. It may take hours to replace just a few lines if the actors can't reconstruct the proper emotional depth.

ADR is used when several actors are available to re-record their lines and play off each other in lip sync to the picture in a mixing studio. High-speed projection is helpful. Each performer has a separate track assigned for recording. A director is generally present since many performers dislike the process and have difficulty dredging up the emotions previously done on location!

Looping

Automatic dialogue replacement without projection and relying on the headset cues for pacing, rhythm, and intonation is called *looping*. A 9-ft continuously running loop is threaded up on the dummies and recorder. The

RYDER SOUND SERVICES, INC.

REVERSE-O-MATIC Dialogue Replacement Cue Sheet

Date

COMPANY __American-Trans-Inter Prod__   Microphones: _____

                                        Equalization: _____

PRODUCTION   " I'll Take The Best "   Start Time: _____ Finish Time: _____

REEL NO   2   Sheet No   1   Mixer: _____

CHARACTER	DIALOGUE	FOOTAGE Start Stop	CHANNELS 1	2	3	MIXER NOTES
CHARLIE	IS IT REALLY TRUE?	START 60-4 STOP 61-6				
HAROLD	I HEARD ABOUT IT, BUT I DIDN'T THINK IT WOULD WORK	START 68-9 STOP 72-4				
BERT	IF YOU KNEW ANYTHING ABOUT THIS TOWN, YOU'D KNOW THAT IF IT'S NEW — AND BETTER THEY'VE GOT IT.	START 110 STOP 126-4				
NORM	WHAT I LIKE ABOUT THAT OUTFIT IS THEIR SINCERE DESIRE TO GIVE YOU WHAT YOU WANT. NO DOUBLE TALK.	START 127-3 STOP 177-6				
CHARLIE	GETTING BACK TO WHAT WE WERE DISCUSSING, I HATE TO HARP ON THE SUBJECT BUT I THINK YOU ARE MAKING A BIG MISTAKE BY . EVEN THINKING OF GOING SOMEWHERE ELSE. HERE, LISTEN TO THIS — NOW LISTEN TO THIS. WHAT A DIFFERENCE.	START 250 STOP START STOP 350-2				
ALAN	MAYBE HE'S RIGHT	START 351-5 STOP 352-8				
CHARLIE	YOU BET I AM	START 353 STOP				WILD
ALAN	HERE'S GEORGE. SEE WHAT HE THINKS.	START 355 STOP 357				
GEORGE	THINKS ABOUT WHAT?	START 358 STOP 361				
ALAN	WE WERE JUST DISCUSSING THE MERITS OF LOOPING DIALOGUE AS COMPARED TO THAT NEW AUTOMATIC SETUP.	START 363-3 STOP 367-2				
GEORGE	I JUST USED IT THE OTHER DAY. AS A MATTER OF FACT - I'VED USED THEM ALL.	START 378 STOP 382				
CHARLIE	WHOSE WOULD YOU SAY IS THE BEST?	START 383 STOP 386-5				
GEORGE	AS FAR AS I'M CONCERNED, THERE'S ONLY ONE OUTSTANDING SYSTEM.	START 387 STOP 395				
BERT	IT MUST BE GOOD. GEORGE HAS NEVER GIVEN ANYONE A PLUG BEFORE.	START 395-3 STOP 407-5				
HAROLD	SO? COM'ON ALREADY GEORGIE. LET'S HEAR THOSE PEARLS OF WISDOM!	START 407-6 STOP 417-5				
GEORGE	THE ENVELOPE PLEASE!	START 418 STOP 421				
BERT	WHAT IS THIS? ACADEMY AWARD TIME?	START 421-3 STOP 425				
GEORGE	GIVE ME A CHANCE! THE BEST AUTOMATIC DIALOGUE REPLACEMENT SYSTEM IS. — REVERSE-O-MATIC AT OYE	START 424 STOP 435-6				overlap

Figure 10-7   An ADR cue sheet. (Source: Ryder Sound Services)

system runs in interlock until a good take is made. Loops are individually edited into separate sound rolls for exact cutting or trim and insertion into the editing master. Looping is usually done if:

- Only a few lines must be replaced.
- The actor feels projection is a distraction.
- All the lines of one actor can be grouped for economy without having any other performer present.
- The budget is limited.

When all the lines to be re-recorded of one performer can be grouped, looping is the practical choice, with projection as an option. The performer can sit in the studio, listen to his or her lines over a headset, and by trial and error try to match the rhythm and intonation on a new recording directly to magnetic fullcoat. Looping is more cost-efficient, but performers operate in something of an emotional vacuum. Often projection is added to help cueing.

ADR and looping result in a master 35-mm magnetic track and a 1/4-in protection copy. An editing copy (dupe) is made to cut into the editorial master.

Here are some do's and don'ts when setting up for dubbing:

- Wind the mag track in a heads-out/emulsion-down position, coming off the top of the reel in "A" wind. (The wind selector must be in proper A or B wind position *before* power is applied to the film transport. The reel rotates counterclockwise.) When threaded properly, the machine equalizer arms are "toed out" and centered between the limiting studs in the panel around the heads. The brake engages when tension is lost.
- Do not insert or remove headphones during recording; this can induce noise.
- Set the level to match that of the incoming signal, but not to peak about +1 dB on the VU meter.
- Set the counter to zero.
- Set the torque motors to the "hold" position.
- Then turn to *record* and allow for the machine to come up to speed.
- Do not vary the playback gain amplifier volume when in direct mode.
- Turn off the record mode before playback, or accidental erasure may occur.
- In *reverse* mode, erase and record functions are disengaged. *Playback* and *record* levels are set separately.

Scoring

Scoring is the recording of the music track. No high-speed projection is required, but a very good acoustically treated recording space is essential. (See Figure 10-8.) The musical group or orchestra may audition to the picture as an

Figure 10-8   A scoring stage. (Inset: A mix console.)

option. All instruments are miked separately or in sections, and assigned to individual tracks in the machine room. One school of thought is that, the better the separation of orchestral parts and instrumentation, the better the recombining and blending. Coverage with one microphone on one track leaves no room for enhancement or correction.

Voice-Over and Narration

Voice-over (or *narration*) is the addition of narrative to the mix. A ¼-in reel-to-reel Nagra and a quiet room would suffice, but a good studio recording of voice can have exceptional impact. Recording directly to fullcoat always gives better response and clarity. Projection is generally not needed, but adequate coaching and direction significantly relaxes the speaker and allows for precision. It would be nice to hear the recording in the studio played against picture for a sense of mood. (See Figure 10-9.)

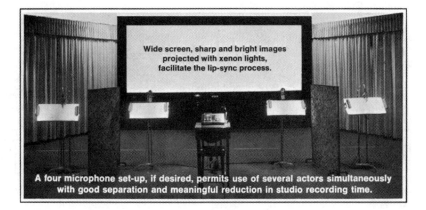

Figure 10-9   ADR studio.

Video Sweetening Versus the Film Mix

Sweetening is the term for mixing video sound tracks. Two systems may be used:

1. Film dubbers interlocked with time code to videotape recorders and/or a multitrack recorder.
2. Video source machines interlocked via synchronizer with a multitrack recorder, a compact disc recorder, and/or a tapeless digital system.

Monitors replace the screen, but a large-scale video projection is helpful. Other source machines with audio may be used including MIDI devices such as synthesizers and sequencers. Time code holds everything in sync (but don't bet on it against the surety of a sprocket hole). MIDI allows you to compose and mix on the spot—at once, seemingly more creatively—but generally the mixing is done with less care for detail and control of the multiple tracks. Even with the advent of stereo broadcasting, video sound appears to be mixed less critically; it seems to be more of an editorial function of cleansing and clarifying.

Direct Recording on Sprocket-Driven Recorders

The basic recorder uses torque motors, which maintain tension across the heads, on the displacement and takeup spindles. The actual sprocket drive is a DC sync motor. The microphone inputs may first go through a mix bay or into the single 600-Ω microphone input. VU meters are standard. The recorder needs approximately 1 sec startup time to reach speed. The machine may be

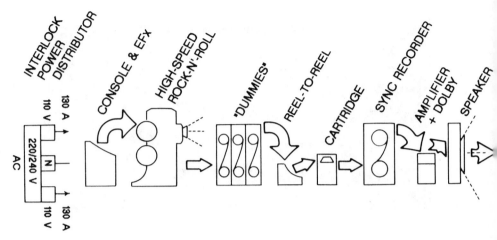

Figure 10-10   Interlock studio flow. Each unit to common ground prevents dangerous differences in electrical potential between machines.

interlocked to a videotape recorder, an audio tape recorder, other "dubbers," the console, cartridge machines, a synthesizer, and other units. (See Figure 10-10.)

Noise is the chief problem in these reel-to-reel recorders. Some of it can manage to get onto the tape. The sources include:

- Even-order harmonics of the bias or erase signal.
- Jitter in the bias or erase signal.
- A lack of symmetry in the bias or erase signal.

A crystal-controlled perfect square wave generator puts out no even-order harmonics, has no jitter, and is symmetrical.

Certain techniques can help you to eliminate noise: On inserts, use short start and stop times. During deletions, match the level of the insert to the level of the erasure. By *ramp switching,* use linear ramp generators to control the turnon and turnoff of bias and erase signals occurring at about a 20-Hz rate. What can go wrong with the insert? (See Figure 10-11.)

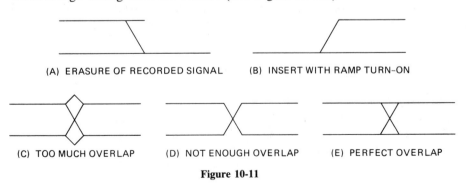

(A) ERASURE OF RECORDED SIGNAL   (B) INSERT WITH RAMP TURN-ON

(C) TOO MUCH OVERLAP   (D) NOT ENOUGH OVERLAP   (E) PERFECT OVERLAP

Figure 10-11

Single-System Recording and Displacement Recorders

During the heyday of single-system newsreel sound recording, the common practice was to use the displacement recorder to reposition sound from the magnetic stripe of the newsreel footage back to its mechanical sync position. Editing techniques developed whereby interviews relied on cutaways from the reverse angle (so that you could not see the speaker mouth out of sync!), used with the sync take for which original frontal picture was cut out to save the sound. Cumbersome as this may seem, it was standard practice until the advent of displacement recorders, which repositioned the sound track back to *editorial sync* by means of a retarded head position. After editing, the track was repositioned back to *projection sync* for broadcasting. Today, single-system sound-on-film cameras advance the sound in relation to picture due to the placement of the sound head in relation to the aperture gate. The frame advance is fine for projection, but it causes editing problems since the sound is not opposite the picture but a bit ahead of it.

The problem of sync reference points and synchronization can be avoided by utilizing a sound-on-film recording process, either optical or magnetic. In the magnetic method, a sound emulsion is applied to the raw camera stock and the sound signal is recorded on it in the camera housing. *The distance from the frame in the gate to the magnetic recording head is 28 frames.* (See Figure 10-12.) This system is particularly well suited to news filming.

After development, the film is ready for projection (reversal stock); this is also desirable for situations where only one copy is needed. The professional magnetic striped stocks available are Kodak's.

Ektachrome EF 7241

Ektachrome EFB 7242

ECO Commercial 7252

Video Newsfilm 7240

Video Newsfilm 7239

Hi Speed Newsfilm 7250

Although all expenses of separate sound recording are eliminated, this method introduces editorial problems. The sound is positioned 28 frames ahead of the corresponding picture. Therefore the sound must be transferred back to fullcoat and edited as double system! The advantages of the single-system process are:

No sync system is necessary.

No start marks are needed.

No editing or syncing delays are incurred.

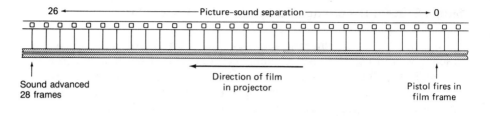

26 ←———————————— Picture–sound separation ————————————→ 0

Sound advanced
28 frames

Direction of film
in projector

Pistol fires in
film frame

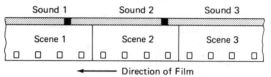

Scene/Sound relationship as photographed on 16mm film.

Sound 1   Sound 2   Sound 3

Scene 1   Scene 2   Scene 3

←——— Direction of Film

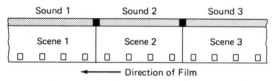

Magnetic sound track repositioned to *editor's sync* with corresponding picture frames *in line*.

Sound 1   Sound 2   Sound 3

Scene 1   Scene 2   Scene 3

←——— Direction of Film

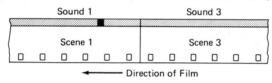

Scene 2 and Sound 2 edited out. Magnetic sound track repositioned to *projection sync*.

Sound 1   Sound 3

Scene 1   Scene 3

←——— Direction of Film

Figure 10-12   Editing single system.

Its disadvantages are:

The emulsion is not as consistent as 1/4-in tape, narrower with a stiff base.

The signal-to-noise ratio (dynamic range) is narrower.

The frequency response is not as good.

Extra handling of film is not advisable.

Certain emulsions cannot be mag striped.

The best quality is for full-level voice recordings only.

Although considered by many as outmoded, the Auricon single-system sound recording outfits are in constant use throughout the world—and have been in use since 1931. The chief disadvantage is weight. A discussion follows of only the basic features. Refer to the Bach-Auricon Equipment Catalog for

Figure 10-13   Auricon sound-on-film camera.

detailed description. The *camera* incorporates both a magnetic and optical head assembly. (See Figure 10-13.)

Model NR-25 sound-on-film recording amplifier.   Bulky and external to the camera, it affords variable area or variable density modulation and has two inputs, speech and music for separate control of mike and other audio equipment such as turntable-amp and mixer boxes. Both HI and LOW impedances.

Exposure lamp settings are made in accordance with published recommendations for each stock (16 mm). Entire system is battery operated. Noise-reduction and filters are built-in. AC operation is optional. A galvanometer modulates recording.

Filmagnetic sound-on-film recording amplifier MA-11.   The heart of the system is the Twin-Head Camera recording assembly and the MA-11 amplifier which is battery operated, transistorized with a response to 12,000 Hz. In use since 1955, it utilizes pre-striped 16 mm stocks. On AC mode the camera may be used for studio sync-re-recording and dubbing from transfer equipment. Filmagnetic "master original" sound track can be re-recorded without loss of fidelity onto 35 mm optical or magnetic sound-on-film!

The variable-area optical system incorporates a noise-reduction shutter.

Simple Interviews with the Single-System
Sound-on-Film Camera

Single-system film may still provide archival quality recording services for ethnographic, scientific, and industrial (medical, judicial, police, etc.) record-keeping purposes. Since single-system optical film guarantees first generation audio and visual recording, it still produces fine clarity and has longer storage potential than magnetic media.

The original Bach-Auricon single-system camera, in use since 1931, provides for both direct optical or magnetic sound recording. The system includes an amplifier, galvo and magnetic recording head built into the camera, microphone inputs, a 1,200-ft continuous magazine roll of 16-mm film, and all the other benefits of 16-mm cinematography, except that it runs AC/DC and is not very portable. Variable track area or density modulation is possible, and separate bias adjustment can be made for speech or music. In use since 1951, the film magnetic system uses prestriped 16-mm film stock. The camera is nonreflex but can be made to run synchronously. The reflexed, crystal-controlled silent update of the basic Auricon is the CP-16RA camera. This provides all the basic features of a single system, plus portability and 30-fps operation for video transfer.

Here is the basic interview recording technique from the classic era of newsreel operation:

1. Set the camera at eye level.
2. Shoot over the interviewer's shoulder so that you can see both eyes of the interviewer's subject (no profile shots).
3. Try to keep the subject some distance from the wall (4–5 ft), to prevent "ugly" shadows.
4. At the beginning of the interview, shoot a 2-shot, establishing the interviewer's relationship to the subject.
5. Don't be afraid of coming in close to the subject, eliminating the interviewer. The camera operator should listen to the interview.
6. The soundperson should jot down questions.
7. Make sure the interviewer is facing in the correct direction. Don't cross the conversational line. You may have to shift the position of the interviewer because of unique conditions of the room.
8. Stay off an extreme close-up of the interviewer, who is not the important person in the interview. You should see both eyes, no profiles.
9. If at all possible, keep the subject around during reverse questions. You can shoot over his or her shoulder and thereby eliminate extreme close-ups of the interviewer.
10. Important: Because of the 26-frame advance of sound, the interviewer *must* pause a little (over a second), listening, before asking the next question.

11. Shoot the interviewer listening; try to avoid his or her nodding, which is an indication of approval of what the subject is saying.

12. Shoot about 10 or 15 ft of a long 2-shot over the shoulder of the interviewer asking questions. Shoot in such way as to see the interviewer's jaw moving but not his lips. The subject should remain silent. With this shot you can "cheat" any questions against it. This in no way eliminates the need to shoot reverse questions.

13. Remember the TV aperture, but do not leave too much head room. Keep the microphone unobtrusive.

A double-band projector was the chief editing tool for single-system sound-on-film and often the edit was telecast directly from the projectors.

Editing Single-System Sound Film

Single-system film operation enables you to film action and sound simultaneously on a single strip of film. The edge of the film is coated with a magnetic layer, similar to $1/4$-in tape, which records the sound. However, because the film travels through the camera picture gate in an intermittent action (one picture is taken, the film moves on, then another picture is taken, etc.), it is impossible to put a sound recording head in that position in the camera. (The film needs time to "smooth out" and run continuously.) Therefore, the sound head is placed 28 frames (or a little over a second) *ahead* of the picture gate. The film looks as is shown in Figure 10-12.

Single-system recording presents severe problems to you as the editor. When you make the desired cut in the film, the image probably jumps; that is, the eye, lip, or head position changes abruptly. This is called a *jump cut* (a discontinuity in space and/or time). Another possibility is that the speaker's lips move without sound. This is called *lip flap* (lip motion with no sound).

The solution is to have two interlocked projectors. During the interview, the director switches from one to the other and back again to avoid jump cuts and lip flap. During editing, the necessary cuts are made in the sound track (the most important element in an interview), and the reaction shots are used to take up the difference between the sound and picture. Figure 10-14 shows how the cuts are made.

Narration, music, sound effects, and other sound elements can also be added. You simply use the picture from one projector and the sound from the other. (See Figure 10-15.) Dissolves are also done by overlapping or superimposing one picture on another. (See Figure 10-16.)

A typical single-system news and studio camera is the CP-16 reflex. The heart of this system is the crystsound amplifier, a modular unit with the configuration of a camera body side cover. It takes the place of a case load of equipment and cabling formerly in use with the Auricon Pro 600 System, which had been in use up to the introduction of this camera in the early sixties. (See Figure 10-17.)

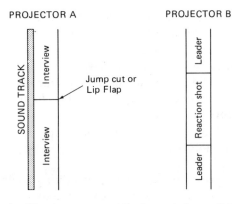

Figure 10-14   Avoiding jump cuts and lip flaps, via butt splicing with cement.

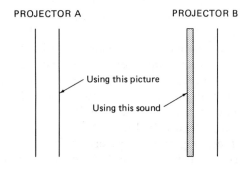

Figure 10-15   Adding sound elements to the interview in live broadcast setups, circa 1960s.

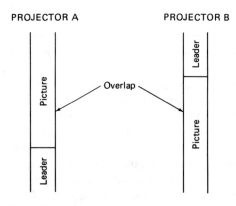

Figure 10-16   How dissolves are done in single-system editing.

Figure 10-17   CP/16 reflex dc single system, with built-in amplifier/mixer, was the news gathering mainstay for twenty years.

EDIT

Logging and preparing sound tracks for the editing process are covered, with reference to the do's and don'ts recommended in The Association of Cinema Labs Manual. Following an operational overview of automated editing systems, time code is again discussed in relation to those systems. In a section on preparing sound tracks for the mix, emphasis is on eliminating possible noise-inducing hazards of the process. Music and effects editing is also considered, with the projector as an editing tool. The goal is to understand the mechanical editing process as a sorting and classification of data for the eventual creative recombination in the mix.

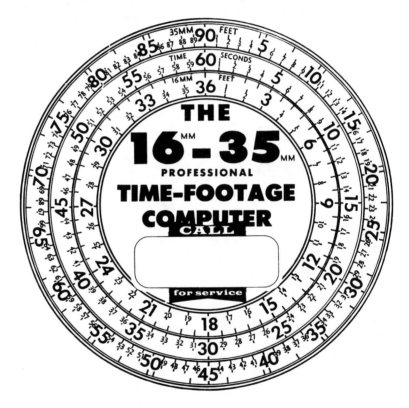

The concept of editing seems simple enough. The semantic root comes from the Latin verb *edere*, to cut. The time has long since passed, however, when the editing process was merely to cut bits of film together (or bits of tape, for that matter). Time code, synthesizers, synchronizers, and computers have radically changed the editorial practices in film and video, obscuring somewhat the audio design function of *editorial content*—narrative elements created through the process of editing. Film and video editing has reached an interface point. Many proprietary systems have come into being, each with a unique marriage of film and video technologies enhanced by computer-assisted methodologies.

Editing Sound and Film/Video

Techniques

The editing function has three fundamental levels of sophistication:

1. *Cutting:* The selection and arrangement in time of the bits and pieces of sound and visual.
2. *Processing:* The creation of physical or electronic effects and "bridges" which link time, space, dramatics, etc.
3. *Composing-synthesizing:* The shaping of sound materials into unique narrative elements classified in terms of dialogue, music, and effects.

On any of these levels, the techniques employed to achieve the desired results—and the only test is that the "cut" produce the desired response from the audience—include but are not limited to the following inventory of editorial forms:

1. *Continuity cutting:* A style of editing marked by its emphasis on maintaining the continuous and seemingly uninterrupted flow of action in a story. However, the continuous time is apparent, not the "real time" (as within the long takes of cinema verité, for instance).
2. *Dynamic cutting:* A contrasting type of editing which, by the juxtaposition of opposites (shots or sequences), generates new ideas in the viewer's mind, ideas which were not latent in the shots themselves. Eisenstein's

example: close-up of man plus close-up of peacock equals an egomaniac. Eisenstein thought of this kind of creative editing as *montage*.

3. *Montage:* In Russia, montage means dynamic cutting. In Europe it means the act of assembling. In Hollywood it denotes a sequence of rapid superimpositions, jump cuts, and dissolves creating a kaleidoscopic sense of motion—all significantly far away from the original notion of narrative meaning by association of images.

4. *Decoupage:* In classical terms, this theory of editing holds that narrative flow is created and preserved through strict straight match continuity in time and space in contrast to Montage which holds that meaning can come through the association of dissimilar images placed next to each other.

5. *Cut:* A transition made by splicing two pieces of film together. Types of transitions defined in this glossary are:

   Cross-cutting: Switching back and forth between two or more scenes, such as a serial episode that alternately shows the heroine nearing the waterfall and the hero galloping to the rescue. Cross-cutting can create parallel action, time, and space. In such cases as the last-minute rescue, excitement and tension are often increased by shortening the shots and accelerating the rhythm of the cross-cutting. The essence is a feeling of equal time/measurement/action on two levels. Thematically unconnected incidents are developed by means of common element—a clock, bomb, gun.

   Cut-away: A shot of short duration that supposedly takes place at the same time as the main action, but not directly involved in the main action. For examples of cut-aways, see reaction shot and insert shot. Cut-aways are sometimes used less for artistic purposes than to overcome continuity gaps when some footage is bad or missing. If ex-president Nixon picked his teeth while speaking, a sympathetic editor would keep the sound but visually cut away to a shot of someone listening that was taken earlier to cover up such routine mishaps.

   Cutting on action: Cutting from one shot to another view that "matches" it in action and gives the impression of a continuous time span. For example, the actor begins to sit down in a medium shot and finishes in a close-up. By having an actor begin a gesture in one shot and carry it through to completion in the next, the director creates a visual bridge that distracts us from noticing the cut.

   Form cut: Framing in a successive shot an object with a shape or contour similar to an image in the immediately preceding shot. In Griffith's *Intolerance,* for example, the camera cuts from Balshazar's round shield to the round end of a battering ram pounding the city gates. The circumference and location in the frame of the two circles are identical.

   Hidden cut: An inconspicuous cut, usually in a fast-action scene, with which the director accelerates the action without significantly shifting the angle or distance as required for a more noticeable cut.

Familiar image: Repetition of an image throughout a program with slight modifications to duration or composition. With each use the meaning of the shot is altered until the concluding image discloses a new meaning.

Jump cut: A severe break in spacial and temporal continuity. This editorial form is perceived as a jump on the screen as if a slice of continuous action has been lifted out of the sequence and the ends joined. Time is compressed and extended. Godard's *Breathless* concludes with the never-ending flight of Belmondo in jumpcut.

Parallel action: An effect created by cross-cutting that enables the audience to perceive action occurring in two distinct places simultaneously. Screen time is created by extending or condensing the duration of these juxtaposed actions in different places. The assumption that both are happening in the same time frame is purely coincidental. Altering the intercutting can create a sense of movement back and forth in time as well as in space. A cliche of parallel action would be in the creation of suspense by intercutting shots of viewers in four different cities watching and waiting for their friend on a quiz show to give an answer before the 30-second bell rings.

Separation: Any shot may be broken down into component details, which when viewed one after the other bring the spectator closer to the subject than he or she would have been in the master shot.

Transition: Any use of optical linkages to denote a passage of time (indefinite or definite) or a displacement in space (real or imagined) including the use of fades, dissolves, iris, wipe, rear projection, traveling matte, aerial projection, and superimposition.

6. *Insert:* An insert is a detail from one of the shots in a specific sequence that is placed within the sequence for timing purposes, or to focus audience attention on one area. For instance, a close-up of dripping water in a bath sequence may be used to build suspense.

7. *Reaction:* Any shot that implies the completion or closing response to a previous action shot. Generally it is a close-up of the response of one character to another but it can also be a shot that defines the result of an action, such as the explosion following a close-up of someone pressing a button.

Film and Video Editing Systems

Editing systems vary in sophistication and characteristics.

Cut and paste. The conventional *cut and paste* technique utilizes basic tools—a razor blade, cement (now replaced by mylar tape), positioning equipment, and a viewer. Sound is *physically* measured and marked, sections of magnetic film deleted or added. The physical sound cut is slanted to reduce friction noise as the splice runs over a playback head. Conventional cut and paste uses flatbed or Moviola upright editors for multiple track editing. Up to three tracks may be physically edited in sync against picture. In the early days, even videotape was physically cut.

The *Moviola* is the motorized version of the table-top editing array. Unfortunately, the machine allows for the (comfortable) editing of no more than two tracks in addition to picture. The system runs sound at 24 fps only, while the picture can be run at 24 fps interlocked to sound or at variable speeds from 2 to 30 fps. As the basic industry tool, the Moviola has the tendency, if misused, to chew up film.

To operate the Moviola:

1. Turn off all switches.
2. Clean the film path of oil and grit.
3. Turn on the power switch; then turn on the amplifier and set the volume level to low.

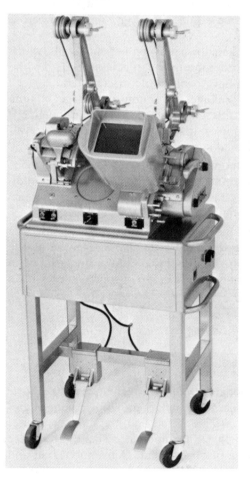

(A)

Figure 11-1 (A) The Moviola; (B) threading the Moviola.

1. On-off power switch.
2. Lamp on.
3. Reset knob for counter.
4. Footage/frame counter.
5. Mag volume and exicter lamp control.
6. Sound motor forward/reverse.
7. Sound motor off/on.
8. Master volume.
9. Pix motor on/off, forward/reverse.
10. Screen lamp.
11. Pix motor on/off, screen on/off.
12. Image bright rheostat.
13. Headset input.
14. Mag/optical mode selector.
15. Tone adjustment.
16. Sound motor pedal control.
17. Pix motor pedal control.
18. Interlock clutch.

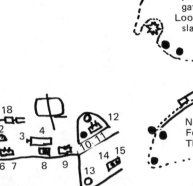

PIX
Loop to outer edge
 pix right side up in
 gate
Loop large enough for
 slack w/o scratching

Sound
No loop
Feed from bottom
Thread above roller

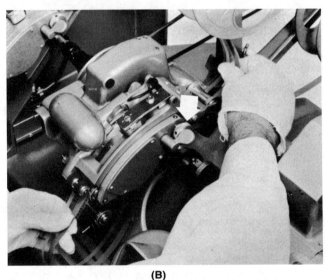

(B)

Figure 11-1   (continued)

4. Check the brightness level of the pix side viewer bulb by turning it on!

5. After threading (see Figure 11-1(B)), engage the interlock clutch, locking the shafts.

6. Set the footage counter to zero.

7. Select Mag or Opt playback mode.

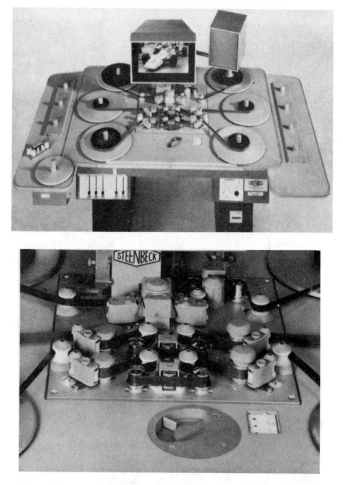

Figure 11-2   Flatbed editor. Horizontal transport is easy on film.

8. Turn up the amplifier and tone controls.

9. Disengage the interlock if you are running sound alone.

10. Change from forward to reverse mode only when the motor is stopped; riding the clutch causes gear damage and sprocket jumps.

11. The motor switch instantly sets transport to 24 fps on the sound side; so it is better to start the machine with the picture side drive set at low speed. Depress the foot pedal until the transport gets up to speed; then switch on the sound motor. This avoids the sudden jump of the sound motor and possible sprocket tears.

12. The picture motor is adjustable by means of a rheostat control for both speed and image brightness.

13. Using the Moviola, instead of the table winds, to rewind causes over-heating.

14. Grease in the gear box tends to liquify after long periods of use, and it drips under the sound head onto the mag film if it is not wiped away.

15. Turn off all switches. The machine is an editor, not a projector.

HINTS:

Use only split aluminum reels.

Use Sharpie ink markers, not a grease marker.

Never run motors against each other in opposite gear.

The cut and paste method achieves very exact edits, and it is cheap. Fast edits with multitrack capacity are also a benefit. However, the disadvantages outweigh the perks: It's messy and tedious, and it causes or induces noise. The physical handling of sound materials presents the possibility of damage from dirt or demagnetization.

Cut and paste (mechanical) editing, set-up and procedure. A multigang synchronizing block (4, 6, 8 gangs, one gang per track) holds tracks in place with sprocket teeth. A footage/frame counter lines up with a frame marker. A magnetic sound reading head sits above the gang lock on each track. The pressure of each head must be adjusted to avoid scratching the emulsion while obtaining a clear audio pick-up, which is amplified by an external "squawk box" sound amplifier/speaker. Using conventional rewinds, wind the tracks through, mark edit points with removable grease marker or Sharpie ink markers.

The process is tedious but accurate. It allows the physical removal of unwanted sound, spots of noise (which are either cut out or *blooped*—covered with tape or ink), and precise frame-to-frame matches. A noise occurring inside the length of one frame must be removed with a punch.

The chief disadvantage is handling the track without damaging it with dirt, grease, grit, scratches, dust, smoke, ripped sprockets. Hence a dupe copy of the track is usually made as backup.

The editor receives a work print reel of approximately 10 min in length (35-mm sprocketed film). This is then previewed on a Moviola, and notes are taken of the sounds required and the footages needed. A tentative list of library effects is made and most are auditioned.

The tape master library may be on ¼-in tape, cartridge, disc with the effects once transferred to mag stock, separated by leader and a tone burst reference. If the budget allows, a duplicate transfer (protection copy) is made of the desired sounds. The editor begins the cutting process manually.

One 10-min reel of picture may require any number of sound tracks and classes of sounds (such as interior, animals, wind, and atmosphere), separated onto discrete tracks for greater mixdown control. The physical distance between sounds on a given track must be adequate to allow the mixer to adjust the board controls, if necessary, from one sound to the next.

If the required sound is too short, a physical *loop* of tape must be made, to allow for the repeating of the sound. Synchronizing sound to picture is a trial and error manual function, which can be aided by using a flatbed editing table. Sound transfers are spliced to a leader (white emulsion tape), base to emulsion, and aligned to a picture sync point.

The final task is to assemble the edit cuts into 10-min reels maintaining sync with picture. These effects tracks are later mixed with music and dialogue tracks.

Sound quality is degraded with each transfer from library master to work copy to final mix due to cumulative signal-to-noise ratio loss. In addition, the mechanical process of constantly running mag film across sound heads for days on end contributes noise from abrasion and creates the risk of breaks and "Moviola chews." Ergo the advent of flatbed editors.

Since the tracks must be marked with crayon pencil, cut, and spliced, they often need to be cleaned of dust and dirt; they could also stand some light lubrication to prevent drying and shrinkage. The least hazardous cleaners are *Tuffcoat Ecco 1500, Freon TF,* and *Renovex* (some other cleaners may remove printed edge code numbers).

The workprint and sprocketed mag track are synchronized by lining up the picture of the slate just as the clapstick is closed with the sound of the closing clapstick: first frame of sound with first frame in which sticks are closed. The film perforations and a marking pen aid in the process.

The synched mag track and workprint are then *edge coded* (see Figure 11-3), so that they have corresponding numerical references when placed in a multigang synchronizer and thereby considered in "editorial" sync or "dead sync."

Transfer.   Film is transferred to videotape and sound is transferred to either a multitrack recorder/reproducer or videotape deck. Simple edits may be done from deck to deck with one track. The multitrack recorder allows for the manipulation of many discrete channels of sound information kept in sync with videopix via a synchronizer. Finding edit points on the multitrack, however, can be tedious and time-consuming. Sound is repositioned using a process of punch-in/punch-out recording. An alternate method is to interlock 16/35-mm magnetic film dubbers with a videocassette deck via a synchronizer.

Synthesizing.   An analog or digital synthesizer (essentially a musical keyboard instrument with memory capacity) can be interlocked via the hybrid SMPTE/MIDI interface code to a film projection and audio console or to a video projector/monitor with console. (See Figure 11-4).

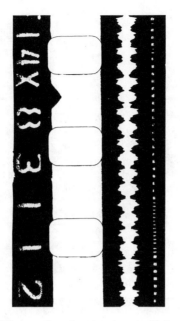

Figure 11-3   Edge numbers imprinted every 40 frames in 16 mm.

Computer editing.   This may be done by means of a sophisticated controller and synchronizers interlocking videotape recorders, playback, dubbers, or multitrack. Sound may be digitized and edited completely in digital form, with picture, and then mixed and transferred to 35-mm magnetic masters or 1-in videotape masters.

Time Code

Time code, a numerical calendar, was developed in the aerospace industry as a response to the need to accurately determine and record the time sequence of events. In the late 1960s, the television industry discovered that videotape was difficult to edit. By 1969, video engineers had come up with a suggested *Standard Time and Control Code for Video-Tape Editing*. In the early 1970s, the EBU (European Broadcasting Union) implemented a time code suitable for film. In 1975, *SMPTE Time Code* was adopted by the American National Standards Institute. (See Figure 11-5).

In 1978, PBS commissioned a study to develop a closed-captioning system that resulted in an optical data track on the film next to the optical audio track. The activity led to the creation of many proprietary time code systems including the quasi-code AATON Clear-Time Code system, which recorded codes once per second on the film. This evolved into a once-per-frame-code. This led, in

Figure 11-4 (A) The Synclavier 9600TS combines sampling, synthesis, sequencing, synchronization, and live recording; (B) the sequence editor screen.

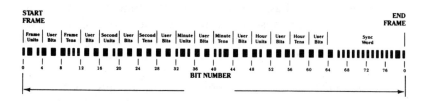

Figure 11-5 SMPTE time code.

turn, to the outfitting of cameras and the basic Nagra field recorder with time code generators set from a mutual master clock.

Time coding is a system used for synchronizing magnetic tape and magnetic film transports—thus synchronizing picture and sound, a long-standing problem in film making. (Previous synchronizing methods lacked the ability to cue several tape transports, automatically and simultaneously, to designated locations, as well as to accurately synchronize and keep locked together in absolute lip sync. This application is of particular interest to the film industry where synchronization between sprocketed and nonsprocketed equipment is beneficial in editing.

Code structure.   In NTSC video, each second of time is divided into 2,400 equal segments, which are equivalent to 80 bits per frame. Time code format shows real-time hours, minutes, seconds, and frames with bits set aside for other noncalendar data. Referred to as SMPTE/EBU, the code consists of 80 bits (2,400 segments) per television frame. This is a biphase mark, or Manchester II, code. These 80 bits are divided into a 16-bit sync word, a 32-bit user word, and a 32-bit time code word:

- The *16-bit sync word* is coded so that there is no possibility of the same code being generated by any allowable combination of user and time code word bits. The sync word also contains information that defines whether the tape is moving forward or reversed.

- The *32-bit user word* is divided into 8 groups of 4 bits each, which the user may code in any way.

- The *32-bit time code word* is also divided into 8 groups of 4 bits each, with each bit defined. The time code word uses a binary-coded decimal format to denote hours, minutes, seconds, and frames. One bit (bit 10), called the *drop frame bit,* is used to identify whether the time code is in drop frame or nondrop frame format (technically called *compensated* and *uncompensated* modes). The drop frame is used optionally on NTSC and PAL-M television systems to compensate for the discrepancy between a "color-time" vertical frequency of 59.94 Hz and a time base of 60 Hz. This is accomplished by dropping two video frames every minute, except every tenth minute. Thus, over a long period of time, the code remains close to real time instead of slowly accumulating an error. Bit 11 is used for color framing with a 1 indicating that 4-field color framing form NTSC applies. The final 15 bits of each frame are for time code.

Data in the various bit positions are counted only when there are differences—that is, a change from 1 to 0 or 0 to 1 in the middle of the *bit period*.

Each 4-bit group is called a *user bit*. VITC has 10 extra bits of data. Two sync bits are inserted before each time segment. Bit 27 is unassigned in LTC as a *Video Field Mark* with 1 (one) indicating color field 1 or 3, and 0 showing field 2 or 4. Bits 82–89 are for *cyclic redundancy checks* (CRC), that is, for error correction.

There are two classes of time code (see Figure 11-6):

1. *LTC Longitudinal* (*Serial*) *code* is recorded along the length of the tape as an audio signal.
2. *Vertical Interval* (*VITC*) *code* is generated and inserted into an unused line of the video vertical interval, and then recorded as part of the video signal.

Here are the basic differences between the two types of codes:

- LTC requires an audio track on the tape, and some systems are designed for special head and track units. VITC is part of the audio and doesn't need special head/track set-ups. (See Figure 11-6).
- LTC may be prerecorded with *video black*. Video is later placed with respect to the code. User bits must be included when the code is originally recorded; then, when it is changed, the entire code strip must be re-recorded.
- LTC works over a wide range but is not effective at *still frame* and very low speeds. VITC is not as effective at very high speeds.

Application.   With a time code synchronizer, musical overdubbing and sweetening can be done by locking sound and picture. As part of the synchronizing equipment, a cueing device enables the operator to run the machine back and forth over a selected interval while laying in various cues of music, dialogue, special effects, etc. After the desired scoring and effects have been added to the various tracks of the multitrack, a final mixdown is made on one of the remaining tracks. When mixing is completed, the same synchronizing equipment is used to lay back the completed mixed track onto the master.

Synchronization.   A MQS-100 series microcomputer synchronizing system reads the time codes from each machine and directs the tape to specifically assigned cue points on their tapes. The transports move forward to

VITC
Vertical Interval
Time Code

LTC
Longitudinal
Time Code

VITC BIT NO					BIT NO
0	"1"	—	SYNC BIT		
1	"0"	—	SYNC BIT		
2		1		1	0
3		2		2	1
4		4	UNITS OF FRAMES	4	2
5		8		8	3
6					4
7					5
8			FIRST BINARY GROUP		6
9					7
10	"1"	—	SYNC BIT		
11	"0"	—	SYNC BIT		
12		10	TENS OF FRAMES	10	8
13		20		20	9
14		DROP FRAME FLAG			10
15		COLOR FRAME FLAG			11
16					12
17					13
18			SECOND BINARY GROUP		14
19					15
20	"1"	—	SYNC BIT		
21	"0"	—	SYNC BIT		
22		1		1	16
23		2		2	17
24		4	UNITS OF SECONDS	4	18
25		8		8	19
26					20
27					21
28			THIRD BINARY GROUP		22
29					23
30	"1"	—	SYNC BIT		
31	"0"	—	SYNC BIT		
32		10		10	24
33		20	TENS OF SECONDS	20	25
34		40		40	26
35			FIELD MARK		27
36					28
37					29
38			FOURTH BINARY GROUP		30
39					31
40	"1"	—	SYNC BIT		
41	"0"	—	SYNC BIT		
42		1		1	32
43		2		2	33
44		4	UNITS OF MINUTES	4	34
45		8		8	35
46					36
47					37
48			FIFTH BINARY GROUP		38
49					39
50	"1"	—	SYNC BIT		
51	"0"	—	SYNC BIT		
52		10		10	40
53		20	TENS OF MINUTES	20	41
54		40		40	42
55		UNASSIGNED ADDRESS BIT			43
56					44
57					45
58			SIXTH BINARY GROUP		46
59					47
60	"1"	—	SYNC BIT		
61	"0"	—	SYNC BIT		
62		1		1	48
63		2		2	49
64		4	UNITS OF HOURS	4	50
65		8		8	51
66					52
67					53
68			SEVENTH BINARY GROUP		54
69					55
70	"1"	—	SYNC BIT		
71	"0"	—	SYNC BIT		
72		10	TENS OF HOURS	10	56
73		20		20	57
74		UNASSIGNED ADDRESS BIT			58
75		UNASSIGNED ADDRESS BIT			59
76					60
77			EIGHTH BINARY GROUP		61
78					62
79					63
80	"1"	—	SYNC BIT		
81	"0"	—	SYNC BIT		
82					64
83					65
84					66
85					67
86			CRC		68
87					69
88					70
89					71
					72
			SYNC WORD		73
					74
					75
					76
					77
					78
					79

Figure 11-6 LTC versus VITC code.
(Source: ECCO)

synchronize, as the synchronizer first uses the tape codes as address references. The slave transports are speeded up or slowed down as much as 50 percent for normal play speed until they are the same distance from their assigned cue point. The synchronizer then uses the tape codes as electronic "sprockets" to keep the tapes synchronized in a phase-locked mode, in which the synchronizer keeps the plane rates of the slave tapes identical to the master tape with an accuracy of ± 100 μs. The synchronizer control is based on a time reference, either the house composite sync/video or the internal crystal. This prevents an additive wow or flutter that could increase as the slave transports react to deviations in the master transport. The times recorded on the different tapes need not be identical; an offset of up to 24 hr is permissible. The synchronizer handles the calculations needed to bring the slave tapes into synchronization with the master tape regardless of differences in time code indexing.

Types of errors. A number of tape speed errors can have a major effect on the amplitude and distortion of the biphase signal. The SMPTE/EBU time and control code, recorded on audiotape, provides precise indexing needed for automatic synchronization and sophisticated electronic editing. The time recorded may be the actual clock time or elapsed time.

- At fast tape speeds, the amount of energy picked up from the tape is large and the frequency of the signal becomes very high. At some point the readability of the code becomes marginal, and above this speed there may be no readable code. To minimize or eliminate these errors, wideband amplifier circuits can provide optimum processing of the signal.
- At lower-than-normal speed, the opposite phenomenon occurs. Amplitude and frequency decrease, and, below a certain speed, no code may be read. Just above the dropout point, intermittent reading may take place.
- Every time the tape direction is reversed, two potential sources of error are encountered. First, the tape speed must reach zero in order to change direction. Second, the data shift register must be switched in the opposite direction, and at least one valid *sync* word must be detected after the change in direction before a valid code is read.

Noise from various sources can interfere with the continuous reading of code, causing random or extended dropouts. Drop frame is an example of this type of discontinuity.

Discontinuity errors are those found on tapes edited with no regard for time code audio protection or with different codes purposely edited in. Often tapes are generated by intermittently making recordings at various times of the day with the time code generator running continuously so as to generate actual clock time. This creates discontinuities or gaps of the time between scenes.

Finally, there is a discontinuity referred to as the *midnight phenomenon*, which can cause processing problems. The phenomenon occurs as the tape progresses in either forward or reverse through a midnight time code. At this time, a 24-hr discontinuity occurs which could not only appear as a valid in code but also cause difficulty in determining the direction (forward or reverse) to the other side of the void. (Some systems deal with the midnight discontinuity automatically while others do not.)

Errors and discontinuities can cause a multitude of problems in editing. An erroneous code may cause the system to act as if it has arrived at an *in* or *out* edit point, when in fact it has not. Errors may also prevent the source from properly positioning themselves with respect to each other and with respect to the record VTR. Any of these conditions makes accurate editing impossible.

Two methods are available to solve the problems of errors: vertical interval code and correlation. *Vertical interval code* solves only the problem of medium- to low- or zero-speed tape motion; fast-forward and fast-rewind speeds are still a problem for vertical interval code. *Correlation* does not require the processing of video, which can cause degradation. The *best* approach is to combine the two, but it may not be cost-effective. The time code indexes used for indexing the tapes need not be identical (time offsets are allowed), and tapes with drop-frame and nondrop-frame formats can be intermixed. System modes include high-speed search and cue, chase mode, synchronized playback, fast and slow resynchronization. The chase mode directs the slave transports to follow all master transport actions. This permits the operator to control cueing and synchronizing at a front panel of the master transport.

This microprocessor-based synchronizing system can cue and synchronize any three magnetic tape transports simultaneously, including video, audio, and magnetic film. Lower cost, less complex hardware, and less complex operating procedures are other advantages in using this type of system.

SMPTE test materials for motion picture and TV. The following test materials are used to determine the efficiency of the playback chain:

- *Buzz Track Test Film:* Determines proper lateral placement of the scanning beam slit in relation to the film path in the projector. The sound record area is opaque and no sound is heard when the slit is correctly positioned. Each side has a square wave, 300 Hz on the pix side and 1 kHz on the film edge. By identifying the tone, the user can determine the lateral direction of slit misadjustment. (See Figure 11-7.)
- *Scanning Beam Test Film:* Checks the uniformity of illumination across the scanning slit. Commonly and incorrectly called the "snake track," it has an 0.003-in wide variable area record of a 1-kHz pulse on the film edge traveling at a uniform rate to the other edge. A standard volume indicator meter is used. (See Figure 11-8.)
- *Multifrequency Burst Test:* Adjusts reproducers and production projectors. It contains series of full-range frequencies. Initial gain adjust-

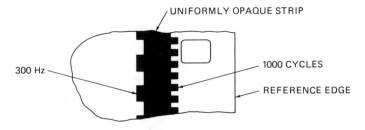

Figure 11-7   Buzz track test film. (Source: SMPTE)

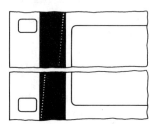

Figure 11-8   Scanning beam test film. (Source: SMPTE)

ments and range selection of the output meter are made with a reference tone. Film is calibrated and provided with correction values.

- *Signal Level Test:* Measures and balances the power level. It provides a reproducible reference to which a program level can be related, but does not itself indicate a program level.
- *Flutter Test:* Measures flutter introduced by sound reproducers. The reference is a 3,150-kHz variable area recording. It requires a flutter meter.
- *Sound Focus and Azimuth Alignment Test:* Adjusts focus. Type A is for labs, type B is less precise. When exposing 16-mm single sprocket film, the emulsion side must face the light source so that every generation undergoes a change from A to B wind. (See Figure 11-9.)

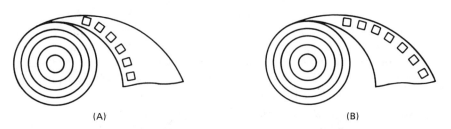

(A)   (B)

Figure 11-9   A and B wind—Emulsion Side In.

Sound Editing

In sound editing, the first concern is the syncing of dailies, the basic location production tracks to the picture. The physical sync reference points—clapboards, beep tones, hand claps, electronic slate marks, and the like—provide the references for alignment. This basic task becomes troublesome if sound was transferred improperly due to the inability to resolve speed fluctuations or due to a loss of sync signal.

Nonelectronic editing presents some real physical hazards:

- Heat, stray magnetic fields, or magnetized cutting blades may induce noise onto the track.
- Cigarette smoke, coffee, grease, and other physical residues are audible on the track.
- Torn sprockets, sync marks, emulsion scratches, and tears must be repaired with care since they may cause further damage. In addition, the mag film may become dry and brittle during months of exposure to the average editing environment. (The sound image in the oxide can be made visible to facilitate the search for start marks. See Figure 11-10.)
- Start points on the mag film do not correspond to the picture start (the first frame of usable image). Frame advances, due to reproducing head displacement, must be ascertained and marked on the base side of the track. (See Table 11-1.)

Here are some technical hints:

- Indicate all areas of silence with white emulsion leader, splicing it base to emulsion to avoid damage to magnetic heads and induced noise.
- Use a pencil degausser to demagnetize all cutting blades, recording/playback heads, and even to erase a section on the mag film if you are careful. (Magnetization of the track sounds like rushing water when played back.) Approach the area to be degaussed with the pencil very slowly holding the tip flush to the magnetic tape. Move the eraser back and forth across the width of the tape. The movement of the pencil realigns the magnetic oxide particles. The rate of advance should be about 3 in/min. Faster movement may induce a signal. Withdraw the pencil slowly with the switch still in the On position. In demagnetizing metal objects like magnetic heads, no contact should be made.
- Use only aluminum split reels for mag stock to avoid induction.
- *Split off* a sound element to a separate track if the element requires EQ or processing, blends or combines (overlaps with another element), presents a significant change in level, or is of indefinite duration.
- Group generically similar kinds of sounds—such as all traffic effects—on one track.

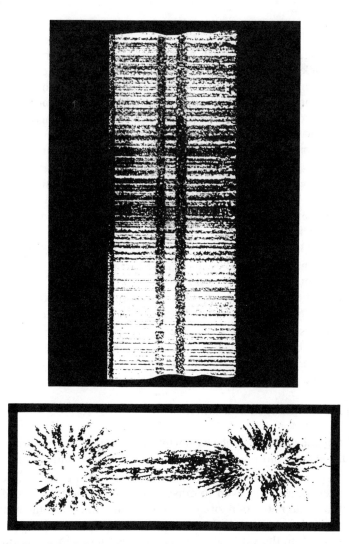

Figure 11-10   Location of the actual recorded region on mag film. (Source: Eastman Kodak)

- Where no dialogue, music, or effects occur, but where there is also no silence, cut in room tone or environmental ambiance to avoid dead spots (areas of no auditory data). Dead spots read as distracting amp/speaker breathing in the mix and in the theatre.
- For absolute editing (dead sync), the start mark is zero (0). When setting up the mix log, begin from 0 relative to the point where the recorded beep tone occurs (opposite "2" on the picture Academy Leader). Then count from the beep as frame 1 back 3 ft (24 frames for 16-mm) and mark the very next frame "start." Count from this start mark 4 ft (32 frames) and line up the first picture frame.

TABLE 11-1 Frames of separation between sound and picture for
projection sync

Super 8	16-mm	35-mm	Gauge
18	28	28	Magnetic
22	26	20	Optical

- When using a *guillotine*-style splicer, take care to insure all sprockets are punched out cleanly. The splicer must be reversed to do this.
- A 16-mm track has one perf for each frame and falls in the middle of the frame line, which is not a problem for narration or dialogue. For syncing an effect, however, 35-mm tracks are more precise a medium because it has 4 perfs per frame and you can therefore make four possible cuts within the 35-mm frame. The 35-mm track also has greater fidelity, and most music libraries supply selections in 35-mm or disk.
- Editing (printed) code numbers are placed at every foot of picture and sound track. After the final edit/mix, if you are using the latent edge numbers of the picture negative instead of any other code, opticals must be measured and ordered using *inside counts*, that is, the first frame and the last frame of the effect as you read in editorial sync.
- Cataloguing standards for work prints and mag tracks should run something like this:
  Reel 1 code # 1000
  Reel 2 code 2000
  Reel 11 code #A1000
- Many labs have discarded the A/B reel leader system and now print on 2,000-ft reels. Reels one and two are spliced together and printed as one. The sound track pull-up is accomplished by adding the first 20 frames of each reel to the preceding reel before transferring to optical negative. A one-reel transfer is made of the first 20 frames of each reel and spliced onto the end of each reel. In release printing, any number of reels may be joined without causing a *sound bump* or loss of clarity.
- For mag film, *butt* (straight cut) splicing uses perforated tape. A razor cut diagonal guillotine is preferred since the cut is cleaner, the tape is thinner, and the splice resists peeling up. Opaque white mylar tape is used so that the splice can be found later.
- Blooping tape, an opaque thin black tape may be placed at the edge of the physical splice on the emulsion side to quiet the cut. (See Table 11-2.)
- Projector wind is the opposite of Moviola wind. Be certain all reels of sound are one or the other before going to the mix session, or you may lose an hour of machine time rewinding instead of mixing.
- Since a spliced picture work print tends to get stuck in the projector gate if splices are not perfect, a *sloppy dupe* is usually made (a cheap and dirty contact print) for mix projection only.

TABLE 11-2 Selected editing hardware

Bloop punch	Makes a wide punch out at the edge of mag film, eliminating a rough cut or noise pop. Triangular and custom shapes are available.
Blooping ink	Opaque paint applied to the optical negative track area to create silence.
Cue punch	Available in several diameters, this circle punch marks sync points and music cues.
Freon TF	Flourocarbon solvent used for cleaning magnetic tracks.
Stop-in-cue	Metalized sensing tape used to mark edge sync points; triggers automatic sensors in certain recorders and playback systems.
Blooping tape	Opaque thin film tape applied over noise and bad cuts to silence them.
Bloop tones	Prerecorded 1,000-Hz pulse tones used for marking sync points, test, and start marks.
Streamers	1-ft gummed lines used as a diagonal cue on picture track.
Music cue punch	Three rectangular hole punch for cueing music tracks.
Audio swabbles	Lint-free cotton tips for cleaning mag heads.
Demag scissors	Brass demagnetized shears for cutting mag film.

- Most studios require the sound rolls to be on cores, with tails out and the projector wind ready to thread up on dubbers. All cue sheet footage must be in 35-mm count regardless of print gauge. If there is any single perf leader in the track, the head and tail leader must be single perf on the same side to avoid any unpleasant accidents in the machine room due to the surprise appearance of the unperforated side being slit by the sprocket tooth drive.

TABLE 11-3 Typical cutting room equipment and prices

2 editing tables with light box and drawer
2 pair long shaft rewinders and spring lock clamps
2 back racks for the editing tables
2 table lamps and 2 editing chairs
2 trim bins
2 film racks
2 double tape dispensers
2 4/gang synchronizers
2 sound heads and arms for each synchronizer (a total of 4)
2 amplifiers (2-channel)
2 C/R straight razor cut splicers
2 split reels
1 flange
1 telephone

The above equipment, along with one editing machine, as listed below, will determine the cost of the space and equipment rental. Additional equipment, other than what is listed above and below, is billed at normal rates. During peak production season upright 35 Movieolas became scarce.

	1 Month	1 Week	Daily
Upright Moviola	$1,127.00	$432.50	$106.00
4–16 mm Steenbeck	$1,227.00	$470.50	$116.00
8–35 mm Steenbeck Hi-Speed	$2,327.00	$912.50	$226.50

- All tracks should be cleaned with Freon TF solvent prior to the mix. In some cases, specific tracks may be so overworked that the dupe protection copy must be cut, conformed, and used in its place to provide a noise-free track.

- Uniformly label all tracks and place a beep tone, as well as punch marks, in identical start marks on each track.

- A good practice is to have a final check interlock screening prior to the mix to avoid any mix time expended to correct editorial mistakes. This premix review is essential and should be booked at least a week in advance of the mix. It could avoid a major embarrassment and costly downtime.

Sound Effects

Each sound track must be the same length as the picture workprint, with corresponding sync markings, unless a continuous loop of one repeating effect is used. (This is run on one machine via a 9-ft strand on a core with sufficient leader to make the loop.) Creating several loops of room tone and ambiance is essential since the mix tends to reveal areas in which ADR has eliminated background.

Effects groups should be separated onto discrete tracks for proper mix control. These groupings may be organized according to *level*—interior/exterior, location, dialogue background, short or long repeatable, dissolves and fade-ups/-ins, etc. Whatever makes sense in terms of the material presented.

If sounds are to overlap, such as gunshots fading into music, each element must be placed on a separate track with sufficient length to cover the fade-up. Fade-ups start from low modulation, are brought up to full modulation at the *center* of the fade, and then diminished to the midpoint of the music fade-up. This generally means that the required element may be twice the length of what is actually heard in the theatre. The *overlap begins before the effect is heard.*

Finally, when the perspective and clarity of voice do not apparently match the background, the voice should be split off to a new track for blending and processing of ambiance.

All sounds have a definite beginning, development, and conclusion.It is less noticeable to trim from the center than from the very perceptible aural entrance and exit which psychoacoustically does not seem to tolerate adjustment of duration. Center portions are generally repeating patterns, which may be shortened without adverse affect.

The precise matching of concrete, nonrepeating sounds—such as gunshots, footsteps, punches, and other sounds that must "hit the mark," so to speak—often do not ring true if spliced to the exact point (frame) of impact. Due to psychoacoustic factors and the differences between the speeds of light and sound, it is recommended that the sound impact point be cut in several frames before the visual impact point to accommodate the delay in the theatre. The slap in the face won't then seem to come too late when you sit in the back of the theatre.

TABLE 11-4 A variable click track conforms to the precise rhythms of picture. Computations of intervals can be quite complex.

Click Number	Intervals to Next Click	Timing	Footage	Frames to Next Click	Actual Tempo	How to Correct	Adjusted Tempo
1	30	0:00	000	624	20.800	Must gain 12 eighths	18 clicks @ 20/6 12 clicks @ 20/7
31	41	0:26	39 + 0	866	20.750 × 30 = 622.500 21.121951	Must lose 1 eighth	40 clicks @ 21/1 1 click @ 21/0
72	21	1:02.1	93 + 2	427	21.125 × 41 = 866.125 20.333333	Must lose 7 eighths	14 clicks @ 20/3 7 clicks @ 20/2
93	8	1:19.9	119 + 13	164	20.375 × 21 = 427.875 20.500	as is	7 clicks @ 20/2 8 clicks @ 20/4
101	53	1:26.7	130 + 1	1116	21.056603	Must gain 24 eighths	29 clicks @ 21/0 24 clicks @ 21/1
154		2:13.2	199 + 13		21.000 × 53 = 1113		

Source: Milton Lustig, *MUSIC Editing.* (New York: Hastings House).

Music

The composer requires from the director/editor a breakdown of each musical section. Cue points indicate where music starts and stops, dialogue overlaps, scenes cut, and cameras move, in that order. All this information is included on the *timing sheet*.

Timing for the cue starts at zero and is rounded to a fraction of a second until the music ends. Notations regarding emotional content must be in clear narrative form.

A *click track* may be required. This is a timed series of measured audible clicks running in exact frame-to-frame sync with the picture cue points indicating *rhythm, meter,* and *duration.* Clicks are fed to the monitor earphones of the composer/conductor. The composer can then orchestrate measurable amounts of melody to fit within a precise period, permitting embellishments at cue points, if necessary and appropriate, and resulting in very precise performances during scoring sessions.

Playing to clicks engages the whole orchestra to a precision beat. Following the conductor's expressions and dynamics, the orchestral elements may be separated for clarity and still maintain unity through the click beat. The music editor attends the scoring session and is responsible for the precision of the product. The music tracks are then built up into master tracks to run in sync with picture. (See Table 11-4.)

Using time code to augment music for video. After studying the program and determining a key and tempo, the composer translates the tempo into a *frames-per-beat* equivalent by timing 24 beats. If 24 beats take 12 frames, the *click rate* is half a frame per beat (a 12-frame click). The smallest click rate possible in film is 1/8-frame.

A click book (a table of references for all click tempi, showing the number of beats and elapsed time in seconds and frames) is often used to locate the points of action in the program. Taking an average of all the most important cues, the composer selects the closest click rate, such as 12.2, which catches most of the precise cues.

The click can be played back (if evenly divisible) with either an audible click from a Synclavier or other digital audio device and/or a visual cue that shows a tempo.

A layout sheet is created showing where *barlines* should be. A cue pulse could be used by inputting a location, but since SMPTE time code is a constant, you should be able to specify locations by hitting a key at the right visual frame, not by inputting a number. The audible click must be available from the video work print, a digital clock generator, or a prerecorded tape slaved via SMPTE to the picture for studio recording with live musicians. Time code offers more precise cueing for the composer and is a decided aid in creating sonic maps.

VIDEO INTERFACE

Electronic synthesizers allow for the marriage of film and electronic technologies in a unified postproduction process. Success depends on synchronization, and synchronization depends on the proper use of time base code. Toward this end, we discuss synchronizers, time base correctors, and time code reader/generators. Audio sweetening methods are also explained, in connection with some basic "personalized" editing set-ups that can move the process from the studio into the home/office.

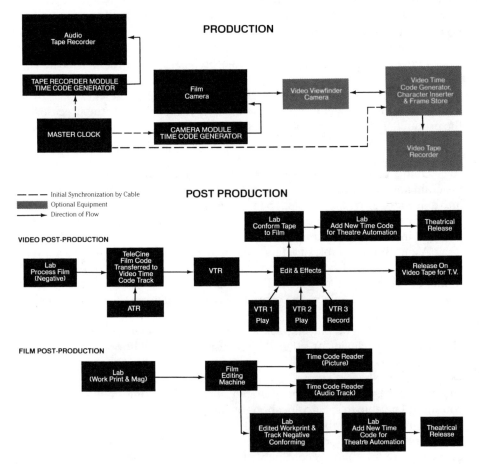

Synchronizers

Reliable synchronizers "make" video/film postproduction work, and time code determines the accuracy of synchronizers. Microprocessor-based synchronizers automatically search audiotape to designated program points, while controlling the VTR. Addition, deletion, blending, and enhancing functions are controlled for up to three discrete tracks. These units place each SMPTE-coded source track onto a single multitrack tape in exact time relationships with the final mixdown. Audio is routed from each source through a mixing console back to a fourth track on the multitrack deck. During the mix, the synchronizer uses time code to lock audio elements to video. The final control step is the *layback* of the mixed master to the master videotape. Since all materials handled by the synchronizer must be striped with time code, differences in time code values from varying source tracks are recalculated by the synchronizer to bring all source to uniform sync.

Three types of synchronizers are in current use:

1. *Play Speed Only:* Requires the machines to be manually cued closely enough together so that the slave machine can be *slewed* into lock by varying the capstan speed.
2. *Chase:* Requires the slave transports to "chase" the master under all conditions. Control of the master is from the machine, while the slave response is delayed because it cannot park until it knows where the master is parked. (See Figure 12-1.)
3. *Control (Q-Lock):* Audiokinetics developed a production editing control system around a synchronizer (Q-Lock) that interlocks film dubbers and recorders with VTR and VCR units. Here is the basic configuration for audio sweetening setup. Q-Lock uses recognized pulses to drive all interlocked tape machines, dubbers, and recorders. By varying the frequency, slew commands (from film transports) can be issued as the Q-Lock generates pseudo-time code for the slave machine and slews that time code into lock. Multiples of the frame rate of that pseudo-code are then output to the film transport. The set is conventional—aligning a series of machines, parking on start marks followed by sync mode selection.

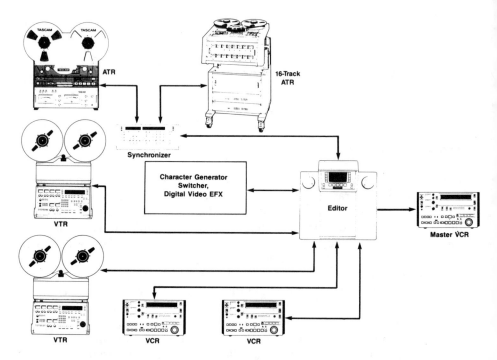

Figure 12-1 Typical studio interlock edit system, with computer controller, multitrack recorder, and VTRs.

A data interface system allows an external computer to access and control all the functions of the Q-Lock synchronizer. The computer may be another Q-Lock, an automated console, or an external PC. Interlocking two Q-Locks permits control of five machines.

Differences between machines, however, are mechanically and electronically complex, and problems may occur despite all the talk about fully automated trouble-free systems. If all machines were perfect, there would be no need for synchronizers or time base correctors.

Time Base Correctors (TBCs)

Videotape editing systems are subject to mechanical error or change called *time base error*. Introduced by temperature, humidity, drag, and tension changes, these errors alter the physical size and shape of tape during recording and playback. Differences in the mechanical sizes, shapes, and conditions of VTRs' tape *paths* can alter the size and shape of the tape during playback relative to the same parameters at the time of recording.

AUDIO SWEETENING

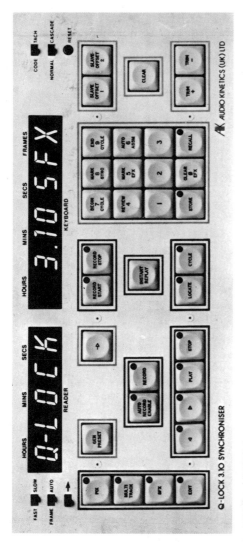

Q-LOCK 3.10 SYNCHRONISER

AUDIO KINETICS (UK) LTD

SOUND EFFECTS ASSEMBLY

SOUND EFFECTS ASSEMBLY and **AUDIO SWEETENING** are techniques for 'building' a series of sounds into a coherent effect or mood in sync with a picture source. Previously, numerous sound sources, e.g. film elements, cartridge machines, audio tapes, Foley and live action audio, were required to occur in time with a picture (film or video). This often occurred without the benefit of controlled synchronism. Recent productions have required up to 90

simultaneous elements to create a single composite effect.

This unique **Q-Soft** program configures the **Q-Lock** control unit to simplify and automate the transferring of sounds from library tapes, and other sound sources, to a multi-track recorder in perfect sync with the picture (film or video).

The major features are:

● Single frame frame crawl mode for exact cueing of picture for both film and video

tape machines.

● Completely eliminates keyboard numeric entry if desired.

● Multiple mode auto assembly: Review can be chosen to be manually controlled or automatically called up after a record function.

● Special memory allocation for marking picture and sound edit points.

● Point of reference for synchronization is completely variable with automatic offset adjustments for each edit.

● Edit parameters may be rehearsed and varied, if necessary, using standard keyboard functions without changing other established parameters.

● Machines are automatically brought on line in correct sequence for editing and assembly.

● End cue may be redefined on the fly during an auto assemble.

● Relay closures available for carts and other effects.

Figure 12-2 (A) The Q-Lock audio for video interlock system allows the linkage of traditional film dubbers and source machines to videotape recorders. Magnetic film dubbers afford the advantage of fast access and insertion capability, high audio quality, and multitrack interface.

(B) The Q-Lock Audio Sweetening module with sample operational program highlights. This is typical of the first generation auto-assembly edit/control/synchronization systems designed around digital technology. [Courtesy of Audio Kinetics (UK) Ltd.]

273

As the program is based on the standard **Q-Lock** coordinator, most functions and facilities are the same. Machine selection hierarchy, loading of offsets, trimming of memories and machine commands such as Locate to Play are all unchanged.

POWER ON

Load tapes on their respective machines and play each for a couple of seconds to allow **Q-Lock** to automatically correlate incoming time code to machines tach pulses. This need only be done when the system is powered up or the tapes are changed. Press the **PIX** button.

Quick reference:

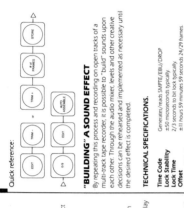

MAKING AN EDIT

Wind or locate the picture in the normal way to the start of the section to be worked on. Press **EDIT** and use the **TRIM + TRIM –** keys to crawl the picture forward or backward until the precise entry frame is visible. Press **BEG CYC.**

Quick reference:

Wind the picture to the end of the section and again use the **TRIM + TRIM –** keys to crawl the picture until the precise exit frame is visible and press **END CYC.**

Quick reference:

Next, after winding the picture to the point where the effect is to be synchronized, use the **TRIM + TRIM –** keys to find the exact frame and press the **MARK SYNC** key. The **LIBRARY** machine will be automatically selected for you.

Quick reference:

If Your Sound Effects Library Has Been Time Coded and Logged

Press **EDIT.** Use the numerical keyboard to enter the time code address of the desired sound effect from the log into the keyboard display. Press **LOCATE.** Press **EDIT** and **MARK EFX.**

Quick reference:

If Your Library Has Not Been Logged

Audibly cue the library machine to the start of the sound effect and press only the **MARK EFX** key.

Quick reference:

PERFORMING THE EDIT

Pressing the **AUTO ASSEMBLE** key will bring all machines on line and cue the library machine to the edit point by the value in the preroll memory. The machines will then enter synchronized play and upon reaching the edit point, automatically transfer the sound effect from the library to the multi-track tape onto the track which you have selected. When the end of the edit has been reached the machine will automatically terminate the transfer but continue to play through the post roll. At the end of the post roll, **AUTO-RECORD** will be cancelled and the system will immediately enter the review mode and again replay the edit.

Quick reference:

Changing The Sound Effect

If it is desired to try a different effect from the library using the same edit points, press **STOP,** then **CLEAR EFX.** Find the new sound effect and press **MARK EFX** followed by **AUTO ASSEMBLE.**

Quick reference:

Modifying/Trimming The Edit

Trimming of any of the edit points is easily done using the **TRIM + TRIM –** keys with the edit mode turned off. Press **EDIT** (turning off the EDIT L.E.D.) and press **TRIM –** or **TRIM +** followed by the number of mins, secs and frames, then **STORE** followed by the appropriate memory. Now press **EDIT** (turning on the EDIT L.E.D.) and **AUTO ASSEMBLE** to continue.

Quick reference:

"BUILDING" A SOUND EFFECT

By repeating this process and recording on open tracks of a multi-track tape recorder, it is possible to "build" sounds upon each other. Through the audio mixer, levels and other creative decisions can be rehearsed and implemented as necessary until the desired effect is completed.

TECHNICAL SPECIFICATIONS.

Time Code	Generates/reads SMPTE/EBU/DROP
Lock Stability	±50 microseconds (typically).
Lock Time	2/3 seconds to hit lock typically.
Offset	±11 hours 59 minutes 59 seconds 24/29 frames.
Capture Window	±11 hours 59 minutes 59 seconds 24/29 frames.
Code Read Limits	−30 to 0 dBm standard or slew limited
Varisped Lock	±33% from play speed.
Fast Lock	±50% capstan slew rate.
Slow Lock	±1.25% capstan slew rate.
Wow & Flutter	0.01% added to slave machine typically.
Outputs	3 generator outputs, adjustable to max +20 dBm (Requires female XLR-3) Video out-looped from video in (Requires male BNC). Video in (Requires male BNC).
Inputs	3 code reference inputs (Requires male XLR-3). Video in (Requires male BNC).
Data Interface	3 machine control inputs (Requires 25-way male D). RS232C
Mains	115/240 VAC 50/60 Hz 45 watts (Requires 3 pole IEC).
Size	Controller: 13.5" x 5-3/4" x 3" max. Computer: 19" x 5-1/4" x 15" (3u rack)
Weights	Controller: 5 pounds. Computer: 25 pounds. Shipping: 55 pounds.

AUDIO KINETICS
4721 Laurel Canyon Boulevard, Suite 209
North Hollywood, California 91607
213/980-5717
Toll Free outside of California
1-800-423-3666
Telex—194781

Figure 12-1 (continued)

Unwanted picture distortion can result from changes as little as one-thousandth of an inch, manifested in the image as a geometric distortion—a bend or curve in the vertical line of the video raster when displayed on a monitor. Playback errors often look like a wave at the top of the raster area. By converting video to digital data, a perfect frame is created.

A *time base corrector* (TBC) straightens out the line. The early digital TBCs (1973) made electronic news gathering (ENG) a reality by eliminating the small, rapid time base errors in portable, economy equipment for field recording. In addition, several other features developed with this technology: TBCs made clean videotape edits possible by locking the VTRs to the same *external sync generator.* Next-generation TBCs incorporated a sync generator that reinserted clean horizontal and vertical sync and burst on the video signal. Synchronizers were developed to lock remote feeds to local station sync, making possible clean switches, fades, splits, and other effects between local and remote nonsync picture sources by removing large, slow time base errors from cable, microwave, and satellite transmissions.

Time Base Correctors/Synchronizers

Synchronizers and TBCs are now generally combined into one multifunction digital system, which makes possible so-called A/B *roll edits* between noncapstan-servo drive videotape recorders. Digital effects components are offshoots of these hybrid super full-frame time base corrector/synchronizers. (See Table 12-1.)

The standard NTSC *full frame* video consists of 525 horizontal lines made up of two *fields,* each of $262\frac{1}{2}$ horizontal lines. Every 1/60th second, one field is inscribed on all of the picture tube's *even* horizontal lines. During the next 1/60th second, the other field is inscribed on the odd lines. The full picture, or

TABLE 12-1 Basic digital effects

Posterization	Digital bits are dropped, resulting in lower-definition contour, or "poster" graphic, look.
Sepia	The color spectrum is converted to a brown tone.
Mosaic	The image is converted to pixel blowups resembling mosaic tiles, which may be increased or decreased in size.
Combinations	A mix of poster, sepia, and mosaic.
Freeze-frame	An entire 525-line TV image is frozen in a full-frame digital memory, with attendant high-clarity vertical resolution.
Freeze field	Removes flicker from a video frame created when a picture with moving objects is frozen.
Strobe	A variable freeze rate repeatedly freezes the incoming video signal; varies from real time to fixed frozen picture rates.

frame, is made up of two fields, inscribed in 1/30th second. A full frame has double the vertical picture clarity of a field.

Digital technology has produced *digital video mixers,* which incorporate all the functions of TBCs while mixing audio and video sources without the need for synchronizers or external sync devices. The inventory of *effects* includes wipes, dissolves, fades, digital strobes, beat freezes, scene cuts, and audio mixes. Systems like the Numark VAM-2000 combine information from video cassette, video disc, CD video, or live satellite feed, broadcast or camera inputs. Custom titling devices may be interfaced.

The chief feature of the digital video mixer is the ability to create glitch-free frames and strobe freezes to audio (freezing video to the beat of audio). Three stereo inputs accept audio source material from another mixer, CD players, reel-to-reel recorders, and cassette decks. An audio effects loop allows connection to compressors, digital delay, and equalizers.

A sample input device that can be interfaced is an Eventide Ultra-Harmonizer, which can change pitch (pitch shift) in stereo program material or make two-channel pitch shifts *diatonically* to any user-specified key. The unit can also be controlled by MIDI interface and all the related options.

Editing with Time Code

The control track on videotape contains a series of electronic pulses that are meant to be read by all VTRs in the editing system. Noise or distortion in the pulse signal, resulting from a variety of internal/external causes, reduces the reliability of conventional two-CTR electronic cut-and-paste systems to the craft of the operator. Some editors develop a "feel" for the shifting peculiarities of the machines, are able to overcome the deficiencies, and produce acceptable (simple) edited programs. Essentially for this reason, TV programs seldom play with time and space in the style of filmic structure. Because of the lack of a homogeneous, accurate, and inexpensive editing system relying on "control track" technology, editing with time code has been recognized as the only precise option for film/video postproduction.

In connection with fully automated computer-assisted editing systems, time code becomes a *logging* and *searching* vehicle. Once all time code references points for each shot and sound take are entered via the keyboard of the editing system, the controller can find and position any element anywhere. Accuracy and repeatability are assured.

What Can Go Wrong with Time Code Editing

Time code editing has its drawbacks:

1. The recorded level of the time code can fall below 3 dB over 0 on the VU meter and not be read.

2. The precision of the time code recording may be low in clarity, with distortion causing edit aborts.

3. The time code may be nonsynchronous due to the fact that the recording's not being locked to a *stable* reference signal. This causes drift between frames. The only way to solve the problem is to re-record the entire time code via a slaved sync generator; this is called *restriping*.

4. Uncalibrated VTRs may cause edit aborts. Also, dirty heads may cause distortion in both the recording and playback of time code. Misalignment errors also cause distortion. A recording limiter may drop the level below 3 dB.

(*Note:* When time code editing first appeared in 1967, it was called *continuous* or *color* time code; today it is referred to as *nondrop frame* time code. All nondrop or color time code is recorded at a little slower rate than actual clock time—3.6 sec/hr slower (108 TV frames). Each minute around the clock, except the tenth minute, requires a two-frame drop totaling 108 frames (54 minutes times 2 frames). This occurs only at one point: As the time code changes from 01:05:59:29, the next frame is displayed as 01:06:00:02 (00 and 01 do not exist in drop frame time). This shortens the code to agree with standard clock time. Editing systems read the bit that identifies drop frame or nondrop frame, allowing it to compute durations and print out a truly frame-accurate edit list.)

With control track editing, each VTR is connected to a "joystick" control device enabling movement of the tape between two VTRs in either direction. After a scene has been recorded on tape, the VTR is placed in joystick mode. The exact frame at which the edit is to be made is located using the joystick, and the VTR is left in still frame position (on hold). Using the joystick with the playback recorder, the exact insert point is found. With both VTRs in still frame, back up both about five seconds, stop them, and then play. Play output VTR until the edit point, then input VTR until the end of the edit. After the audition, repeat and record the entire process. Some decks have variable pre-roll capability, making this process smooth. Everything is fine as long as all units are working! Frame-accuracy is not guaranteed. Anything that interferes with the VTR counting of control track pulses causes a one- to seven-frame error.

The two methods of editing videotape are assemble and insert.

In the *assemble* method, you select and arrange all signal information (control track, video, address track, audio) simultaneously and inseparably. Each edit follows a linear progression attached to the previous cut.

In *insert* editing, the control track signal is already on the tape; audio and video may be edited as separate tracks and inserted at any point in the tape. The postrecording of time code, called *striping,* may be accomplished while recording video in the assemble mode, or later as an audio-only insert on the outside audio track.

Time code editing allows for the use of more machines and therefore for more sophisticated selection and the arrangement with frame-accurate precision. In assemble editing, tapes may be *striped* with time code while recording original footage in the field or while preparing a tape with video black (the recording of a blank signal on the tape). This tape provides:

- A control track to make the tape run at constant speed.
- Time code to allow locating of any frame.
- A video signal reference that enables the system to stabilize (video black or color bars).

Tape that is striped after the video has been recorded loses one audio track to time code unless address track striping is done as part of the video track (only in assemble mode).

An audio insert is not possible because some of the video may be erased. A master video, however, can be assembled with video black and time code on the address track for editing; a dub of the original material can have visual time code *burned in*. This workprint is called a *window dub*. A character inserter (time code reader plus character generator) produces visible time code numbers surrounded by a rectangular box (or "window") separating them from background video.

Editing can be "on-line" or "off-line."

- *On-line editing* refers to the process of manipulating material that is or will become the finished program.
- *Off-line* is the process of editing a copy of the program, usually on 3/4-in tape and then conforming the original to the edited work print. The ability to work off-line came about as a result of computer-controlled time code indexing. (In the earliest days of video editing, every time a sound element was added to the edited program, it had to be re-recorded. Clarity/quality loss was more a function of careless processing/transferring than of producing generations. The current practice of "sound sweetening" involves the separation of discrete tracks to high-quality audio recorders for processing and mixing.)

Window dubs are used only for preliminary off-line editing, which uses 3/4-in or Beta decks. Work tapes are edited and revised until a list of time code numbers, representing the way the master tape is to be assembled, is generated.

The product of on-line editing is the master tape. Once all decisions have been logged, the on-line editing process may be completely automatic. Since the list of edit points has been stored (on tape, paper, or disk), the computer-editor simply calls up each element from the order of the list. In Table 12-2, for example, the columns from left to right are as follows:

TABLE 12-2   Sample edit lists

1	2	3	4	5	6		7		8
01	BL	V1	C		00:00:00:00	00:00:10:00	10:00:00:00	10:00:10:00	NN
002	01	V	C		01:25:02:19	01:25:07:13	10:00:10:00	10:00:14:24	DN
003	02	V	C		05:00:41:09	05:00:44:25	10:00:14:24	10:00:18:10	NN
003	01	V	D	030	01:25:07:13	01:25:14:04	10:00:18:10	10:00:25:01	DN
004	99A	VI	C		18:02:52:17	18:03:17:19	10:00:25:01	10:00:50:01	DN
005	01	VI	C		01:26:04:06	01:26:09:13	10:00:50:01	10:00:55:08	DN
006	02	VI	C		05:00:51:16	05:00:56:23	10:00:50:01	10:00:55:08	NN
006	99A	VI	C		18:03:17:19	18:03:18:24	10:00:55:08	10:00:56:13	DN
006	02	VI	W118	045	05:00:56:23	05:01:03:05	10:00:56:13	10:01:02:25	NN

1. The edit number.
2. The source reel number.
3. The type of signal being recorded (V for video only, V1 or V2 for video with audio 1 or 2).
4. The type of edit being performed (C for cut, D for dissolve, W for wipe, etc.).
5. The length of special transitions measured in frames.
6. The time code numbers for the *in* and *out* points for the source.
7. The *in* and *out* points for the record tape.
8. In autoassembly, a computer-controlled editor follows the numbers.

Time Code Reader/Generators

A typical time code reader/generator provides the following functions:

- Reading time code from a replayed tape.
- Generating original time code.
- Regenerating replayed time code (jam sync).
- Burning in display of characters and time code.
- Generating user bit information.

Since digital time code signals have very fast edges, requiring high frequency response in the time code replay amplifier, it is standard practice to regenerate, not transfer, time code from the camera master to the editing master. This is done by making the source time code signal trigger a local time code generator in sync with the original code (jam sync). If there are gaps in the replayed code, the generator follows the changes in digits.

In multi-VTR edits, it is often necessary to time the length of a shot whose start time code is not zero, or to compare two shots with different code counts. A built-in *offset* generator in the reader/generator unit handles this.

Hybrid generators also act as synchronizers and communications link among VTR editing components. They allow for rapid locate and sync lockup via the very code it reads or generates. They can be used as a *speed-only resolver,* using time code or sync tone inputs as the reference, and they perform an automatic switchover to sync tone input when time code is lost. The system interfaces with professional audio consoles and recorders (such as Ampex, Studer, Sony, Tascam, Mitsubishi) while generating worldwide standard codes (SMPTE, EBU, and film).

For field recording, a number of portable readers/inserters provide monitoring of SMPTE/EBU and control track pulses. These systems may be used for cataloging, reviewing, or preparing tracks for editing.

Audio Sweetening for Video

Sweetening is the upgrading of the location audio track recorded with either a single- or a double-system on location. After transfer with time code to a multitrack recorder, replacement and supplemental audio elements can then be systematically added to each vacant channel.

- *Replacement audio:* The substitution of the edited (multigenerational audio) with the original first generation audio from the master protection copy.
- *Background music:* "Wallpaper" music is timed and recorded. Audio tracks may be laid over this music track, or the music track may be combined with other elements in the mix.
- *Effects music:* Source music, emanating from things seen in the program or music used in fragments for effect, is recorded discretely on separate tracks.
- *Sound effects:* Live and prerecorded natural or artificial sound elements are split off and recorded with time code on several tracks.
- *Voice effects:* Off-camera voice noises and vocal sounds occupy a separate track.
- *Ambiance:* Location background sound and room tone may be run on electronic loops for insertion any place in the program. These elements, such as shopping center ambiance, are recorded separately. Controlled introduction of realistic sound creates a strong sense of authenticity.
- *Applause and laughter:* Crowd reactions, audience cues, and other traditional uses of applause and laugh tracks may be combined on one track to be inserted at specific points in the narrative or nonfiction program to heighten the mood and create a participatory ambiance.

- *Foley effects:* Prerecorded in sync to picture, it occupies a primary track.
- *Automatic dialogue replacement:* Dubbed lines are separated for more accurate blending with original dialogue. The addition of ambiance is critical to the acceptance of the dubbed lines.

Audio for Video Post-Production

Audio for video evolved from the music/variety specials of the late sixties, in which prerecorded music was played back on the set where live vocals were added. Video editing began as a reel-to-reel function, and final edits often went through six generations before a final broadcast with a frequency response out to only 6 kHz. The first improvement was the move to get a first-generation dolby encoded tape from the record company and lay back that onto 1-in video masters. Computers entered the process, allowing soundtracks to be precisely conformed to video and then laid back film-style from the original tapes onto the finished master reel.

Eliminating studio rewinding of tape saves half of the available studio post time. Computer-assisted systems run the consoles, the editors, the synchronizers, the storage media punch-in and punch-out recording, and speeding up recording of sound tracks that constantly change rhythm. A 16-bar click rate changes to 32 bars at another click rate, then back to 16 bars at another. Software-controlled machines simply click to a point and the band records to that point. The machine backs up and counts off however many beats the conductor wants at the new click rate, sets it up so the downbeat corresponds to where the first click left off. This process greatly aided the production of concert movies.

While time code became the standard reference for post-production, it introduced new problems. For one thing, because the pulses are square wave, they tend to get wrecked and lost going through a multitude of systems. Jam-synching requires a clock to hold together the old code and new code (corrected or regenerated due to loss). A 59.95-Hz video sync signal is placed on a separate track to provide a backup should code ever be lost. Standards interchange between machines suffers due to nonstandard head positions in various systems. Split-head two-track machines, like the Nagra T Audio and Studer with the time code in the center, help relieve the problem and allow for keeping machines on pitch while monitoring (A and B tracks) between 24 tracks and the final mix.

As in film, sound post-production for video includes Foley sessions, commercial libraries, and custom libraries (now on disk). The foley actor is, however, fast being replaced by the "sampler operator" who composes effects with samplers, synths, and computers, the fourth wall of sound for video post-production.

Many new tools are available that make even the small sound studio a powerful sound processing and origination bay. MIDI interface opens the gateway to even more options. Two primary production instruments are the Emulator and Synclavier:

- The *Emulator* is a hard disk system allowing quick loading of 30 minutes of sounds, which may be truncated/re-edited and laid back onto tape. It triggers off time code.
- The *Synclavier* allows multichannel effects generation for an entire show without having to dump sections onto tape until the end.

Effects prelays can become a one-person operation with the direct-to-disk option, which allows for the building of effects for an entire show in real time at a 100-k sampling rate then mixed straight to 1-in video masters.

Analog synthesizers like the Prophet, Roland Moog, and ARP are still in demand as unique signature sound generating instruments.

A popular system for effects is a Macintosh computer with thousands of effects on a hard drive, fired by time code using new software like Digidesign's *SMPTEcue* and *Sound Designer* programs. The effects lists on the SMPTEcue are searched, the proper category (office sounds) is *downloaded* by the Macintosh into a recorder, such as an Akai S900, for playback audition. A Technics class CD player may be used for CD library playback. Pitch shifting and other sound manipulation techniques can then be accomplished on a wide range of processing gear.

The Fairlight expandable sound synthesizer systems allow for performance of "dynamic" effects (wind, trains) to picture for fluid, accurate positioning. "Static" canned effects may be sampled and simply laid in. Real-time effects allow complete control of attack, decay, and vibrato for a realistic feel to the sound elements. SMPTE chase/lock provides a setting for structuring musical scores, laying in sound effects, and synchronizing to multitrack tape

TABLE 12-3 Video post sound generation options

- Analog synthesizers.
- Digital synthesizers.
- Conventional reel-to-reel recording to ¼-in tape and time code.
- ¼-in tape library masters loaded to cartridges and locked to video.
- Compact disc.
- PCM-F1 digital field recording to multitrack or "synths."
- Multitrack.
- PCM-F1 digital to Emulator II + EQ + sampling, loaded into Macintosh to truncate, clean, loop, edit.
- Redraw waveforms of original sources (78-rpm record, ¼-in or 3/4-in video, 16-mm magnetic, CD, etc.) on Fairlight with a Sound Designer program.
- Sample an effect from a CD library, then perform it like foley to picture using the Emulator.

and disks. Stereo sampling, waveform editing, and sequencing are other processing options.

A Typical Post-Production Method of Audio for Video

First, begin with a still frame storyboard and an inventory of the sounds needed. Then:

Step 1—Create: Sounds never before created from familiar but unrepeatable acoustic events, such as sounds recorded at the Jet Propulsion Labs, the telephone company switching center, a computer factory. You can:
— Synthesize sound from scratch or process real-time acoustic events.
— Create conventional foley stage effects live or with analog/digital synths.
— Generate sounds with voice, noisemakers, or instruments, and then process.

TABLE 12-4   Examples of customized digital post-production systems

---

System 1

48-input SSL6000s computer-assisted console
Sony Digital multitracks
1-in type C videotape recorder for layback
Adams-Smith sync interlock for all machines in all rooms
Sound effects accessed from compact disc library or Compusonics hard disc based
   workstation
A bank of 8 Magna-Tech dubbers interlocked to the digital multitrack.
Workstation*

Every mono track on a film dubber exceeds a single track on an analog 24-track
   machine by 7.3 dB SN, and 35-mm stock has no printthrough.

System 2

R-DAT rotating-head digital audiotape recorder and workstation* with transport sync,
   confidence listening (read-after-write) and editing (write-after-read).
Uses data compression to write SMPTE/EBU time code within the subcode area above
   and below the encoded audio on each track (1/4-in) without conflicts.
R-DAT original is transferred digital-to-digital to a workstation or open-reel recorders
   for processing.

System 3

Pro Digi Mitsubishi and Otari recorders (32- and 16-track).
Neve Necam 96 automated console.
Synclavier with Harrison Raven Console.
Sony MCI 628 for video sweetening.

---

*Some digital computer-based workstations are: AMS Audiophile, Audio + Design Sound-
maestro, Digital Audio Research Soundstation II, Fairlight Series III, Lexicon Opus, Solid
State Logic Digital Production Center, Synclavier, Audioframe.

Step 2—Electronic sound assembly: Set up a basic *edit bay* made up of two videocassette decks, a controller, a synchronizer, a multitrack deck, a mixer, a master recorder (Ampex 16 track 2-in tape recorder).

Step 3—Save and store: Keep elements and edits in an audio library that is slaved to the VTR. Tracks are staggered to avoid crosstalk vis-a-vis an arrangement like this: 3-4, 7, 8, 10, 14, 15 open, 16 (SMPTE CODE).

Step 4—Assign a zero point: With a zero point assigned for the program:

—Assemble according to the edit list time code numbers, which are punched in, triggering the automatic loading of elements to edit points.

—*Crawl and fly:* Incrementally controlled variable speed positioning allows minute speed changes to visuals.

—Play back to video and compose on-the-spot via analog synths (Moog, Prophet) or digital synths (Synclavier, Fairlight).

—Edit with the computer and hard disk (such as the Atari 800, which can offer four sound registers via a sound chip with amplitude, velocity, frequency modulation). The computer *logs and sorts* according to (1) sound name, (2) number, (3) category, (4) reel number, (5) track number, (6) clock number, and (7) visual reference.

Step 5—Layback: Lay back the master tracks to 1-in videotape. Off-line/on-line edits and sweetening are creative as well as organizational processes. (See Figure 12-3.)

Sample Audio-for-Video Post-Production Techniques

POST-PRODUCTION MUSIC EDITING AND SOUND CONTINUITY

• Live audio is recorded on location on a mobile truck.

• The automated audio processing system allows the signal to be as loud as necessary without hazard of overmodulation.

• The signal passes to a pair of Ampex 24 track recorders with Dolby NR on each channel. Recording is done at 30 ips.

• A ¼-in machine is used to record a reference *monomix.*

• SMPTE time code is recorded on a separate track on the 24-track deck.

• The time code readout is slated visually from clocks to film camera.

• Btx time code readers are used to synchronize mixdowns onto two multitrack recorders interlocked to a 3/4-in VCR.

• A 24-track master is relayed in sync via time code to VCR.

• To add *inserts* of sound takes recorded on different days, locate the cut point on video and enter the code numbers into the synchronizer. A second tape track is manually synched to the VTR. The synchronizer automatically calculates the offset between the two time codes and keeps new audio and new code in sync with old pic and its code.

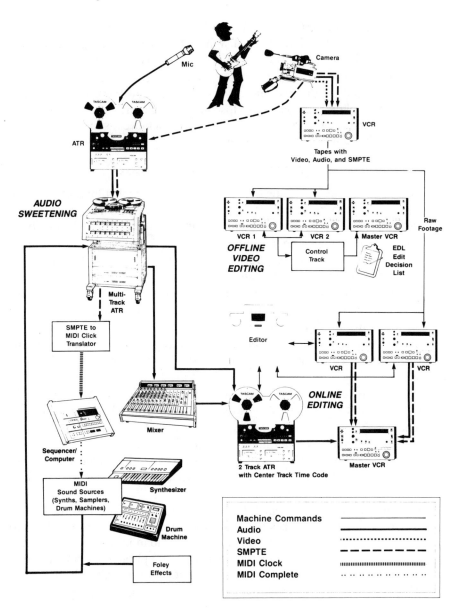

Figure 12-3 MIDI interface allows for the connection of instruments and effects generators to a standard multitrack recorder or VTR via a mixer. (Courtesy TEAC)

INCREASING EDITING SPEED TO MODIFY TRACKS

- The original recordings are made at 30 ips for best fidelity.
- Play them back at normal speed.
- Time code is fed to a ¼-in machine running at 7½ ips.

- The master tape is then played at 15 ips and time code re-recorded onto the master on an unused channel. When the master tape is played back at the normal 30 ips, the time code is twice as fast.

- During editing, the 1/4-in tape with code at 7 1/2 ips is played back at 15 ips and used as the master to sync up the multitrack recorder. The multitrack plays back only at 15 ips and is in sync with all other machines linked with the synchronizer. Therefore, you achieve faster recording and speed with slower precise editing rates.

1/4-IN OR 16/35-MM MAGNETIC FILM TO VIDEO TRANSFER

- Nagra 1/4-in sync is transferred to 16/35-mm magnetic film and edited to picture. Sync sound effects are transferred to 16/35-mm mag and edited to picture. Selected music is fed by the same route and edited to picture.

- As many as ten elements are assembled into a *dirty mix* and used as a reference. Picture and reference mix are transferred to 1-in VTR for assembly to the *composite master.*

- Ten sound elements are also transferred discretely (track by track) onto a 24-track recorder, along with pilot tone; then the tape is resolved and striped with SMPTE time code.

- The master 1-in VTR is assembled with other studio tape sources (carts, disks, etc.). Audio is *laid over* to another 24-track machine with time code.

- Film sound 24-track is synced with the composite master 24-track machine using the 24-track dirty mix as reference for checking *lip sync.*

- The results are a 24-track *tape* with *film* sound, composite dialogue, a guide track, and SMPTE time code, which can be run in sync with a 3/4-in cassette workprint. More music and effects may be added to left-over track areas on the 24-track tape. Each track is equalized and processed for balance and tonal clarity.

- Mix music and effects, which have been separated onto two tracks and which can then be run back to make corrections. Shuttle back and forth to find edit spots. Either *punch-in on the fly,* or load in time code numbers and have the machine go into record mode. An option is to load time code numbers to roll a given effect or music cue from the cartridge or 1/4-in.

- Then lay back the 24-track to the 1-in VTR master with Dolby.

THE MIX

Understood primarily as an operating room for saving, blending, and positioning audio tracks, the mixing process is discussed in terms of creative options. The roles and talent of the mixer are expressed in terms of quality control and poetic juxtaposition of sound data. The functions of the mix console are diagrammed and explained as a step-by-step combination of many tracks into one master. A sample mix and instructions on how to create it are presented. The practical aspects of setting levels, compression, balance, layering, and transitions are discussed as principal functions of the mix. Both the directorial and the technical options are detailed to suggest ways of saving valuable time in the mix.

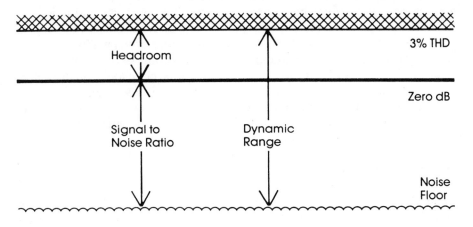

Mixing is the combining and blending of many sound tracks into one master soundtrack. The final composite track is recorded on 35-mm fullcoat magnetic film and a 1/4-in protection copy is made. Understood primarily as an operating room for saving tracks, mixing provides more opportunities for creative alteration of the narrative than any other process. The craft of the mixer can make or break the program. Mixing can create the kind of multidimensional experience that converts sound into a strong narrative element. Yet the role of the mixer has incorrectly been defined in terms of quality control. As we can see, the process is more than merely "cleaning up" mistakes and noise.

However, one cannot lose sight of the fact that the mix is also the stage in which the soundtrack is conformed to the limitations of the exhibition space. While acoustically the mixing studio is the ideal screening space for the program being mixed, the average theatre does not even come close to the quality of this space. Somehow the mixer must find a happy technical median between the best and worst of all possible playback systems, one that also accommodates the very real limitations of the broadcast airways and home video centers.

The Mixing Process

Dialogue is worked on first, with music and effects more or less being "conformed" to preserving the intelligibility of the dialogue. If anything is going to be sacrificed in terms of fidelity, it will be effects, then music.

The Mixing Console

The mixing console controls the machine room playback machines, the recorder, and the high-speed projector. Before the advent of high-speed systems, much time was consumed by real-time rewinding after every rehearsal prior to recording. The recording is done in discrete bits and pieces, one shot or one segment of a shot at a time. The specific segment being mixed is then auditioned against the shots before and after it to obtain a perspective on how well it is integrated into the whole composition.

The consoles through which prepared tracks are mixed are now computer-assisted with memory features that allow for repeatability and greater

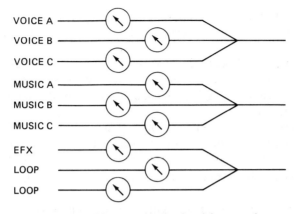

Figure 13-1   Diagram of a simple mixing console.

control of multiple functions. Each input has filter networks, equalization, and reverb. A schematic diagram of the simplest kind of mixing console is shown in Figure 13-1.

The *component functions of a console* are as follows:

- *Channel:* An electronic signal path that is assigned a specific sound element. The track layout on the "dubbers" should match the channel assignments on the board. The board layout should be basically the same in terms of how elements are grouped for each 10-min reel to be mixed. Channels flow to busses.

TABLE 13-1   Why audio must be better

1975	PBS introduced satellite program distribution with 15-kHz audio bandwidth.
1978	Cable invests in higher-quality sound gear for broad-based satellite distribution.
1980	MTV went on air with stereo TV.
1984	FCC establishes a de facto stereo TV standard.
1988	CBS broadcasts all prime time in stereo.
1988	Super VHS enters home video with higher-fidelity playback.
1988	Cineplex-Odeon begins renovation of 1500 theatres in the United States.
1988	Dolby introduces spectral recording.
1988	Direct-to-disk (tapeless) recording available.

TABLE 13-2   What the mix/mixer/mixing console must have

Lightness	Logical and clear configuration.
Quickness	Easy control of all inputs and functions.
Exactitude	Precise calibrations and specifications.
Visibility	Easy-to-learn color coding.
Multiplicity	Capability of extending to external units and new technologies.
Consistency	Ruggedness, reliability, repeatable quality.

- *Buss:* A summed signal path that usually begins with feeds from channels and ends in output connectors. They also pass their signals to other busses:
  —The *master buss* conforms to the final program configuration—mono, stereo, 3-track, 6-track, etc.—and is considered a program buss.
  —A *mono buss* is a single path used primarily for the main house speaker or stage monitor.
  —A *stereo buss* is a 2-buss system that keeps left/right information separated (split) for monitoring the stereo image for broadcast stereo or stereo dolby magnetic and optical release formats in film.

- *Submixers:* Mix systems within the mixer console that perform three tasks:
  —*Auxiliary:* Takes channel signal, sums into mono or stereo Aux Buss, sends buss signal to Aux output used for effects mixes, monitor mixes, Cue or Foldback mixes.
  —*Effects submixer:* Used with external effects devices with *effects returns* that bring processed signals back to the mixer.
  —*Monitor:* Audition and evaluation submixer.

- *Faders:* Sliding pan/pot program level adjustments that control:
  —*Channel fader:* The level of the signal-to-mix buss.
  —*Group fader:* The level fed to recorder tracks and meters.
  —*Monitor fader:* Provides independent mix to machine room for the required recording level (not the listening level).
  Faders cause loss to control the signal level, and some add noise. Some systems use voltage-controlled amps, so that no audio ever passes through the fader, but the signal may be boosted or cut at the input level.

- *Pan pots:* Position the input channel signal between any odd/even combination of subgroups and may be used simultaneously to position within the stereo panorama between left/right stereo outputs. Often they control two faders that are wired back-to-back, rotating fades up one and fades down the other simultaneously; at center, each is not quite off and is still reducing the signal slightly so that the signal transition thru the center does not get louder as one pans through it. Positions may be fixed at stereo or mono, left or right.

- *Equalizer (EQ):* Controls boost or cut portions of the audio spectrum. The in/out switch allows for the quiet comparison of program with and without EQ. Normally a three-band parametric system works on high, midrange, and low, left and right input channels. The average boost/cut maximum is 12 dB shelving at 100-Hz and 10-kHz positions. Midrange sweep frequency and dip-type are active from 300 Hz to 6 kHz. In center "detent" position, EQ is usually out of circuit. In a dual piggyback design, the top selects band, and the bottom selects level of cut or boost.

- *Echo send/return:* Derived from composite of left/right signals in stereo boards sent to external echo, reverb, or effects signal processor unit. Each send may be reprogrammed to the *prefade* position. The return button sends the processed signal back to a combination of two program busses and two audition busses with level control at the input and mixed with the original signal. This delay can be created in several ways:

—*Fed to actual room:* A fixed reverberation time created by feeding to a loudspeaker at one end of a room and recording with a microphone at other end. (See Figure 13-2.)

—*Variable reverb time created by reverberation plate.* (See Figure 13-3.)

—*Tape delay:* Running across a series of heads via a tape loop. (See Figure 13-4.)

—*Digital delay:* Via assigned timing codes. Delay may be varied from microseconds to 4–5 sec. Some computer-controlled systems have as many as 19 delay elements that can add colorless reverb, 10-sec "space" effects, "chorus" group impressions. Some processors synthesize actual room ambiance in stereo with internal mix amps and decay con-

1. AN ACTUAL ROOM (FIXED REVERBERATION TIME)

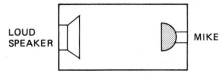

ROOM DELAY

Figure 13-2 Room delay can be accomplished by recording in an empty room from a speaker input.

2. REVERBERATION PLATE (VARIABLE REVERB TIME)

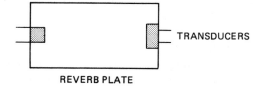

REVERB PLATE

Figure 13-3 With a "reverberation plate," a transducer picks up the delayed signal from the edge of the plate.

Figure 13-4 In a tape delay, magnetic tape passes over a series of mag heads, one of which punches in at the desired delay interval.

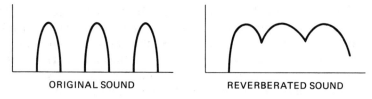

ORIGINAL SOUND   REVERBERATED SOUND

Figure 13-5 Comparison of original and delayed signals.

trols; these create the illusion of a new or similar space where on-location recording cannot be matched or balanced for voice or music. (See Figure 13-5.)

- *Input pad* (*trim*): A 20-dB attenuator prevents overloading from high-output devices or loud signals.
- *Mute:* Allows muting of postfader functions of input channel including channel output, Aux output, effects output, subassign, L/R stereo assign.
- *Solo:* Sends a postfader, post-EQ signal to monitor the buss for individual audition of each input.
- *Monitor:* The master control sets the overall output level derived from the input channel monitor sends.
  —*Monitor cue:* Provides foldback of the monitor mix (composite signals) so that a musician or narrator may hear sync tracks while overdubbing.
  —*Control room monitor:* Gets the signal from headphone mix and studio selector (left/right).
  —*Studio monitor:* Selects stereo program busses, mono Aux input, stereo Aux input, or stereo audition buss, and sends to left and right output jacks (to studio speakers).
- *Talkback:* Allows for communication with machine room via a built-in microphone in board. Also provides a verbal slate for each channel or track. The mixer may also speak through studio speakers.

Many personal computer workstations now feature program software that provides for digital manipulation of the waveform with commands centered around a simulated mix panel display on the PC monitor. (See Figure 13-6.)

The Computer Command Module: Computer-Assisted Sound Mixing Functions

A computer memory can greatly aid the mixer in recalling all previous control movements on the board, thereby enhancing manual dexterity when balancing complex inputs to a 3-track master mixdown. (See Table 13-3.) Considering

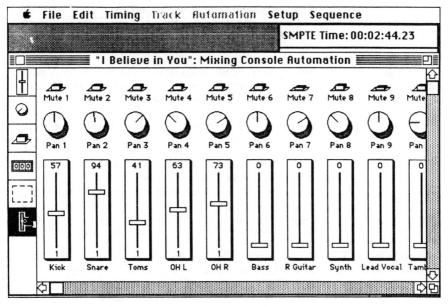

Figure 13-6 PC mix display software by DigiDesign.

that many features begin with over 100 discrete tracks, the system for film and video postproduction appears invaluable. The principle of a typical computer-assisted dubbing system (Necam) is to memorize fader levels and channel mutes, then repeat these movements and positions in frame-accurate synchronization with picture and sound. This not only allows for quick audition, instant replay, and recording, but it also allows the mixer to go back to that section to remix or duplicate the settings in a future scene without having to guess at the approximate settings.

These time-saving features provide a gradual increase in the number and quality of functions a mixer can handle. Consider what it would be like to go back—after spending days mixing 64 tracks down to the individual 3-track master—to make a last-minute change in the editing of picture, relying only on your log and memory for the related adjustments or modifications! Since this is common on most feature-length films, having all those creative decisions on a floppy disk is critical.

Some functions include:

- Manual override of the memory controls at any time to make changes during the mix.
- The fast autolocator facility to control the synchronized recording machines, using simple numbered location points that are identified by the mixer and adjusted in real time.

TABLE 13-3   Computer-assisted mix functions

Mix list	Contains the names of all complete and partial mixes, updates, and trims. All may be updated. Because all faders in the trim mode are automatically "nulled" no matter what their positions, most updates can be written simply by listening to a mix play-back and instinctively making moves as the inspiration moves you. Earlier mixes are protected during updating and may be compared.
Advanced update	While refining mixes, it may be useful to place some channels in the absolute and others in the trim, or isolate, mode. Per-haps you may want to rewrite fader levels on some tracks and only change cuts on others. A fourth fader status, auto take-over, enables you to trim a level during part of a pass and re-turn exactly to its previously stored level at a precise point without stopping the tape.
Mix editing	Partial mixes may be joined together and "inserted" into longer mixes. Specific sections of any past mix may be inserted into the current mix.
Rollback and preview function	Permits rollback of all tape machines and the mix data simul-taneously, allowing pick-up recording to be performed automat-ically within the computer. As the entire mix assembly takes place within the computer, the final mix layback to video can be first-generation.
Total recall opera-tions	All settings are stored in a set-up list. Displays provide an in-teractive real-time comparison showing all differences between the way the console was set up and the way it is now set up. Detail displays provide, for instance, comparisons of all gate settings for one channel. Minor revisions can be made at a later date since the instant recall allows for quick set-up on another scheduled worksession, and the total recall system is completely independent of the audio signal path.
Dynamic mixing sys-tem	There are three basic fader statuses: —*Absolute:* All fader moves are written exactly as performed. —*Trim:* Previously stored fader moves are updated by using the fader to trim their gain patterns up or down. —*Isolate:* The fader may be used to monitor a track but is iso-lated from the computer. Additional statuses permit channel and group cuts to be written separately from fader movements so that the system may be preprogrammed to automatically switch all channels on and off as needed. Fader values may be written separately from cuts.
Basic updating func-tions	Once one is happy with the mix, it is filed on the production disc. In trim status, the computer plays back the original mix and simultaneously copies it into a temporary update file ex-actly, until a fader is moved. If and only if a fader is moved, its previously stored value is altered. The trims are summed with the original values, and the result is heard on the monitors and stored in the update file.
Events controller	Provides electronic manipulation of cues for all playback ma-chines interlocked to the console (cartridge, ¼-in, cassette, etc.).
On-line events control	Facilitates the control during broadcast of reel and cart ma-chines for prelays to be run against master production dialogue tracks.

TABLE 13-3 (continued)

Off-line revision of events timing	The timing of events entered on line may be adjusted frame by frame (electronic editing of cues).
Events control mixing applications	Moving or replacing an effect. The effect may be dubbed off a multitrack onto ¼-in tape or derived from an original source tape. The new cue is placed on a machine under events control with new start and stop times entered into the events list. This machine may then be activated in conjunction with the drop-in program to automatically replace previous cues on the multitrack. This eliminates the physical removal, editing, and reloading of sprocketed track.
Preset	A preset is a map of the channel, group fader levels, and cut settings at a given time. Transitions between presets may be entered as hard cuts or crossfades as short as a single frame. Presets may be edited into the sequence list as often as necessary. Transition and crossfade times may be changed frame by frame. Each sequence list can store up to 100 presets and 128 events.

- Spot sound effects automatically triggered by "event triggers" at specific SMPTE time code or film frame counts for rapid insertion into the mix.
- Placement at any time of the physical position of the faders in memory and their instant reproduction. Correct sound levels are assured through every repeat.
- Dynamic recording of movements of the faders in exact sync with the sound tracks. On replay, updates are possible via simple manual override. Faders can be grouped so that moving one controls several other channels. All effects channels, for instance, can be controlled after presets by one fader and repeated.
- Storage of hundreds of attempts at mixing a sequence, in addition to their being named, listed, recalled, and compared to determine the best settings of a group. This audition feature greatly expands the creative possibilities by freeing the mixer from the tedium of mechanically resetting and rewinding each attempt while trying to remember every position (using pieces of tape on fader marks).
- Combining the chosen sections of two or more dubbing sequence mix attempts using a merge facility to give optimum balance.
- Other controllable functions, such as pan pots, graphic equalizers, and delay times on a digital echo unit.

The Principal Functions of the Mix

The following are the chief functions of mixing in their order of importance:

1. Compression of the dynamic range.
2. Balance of levels within each track.

3. Enhancing speech through equalization and filtering.

4. Layering or balancing of tracks against/over each other.

5. Creating perspective or positioning sound in the field.

6. Creating transitions between elements of sound data.

7. Adding more effects or music elements.

8. Eliminating noise.

The first six functions are discussed in this chapter; the last two are not because they are explained elsewhere in the book.

Compression

The playback medium cannot reproduce the range or depth of amplitudes that may have been recorded and preserved throughout other stages of the audio design process. Because the ear can more readily accept a uniform change in levels across the frequency spectrum, an attempt is made to preserve and retain the pattern of frequencies while redistributing the energy levels uniformly across a given spectrum. (See Figure 13-7.)

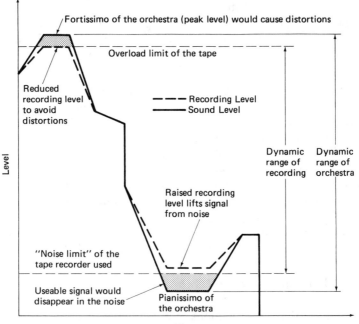

Figure 13-7   Compression of dynamic range for tape recording.

ISSUES

- How do you determine the correct compression ratio to use?
- How do you set up the levels and threshold of compression?
- When is slow attack time better than fast?
- Are there any guidelines to setting release time other than by ear?
- What can de-essing really achieve?

A compressor technique is very subjective. Each situation is different and good judgement is only a function of listening and experience. The following guidelines are relative, but they provide a valid structure from which to make specific alterations for unique problems.

Compression ratio.   A 2-to-1 ratio means that for every 2 dB of level increase, the result is only a 1-dB increase after compression. This is a very mild effect that is extremely "inaudible" and usable over a very wide spectrum (dynamic range of 4 dB). It is probably a good ratio for people who really don't want to use a compressor in situations where the program material has such a wide dynamic range that it will not "fit" on tape with signal-to-noise problems. A 2-to-1 ratio is quite often used for voice and is very useful for piano and similar instruments where peak levels are much higher than average levels.

A 4-to-1 ratio means that for every 4 dB of level increase, the result after compression is a 1-dB increase. This most popular ratio does not give the sound of a "limiter" but is excellent for singing and tape-to-tape transfers. 4-to-1 is used for subjective compression to permit recording a wide dynamic range without exceeding the limits of recording equipment and without a noticeable change in the upper end of the range. A higher ratio limiter prevents a vocalist from overloading a tape machine, but it also causes a noticeable loss of dynamic range at the levels above threshold.

Setting levels and threshold (compression).   Set the input level control to achieve about +4-dBm output or higher with the compression control maximum counterclockwise. With the GR button *in,* advance the compression control clockwise to achieve the desired gain reduction. Then, as program material changes level, you can use the input control to "trim up." Now judgement prevails! (See Figure 13-8.)

The GR button can be used to compare compression with no compression. Output noise is constant and does not change with any settings at 86 to 91 dBm.

In the 4-to-1 ratio, operation with much of the program is achieved below threshold where compression occurs only at the higher-level passages. Some of the lower-level passages may be brought up as well as compressing the higher passages down.

In the 2-to-1 ratio, most of the program material should be well above

Figure 13-8 Compression-filtering module from a Solid-State Logic mix console.

threshold. You see quite a bit of VU meter deflection with less noticeable audible effect.

Attack time control. This is probably the least understood but most important control for achieving "unhearable" compression. With high ratio (12-to-1, 20-to-1) limiters, fast attack times are necessary to prevent any unlimited material from overloading the amplifier or output circuitry, since the unlimited material is considerably higher than the limited level. This results in a complete loss of transient dynamic range. This is the cause of the familiar "constricted sound" of most limiters.

Now consider that we have only two ratios to work with, 2-to-1 and 4-to-1. If we deliberately slow down the attack time, we allow some transients to "leak through" at the uncompressed level. Since the uncompressed level is not extremely higher than the compressed level, these transients do not overload the amplifier or output circuitry, but they do recreate a more natural relationship of peak material versus average power level material. Hence no *constricted sound.*

If you set up your compression with fast attack time and then "back off" on the attack control, you hear all the transient dynamics return, but the VU meters (average power level) remain compressed.

Release control.   The subjective use of the release control needs little explanation. The only precaution required is to avoid extremely fast release times on low-frequency program material. The low-frequency effect causes an increase in distortion at low audio frequencies, notably below 100 Hz due to ripple in the control voltage. This causes the compressor to attack each cycle individually, and not compress the signal as a whole. At 50 Hz, with the compressor on fast attack and fast release with 10 dB of gain reduction, THD can be as high as 6% due to this effect.

Another precaution when using any compressor with fast release times is that the unit responds faster than the meter indicates.

The minimum release time is intentionally calibrated to 100 ms for music recording. If shorter release times (25 ms, 50 ms) are desired for dialogue recording, strap pin 5 to pin 1 (in the Quad Eight Auto Mix).

The use of too slow release times causes level dips in the program. When using the de-esser feature, always use the fastest release time.

De-essing feature.   Sibilance ("sss" sounds) never occur at the same time as vocal sounds. The compressor is set up for *fast release,* and the de-essing circuit boosts the high-frequency response of the control amplifier. Thus, the compressor now responds to high frequencies more than others. This is sufficient to cause the gain reduction to occur only on the "ess" sounds, and then release quickly enough for the vocal sounds to be unaffected.

Good control of sibilance requires the use of a rotary selector switch with the different capacitor values as a "curve selector." The level of the "esses" can then be controlled independent of the vocal sounds. For example, the distracting effect of vocal esses on echo chambers may be eliminated, permitting more high frequency equalization of the vocal chain.

Balance of Levels

Program material is usually transferred "flat" but with some care to amplify or demodulate any segments that fall outside the dynamic range of the tape medium. Suffice to say that before any other actions can occur in the mix, extremely low or loud sounds must be adjusted in relation to other sound in the section and in relation to other sounds in proximate shots, and from scene to scene.

Enhancing Speech

Motion picture release prints have a narrower frequency range than certain other types of sound recording or transmission. They do not, however, have to "sound" as if they haven't a wide bandwidth. During the master mix, the frequency response range is limited with sharp cutoff filters to the range of playback systems. Within this range the tonal balance is equalized to produce the best compromise between intelligibility and *naturalness*.

A typical optical track has a crisp, undistorted response from about 60 to 8,000 Hz on color positive and black and white positive and negative, 80–6,000 Hz on color reversal stock, and 50–8,000 Hz on 35-mm color.

Equalization alters harmonic structure. A change between 1 dB to 3 dB is not perceived. Therefore, no *large* changes are made. Each track should not have similar changes occurring at similar frequencies. That bias ultimately reduces intelligibility and increases the hazard of masking effects of high frequencies. (See Figure 13-9.) In a given element, the absence of frequencies below 600 Hz causes poor articulation of vowels, while absences above 600 Hz produce poor transmission of consonants. Equalization within the range of 400–2,000 Hz is more noticeable than outside that range.

Layering and Blending

To blend tracks, the mixer must be careful to select the proper general level for classes of similar sound elements. Since voice should dominate, music and effects are recorded one to two times down from the level of voice. Since *masking* (two similar frequencies residing at equal levels) may occur anywhere, adjustments of a nonuniform nature must be made to avoid cancellation or muddy articulation. The psychoacoustic effect called *masking* can also be used to hide unwanted noise. The mixer may find a frequency close to a noise element's frequency and match levels, thus making it more difficult to distinguish the noise. (See Figure 13-10.)

Positioning and Perspective

When one considers the structural uses of sound, the most easily created element in the mix is space, whether screen or off-screen space. The manipulation of faders (see Figure 13-10) alone is sufficient to give an elemental sense of position and depth. All that is required is a sensitivity to the relationships of *pitch to distance,* and of *intensity to duration*—an understanding of the Doppler effect.

Audiences generally read a low-level sound as emanating from a distant source if the source is not visibly in the field of view. Creating an imbalance in levels often displaces the viewer into a new position in relation to the scene. This can often be confusing if the visual data contradicts the aural. Positioning

Figure 13-9 Equalization module for the SSL board. 4-band equalization: HF 1.5 to 16 kHz; HMF 1.5 to 7 kHz; LMF 0.2 to 2.5 kHz; LF 30 to 450 Hz. Low- and high-pass filters attack at HMF and LMF groups.

can become a tedium of trial and error. Codes of perspective must be given to the viewer through the discrete modification of particular frequencies that hint at the location of sound sources.

Furthermore, contradictions between aural and visual data may indicate an *emotional perspective*. This must be further reinforced with repetition and juxtaposition with a stated sonic reference that makes it clear how the change in perspective on the track represents a change in mood, state of being, characterization, or time.

Imagine the sound of water dripping played back at a high level while the dripping water spout is seen in the distance. The physical contradiction suggests that something other than strict continuity is at work. The job of the mixer/designer is to make this contrast work and serve a narrative function. The

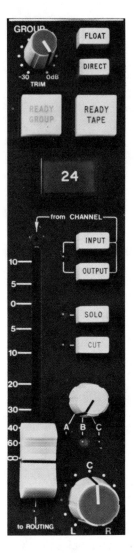

Figure 13-10   Fader and trim group modules: A pan control would allow the mono microphone signal to be positioned anywhere within the stereo panorama.

meaning of this aural contrast is defined the second time the pattern is heard in, perhaps, a new context. If it is not repeated narratively, the mixer must trust in the imaginative capacity of the viewer.

Creating Transitions

Not only is it necessary to separate and establish sound elements as articulate entities that tell a story, but it is also critical to create *sonic crossover* from sound to sound and from shot to shot. These transitions must be made perceptible (so that it is clear that a spacial-emotional change occurs) or imperceptible (so that it is clear that no narrative change has occurred).

Manipulation of the board faders and equalization-plus-reverberation can produce four types of transitions:

1. *Segue:* A sharp break from the last element directly to the next without concern for the disparity of levels, quality, tonality. This makes the visual cut very noticeable. Likewise, a spacial/sonic change is very apparent. This implies a time elipsis.
2. *Fade-out:* A gradual diminishing of the signal. If the transition is rapid, a short time change is implied. If it is long, a jump in time is suggested that may be definite or indefinite, within the location, or transferred to a new location. Duration may also imply simultaneous action—events occurring together at the same time in different places.
3. *Fade-up:* An increase in level from silence to audibility implies time changes similar to the fade-out.
4. *Crossfade:* Overlapping of the fade-out and fade-in (also known as fade-down and fade-up) while maintaining a balance of level to background by never traveling through the whole range of the fader. This transition can be definite (giving a measurable or "felt" sense of time movement) or indefinite (implying a leap in time), and this compression can be either forward or back in time.

Edit Point Match

Since sound travels slower than light, it is possible psychoacoustically for the experience of the screened image to be out of sync with sound when auditioned in the ideal situation of the mixing room. The elements may be in editorial sync, but the *experience* may be asynchronous (especially for people with perfect pitch). The mixer must reposition some sync points by advancing or retarding the sound several frames in order to make up for time delay phenomenon in the theatre. The projected image is reflected back from the screen to the viewer at 186,000 mi/sec while the sound reaches the speaker system in electrical form at about half the speed of light. Translated into physical soundwaves, the aural image is dispersed within the theatre at 1,127 ft/sec. If someone is seated at the center of the theatre audience 47 ft from the speaker system, a 1/24-sec head start must be given the sound. If the average patron is seated 94 ft away, another frame advance is required for things to "seem" in sync!

Mix Modules

The audio sweetening console has evolved into a highly sophisticated processor of sound data. Modular design allows for the addition of many basic units. (See Figure 13-11.) Many boards are now computerized, as the Neve and Solid State

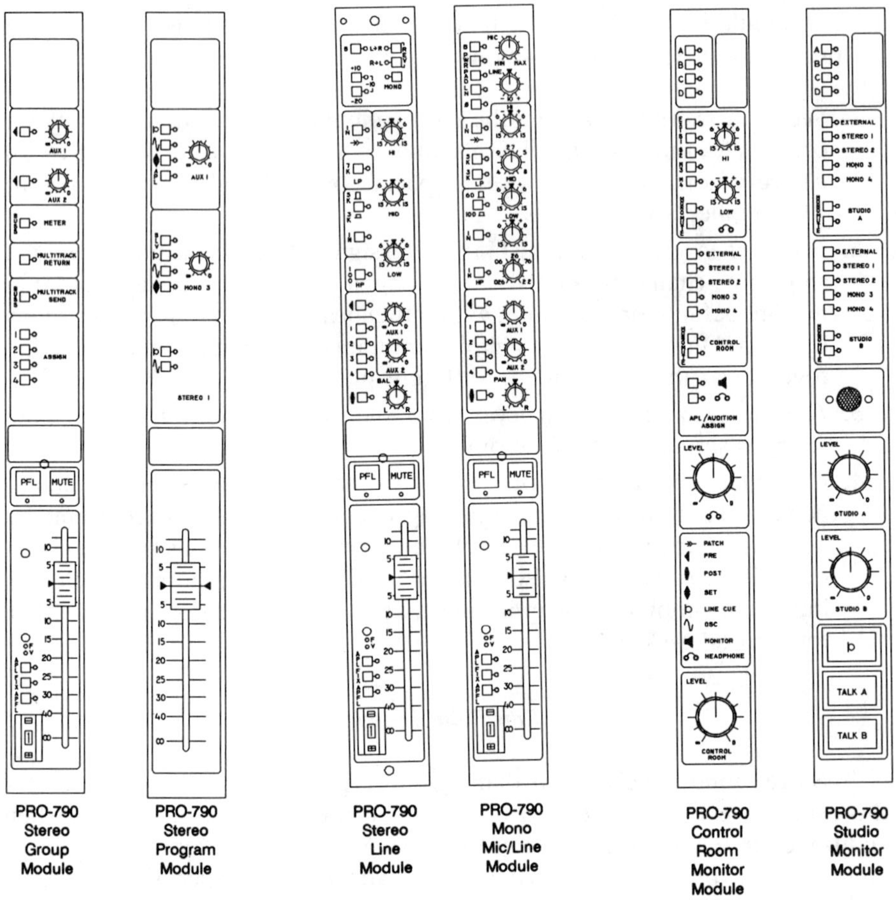

| PRO-790 Stereo Group Module | PRO-790 Stereo Program Module | PRO-790 Stereo Line Module | PRO-790 Mono Mic/Line Module | PRO-790 Control Room Monitor Module | PRO-790 Studio Monitor Module |

Figure 13-11   Modular units from an audio sweetening console.

Logic boards, which feature a fully programmable central command module and attendant functions.

Some of these additional units are:

- *Stereo line module:* Used to assign inputs and provide trim of line level. The sample shown in Figure 13-12 from a Harrison Board also links the EQ patch to this stage.

- *Mono mic/line module:* Accomplishes the same functions of organization as the stereo. Pan control moves mono into stereo format. The Aux level control sends a sample of the input signal to external processing units (reverb, digital delay, de-ess, etc.). The line input may accommodate other audio sources (MIDI gear, recorders, cartridge machine libraries, etc.).

- *Stereo and mono group modules:* Provide access to multitrack recorder send/return, as well as console output monitoring.
- *Stereo program module:* Implements level control over primary stereo output; also allows talkback (line cue) functions.
- *Control room monitor module:* Loudspeakers and headphones are fed stereo data for monitoring through this stage. Levels and mute control with meter display are selectable.
- *Studio monitor module:* Requires external power amps but sends stereo data to external studio speaker/monitors; contains talkback circuit for communication to machine room and elsewhere.

Preparation for the Mix

Mix Spaces

There are basically two schools of thought on the "ideal" mix space—old and new.

The old mixing studio at MGM has been in continuous use for more than 40 years. Very few physical changes have been made to the basic room, which is

Figure 13-12 (A) SSL 4000G computer-assisted console. (B) Computer command module of Solid State Logic Series 6000. (C) Advanced locating functions of an SSL board.

The Computer Command Module

The various Lists are entered via the Computer Command Module. This module includes the Computer Master Status buttons which allow the system to access the master machine synchroniser, transport controls and record bus. Buttons are also provided to place the system in Automated Mix mode, control the fader automation master status, and switch between large and small timecode displays.

The Command module also includes an alphanumeric keyboard and a field containing 33 dedicated keys with a single word engraved on each button. These dedicated buttons are the keys to the simplicity of the SSL Studio Computer. Using them, the engineer constructs common-sense English phrases and sentences which tell the computer what to do.

For example, with the tape parked at the top of the reel, ready to record prelays for a documentary segment, the engineer keys in the sentence NAME TITLE **Scandals In High Places** EXECUTE (The EXECUTE key tells the computer to carry out your command.)
The computer notes the Title's name and starting tape location, then enters both into the Title List. When the length of the segment is determined, the engineer positions the tape at the end of the segment and keys in the phrase TITLE TO HERE EXECUTE.
This instructs the computer to append the end time to the list.

The Computer Command Module also incorporates a set of transport controls for the master machine. These provide parallel manual and computer control over the master and slave machines, permitting advanced features such as the ability to perform rollbacks and pick-ups within the automation system. This feature is detailed in the section on Post-Production applications.

Figure 13-12 (continued)

Advanced Locating Functions

Title "From" and "To" times, and Cue "At" times, are displayed above in SMPTE timecode, but may also be entered in 16 or 35mm foot/frames and freely converted between standards. You can also ask the computer to calculate and display the length of time between any two Cues or other location points.

The SSL allows Titles, Cues and time values to be freely intermixed within command lines, allowing the engineer to instruct the computer without having to think like a computer. Commands such as [CYCLE] [TITLE] [EXECUTE], [PLAY] [CUE] 7 [EXECUTE], [GO TO] 18:36.02 [EXECUTE] or [PLAY] [FROM] [HERE] [TO] [CUE] John Exits [EXECUTE] provide only the basic vocabulary of the system.

More elaborate commands such as [CYCLE] [FROM] [CUE] G + 0:07.12 [TO] [END] [TITLE] −0:03.21 [EXECUTE] may also be used if the engineer finds them useful. The SSL will instantly calculate the timecode values of Cue G and the end of the Title, perform the requested math, locate to the first point specified, play to the second point, and repeat the cycle until you tell it otherwise. It will even display the calculated time values on the screen, so that the engineer can name these as Cues and avoid that particularly long command line subsequently. A REPEAT key is also provided which repeats the last command to the computer, thus minimising keystrokes still further.

Programming Drop-Ins

To simplify prelays, dialogue splitting and other insert recording, the computer may be given control of the master record bus. Drop-ins can be rehearsed while the tape is rolling, or they may be entered off-line.

When the tape is rolling, the command [DROP-IN] [EXECUTE] names the Record In time; the Record Out time is entered by pressing the [EXECUTE] key a second time. To enter Record In and Out times off-line, the command structure is [DROP-IN] [FROM] I [TO] O [EXECUTE], where "I" is the frame at which the insert recording is to commence, and "O" is the frame at which the machine is to drop out of record. These values can be entered as timecodes or using previously stored Cues, as in the command line [DROP-IN] [FROM] Police Sirens [TO] Lady Di Waves [EXECUTE].

Figure 13-12 (continued)

---

a large, full-sized 1950s-style theatre with a large screen (over 50 ft wide), and more than 20 speaker clusters surrounding the room. Behind the screen are interspersed hard and soft surfaces, cantilevered walls that can be angled, isolated air conditioning vents, and an overall "average" theatre ambiance, neither too dead nor too live.

The new ideal mix space appears to lean toward rooms with very few if any reflections. This *LEDE* concept (live end, dead end), pioneered by Chips Davis, postures an anechoic chamber as the most efficient listening space where reflections from walls, ceiling, and objects are minimized and controlled so that they are phase or time coherent, creating "neutral" uncolored spaces. This is an attempt to free the mixer to deal with subjective creative decisions in an intimate space.

While both the old and the new have limitations, the primary criterion is the reality of the exhibition medium. The bottom line for television is the home receiver. Most of the "quality" mixed into a given program doesn't make it into the living room. Should the mixer care? Yes, because:

- The quality of reception, the broadcast bandwidth, and the sensitivity of home entertainment playback (component) systems are improving every year.
- Stereo demands a higher level of precision.
- Marketing needs demand better sound quality because many dramatic shows may be distributed on videocassette, fed by cable, or given a theatrical run in the theatre. For example, many *American Playhouse* productions debut on the tube, are given a short-run theatrical release, then are distributed on videocassette. The sound track must accommodate all possibilities.

On the other hand, the limits of home playback provide a rationale for limiting budgetary expenditure for better sound since some projects appear simply to not be worth the effort. Nevertheless, it may be more profitable to monitor the mix through a television set speaker than through the ideal clusters of the mixing theatre to determine what is being *lost*.

Mix studio time is costly. It is to your advantage that the session go as smoothly and rapidly as possible. Don't give the mixer editorial or machine room problems with which to contend.

Track preparation is probably the most important time factor when getting ready for a mix.

Dialogue: Every time there is a shot change, a change in equalization, or a sudden change in level, the element should be *split off* to a second dialogue track. If the changes don't occur too often, two dialogue checkerboarded tracks should be sufficient. The idea is to allow the mixer to preset as much of the level and equalization as possible; so many very rapid changes may require a third track. A narrator should have his or her own track.

Music and effects: The elements should be split off whenever they butt up against each other, overlap, or are crowded into a short length (which is usual for effects). It is not unusual to have five or six effects tracks for a complicated scene.

Loops: Continuous runs of room tone or environmental ambiance may be easiest to handle in the form of loops. However, effects loops should be avoided as they force the mixer into an editing function. It is always better to lay in any sound on a roll, especially if it must begin or end in an exact spot. It is easier for you to cut a sound to a spot than for the mixer to key in the sound on an exact cue. Changing loops in the middle of a mix is also time-consuming; everyone sits sipping coffee while the projectionist is threading up the next loop. Loops can be no shorter than 2.5 ft and no longer than 75 ft. The ideal length is 4–8 ft. A 10-min reel is the preferred length for maximum control.

Leader Marking and Identification

The laboratory prefers that all picture be submitted with Academy leader. This assures in-sync printing. There should be:

- 7 ft of leader before the Academy start mark.
- A beep tone on the tracks all at the proper spot (all should beep simultaneously when projected).
- A cue punch on the picture leader opposite the beep.
- Runout at the end of tracks of at least 10 ft of leader (white emulsion). (It is very frustrating to try to remix the last 5 sec of a reel only to discover that the track has run off the dubber. (See Figure 13-13.)

Fill Leader on Tracks

All silent areas on the track should be filled in with white emulsion leader. The leader emulsion is spliced to the track base to avoid the emulsion's clogging the head gaps and causing abrasion or emulsion noise over the record/playback heads.

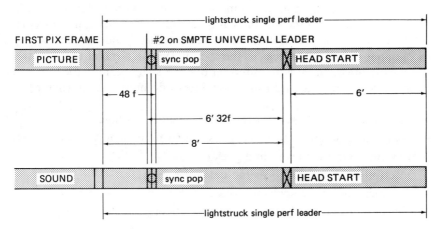

Figure 13-13 Preparation of leaders for mixing (16-mm footages).

Workprint Prep

The picture should be mounted heads up, projection wind on a reel. All splices must be checked that they can withstand the pressure of the high-speed pull of the projector. Check for overlapping tape, which should be trimmed from sides.

The 3-Track Mix

Despite the heroic protestations of many mixers, it is really very difficult to try to control more than a handful of tracks at one time. A major mix situation employs three mixers working as a team, each assigned a specific area— dialogue, music, effects. They end up with a 3-track master with the major elements mixed down from as many as 120 original tracks. Having music and effects on separate masters allows for ease in the preparation of foreign dialogue masters, transfers to other media (disc), and re-release.

The three-track mix has a number of advantages:

- The mix can be rebalanced without having to remix from scratch.
- The final mix can be changed easily (new narrator, dropping a music selection, etc.) after test previews.
- The same mix may be used for magnetic and optical release formats, television, videocassette, etc.

Mixing Cue Sheets

All of the component sound elements to be mixed are assigned a specific machine (reproducer) in the playback room. These elements generally correspond to a mix cue log written in clear, precise shorthand on cue sheets, a multicolumnar map of the tracks as they run in sync in parallel to each other. The following information is required on the cue sheet: Cue marks are measured in terms of footage and frames or time code numbers (start/stop):

- Point where sound exists in relation to picture footage.
- Point where sound enters and goes out in relation to picture footage.
- How the sound comes in and goes out.
- Description of the sound or the desired effect.
- Identification of the speaker, voice, object.
- Reel number and roll number for each sheet.

A separate sheet should be made for each 10-min sound roll; number the sheets if there are more than one to a roll. (See Figure 13-14 and Table 13-4.)

Reeves... the sound choice

Producer _____   Reel No. _____   Page _____

Title _____   Date _____

Job No. _____   Reeves Production Services / 304 E. 44th St., N.Y., N.Y. 10017 / 212-679-3550

NARRATION	VOICE A	VOICE B	EFX A	EFX B	LOOP	LOOP	MUSIC
3.24 beep							
4.32							
16.8							
25.10							
33.9							

Figure 13-14   Mixing cue sheet used by mixer to "map" sound movements. Each element occupies a precise position in the vertical scheme in relation to events listed at the far left. Transitions between sounds are marked by hand and annotated horizontally.

TABLE 13-4   Mix cue sheets (for backup interlock system)

Composite cue sheets require the following basic information (see Figure 14-14):
- Footage at which each sound starts, the way it starts.
- An indication of duration, natural ins and outs.
- The footage at the end point of the sound and the type of transition to the next sound information.
- The applicable relative levels, fade-ups/downs.
- Clearly marked areas where no sound exists.
- Kind of sound: narration, sync voice (dialogue), music (A & B), effects (A, B, C), loops, effects, all loops.

Visual Cues on Workprint

There are two kinds of visual cues on the workprint:

- *Cue punch:* A series of three or four punched holes at ½-sec or 1-sec intervals to warn the mixer visually of an upcoming segment to attack. A rhythm is set up that enables the mixer to hit the cue precisely.
- *Streamer:* A diagonal line scribed into the workprint. This cue occurs the instant the line touches the opposite side of the screen during projection.

Calibration Tones

Prior to the mix, the console must be neutralized or set to zero by turning all controls to "0," "off," or "flat." This establishes a point of reference. Record calibration tones on the ¼-in master and fullcoat master on all channels simultaneously with no noise reduction:

- 1 kHz at 0 VU.
- 1 kHz, 15 kHz, 10 kHz, 100 Hz, and 50 Hz at 0 VU for 7½ ips.
- If Dolby-A is used, record an encoded Dolby tone at 0 VU, followed by an encoded 1-kHz tone at 0 VU.
- If dbx Type 1 is used, record an encoded 1-kHz tone at 0 VU.

The recording engineer uses the 15-kHz tone to align the repro heads, the 1-kHz tone to set the overall level and channel balance, and the other tones to set playback equalization. The playback should then reproduce the same tonal balance as recorded during the mix.

TABLE 13-5   Kinds of effects created with filtering on equalization

Boost	Cut	Result
3–10 kHz	100–300 Hz	Bright articulate "presence rise" for voice.
4–10 kHz	50–500 Hz	Drop muddy sound in percussion and outdoor vocal.
8–10 kHz	100–500 Hz	Deemphasize midrange sweetening strings, reeds (saxophone).
	100–300 Hz, 3–20 kHz	Removes sibilance from voice and background hiss.
	100–3,000 Hz	Corrects imperfect room acoustics, emphasizing highs and mid-lows.
	100–800 Hz, 2–20 kHz	Piano becomes rinky-tink, reduces high-frequency brass bite.
	100–5,000 Hz	Adds "sizzle" to voices.
	100–10 kHz	Telephone sound for voice.
	300–10 kHz	Bass boost for vocals and string bass.

Mixing and Cue Mechanics

Here are some preparation tips (see Figure 13-15):

- The footage should always be marked to within ¼ ft.
- Always parallel all cues and corresponding footages/codes.
- Indicate all pauses in narration 3 ft or longer in duration and *all silences*.
- Show the last word of narration before the pause starts.
- Fill leader used for spacing of the soundtrack silent intervals should

scottsound

6110 SANTA MONICA BOULEVARD • HOLLYWOOD, CALIFORNIA 90038 • (213) 462-6981

RERECORDING LOG

Track No. NARRATION	Track No. DIALOGUE	Track No. MUSIC	Track No. EFFECTS
Reel No. 1	Reel No. 1	Reel No. 1	Reel No. 1
000 Dead Sync			
6'33 SYNC POP	6'33 SYNC	6'33 SYNC POP	6'33 SYNC POP
8 First Pix Fr			
10			
	15' _police_		18 < water fall
	18		
22 last word (fight)	Natural IN	26 Bells, Flute	32
	28		
		50 louder	
65 raise level			fade in
	70 Natural Out	cross dissolve	75 < Birds LOOP
	85 No symbol means 85		86 > fade out
90 Last word (please)	straight cut		
	125	125 HORNS	
135	135	135 >	135
< = FADE IN			
> = FADE OUT			
⇄ = DISSOLVE			
/ = Feet			
x = Frames			

Figure 13-15 Annotated re-recording log.

Figure 13-16   Filtering and equalization module.

always have emulsion spliced away from magnetic heads (base to emulsion) to avoid noise and clogging head gaps.

- Only one sync mark is recommended to avoid confusion as to exactly
  where things begin. This mark should be exactly 8 ft ahead of the first
  frame of picture.

- A fade-up starts *before* the point where it is expected to be at full volume,
  so there must be sound on the track before the fade-up begins.

- A sound comes in automatically when it begins on the edited track. All
  that is necessary is that the pot be preset to the desired volume for that
  channel on the console. This is one area in which computer memory
  greatly facilitates multitrack coordination and repeatability.

    Consider having to audition four or five effects loops that play
simultaneously against each other in a scene from *Star Wars* during a fast-
paced battle sequence. Each element is preset alone, while other pots on
other elements are down. All are brought up, but each mark must be
remembered either by using pieces of tape, making notes on the mix
sheet, or just having a good memory. The loops are balanced against each
other until it appears to blend properly, and the entire effect built-up of

five separate tracks is now recorded. Upon playback against the previous scene and next scene, it is determined that some adjustments are necessary; they are made—but all the marks must be hit again. Later, when music (if it appears) is played and mixed against the effect, *another* adjustment must be made (due to, for instance, a troublesome masking effect). You must then go back to the original marks (if the tapes are still there), or your notes, and remix. Having all these pot points in a console computer memory greatly simplifies these complex tasks.

- A track may be taken in or out *instantly* by means of a console switch. The mixer can hold a track out and then at the cue point switch it in so that the sound begins instantly. Or it can be switched out instantly. If it is expected that a track must hit a cue *exactly* to a frame, edit the track in advance so that it hits the cue automatically rather than tormenting the mixer by making him try to hit the mark during costly mix time.

Laydown of Music for the Mix

Music elements require special handling since, with their generally wider dynamic range than dialogue and effects, they tend to dominate. Separating multiple music elements into three masters greatly facilitates the master mix by isolating classes of sound to be controlled individually against all other elements.

Laydown of music prior to mixing.   The following are some suggested assignments of recorded instrument groupings separated onto discrete tracks to be more carefully blended in the mixing process:

3-TRACK 35-MM STRIPE-COAT FILM

- Right track: strings.
- Center track: keyboard and percussion.
- Left track: brass and woodwind.

STEREO 3-TRACK MIX

- Stereo left: strings.
- Stereo right: brass and woodwind.
- Surround: percussion.

3-TRACK MIX FOR TELEVISION

- Ch-1: strings.
- Ch-2: rhythm.
- Ch-3: woodwinds.

STEREO MIX FOR TELEVISION (LARGE 60-PIECE ORCHESTRA)

- Ch-3: violas, cellos, low bass.
- Ch-1: strings, trumpet.
- Ch-2: woodwinds, French horns, percussion.

Many mixers use a delay of up to $4\frac{1}{2}$ ft for strings, which lends a light and airy ("floating violin") feeling. Television's small format screen demands *isolation* of each section of instruments with mikes close up to enhance *articulation:*

- The closer the mike, the brighter the effect.
- The farther the mike, the more blend achieved.

For the nice, big, warm, fat, punchy sounds needed in the theatre, the orchestra is miked far away and from above using the classic studio multiple microphone technique in which nearly every instrument group is assigned a separate mike. No instrument is ever overwhelmed. MGM pioneered the use of this technique using a "Church" microphone, which was developed by their staff engineer. In the mid-1970s the only existent inventory of these microphones (a hybrid ribbon) was stolen, ending the use of a unique industry standard.

Narrative Functions of the Mix

The meaning of dialogue in the context of the shot and in the context of other thoughts is accomplished through changes in the emphasis on and the intonation of words. Through filtering and equalization, a given phrase may convey a new meaning each time it is repeated. In *The Conversation* (1974), director Francis Ford Coppola disects this aural phenomenon and makes it the subject of drama. A recorded surveillance tape assumes new narrative dimensions each time it is played back and analyzed.

Vowels and Consonants

Altering vowel and consonant waveforms in the mix can produce startling changes in the way a word or sentence conveys emotions. (Consonants contain sounds ranging from 1 kHz to 10 kHz, vowels from 300 Hz to 800 Hz.) Moreover, the presence or absence of the *voice fundamental* in the mix determines the *naturalness* of the voice but not its intelligibility. (In humans, the voice fundamental is rather fixed at the pulse repetition rate of the larynx, which resonates like a double reed between 100 Hz and 300 Hz.) The fundamental carries vocalized soundwaves up through the mouth and nose, which act as modifiers of the sound. To upgrade intelligibility of voice, the mix must emphasize consonants and round out vowels through equalization—rolling off some waveforms below 1 kHz while boosting signals above 1 kHz by 12 to 15 dB.

Reverberation degrades speech intelligibility. Resonating, reverberating vowels mask succeeding consonants. For complex sound such as speech, a late echo, whose level is 20 dB or more lower than that of the direct sound, is ignored by the brain. This is called *forward masking*. Reduced intelligibility results when the brain is confused by a late echo equal in level to the direct signal of the same speaker. If its level is 10 dB or more than the direct sound, the brain accepts the echo as the primary sound (backward masking). It is easy to see then that the mix through digital delay can drastically alter the recognition of certain elements of dialogue.

Time Relationships

Changing the time relationships between shots, by modifying the duration of aural transitions, can also alter spacial continuity or create it. Alain Resnais' *Last Year at Marienbad* is structured on the track as a series of forward/backward time reversals conveyed by means of the differences in the generation of sound elements as well as the duration of dissolves and fades.

Emphasis/Deemphasis

The mix may augment the personality traits of characters by emphasizing or deemphasizing the sonic/musical thoughts, moods, tonalities, presence, and timbre of voice and effects. Robert Altman's *Popeye* can be understood only when the audience recognizes the vocal manipulations between characters and especially within the complexities of Popeye's (Robin Williams') vocal gymnastics which tend to, unfortunately, go unheard due to poor playback.

As another example, in *The Sorcerer* (1977) directed by William Friedkin, various trucks are travelling along rutted dirt roads to the sounds of big rigs, straining motors, gravel spraying—all voluminously recorded. Mixed into these "natural" event effects are tremendously slowed down recordings of leopard and mountain lion roars. The result is that the trucks have a living, breathing voracity about them, an emotional presence no visual could ever convey.

Aural Allusions

The mix can create narrative suspense, a sense of anticipation, mystery, and dread through a combination of fragments and the repositioning of the audience by aural allusions. For example, in *The Birds*, Alfred Hitchcock constantly reverts to the perspective of the menacing blackbirds by focusing attention on the details of their chatter, flapping, and pecking—placing the audience virtually on the perch with them through the aural illusion of intimacy.

The mix function creates the imbalance between the foreground and background detail, raising the background to primary focus.

The narrative mix also serves a number of secondary functions:

- *Narrative content:* The mix supports the space-time reality, and can imply a reality other than what is seen. It determines the audience's perspective through sonic focus, and the audience's attention through aural masking. Silence provides the inference of off-track sound implied by action, movement, color, and shape.

- *Spacial content:* The mix defines on-screen space with on-screen sound, and off-screen space with off-screen sound. The characteristic (uniqueness) of the space is conveyed through *aural texture* created by the mix (muffled, thin, loud sounds, etc.).

- *Emotive content:* The mix isolates sounds *not heard by screen characters* (vocals, music, effects) which convey impressions of the environment, pacing, and/or naturalness. The mix isolates sounds *not heard by the audience* (movements, reactions, actions of players), which may evoke a comedic or horrific response in viewer. For instance, we need not hear the sound of a slap; merely to see it may infer the sound.

—*Aural hallucination* (of characters) uses a sound image to punctuate actions or reactions, to convey mental or physical movement not seen on screen, but felt.

—*Aural allusion* (of audience) uses sound to evoke an image, or a puzzle with length, width, and height interpreted by the audience in terms of what it knows about the character and what it appears the character is feeling.

—*Aural depth-of-field* uses sound to create a focus in the mix by means of left-right, top-bottom, foreground/background localization.

—*Sound masking* makes use of a frequency-based effect whereby certain sounds are made to dominate or diminish in relation to a complex array of adjacent frequencies. This may extend to the representation of certain "unrealities," such as depicting the way a character picks out the words of one person talking in a crowded party sequence.

- *Rhythmic content:* The mix creates the timing and pacing of the film by smoothing out the relationships between editing rhythm, duration of shots, and the symbolic, melodic, metaphorical and narrative use of music.

Narration/voice-over tips.   Voice-over and narration are especially tedious and repetitious to refine and enhance. All console movements must be repeated exactly. During the final blending of tracks during audio sweetening for video, several tips are in order to improve clarity and impact. To keep voice-overs at moderate levels while preserving intelligibility:

- Use soft gating or expand the music track with the voice-over as a trigger.
- Compress the voice-over, the music, and the entire track.
- Use exciters that allow the voice to stand out at a lower volume.
- Try short delay programs and early reflection programs to add depth and apparent loudness to voice.
- Employ tight chorus and pitch shifting programs to fatten the voice.
- Monitor the premix through a compressor to simulate the playback quality of a VCR or TV.

14

OPTICALS

The final mechanical stage of the sound recording process, the optical transfer/playback process is covered in such a way as to provide a basis for determining what can be done in all other phases to maximize the quality of the optical print. Two methods for making prints are evaluated. The series of quality control checks and tests are outlined, and the practical limits of optical sound presented, in terms of recorders (including Dolby spectral recording). The aim is for you to be able to specify the kind of print needed for a particular kind of release format. Notions of "fidelity" are examined as a possible mode of evaluation.

Once the sound mix has been completed, it must be transferred to the desired release format. The current choices include Dolby stereo optical, standard optical, 4-track magnetic, 6-track magnetic, optical or magnetic disk. For television, 1- or 2-in videotape is the master.

Since the primary release format for approximately 75% of motion picture releases is mono optical, we shall confine this discussion to the basic *optical negative*.

The Optical Transfer/Playback Process

Magnetic information (the master mix) is transferred to high contrast black and white film photoelectrically. The exposure is developed into a negative (and in some cases a positive). The negative has a visual representation of the sound track in the form of a contoured sinewave image. The negative is composite printed with picture, resulting in a motion picture release print with the sound-track at the edge.

The playback system contains three elements: lamp, lightbeam, and photocell. (See Figure 14-1.) A beam of light is emitted from an (exciter) lamp of a constant energy. The presence of the optical soundtrack causes the beam to be modulated. Since this optical sound track happens to be a picture of the waveform, the transmitted light varies with the level of sound as represented by peaks and dips. The transmitted light is read by the photocell (which is a transducer that converts light energy into electrical) and converted to an electrical waveform that *approximates* the electrical waveform of the final mix.

Variable Track Area

The optical acts as a mask changing the transmission of light, this can be done in two ways:

- Varying the *area* of the sound track (see Figure 14-2A).
- Varying the *density* of the sound track (Figure 14-2B).

Variable area allows a higher percentage of modulation (90% to 40%), the signal-to-noise ratio is 6 dB better, and the overload characteristic is more

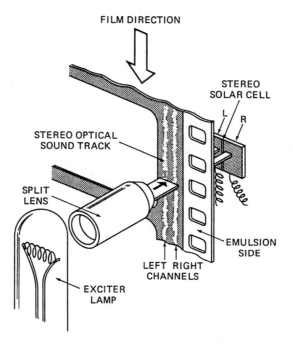

Figure 14-1   Stereo solar cell pickup—two tracks of the stereo optical print.

critical. But the projection equipment must be in top condition (track place-ment, azimuth). If density tracks are made properly, however, they are probab-ly better as they can be played on poor equipment, but the variable area track is in favor at this time. There are two ways of creating a variable area track: with a ribbon (light valve) and a galvanometer. (See Figure 14-3.)

With a galvonometer system, a beam of light is reflected onto film from a

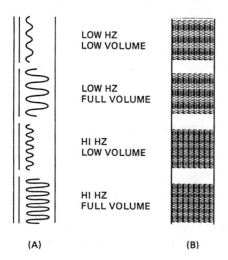

Figure 14-2   (A) Variable area;
(B) variable density.

RIBBON (LIGHT VALVE)

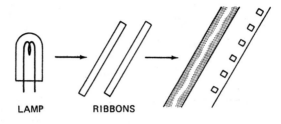

LAMP   RIBBONS

(A)

GALVANOMETER

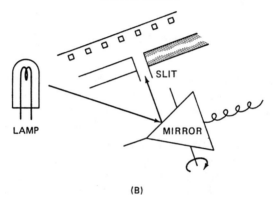

LAMP   MIRROR

SLIT

(B)

Figure 14-3 (B) Ribbon (light valve); (B) galvanometer.

triangular mirror that vibrates according to the sound waveform input. This beam passes through a very narrow slit, creating a narrow beam of light varying with the impressed sound, exposed on a film emulsion of high contrast. (See Figure 14-4.) The sound, unfortunately, moves the mirror both in positive and negative positions. (See Figure 14-5.) This means that the rest position (no sound) is in the position shown in Figure 14-6. The lack of sound creates a clear area in the print (the negative is black opaque) equal to 50% of the area of the

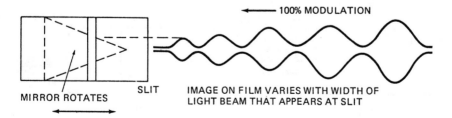

100% MODULATION

MIRROR ROTATES   SLIT   IMAGE ON FILM VARIES WITH WIDTH OF LIGHT BEAM THAT APPEARS AT SLIT

Figure 14-4 Rotating mirror. The image on film varies with the width of the light beam that appears at the slit.

Figure 14-5   Mirror side view.

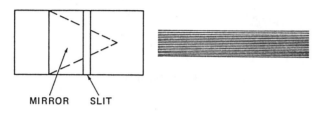

MIRROR   SLIT

Figure 14-6   Mirror/slit.

sound track. It is read as hiss and noise by the photocell and subject to induction of more noise later as it becomes scratched and pitted. Obviously, we want the sound track to be opaque where there is no sound.

In practice it was found that a very small area should be left open to allow for a little hiss to come through. This condition is obtained by using a noise reduction process similar to noise suppression. The galvanometer or light valve is biased (see Figure 14-7) by a direct current to push the mirror up so that only a small portion of it is in the slit scan during the period of no sound. When the sound signal arrives, the bias is reduced and the mirror operates normally.

The system is subject to the problem of attack time/release time control. It is usually set with a 6-dB margin, which means that it wants to anticipate the signal and be 6 dB beyond it at any moment. When the signal is 6 dB down from full modulation, the noise reduction is not in use. On lower-level signals, it is reducing the affected areas on the print.

If the attack time is too brief, the signal may clip, and the word decays. If too long, noise reduction is retarded and syllables may be lost. There is noticeable hiss at the end of each word as the bias line closes down. The lack of a bias line is quite evident as there will be no hiss. If it is too fat, hiss is

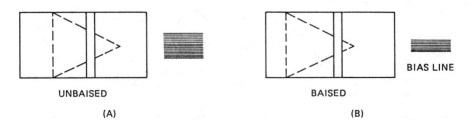

UNBAISED   BAISED   BIAS LINE

(A)   (B)

Figure 14-7   (A) Biased; (B) unbiased.

overpowering. The ideal constants for 16-mm tracks seem to be bias line 3–6 mils. The average times for voice are:

- Attack time noise reduction: 30–40 mils (one frame).
- Release time noise reduction 160–200 mils (4–5 frames).

Low-frequency noise caused by defective noise reduction due to misadjusted attack time is called *thump!*

The Sound Track Negative

Ideally the variable area sound track should be totally opaque in the no-transmission region and perfectly clear in the transmission portion for maximum output (the most light reaching the photocell). Any departure from the ideal renders the optical process inefficient. Since there are no totally opaque or clear films, only varying degrees of gray tones, you must find a condition of exposure and development that gives the highest contrast between the light and dark areas of the optical negative (200-to-1).

In sensitometry, the well-known H&D curve defines density as a function of the log of exposure. (See Figure 14-8.) Normal photographic reproduction utilizes the straight line portion of the curve. A slope can be measured in this region as

$$\frac{\Delta \text{ Density}}{\Delta \text{ Log Exposure}} = \text{Gamma } (\gamma)$$

where Δ density is the change in density and Δ log exposure the change in log exposure.

This ratio γ (gamma) is an indication of relative contrast—high or low. The gamma of the final composite print for picture requires moderate contrast. Color prints for telecine transfer and broadcast must be within 2-to-1 to 4-to-1 ratios of contrast for proper articulation. The sound track, however, wants to be

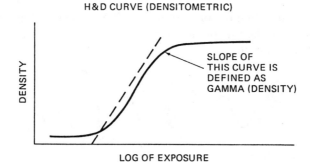

H&D CURVE (DENSITOMETRIC)

Figure 14-8 H&D densitometric curve.

100-to-1. Since we are locked in to moderate contrast for the all important picture element, the only solution is to create an optical negative in such a way that, when printed along with picture and developed for the picture requirements, it also has maximum contrast. This is not easy. Black opaque leader has a gamma of 4.0, and the optical requires 3.0.

Test Negatives

Test negatives are drawn of various densities. The lab (who should be the same lab that does the pix developing) makes a print of each at the standard print density for that lab. Some labs have set a different average gamma for the day's work, so it is not wise to change labs for the sound track work. Subjectively, one of the negatives will produce better results. However, a more rigorous test would involve *crossmodulation analysis* (which is explained later in this section). Since we are limited to an underdeveloped print in the case of the sound, we can overdevelop our negative (see Figure 14-9) and the net result would be a practical advantage. Developing at high densities causes *image growth. Overexposure* and development of the negative foster healthy image growth. In the final printing process there is retraction due to the lack of development time allotted to the sound portion of the composite print process. Since the gamma of the release print is predetermined by the lab, we must work backwards from these constants: That is why the sound studio must send a crossmodulation test to the lab.

This relationship between negative and print density is unique to each lab, each printer, each galvonometer, each negative emulsion, each print stock, and each developing solution. Theoretically, a new crossmodulation test must be made if any of these links is changed. In practice, this is too costly and tests are usually made only when:

- A new emulsion run is delivered to sound studio.
- A new bath is introduced in developing.
- Any great changeover in equipment takes place.

This method assumes that the print stock is uniform, the developer is the same from day to day, and the film being used is printed on the same printer that the track tests were made on.

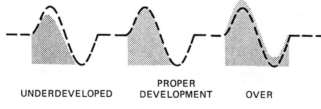

UNDERDEVELOPED   PROPER
                        DEVELOPMENT   OVER

Figure 14-9 Degrees of development.

NOTES

- A negative sound track made for printing on normal black and white stock will not have the proper density for color, another brand of stock, or high- or low-contrast prints.
- After the sound negative is made, the lab cannot be changed.
- Once the test is made, the same printer should be used.

If this critical combination of negative density and print density is not maintained, the sound is less than optimum (actually, it is horrible). The poor combinations give rise to frequency distortion (a raspy and unpleasant sound). If the studio makes a negative for a print density that the lab says is correct in the test (*normal print density*) and the lab cannot hit this density for the release print, the print may be rejected on this basis. Otherwise, the studio is at fault and should cut a new optical. If all goes well the two extremes of overexposure and underdevelopment cancel out and a perfect waveform results.

Undermodulation of the track results in disaster. (See Figure 14-10.) Unlike magnetic recording with a signal-to-noise ratio of 50 dB or better, the best 16-mm optical work is 40 dB and in practice is usually 3–35 dB. An undermodulation of 6 dB raises the noise level by the same amount (doubling). The 16-mm optical negative must be heavily recorded, with the peaks occasionally touching the edge. Sound effects meant to be loud should bleed over from one track to the other.

Crossmodulation analysis. Deficiencies in each stage of the optical recording process can be minimized by careful selection of the best negative and print densities in the final stage. Since relative contrast is fixed as a function of either the color or the black and white image quality desired, neither the negative nor the print image can be absolutely sharp and clear. Distortion resulting from the scattering of light at unsharp edges of the waveform image is called *crossmodulation*.

A test exposure is made using either the Westrex light valve or RCA Galvonometer combining mid-frequency 6,000 Hz and low-range 400 Hz at several levels between 2.4 and 3.2. Each of the resulting negatives are developed in the standard bath at the standard temperature. The prints are drawn

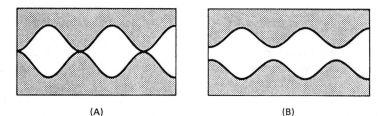

(A)   (B)

Figure 14-10 Dual bilateral sound track: (A) fully modulated, (B) undermodulated.

Figure 14-11   Variable area optical resembles a bar code
grid with some blurring.

covering a range of densities usually from 1.0 to 2.1. They are auditioned on an
optical sound reproducer, the output of which is fed to a volume meter through
a filter that passes only 6,000-Hz or 400-Hz signals. The best combination is
achieved when (a) the lowest output at 400 Hz is obtained with the best output
for 6,000 Hz, and (b) the test results show that, for each negative density, there
is a print level at which the 400-Hz component is at a minimum. The reduction
of this component relative to a reference tone is termed the *cancellation*, and
the print density to be selected for a particular negative is that in which this
cancellation is most effective. (See Figure 14-11.)

The adoption of a 24-fps sound speed was made during the early days of
sound-on-film (1927–29). It was chosen as the standard for the Western
Electric transfer system, which was used for both the Fox Movietone News and
the Vitaphone (Warner Bros.) system. Projections speeds were variable, subject to the hand-cranking interpretation of the projectionist of the screen
action. From historical records, an opinion poll was taken of technical people in
the young industry to arrive at the happy median of 24 frames per second which
was more suited to voice fidelity than it was to sharpness of the image. To avoid
wow and flutter due to the intermittent action at the film gate, the optical track
was advanced ahead of the picture on the composite for projection. Since that
time, several types of optical tracks have evolved to meet exhibitor needs and
developing technologies. Economics of the marketplace dictated. (See Figure
14-12.)

The Optical Recorder

Sound studios employ a variety of equalization and compression circuits at this
stage with either the Western Electric light valve or RCA galvo.

- A high-frequency *preemphasis* circuit (film rise) compensates for loss in
  recording definition caused by the width of the optical recorder aperture.
- A high-frequency preemphasis compensates for the width of the replay
  slit or the "Academy Rolloff." This induces clipping problems and cannot
  be used with flat equalized tracks.
- A high-frequency "chopper" circuit operation, between 7 and 9 kHz cuts
  off high-frequency signals that might cause distortion from inadequate
  printer control.

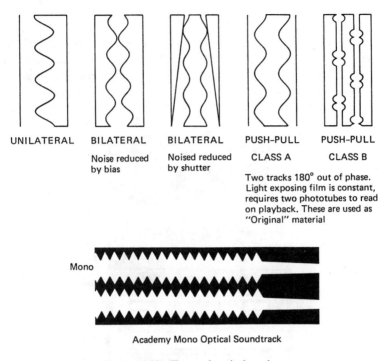

UNILATERAL	BILATERAL	BILATERAL	PUSH–PULL	PUSH–PULL
	Noise reduced by bias	Noised reduced by shutter	CLASS A	CLASS B

Two tracks 180° out of phase. Light exposing film is constant, requires two phototubes to read on playback. These are used as "Original" material

Mono

Academy Mono Optical Soundtrack

Figure 14-12 Types of optical tracks.

- Limiter or compressor use prior to the optical recording avoids overloading.
- Ground noise reduction is accomplished by a delay record system. The object is to reduce to a minimum the amount of transparent track with under zero signal conditions. Grain noise, abrasion noise, and replay cell noise are all proportional to the width of the track being replayed. The disadvantages of this type of noise reduction are:

    —The risk of low-frequency "thumping" if the action of "delay-record" is too fast.

    —Clipping of the front edge of waveforms if the action is too slow.

    —The risk of noise "swishing" (modulation effects) if there is too much noise reduction. Current monoaural and stereo Dolby-encoded variable-area tracks are being made with a bias line in each half track of 2 mils. Bias lines narrower than this can cause swishing.

Printing and Resolution Quality

Better high-frequency response is obtained with contact printing, but there is risk of wow and flutter from the nonsprocketed drive, negative-positive contact; the system is also slow. High-frequency response seems to be better on black and white stocks, but the difference is very close to color.

RCA Optical Film Recorder

At the studio a voltage level is chosen for exposure of the high-contrast film stock used in the optical recorder (really a camera). This level is usually graded as an index number: 5.9, 6.9, 6.1, 6.2, 6.3, etc. Each lab has a recommended development index rated in gamma: 2.35 to 2.60 are the standard densities. During the transfer the signal may be compressed or limited. The

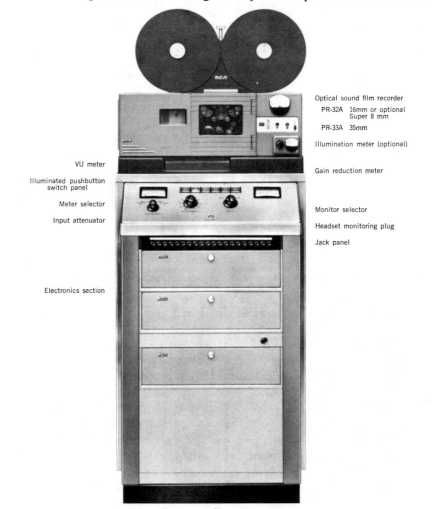

Optical sound film recorder
PR-32A   16mm or optional
            Super 8 mm
PR-33A   35mm

Illumination meter (optional)

VU meter

Illuminated pushbutton
switch panel

Gain reduction meter

Meter selector

Input attenuator

Monitor selector

Headset monitoring plug

Jack panel

Electronics section

Figure 14-13   RCA Optical Recorder. (Source: RCA)

wind (A or B) must be specified prior to the transfer. The possible formats include 65-mm, 16/32-mm, 16/35-mm, double rank, and 4-strip Super 8.

The camera is capable of producing a bilateral negative or a bilateral direct positive variable area optical. Change-over from modes is done by tilting the galvo and reversing the motor. Maximum reel length is 1,000 ft for a 35-mm print. The basic components of the system are:

- Recording amplifier.
- Noise reduction amplifier.
- Compressor amplifier.
- VU switch and meter control.
- Recorder.
- Galvo.
- Magazine.
- Headphones.

A selector switch permits measurements of audio levels at the system input jack, compressor amp output, galvo input, and ground noise reduction output. One hundred percent modulation is at 33 dB.

- The *A chain* is composed of (1) the replay slit and (2) the optical preamp. It should be flat, equalized only in the highs, but the range of slit widths found in the theatre varies.
- The *B chain* is composed of (1) the power amp and (2) the loudspeaker.

The old workhorse—the single-system Auricon Pro 1200 Optical Camera—records a sound track on film stock 26 frames ahead of picture exposure. All the advantages of single-system direct sound-on-film do not outweigh the marginal quality of the track, largely because the picture must be developed for best gamma, not for optimum audio fidelity.

When the finished negative is returned from development, the beep or sync start mark is lined up with the magnetic beep in a synchronizer. It is then moved forward so that it is 26 frames ahead of the mag beep. The start mark from the mag track is then marked on the sound negative leader. This is called *pulling up the negative track*. Now the sound is no longer in editorial sync, but in printing or projector sync.

Practical Limits of Optical Sound

The frequency range of optical film is limited by the resolving power of the film stock, which is beyond the range that is utilized. The printer slippage is also a limiting factor. The printing process can add:

- Printer slippage.
- Poor print density.
- Poor focus (involves A and B winds).

TABLE 14-1 Balance comparisons

High Fidelity:	40 Hz–15 kHz	¼-in tape at 15 ips
	65 Hz–11 kHz	
	75 Hz–9.5 kHz	35-mm optical
Medium Fidelity:	80 Hz–7.6 kHz	16-mm optical
	110 Hz–5.3 kHz	
	130 Hz–4.4 kHz	
Low Fidelity:	160 Hz–3.6 kHz	Radio
	200 Hz–3 kHz	
	250 Hz–2.4 kHz	Telephone

What else can go wrong with the optical negative?

- All the motion problems found in magnetic film.
- Wrong density.
- Improper track placement.
- Improper modulation over or under.
- Defective noise reduction.
- Missing bias line.

In the case of 16-mm optical sound, we end up with a signal-to-noise ratio of 35–40 dB and a frequency range of 90 Hz to 6,500 Hz. This is a far cry from the 55 dB and 40–12,000 Hz specs of the ¼-in master. Maximums for optical playback of 35 mm are 50 dB SN and 75–9,000-Hz frequency range. (See Table 14-1.)

What kind of optical should you order?

If your film is:	If your film is:
AB original color	A wind internegative
AB original black and white	Color reversal internegative
Original mastered from original to B wind	Black and white dupe negative
	Material mastered to A wind
Use B wind track.	Use A wind track.
Obtain:	Obtain:
A wind trial print	B wind trial print
A wind release print	B wind release print

If you send your optical track to the lab in editorial sync, do not punch the sync point. Label it as "editorial sync," and it will be advanced to printer sync and punched at the lab.

If you want to advance the track yourself, the printer sync must fall exactly 26 frames (16-mm) behind editorial sync. The dots on the original picture roll stand for editorial sync. The X's stand for printer sync. Consult the *Recommended Lab Standards and Practices Guidebook* available from the American Cinema Labs Association.

TABLE 14-2 Program routes for TV

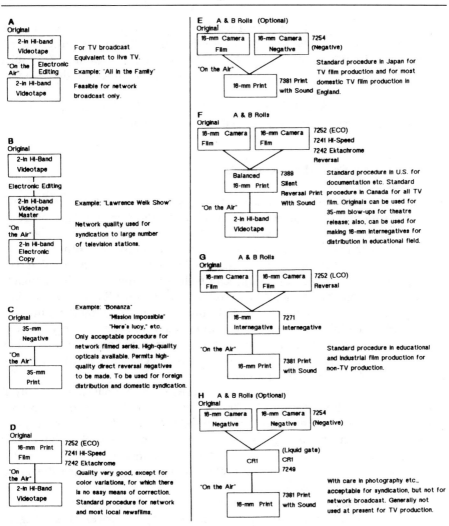

A. For broadcast-equivalent to live TV. Feasible for network only.

B. Network quality used for syndication to a large number of television stations.

C. Acceptable for network "filmed" series. High-quality opticals available. Permits high-quality direct reversal negatives to be made used for foreign distribution and domestic syndication.

D. Good color, very good quality for network newsfilm to tape.

E. Standard procedure in Japan for TV film production and most domestic TV film production in English. Duping not satisfactory. Abrasions show as white marks on print.

F. Standard for U.S. documentaries. Originals used for 35 mm blowups for theatrical release and for transfer to videocassette.

G. Educational-industrial film production standard. OK for limited syndication but somewhat obsolete.

H. Acceptable for syndication but no longer used for broadcast.

When working in the reversal process, a positive sound track must be presented to the lab. The quality control is more difficult since there is no negative density to control. If the lab matches test to print quality, the results should be satisfactory. However, there are more variables in the reversal process.

Video, of course, does not require an optical print. Some probable program routes for audio in broadcast are set forth in Table 14-2.

Dolby Spectral Recording (Dolby SR)

Dolby spectral recording is a studio mastering system that yields recordings with greater clarity and sonic purity and that relies on the principle of least treatment. At the lowest signal levels, or in the absence of a signal, Dolby SR applies a fixed gain/frequency characteristic that reduces noise and other low-frequency, low-level disturbances by as much as 25 dB. Only when the level of part of the signal spectrum increases significantly does the circuit adaptively change its own spectral characteristic. When this happens, Dolby SR changes gain only at frequencies where change is needed, and only by the amount required.

Because Dolby SR increases recording headroom considerably, there is less risk of underrecording in analog and overrecording in digital formats. The prime objective of Dolby spectral recording is to achieve as nearly optimum level as possible at all audio frequencies.

A-type signal processing relies on compression and expansion, but only at low signal levels and separately in four frequency bands. The signal components in each band are integrated; if this level is below a fixed threshold, it is boosted during the recording and attenuated during playback. This classic noise reduction scheme has been taken one step further with spectral recording, which takes into account the limits of the human hearing system (illustrated as a "window" in Figure 14-14).

The playback of an analog recording can be matched against the realities of the hearing window, resulting in several interesting discoveries (see Figure 14-15):

- The noise of the tape is audible only in a restricted range of middle frequencies where the auditory threshold is lowest.
- Noise or distortion components at higher and lower frequencies, even if only slightly below the threshold, are totally inaudible.
- If the audible noise in the midrange frequency band can be reduced by 20–25 dB, no noise is heard at all.

The simplest way to suppress noise and other low-level recording defects is to use as high a recording gain as possible. At very low signal levels, Dolby SR seeks optimum gain. The result is a form of fixed equalization that does not change as long as the signal level stays below a certain threshold. When the recording is played back, the same equalization is applied in reverse and any

The auditory window

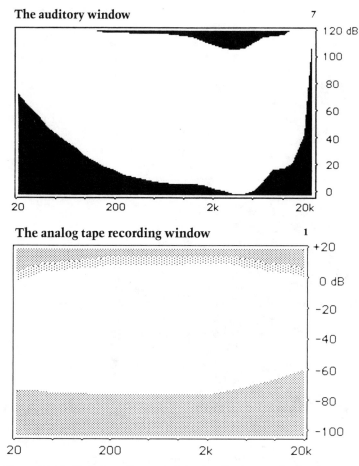

The analog tape recording window

Figure 14-14 Dolby's auditory window visualization graph. Compare this to the analog tape recording window. (Source: Dolby, Inc.)

Playback of an analog recording

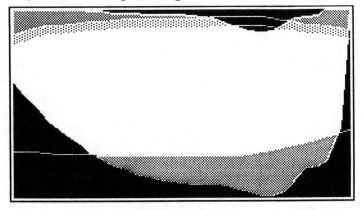

Figure 14-15 Playback of analog recording superimposed.

Figure 14-16 The Westrex optical recorder. (Courtesy Westrex)

background noise is lowered by the same amount. The principal mechanism by which this occurs is a group of ten fixed- and sliding-band filters with gentle slopes.

The changes that take place in the Dolby SR circuit are adaptive—the system filter always adjusts itself to maintain the highest practical gain at every frequency as the signal spectrum changes. The human ear and brain also respond to these changes in the signal spectrum.

One such response is a form of signal processing known as *masking*. The purity of sound of Dolby SR recordings is due to a great extent to this cooperation of adaptive signal processing and auditory masking. In masking, a high-level signal component raises the auditory threshold above and below the signal frequency. Sounds lower in level and near it in frequency disappear completely in this psychoacoustic "shadow." In the Dolby SR circuit, feedback of the signal characteristics determines how each filter in the Dolby SR circuit must change to most closely envelope the masking shadow. This is the way the Dolby SR applies as much gain as possible everywhere in the spectrum. The only region of the spectrum that is not boosted is the region controlled by masking, where audible low-level information does not exist.

PLAYBACK

Knowing the components of a typical projector and how to set one up for operation enables you to understand how they limit what we see and what we hear—and what can go wrong. What happens to the signal in the amplifier and then the speaker systems is often determined by physical and psychoacoustical factors that can enhance as well as often hinder enjoyment in the theatre. Understanding how clarity and intelligibility are affected enables you to backtrack through the entire audio process to locate areas where changes in techniques can improve playback. New technologies that aim to improve sound in the theatre are discussed.

History of Playback

In the early twenties, Western Electric developed the electrodynamic loud-speaker driver. Its developers used edgewound flat ribbon wire as a voice coil, immersed it in a magnetic field, and put a speech current across it, which caused it to move back and forth quickly. Later, Mackenzie looped wire around a post and back parallel to and very close to the first strand, added the same magnetic field, and sent the speech current across it, causing the same vibrations according to the applied electrical waveform acting like a set of vocal chords. A beam of light, shining down through and between the wires, was modulated in intensity by the distance in the gap between the wires. This became the Western Electric Light Valve. No other advances occurred until recently, when work with laser systems as the matrix for playback progressed. (See Arri section in Chapter 16, "Presentation and Projection").

Photoelectric tubes, the heart of the projector transducer apparatus, were understood in principle by the turn of the century based on the work of Albert Einstein and others. When DeForest obtained a patent for the audion tube, the photoelectric tube transducer, the sound track width and location, and projection speed all became standardized.

Sound was considered a novelty in the early days of "sound motion pictures." Silent movies, of course, were never really silent, they always had some form of sound accompaniment. There is much conjecture as to why music essentially became an inseparable component of the theatrical experience of movies. Claudia Gorbman's *Unheard Melodies* (Indiana University Press, 1988) provides a fascinatingly thorough discussion of the apparent rationales at work in the use of music in support of the movies. She points out that a tradition had already existed in theatrical melodrama that seems to have carried over into the "photoplay." Moreover, music served the function, in purely practical terms, of covering up the noise of the arc projector.

Music illustrators were employed to provide musical background with a live instrumental performance. Full orchestra accompaniment became the norm, and by 1911 wonderful "machines" with a unique signature like the *Mighty Wurlitzer* provided both novelty and showmanship. In Japan, performing with the *benshi,* an audio interpreter/performer/narrator, became a high craft that was recognized in many cases above that of the movie actors!

Although there are important structural functions for sound/music accompaniment (which we shall explore later), novelty and showmanship are the keys in understanding the mentality of the exhibition (or playback) space. Throughout the 1940s and 1950s, in the wake of the popularity of the American musical, there was great experimentation with widescreen and stereophonic playback systems. (Refer, for instance, to the discussion of Fantasound in Disney's *Fantasia*.) The 1960s and 1970s saw a retraction from this technological stance of novelty and showmanship in favor of a purely technical improvement of the playback chain. The result was the preoccupation in the 1980s with noise reduction and updating of the theatrical space to bring families back into the movie houses and away from their VCRs. Exhibitors again recognized, as they did in the 1920s, that sound is a marketing tool, in addition to a means toward greater enjoyment and bigger profits.

Playback is, albeit slowly, being improved. In 1979, 25% of all MPAA-rated films were released in the new noise reduction format called Dolby sound, and they accounted for 40% of gross box office receipts. By 1981, more than 100 titles wee released in Dolby stereo and advertised as such. Dolby extends the effective frequency range in playback to 12.5 kHz (6 kHz above the average hometown theatre capability) and reduces high-level noise from the track. But only theatres that are Dolby treated (to the cost investment tune of approximately $20,000) can benefit from the system.

While Dolby is used as justification for higher rental rates to the exhibitor from the distributor and higher ticket prices to the consumer (all in the name of showmanship), in fact Dolby adds very little to the enhancement of the moviegoing experience, except to make dialogue more intelligible. Only a handful of directors have explored the structural potential for improved sound and sonic imagery (Altman, Friedkin, Lucas, Bergman, Resnais, to cite a few).

Each type of format has its own characteristics:

- *4-track format:* The actual recorded tracks are 1.5 mm wide for the three wider stripes (left, center, right—behind screen) and 0.89 mm for the narrow stripe (surround). 4 speaker cluster will suffice
- *6-track format:* Provides signals for five behind-screen speakers plus a surround channel. Two additional behind-screen speakers are driven full range and are intended to provide seemless, stable multichannel spread across a screen perhaps 80 ft wide.
- *Dolby Stereo 70-mm format:* Additional full-range speaker channels are not required; only the extreme left, right, and center channels carry full-range information. Tracks 2 and 4 carry low-frequency data below 200 Hz; they drive the half-left and half-right behind the screen speakers increasing power-handling capability necessary for films like *Altered States*. Low-pass filters reinforce the steepness of the 200-Hz rolloff (to 24 dB per octave), and eliminate the need for noise reduction on these tracks. Track 6 is reserved for surround information encoded with Dolby A-type noise reduction.

Magnetic Playback

The disadvantages of magnetic playback are:

- Magnetic tracks are expensive and time-consuming to make. They are virtually hand-made as oxide is painted on and dried for three days (cured); then sound is transferred in real-time with great precision.
- Stripe wears and flakes.
- Head gaps wear down. They must be maintained very well by the theatre (replacement every 8–10 weeks at $1,200 each).
- There is drastic high frequency loss due to wear.

Audio designers, however, don't have to be demoralized by this state of exhibition. Help is on the way. Moreover, it is their responsibility to take into account the possible *losses* in clarity, frequency response, signal-to-noise ratio and perspective, and find a compromise. This in no way suggests that a quality standard should be lowered. It simply insists that separation and high-frequency response must be programmed in such a way as to be preserved in even the worst of multi-, mini-, closet-sized "showplaces." For this reason, the distributor may provide several different release print formats for specific markets, such as:

- *35-mm optical:* Two separate monophonic (Academy duobilateral variable area) tracks. (See Figure 15-1.)
- *35-mm stereo optical:* Two dissimilar tracks and a stereo solar cell at the projector. (See Figure 15-2.)
- *35-mm 4-track magnetic sound stripe on print.* (See Figure 15-3.)
- *70-mm 6-track magnetic sound stripe on print.* (See Figure 15-4.)
- *70-mm Dolby stereo 6-track.*
- (Proposed) *70-mm 8-perf with 6-track digital audio (disk).*

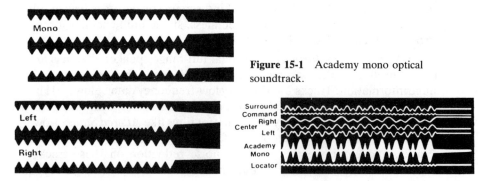

Figure 15-1 Academy mono optical soundtrack.

Figure 15-2 (A) Dolby stereo optical soundtrack; (B) Kintek stereo optical soundtrack.

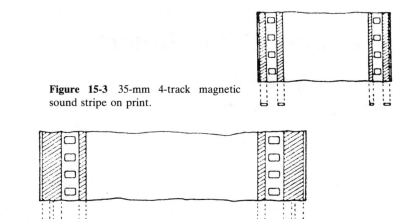

Figure 15-3 35-mm 4-track magnetic sound stripe on print.

Figure 15-4 70-mm 6-track magnetic sound stripe on print.

An average feature has a release with a minimum of 50 prints, and wide release in 35-mm standard optical can reach 1,800 prints. The most rare and costly release pattern is 70-mm 6-track magnetic (normally 50 prints at an average cost of $20,000 each).

Cinema Digital Sound

Theatrical film sound playback technology has incorporated a fixed sound-on-film system (CDS) first used on 70-mm prints of *Dick Tracy* (1990). (See Figure 15-5.) The process involves the decoding of the visually imprinted optical bar code on the release print using a digital reader similar to the system used at supermarket counters. The sound track has been digitally encoded into a pattern of ones and zeros along with SMPTE time code and control channel information. The process, developed by Eastman Kodak and Optical Radiation Corp., provides the clarity of compact disk playback.

Playback in the Average Theatre

The typical arrangement of speakers in a theatre consists of as many as five loudspeakers (but more often one) behind a perforated screen, with two groups (or clusters) to either side of the stage, additional rear speakers, and perhaps a ceiling-mounted "surround" group to the rear. The theatre, ideally, should mirror the mix studio arrangement.

Unfortunately, it does not. The standard for quality comparison is the Academy screening theatre in Beverly Hills or the mixing theatre used to mix the tracks. For directors who have listened to their films in the final mix, the experience in the average hometown theatre can be qualified only as disillusion-

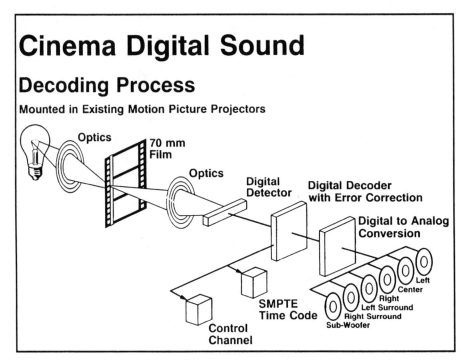

Figure 15-5 Cinema digital sound.

ing. (See Figure 15-6.) Some of the deficiencies in the playback systems of the average theatre are:

- Antiquated speakers and low-wattage amplifiers poorly matched.
- Blown voice coils in the speaker clusters.
- General aging of components.
- Improper placement of speakers causing poor radiation of sound. Clogged pores in the screening material due to the build-up of smoke or dust.
- The wrong type of speakers for the given acoustic space; cheap speakers.
- Dirty exciter lamp and lens.
- Noisy theatre (popcorn level untreated).

Dolby Playback

Despite the clarity derived from Dolbized prints, sound reproduction in the theatre hasn't developed since the late 1920s and has limitations that the audio designer must consider. Reproduction is limited to the relative efficiency of the photoelectric transducer system in the projector, the acoustics of the theatre,

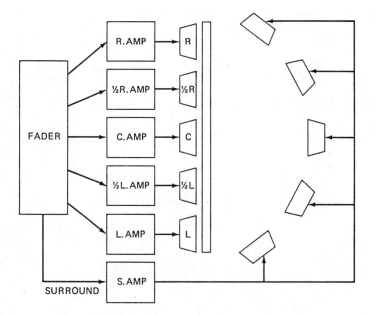

Figure 15-6 Theatre loudspeaker set-up for conventional and Dolby stereo.

and the quality of the optical or magnetic track. (Magnetic tracks almost always provide finer reproduction, but they are more costly, they require good speaker systems, and the oxide wears thin from use.) Moreover, the speaker systems in the Dolbized theatre have a particular equalization characteristic creating a wide-range, clean, balanced sound propagation. Dolby therefore *emphasizes* any problem in the sound system, such as:

- Poor acoustic design.
- Poor maintenance.
- Poor film alignment in the projector or dirt in the path of the modulating light.
- Poorly matched power amplifiers or too few speakers for the size of space.
- Damaged or substandard prints.

While Academy mono optical standard tracks are not wide-frequency range mediums (25 db at 9 kHz maximum—not very "hi-tech"), stereo optical Dolby tracks are wide-frequency range (out to 12 kHz). It has Dolby A-type noise reduction (now spectral recording) via Dolby stereo bilateral variable area—Dolby SVA. Playback in the theatre is reproduced with two discrete channels of Dolby A-type noise reduction. Circuitry derives a center signal (for a central behind-screen speaker) and extracts a fourth surround channel for loudspeakers in the audience area. The surround channel exists within two

Figure 15-7   Academy screening theatre. (Source: JBL)

tracks in the form of a *phase matrix*, which has been encoded with Dolby B-type noise reduction prior to being matrixed. This is encoded by means of B-type NR through a delay line, which minimizes the perception of unintended *crosstalk* from around or behind, and ensures temporal coherence in a larger space.

Effect of Level in the Theatre

Much of the craft of the mixer is sabotaged by improper playback. Blending, matching, focus, perspective, transitions, and movement in time are all "modified" by poor acoustics, projection, and high-level distortion. In particular, playback level in the theatre affects the audience's interpretation of the narrative and mood. When observed at low levels, a subtle film like *Raggedy Man* has the feel of a metaphorical enchanted land; its air of suspense is heightened, its mystery enhanced. It is perceived as a quiet, sensitive fable. If the same print is viewed at another theatre at high sound levels, every noise and sound on the track (interiors particularly) is magnified to the point of absurdity. Every noise appears to have a narrative meaning, but doesn't. Every action is telegraphed—you can hear it coming. Every effect is less natural. The dialogue seems separated from the background in an unnatural, "insincere" way.

Surround Sound

The sound envelope—*sensurround* or *surround sound*—entails a circular aural space in which sound emanates in a free field from all directions. In addition to a minimum of two front loudspeakers, a large rear loudspeaker cluster reproduces conventional stereo and low-frequency boost, with the signals of opposite phase.

The three worldwide playback processing systems currently in use are:

1. *Kintek Stereo:* Synthesizers turn a nonaural print into "facsimile" stereo—left, center, right simulation. A sub woofer system accurately reproduces the lows' "boom" and rumbling bass.
2. *Eprad Starlet:* This system combines left and right of a 2-channel print through one speaker, detects the difference between left and right, and sends it to surround speakers, giving the effect of separation.
3. *Dolby:* This approach utilizes a circular tracking system of speakers around the audience. Four channels of sound are encoded on two optical tracks. They are then sent through preamplifiers, noise reduction gates, and equalizer patch; deep bass is separated and sent by the time delay to rear surround speakers (left rear and right rear). The time-delay compensates for the distance from the screen to rear speakers since light travels faster than sound.

All systems require the theatre owner to do certain things to the exhibition space:

- Install new speakers matched to honestly rated power amplifiers with specific system circuitry. Placement is made for full radiation and coverage.
- The space should be "tuned" acoustically through an analysis of surface reflections, acoustic shadows, and ambient noise level.
- The projector is cleaned and speed-tuned, with the addition of an equalizer to frequency match the anticipated deficiencies in the playback chain. Equalization in the theatre, for instance, enables each print to be "tuned" to match the acoustics of the theatre.

Loudspeakers

Construction.   In its simplest form, a loudspeaker consists of a metal frame with a cone of some softer material suspended from it. The frame also holds the electrical mechanism that moves the cone. The cone movement produces airwaves perceived as sound. If the cone is made to move correctly, any sound may be reproduced. Since no mechanical suspension can stretch indefinitely, there are limits to low-frequency accuracy. Speakers with air in an enclosed frame to provide a suspension cushion exhibit extended bass and low distortion. This is called *acoustic suspension*.

Speakers generate waves through two properties of construction and design: density (inertia) and compressibility (springiness). Using a thin diaphragm in speaker construction improves direct radiation loudspeakers. A conical shape provides rigidity.

However, speakers are nonlinear. Too much drive energy is spent moving the cone and too little moving the air that finally becomes the sound wave. The air in front of the cone exhibits mass more than elasticity. The air inside the box behaves more like a spring and its mass is insignificant. Inner box air is relatively static due to compression and expansion by the cone regardless of whether the speaker design is the *infinite baffle type* (which is sealed) or *reflex* (which allows for air to escape augmenting the sonic wave at certain frequencies). The sound wave is influenced by the properties of the cone and its suspension design, the air pressure within and without the cone the driving electrical current delivered by amplifier-supplied voltage.

Every speaker has a *resonant frequency* at which highs and lows balance each other. The springiness of the air inside the box and cone suspension acts in conjunction with the combined mass of the cone and of the air that moves it to create a resonant effect, like a spring and a counterweight. Very little force produces a large movement at this point.

In most loudspeakers, voltage output represents the frequency content of the audio waveform. (See Table 15-1.) Cone movement is limited as the frequency is varied. The current needed to produce cone displacement varies according to the force needed at each frequency. The rate, not the distance of displacement, needs to be uniform. A low-frequency wave requires a large air movement; a high-frequency wave requires a small, rapid air movement. This movement translates to voltage and force translates to current.

A small force resulting in a large movement at just one frequency can be represented as an analog by a series resonant circuit. The applied voltage is the force, the current is the movement, the inductance is the mass, and the capacitance is the compliance or springiness. But, electrically, movement translates to voltage and force translates to current. A small current produces a large voltage at a given frequency.

TABLE 15-1   Table of mechanical analogies

Mechanical System	Impedance Diagram	Admittance Diagram
Force, f	Voltage, v	Current, i
Velocity, v	Current, i	Voltage, v
Impedance, Z	Impedance, z	Admittance, Y
Mass, m	Inductance, L	Capacitance, C
Compliance, c	Capacitance, C	Inductance, L
Elastic energy $= \frac{1}{2}cf^2$	$\frac{1}{2}Cv^2$	$\frac{1}{2}Li^2$
Kinetic energy $= \frac{1}{2}mv^2$	$\frac{1}{2}Li^2$	$\frac{1}{2}Cv^2$

Types of speakers.   Loudspeakers radiate tones of differing pitch into space in differing *patterns*. The higher the frequency, the more narrowly the pattern is beamed forward resulting in uneven distribution. Equalization is employed to boost high frequencies weakened due to the size of the speaker and certain physical laws. Some systems employ hemispherical domes in place of cones. They are smaller than speakers in transistor radios but are driven by magnets weighing several pounds.

Woofers are speakers that produce low frequencies well because their larger size enables the displacement of large amounts of air. A mechanical force must be present to restore the woofer to its original position. Two methods are used: (1) an elastic ring around the cone, which is stretched by deep bass notes; (2) air suspension making a near-perfect spring, which is very loose.

The location of a speaker has a significant effect on the level of bass. Each speaker has an optimum distance from room surfaces for proper dispersion of sound. Their backs should be against the wall but away from corners. Slight downtilt assures proper address to audience areas.

Tweeters reproduce highs very well, are capable of very rapid vibration, and have small voice coils that tend to overheat quickly. *Dome radiator drivers* employ large voice coils wrapped around the speaker's outer diameter, which can handle heavier current. The small diameter allows wide dispersion with little coloration.

Vocal range speakers reproduce middle and high relative frequencies. They must be solid and small to maintain good aural dispersion patterns. A dome-shaped speaker is ideal, can be driven by a large voice coil, and tends to be expensive. Conventional cones tend to not have enough room for a "spider," which centers the voice coil of the cone and no room for a high-power handling coil.

Efficiency

A speaker should be judged by its absence rather than by its presence. Some speakers convert more amplifier power into sound than others. However, efficiency electrically is not a fair indication of quality. When comparing speakers, you must have them at equal loudness levels.

You must also have controls set that the overall ratio of treble to bass energy is the same for each speaker. Most speakers have backpanel controls for changing the aural shape or contour of frequency response to match or compensate for room acoustics.

Crosstalk

Unstable coupling of the audio signal from one channel to another channel is *crosstalk*. The movement of current through a wire or conductor creates a magnetic and electric field around that conductor. The field is a complete loop, concentric with the conductor, while the electrical component of the field moves out and terminates on surrounding metallic objects.

The flux lines density and number of the magnetic field "cut" the conductor, determining the *induced* current. The electric field induces current in a conductor by electrostatic (capacitive) coupling to that field. Either field can cause current, or flow, in nearby wiring or in the components of another current circuit, creating crosstalk.

Speaker cabling in older installations tends to have trouble spots at terminal blocks, patch bays, poor shielding, or poor grounding. Exposed wires lose the protection of their shielding and should be dressed cleanly.

Floor Plan Isobars

The sound pattern radiated by a loudspeaker can be described by a set of *isobar* curves (sometimes referred to as *pressure contours*). In Figure 15-8, the floor plan isobar curves show the "footprint" of a loudspeaker mounted up in the air and pointed down at various angles. The X marks the spot where the speaker is aimed on axis, and the contour lines represent locations off-axis where the sound pressure level is constant. The inner contour defines where the sound pressure level is 3 dB less than that measured near the center of the contour. The middle indicates 6 dB below maximum, and the outer indicates a 9-dB down level. Isobar floor plans can be useful for ensuring even sound coverage when designing a sound system.

The H represents the mounting height of the speaker above ear level and hence defines the scale of the floor plan. If the speaker height is 10 ft, the resulting scale distances of the marks are 10 ft, 20 ft, 30 ft, 40 ft, etc. The size of the pattern on the floor may be determined for a particular speaker height. If the room is drawn to the same scale, the sound coverage of the room may be predicted by overlaying the floor plan isobar onto the scaled floor plan of the room.

Soundsphere and Spatial Sound Processing

Soundsphere enclosures marry a sphere and a critically shaped reflector, transforming narrow angle playback coverage into a cone of smooth, clear 360° horizontal/270° vertical dispersion field. (See Figure 15-9.) The sphere/reflector propagates sound in concentric waves (circles), simulating a broad source.

A single Soundsphere could provide complete coverage in a simple functional space like a church. (See Figure 15-10.) But, for the theatre, several must be used in combination with specialized speaker systems, which can provide emphasis in specific frequency ranges.

There was a time when the fixed magnetic or optical sound information on the film could not be further modified in the playback mode save for simple noise reduction and equalization. At least one prototype system now allows complex modification of the playback channel, reintroducing the plausibility of true showmanship on the part of discriminating exhibitors.

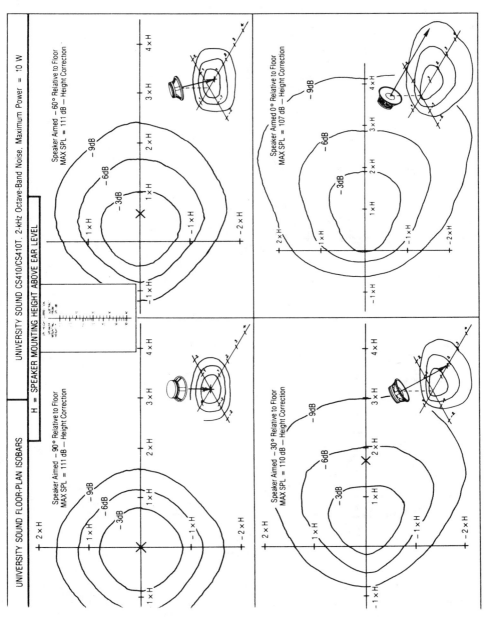

Figure 15-8 Sample floor plan isobars.

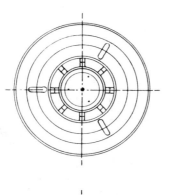

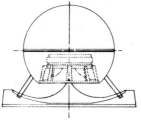

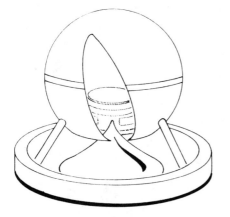

Figure 15-9 The Soundsphere cone of sound. (Source: Soundsphere)

SP 1 Sound Processor

A programmable multichannel 3-D audio simulation system, the Spatial Sound Processor creates sound perspective (movement) in stereo and surround formats from a monophonic track. (See Figure 15-11.)

Intelligent programming of the device, as well as the use of perfectly efficient, extremely flat response speakers like the Walsh 5 from Ohm (Figure 15-12) allows sound data to be "placed" or "moved" automatically or manually.

Figure 15-10   The type of space suitable for one Soundsphere.

Manual operation would require an operator who would be a modern-day audio accompanist in the theatre (like the silent days!).

Regardless of the number of speakers, the processor uses amplitude adjustment to position sound while altering the relationship of direct to reverberant sound. As long as the processor knows the number and the positions of the speakers in the showplace, it can create a three-dimensional sound field according to your design. The "program" also allows for sequence selection (changing order of movement), sequencer speed (changing the rate of change from position to position), sequence direction, scale, expansion, rotation and reverse for up to nine speaker sets. And it can memorize 50 programs.

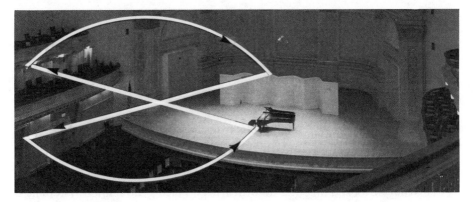

Figure 15-11   Spatial Sound Processor figure-eight sound dispersion pattern.

Figure 15-12   Walsh 5 flat response speakers. (Courtesy of Ohm)

The SP-1 processor can control an external MIDI light system, transmitting via MIDI a series of MIDI messages proportional to the output amplitude of each SP-1 output. These codes are translated into voltages controlling intensity of light sources. Panning of light and sound is possible.

The Acoustic Wave Cannon System

The acoustic wave cannon produces sound using two vibrating columns of air captured in an acoustic waveguide. (See Figure 15-13.) The driver needs only to move a small amount to set the sound-producing air columns into high-amplitude motion. The driver acts as a motor for an acoustic lever. The cannon systems may be locked together to form arrays. Placing the cannon system near

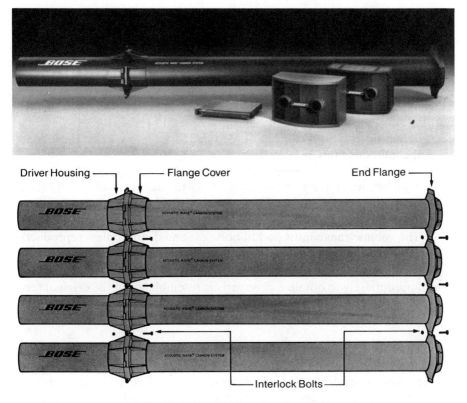

Figure 15-13 Bose Acoustic Cannon. (Source: Bose, Inc.)

TABLE 15-2 An inventory of other functions

Doppler effects	Doppler frequency shifting is created by linking a digital delay box in the signal path and setting duration of the delay.
Expansion	Simulates sounds coming from behind the speaker by increasing/decreasing signal amplitude proportionally with the simulated sound distance desired.
Rotation	Moves the designed spatialization pattern in a two-dimensional mode around the vertical axis and three-dimensional around the vertical/horizontal axis. Reverse the direction of a train.
Scale	Felt "size" is increased or decreased, for example, a spiral of sound descending from the ceiling covering half the space. By turning up the scale, the spiral covers all the space; down, it's smaller until the sound moves in a straight line from ceiling to floor.
MIDI control	Trigger sound movement from a keyboard instrument using such parameters as after-touch, key velocity, note number, and pitch bend.

hard, massive surfaces, such as a concrete slab floor, produces maximum low-frequency output.

High Fidelity

According to Stephen Handzo, in the early 1930s, the first use of the term "high fidelity" was in reference to RCA's improved optical sound system (Weis and Belton, *Film Sound, Theory and Practice*, CU Press, 1985).

"High fidelity" is a concept of *realism*. To achieve realism three fundamental conditions must be satisfied:

1. The frequency range must be such as to include, without frequency discrimination, all the audible components of the various sounds to be reproduced.
2. The volume range must permit noiseless and distortionless reproduction of the entire range of intensity associated with the sound.
3. The subjective aspects involving psychoacoustic effects must be used appropriately to obtain a close artistic resemblance of the original rendition; these include loudness and dynamics, noise, auditory perspective, and reverb.

Fidelity is also a function of "perceived" authenticity, as sound waves reach the ear and are translated into data. However, the entire playback system presupposes a completely linear transfer of the waveform from speaker to ear. It is now known, for instance, that humidity has a marked effect on clarity and fidelity. In a perfectly linear system, molecules of air move uniformly as in the "string analogy" (see Figure 15-14). The sound from the vibrating string reaches the ear through the effect that the string has on the molecules of air around it. When the string is moving up, it pushes on and compresses the air above it, and leaves a partial vacuum below it. Furthermore, during playback in

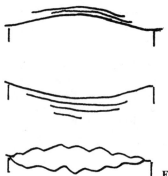

Figure 15-14 The string analogy.

the theatre, sound waves are scattered laterally after transmission through the screen, causing a loss of sound pressure.

With regard to high fidelity in speakers, remember:

- Total *nonlinear distortion* is a function of the frequency supplied, as well as the harmonics/subharmonics produced by direct radiator vibrations, driver, and suspension. The low range amplitude of cone must be inversely proportional to the square of the frequency. Amplitude increases rapidly with decrease of frequency.

- Faithfulness of transient response of the loudspeaker must handle sudden changes in electrical input (tone burst).

- Directivity is a function of the system angle with respect with the reference axis of the system. It can be controlled by diffractors, reflectors, acoustic lenses.

Tracking Loudness

Loudness cannot be directly measured. Loudness is based on the perceptive response of the listener. It has been determined, for instance, that the average listener perceives only a doubling of apparent loudness for each increase of 10 dB/SPL.

Pitch and timbre affect the apparent loudness of a sound. The ear is less responsive to low and high frequencies than to midrange signals; moreover, complex waveforms at a given pitch tend to sound louder than pure tones of the same frequency.

Dynamic range—the overall span of signal levels from softest to loudest—can be understood only in the practical terms of a crest factor. The so-called "peak-to-average" ratio denotes the real difference between the instantaneous peak intensity of a signal and its average (rms) level. All natural sounds have a crest factor, which is a prime aspect of timbre, its distinctive sound. When sound is compressed to meet the limitations of the broadcast medium, the crest factor is modified. The average level of a signal directly relates to its loudness, while the peak level is the instantaneous measure of the signal's electrical intensity.

VU meters are not sufficiently accurate to display loudness. In digital recording, overload of the signal yields greater distortion than comparably overmodulated analog signals.

The Dorrough Stereo Signal Test Set has meters that display response to the entire waveform, showing the true peak level of asymmetrical signals, such as speech or sound effects. On the same scale, the system displays the persistence value of the signal (see Figure 15-15), indicating the average loudness values based on psychoacoustic factors effectively expressing the crest factor of the program. This is the first test system that tracks both aspects of loudness perception.

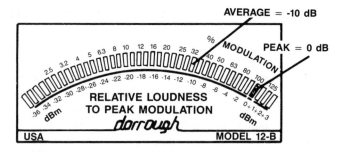

Figure 15-15   Dorrough Stereo Signal Test.

Amplifiers

An increase of 10 dB or 10 phons results in an approximate doubling of perceived loudness. This relationship between aural intensity and perceived loudness requires a tenfold increase in amplifier power (60 × 10 = 600 W, which is twice as loud as a 60-W amplifier). A 3-dB increase, which yields an incremental but significant rise in loudness, requires twice as much power.

Psychoacoustic factors.   The ear seems to discriminate against very short sounds, but clipping and distortion are sensed by the ear as atonal pitch values. According to Harry F. Olsen's *Music, Physics and Engineering*, 13 msec is enough time for distortion to be detected. The ear is almost ten times quicker in responding to distortion than to intensity. An amplifier's ability to cope with severe peaks may not be heard, according to Ralph Hodges, but its *inability* to do so can be heard.

Brief peaks at intensely high levels do not seem unbearably loud. For brief sounds, the perception of loudness depends on duration as well as intensity. According to Wolfgang Ohme in the *1967 Hewlett Packard Journal,* any sound lasting less than about 100 msec (0.1 sec) sounds softer than a steady sound of equal intensity. A 10-msec sound must be at least 10 dB stronger than a steady sound of equal intensity in order to seem as loud. To an amplifier, 100 msec is 100 cycles at 1,000 Hz or 10 cycles at 100 Hz, more than enough for any music power capabilities to be exhausted and for amplifier clipping to set in. Peaks require high-power capability.

Sound reproduced through poor speakers and/or amplifiers does not sound intolerably distorted because of masking, an aural mechanism by which a loud sound can render a softer one partially or completely inaudible. As measured by Fletcher and Munson, *masking* is the amount by which the threshold of hearing is raised by the presence of another sound. Lower sounds can mask higher sounds, but the reverse seems not to be true. The closer together the two sounds are in frequency, the more effective the masking. The best way to unmask sound is to get closer to the source. Thus, distortion can be masked even at normal listening levels. At 100 dB, 1% distortion achieves a 60-dB level, which can certainly be heard.

The ear has another ability that is not yet understood. Sounds are apparently identified by the coincidence of "pulses" received over different sets of nerve fibers, not by recognition of a specific pulse code over a single auditory nerve fiber. You can listen to the entire orchestra or to the violin section, or you can pick out a conversation in a crowded, noisy room filled with other conversations. This isolation demonstrates the existence of a kind of sonic zoom, but the biological mechanism at work is unknown.

Amplifier power transfer. Amplifier output impedance must match the ohms of the speaker system. To get a load resistance that gives maximum current and voltage simultaneously, the load impedance is of the same value as the internal impedance of the original source. Overpowering speakers can cause burnout. Wiring a fuse in-line for each speaker should prevent blowouts. With an 8-Ω speaker, a 1-amp fuse blows at 8 W, a 1½-amp fuse at 18 W. Halving the speaker impedance halves the power level at which the fuse blows; doubling it doubles the power. In most cases the minimum amplifier power needed is the minimum required to drive the speakers.

Musical waveforms have components that peak at about 10 times the average power level of amplifiers. Most amplifiers give the wave all available power and then clip the rest off, distorting it. The distorted peaks pass so quickly, you may not notice them. *Listener fatigue* occurs when the instances of distortion create a cumulative effect after a long day of listening. If your speaker can't handle the power levels needed for accurate listening, a speaker of equal efficiency and higher power-handling capacity, or one of higher efficiency and equal power, should achieve comfortable listening levels without using too much amplifier power.

Power requirements. When calculating power needs, keep the following tips in mind:

- Small changes in loudness demand great changes in amplifier power. In general, the minimum amplifier power required is the minimum required to drive speakers cleanly to average listening levels while also handling peaks. A 600-W amplifier is not 10 times louder than a 60-W amplifier. Every 10-dB increase results in a doubling of *perceived* loudness. This requires a tenfold increase in *amplifier power*. A 100-W amplifier produces only four times as much power as a 1-W system! The maximum acoustic output from a typical speaker with a 40-W amplifier equals 106 dB. With 200 W, you obtain 113 dB. A 3-dB increase requires twice as much power. A very large, high-power amplifier may be better than a lower-power system, but not louder.

- The rated power of amplifiers is not always *continuous* power and may be off by as much as 20%.
- The rated power must be delivered at all audible frequencies.
- Power needs are a function of the space: Live spaces have little absorptive material. Dead spaces have much. To determine the minimum amplifier power required in continuous watts per channel (rms power), divide the volume of the listening space by 4 m³ (15 ft³).
- Too little power causes distortion; too much damages speakers.
- If very high sound levels are demanded from low-powered amplifiers, clipping occurs, which can also cause internal damage to midrange and high-range drivers. Damage is more common in low-powered than in high-powered systems.
- 100 W is more than enough for most spaces and speakers.

Power Requirements for Theatres

John F. Allen of the Klipsch Company devised a system to determine the exact amount of power a stereo playback system requires in a given theatre. The reverberation characteristic of the theatre is not taken into account and is deemed to be a factor that makes the estimate arrived at one with a safety margin built-in.

$$\text{Power required} = 10^x$$

where $x = [106 - (1\text{-W } 4\text{-ft speaker sensitivity} - 20 \log\frac{D}{4})] \div 10$

D = the distance from screen to center seat. For surrounds, D = ½ width of the theatre. For 70 mm, multiply the result by 2.

To find the sound pressure level available from a system:
Available SPL = Speaker's 1-W 4-ft sensitivity + 10 log amplifier power − 20 $\log\frac{D}{4}$

Acoustic Space

The variations in the performance of theatre sound systems result in requirements for flattening the B chain, which varies from site to site. Equalization may be acquired by any combination of slit width and:

Equalization in the preamplifier.
An actual filter unit.
Equalization in the power amp.

A high-frequency loudspeaker pad.

Treble attenuation from the screen material.

Excessive reverberation time constants in most theatres represent a barrier to fidelity. More people complain of the sound's being too loud in theatres than too low. Sound engineers often anticipate low playback levels and therefore restrict the dynamic range of the track in the mix or transfer.

Loudness is associated with distortion. A reduction in sound volume usually is accomplished through the reduced distortion level emanating from flat equalized tracks. Some theatres may incorporate a Dolby-type noise reduction system in the playback chain because the audience rustle may just reach the level of the quietest sound on the track. The unit is used between the A and B chains.

PRESENTATION AND
PROJECTION

A professional projector should have a variable focus with two positions for A and B wind. (Most are focused halfway between the two.) The projector always has mechanical limitations. For example, there is always a slight loss at the top end of the signal, but this is put back in the amplifier (in postequalization). The limitations arise from the fact that the film is coming off the sprockets near the sound, where they can introduce a slight (24-Hz) modulating effect. A flywheel is attached to the sound drum in an attempt to dampen mechanical problems, but often poor maintenance leads to a high incidence of flutter and wow.

Projection Quality

The weak link in the playback chain is the transducer system of the typical projector, whose photoelectric technology has not improved in over 50 years. However, separate magnetic track playback provides excellent sound in theatres that are acoustically tuned and prepared to accept the information on the track. Furthermore, the near future should see the dominance in theatrical exhibition of compact disc and hard disk as source media for sound playback. (See Figure 16-1.)

The quality of projection is based on optical assembly alignment and scanning slit placement over the optical print. If the light beam from the exciter lamp does not focus in the correct plane, the resultant image is soft. This is noticeable in high-frequency loss. Projectors have an averaged focus point to account for slight discrepancies in print emulsion thickness and wind (A or B). It is critical that the optical path be kept extremely clean and constantly tested for proper alignment. There is not much else to worry about save the condition of the transport, which accounts for the relative tightness of the print around the sound drum—a highly polished ball bearing capstan roller that presents the print to the sound head.

In practice 24-fps projection speed is unsatisfactory. The higher the projection speed, the more stable is sound and image playback. Fidelity is a function of many variables, but at higher rates fidelity is definitely improved.

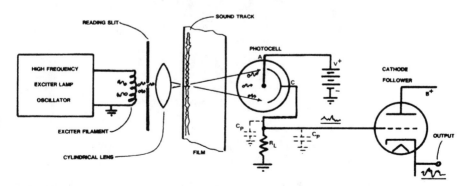

Figure 16-1   Optical relay scanning path.

Quality also depends on the design of the projector:

- Projectors with a *Geneva movement*, a clockwork device stabilizing the rotational aspect of the transport and claw mechanism, provides a semblance of quality. (See Figure 16-2.)
- *Showscan*, a new type of exhibition standard devised by special effects cinematographer Douglas Trumbull, utilizes 70-mm prints cut from a 65-mm negative and projected at 60 fps. The overall effect is to heighten the reality on the screen. Few theatres have the capacity to present Showscan but early tests provided some astonishing results.
- *IMAX* widescreen presentation (70 mm) uses a sandwich of air pressure at the gate in place of friction drive to stabilize the long image over the

Figure 16-2   (A) Geneva projection movement. (B) The 35-mm sound head sits under the picture head. (Source: Kinoton)

aperture. Standard projectors have the mechanical limitation of the film coming off the sprockets near the sound drum, presenting the possibility of induced modulation noise (24 Hz). A flywheel is attached to the sound drum in an attempt to damp any mechanical problems, but there is a high incidence of *wow and flutter* over the head, generally due to poor maintenance. If all is perfect, the signal from the photoelectric cell is "sound"— not much like the original in the mix, but sound nevertheless.

A recent development is the use of magnetic fluid in place of the spider to float the voice coil inside the magnet. The elimination of the spider leaves room for a larger coil. The fluid also helps disperse heat from the coil.

Tuned and acoustically treated theatres, such as the Academy "THX" model, employ a mix board with a graphic equalizer to acoustically tune (pre-emphasize) the showplace for each film.

In addition, graphic equalizers, used in the playback chain, offer a number of advantages. They:

- Eliminate tonal imbalance in playback due to acoustic deficiencies of the exhibition space.
- Help realize the full acoustic potential of the speaker.
- Modify sonic balance to prevailing tastes of a particular region or nation— year to year!
- Control rumble, hiss, and surface "popcorn" noise from old prints and poor new ones.
- Disguise losses due to incompatibilities within the playback system.
- Correct imbalances in stereo reproduction or speaker placement.
- Match the enhanced properties of a well-mixed track.

Signal Transmission

Power is transmitted from amplifier to speaker in one of two basic ways: constant impedance or constant voltage networks. Loudspeakers are wired in a series-parallel arrangement so that their impedance is matched individually and combined while all play at the same level. Loudspeakers, connected via transformers to a constant voltage output from an amplifier, avoid unequal or wasted power output.

Surround Sound

Surround or *sensurround* employs the placement of side and rear loudspeakers creating a sonic envelope around the audience in the theatre. In addition to the clusters of speakers behind and/or above the screen, these speakers provide enhanced spacial reproduction of sound. This is not to be confused with *quadrophonic* sound, which utilizes a stereo pair in the front and rear of a theatre. Nor is it true stereo, which is merely 2-channel playback, sometimes with a third external rear speaker duplicating some of the left or right channel sound. Sensurround employs discrete channel separation with sonic data not present on other channels.

In 1953, *WarnerPhonic* sound accompanied the 3-D release *House of Wax*. One of the two projected picture prints had an optical track with the sum of all other channels as backup. The magnetic track was 3-channel, played back on a separate interlock dubber. The right-side picture print carried the surround sound on an optical track. *Cinerama* and *Imax* formats utilized a separate 35-magnetic-track with the surround sound data.

Standard practice for surround sound was to use magnetic 4-track 35-mm

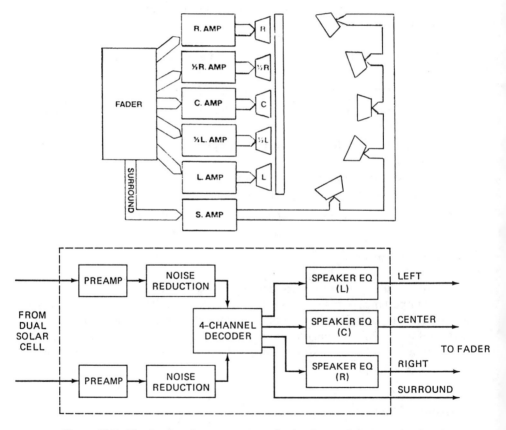

Figure 16-3 The loudspeaker arrangement in the theatre for conventional and Dolby stereo 70mm release prints. For the Dolby stereo format, the half-left and half-right speakers reproduce only frequencies below 200 Hz.

playback using the thin magnetic stripe, which was squeezed between the right edge of the picture and the sprocket holes for the surround information. Similar 4-track optical tracks were also employed. Some pseudostereo techniques use center channel (of a 3-channel stereo print), and surrounds from left and right channels sacrificing stereo "effect."

Six-channel 70-mm adds two more frontal channels with the usual 4-track set-up. (See Figure 16-3.) In 1975, left and right surrounds were split and fed matrix-encoded signals from magnetic sound on 35-mm fullcoat in the release of *Tommy* (erroneously termed quadrophonic). In 1977, the 70-mm release *Star Wars* employed discrete tracks on the 70-mm print with left surround data above 500 Hz on channel 2 and right surround data above 500 Hz on channel 4. Surrounds below 500 Hz played back in mono on channel 6.

Ambisonic surround sound technology uses conventional 2-channel stereo utilizing both amplitude and phase to convey a full 360° (pantophonic) horizontal sound enhanced by adding a third channel. Unlike other surround systems, Ambisonics also employs a supplementary channel with *height* information. Horizontal directivity of a sound is sensed by differences in magnitude (sound level) between the ears and differences in phase (slight path length differences from source to each ear). Vertical source direction is much more complex perceptually. The outer ear is quite different in size and shape above the auditory canal. These physical structures set up reflection trains toward the inner ear, which decodes the pattern into a determination of vertical source height. Most surround systems do not exploit the vertical component chiefly because the mixer fails to consider its narrative significance. This is one area that deserves further experimentation.

Both *2001: A Space Odyssey* and *Apocalypse Now* demonstrate the enormous dramatic potential of surrounds, as Hal the computer speaks through the surrounds and jungle pin-point ambiance is layered through the surrounds. In the first film, the surrounds act as an "effects" concept adding to the characterization of Hal; they offer "ambiance" by creating a psychoacoustic space with dramatic power.

According to Ted Uzzle of Altec-Lansing (the speaker manufacturer) the basic requirements in surround technology are:

- Speakers must be able to handle short-term, high-power audio signals.
- The system must convey a wide frequency range even though bass is less directional than the highs. The power needed to generate bass at a given level throughout the theatre is generally greater for speakers behind the screen than if side and rear speakers are used.
- High-frequency dispersion, which disguises any speaker as a point source spreading out the sound field.
- Ideally, cluster speakers should be angled toward the audience. This tilt is often calculated as:

$$\text{Tilt} = \frac{\text{Cabinet height} \times \text{Hanging height}}{\text{Hanging height}^2 + \text{Aiming distance}^2}$$

The distance between speakers is twice the average height from the floor to the lip of the balcony.

Sensurround

In *The Poseidon Adventure* (1974) Universal experimented with high-level surround effects in the recreation of the sound of an earthquake. Studio trials utilized bass horns driven by 18-in speakers, two 28-Hz corner horns via a bank of 1200-W amplifiers. Sound levels in excess of 120 dB SPL shook the walls. The core reference was the tape recording of the 1971 Sylmar, California earthquake, analyzed to determine the frequency distribution. A control system was developed to overcome the Academy standard rolloff. However, the playback requirements for the effect included very high-power amps and a speaker system capable of handling bass fundamentals down about 16 Hz, necessitating a supplementary portable system to be leased to theatres without the necessary gear.

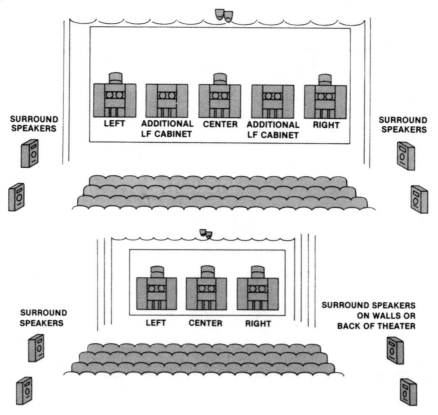

Figure 16-4 (A) Correct sensurround set-up; (B) incorrect set-up.

High-performance of the surround channel is increasingly more significant since very low-volume subtle effects are assigned to surround for environmental participation of the viewer. Some decoder/processor units reproduce only loud surround sounds. In the *Empire Strikes Back*, several sequences are in the swamp-like home of Yoda in which distant cries of weird creatures and other eerie sounds should envelop the audience making them participants in the environment. The experience is missed if correct surround radiation is not achieved. The full coverage would look something like that shown in Figure 16-4.

Too many speakers (multiple sources) result in the apparent source of sound being smeared across the total array with concomitant time and amplitude distortions. The requirement for multiple low-frequency units is a function of the acoustic power at the lowest frequencies (below 80 Hz). For equal loudness at 30 Hz, the SPL must be 15 to 20 dB greater than at mid-frequencies, due to the relative insensitivity of the human ear to bass.

Crossover Networks

High-fidelity recordings cover a range that no single element in a loudspeaker can reproduce. Each driver in a given system is assigned a particular bandwidth that it must handle instantly, while filters roll off out-of-range frequencies. This is called a *crossover network*, and it is between the woofer and midrange that passive crossovers have not been able to eliminate phase distortion (time delay). (See Figure 16-5.) This occurs because the midrange driver is usually wired out-of-phase with the woofer to maintain *amplitude linearity*. In new systems, a dynamic filter driver can eliminate phase distortion by producing a compensating signal.

Flat loudspeaker power response, as well as axial response, is desirable for full tonal balance everywhere in the audience. Accordingly, elimination of crossover networks improves speaker quality by reducing the loss of power and electrical damping. Individual power amplifiers—biamps—for stage and all surrounds should provide 20-dB headroom and contain bandpass filters to protect loudspeakers from input signals outside the components operating

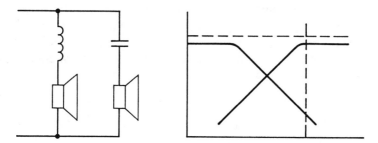

Figure 16-5 A speaker crossover network.

bandpass. Even high-quality loudspeakers require simple response-correcting equalization in a theatre, since systems that have flat (uniform) response do not necessarily have flat power response.

Speakers do not present the amplifier with a purely resistive fixed load; the speaker load is dynamic and highly reactive, resulting from a complex of interrelated electrical, mechanical, and acoustical factors. Most power amplifiers operate on the principle of constant voltage. Speakers, on the other hand, need a current-controlled drive if they are to *accurately* reproduce complex audio signals. When a speaker is coupled to a constant voltage power source, the speaker receives instructions in "amplifier language" when it really needs "speaker language." A correction is available with the Barcus-Berry Dyna-Sync command module, which converts amplifier language to a current-controlled drive. The module directs the amplifier whenever program input doesn't match amp output, to generate a corrective drive signal.

Electronic crossovers consist of a series of active filter circuits placed in front of the power amplifier, generally in the projector preamplifier. The purpose of such networks is to channel specific frequencies to the appropriate speaker drivers—treble to tweeters, bass to woofers, midrange to midrange. *Passive* crossover networks are composed of inductors (coils) that pass bass signals and block highs. (Capacitors block lows and pass highs; resistors attenuate all audio tones.)

Loudspeakers sound best when properly damped, vibrations ending when there is no electrical stimulus applied. Low-impedance speakers exhibit this damping. When a crossover network is placed between the amplifier output and speaker input, the speaker no longer "sees" a low-impedance circuit and damping characteristics are reduced.

When Playback Systems Fail . . .

When playback systems fail, certain perceptual phenomena are enhanced, and the entire perception of the program may differ from print to print, medium to medium. Two results are:

1. *Sonic apparitions:* When stereo imaging becomes positioned at a spectator-to-subject distance that does not correspond to what is seen.
2. *Skewed spatialization:* A special case of reverberation effect that denotes an angular field of perception. An oblique angle is suggested as the point of view of an unseen character, of the director, or of the audience forced to "psychologically" change its position from "witness" to involved spectator.

This point is illustrated by a comparison of sound track data on the 35-mm and 70-mm prints of *Star Wars* (1977). Playback variances between differing formats for the same print of many motion picture releases may be a function of directorial alteration, mixing compensation for small theatres, masking, and other inefficiencies in a theatre, in addition to human perceptual errors. Here is a sampling of track differences by David Beraru et al. for a section of *Star Wars*:

70-mm 6-Track Magnetic	35-mm Optical
In the opening sequence the alarm on the Blockade Runner is a loud whooping.	Alarm is a gentle whoop.
When R2-D2 is struck down by Jawas, a hollow thud.	A metal trashcan sound.
When the Jawas unload the droids, the outside door to the sandcrawler makes a noise.	No noise.
The stormtroopers' lizards make odd sounds.	Virtually no sound.
The voice of Aunt Baru is totally dubbed.	Not dubbed.
No excess static.	The 3-D image of the Princess buzzes with static between transmissions.
Luke's binoculars make a lot of noise.	Almost none.
In the conference room on the Death Star, Darth Vader's breathing is much louder.	There, but subtle.
When Luke and the others enter Mosse Isley the traffic background is loud.	Two cantina scenes have different backgrounds. Millenium Falcon's engines sound different during the emergency takeoff from Mosse. Background is filled with high-pitched radio squeaks. Different sounds as the ship makes the jump to light speed.
The Death Star's Beam has a much more distinct tonality.	
Luke's Lightsaber scene with blast shield down lasts 23 seconds.	Lasts 16 seconds.
No change.	Falcon's engines wind down coming out of light speed.
No extra sound data.	Tie Jet fighter tries to escape as Solo jams its transmission—electronic wave sounds.
Constant whine	Intermittent gear shifting as Falcon is pulled into Death Star.
Line is cut out.	3-PO explains how tractor beam can be cut off as R2-D2 looks on.

70-mm 6-Track Magnetic	35-mm Optical

C-3PO

"The power beam is coupled to the main reactor in seven locations, a power loss at one of the terminals will allow the ship to leave."

Over Intercom

"We have an emergency in detention block AA-23."

70-mm 6-Track Magnetic	35-mm Optical
	The Wookie yells louder in the trash masher.
	More rumble in the tractor beam shaft when O Bi Wan uncouples it.
Luke and Leia have a double echo in the air shaft.	Simple reverb.
Line is cut.	"Close the blast doors!" Vadar's breathing is louder during combat with O Bi Wan. Footsteps are heard when the group runs to the Falcon.
No sound.	After escaping, Solo charges up the main guns, eliciting an electron sound.
One long whine.	A separate whine for each X-wing.
As ships pass through field, fighter's voices warped.	No change.
Death Star Narrator is not same as on 35-mm.	
Over the Death Star, Luke yells for help— "Blasted Biggs, where are you?"	"Blasted Wedge, where are you?"

Note: The 35-mm print was made available during a Screen Actor's Guild screening. The 70-mm print was seen in a Los Angeles theatre during the first days of release.

Recuts, re-releases, reconstructions, and varied distribution patterns account for changes in the sound track, but they appear less noticeable than picture edits.

Industry Standard

By adopting an industry standard, a sound technician in New York can listen to a track and have a fair idea of what the soundperson in California had in mind. Since speakers assuredly add so much coloration, it is probably best that there is a standard determined. (See Figure 16-6.)

The following are the accepted German DIN standards for European high fidelity for speaker performance comparison:

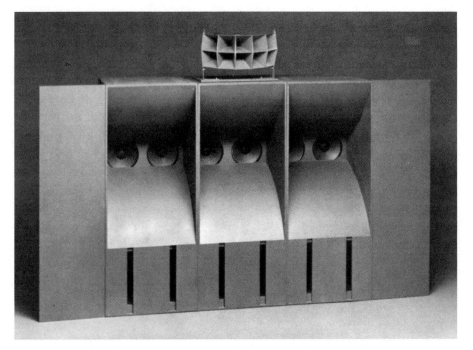

Figure 16-6   Altec Lansing A1 System. (Source: Altec Lansing)

- *Frequency range:* Limit or range are those 8 dB lower than the average level over 100 Hz to 4,000 Hz.
- *Impedance:* Nominal resistance of the system—16 Ω.
- *Sensitivity:* Number of watts required to produce a 96-dB SPL.
- *Nominal power handling:* Number of watts of a noise spectrum that the system can withstand for one minute in every three over a total time of 300 hr.
- *Maximum power handling:* The maximum burst of power (no more than 2 sec in duration) withstood at 250 hz and its low-frequency limit, without distortion caused by such factors as limitations of coil or cone movement.

If there were an industry loudspeaker standard, it would be an Altec *Voice of the Theatre* speaker.

Loudspeaker Care and Handling

- Never hook up a speaker when the amplifier is on and being driven by a signal.

- To protect high-frequency compression drivers from turn-on transients and spurious low-frequency signals, use a DC blocking capacitor when *biamping*.
- Never turn on low-level electronics (preamps, mixers, stereo synthesizers) *after* the power amplifiers are on.
- Keep dust, dirt, smoke, popcorn, dead mice out of the throat of the high-frequency horn. They reduce high-frequency output.
- Use connectors that make ground connections first, like the XLR type, to avoid ground loops.
- Excessive low-frequency signals can cause severe cone damage. Special "surround" speakers should be used.
- Use a large enough power amp, and check it often with an oscilloscope. Clipping in amp and loudspeaker reduces their life.
- Bloop print repairs. An unblooped splice can cause a large signal spike, which blows out the voice coil.
- Loudspeakers don't like high humidity or salt air.
- Avoid excessive equalization since most speaker/amps can't handle frequency extremes.
- Support loudspeakers on solidly braced brackets, and check for loosening of bolts and clamps due to vibration.

THE EAR AND HEARING

The functions, sensitivities, and limitations of the human ear—
the final link in the sound chain—are explained with
illustrative graphs. The Doppler effect and the detection of pitch
are also presented in terms of how they modify the subjective
quality of sound in the theatre.

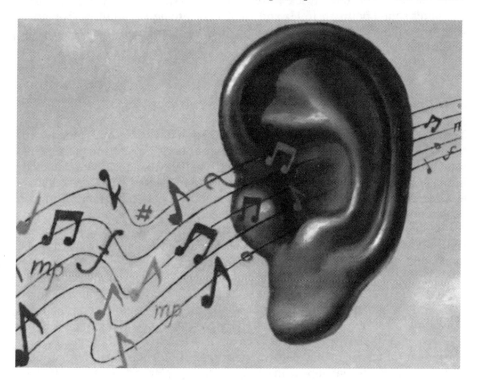

The chain of aural black boxes concludes with the human ear, which translates sound between 16 Hz and 20,000 Hz into nerve impulses. Together with the auditory centers of the brain, it is an instrument that is not only sensitive but highly selective.

How the Ear Works

The ear canal acts as a broadly tuned resonator that intensifies by as much as 10 times the pressure variations of sound waves over fairly broad band of frequencies (greatest at 3,400 Hz). (See Figure 17-1.) High frequencies are detected inside the cochlea just behind the oval window. (See Figure 17-2.) Low frequencies are detected deep inside the cochlea spiral via hair cells transmitting to nerve endings, which are bundled or harnessed into a kind of nerve leading to the brain's central nervous system center where digital filtering occurs. Chemically encoded data are held in a brain buffer, and assembled into word fragments and then full words, thoughts, perceptions, images/facts.

The mechanism behind all this data processing is a profound but simple hydroelectric system in which specialized nerve cells convert fluid movement in the spiral cochlea into impulses. The cilia or hair cell position along the trail constitutes a set of highly selective frequency filters. According to Bell Labs research, the selectivity may approach several hundred decibels per octave dependent on the frequency decade considered. Loud noises kill off hair cell detectors and the resonant peak in young humans (3 kHz to 4 kHz) falls off with age. A *notch* forms around 4 kHz, which widens and deepens with continued exposure to severe sound level pressure. Sensitivity appears also to wane with age. In childhood some individuals can hear a 40,000-Hz tone. A child, for example, can hear a mosquito singing outside a window when the eardrum is receiving less than one quadrillionth of a watt of power, virtually the level of the imaginary. But then the average drop in upper frequency discrimination is about 80 Hz per year. (See Figure 17-2.)

The eardrum is not the only auditory transducer. We also hear through the skull by means of bone conduction, and there is strong evidence for diaphragmatic sensation of low frequencies. As we normally hear ourselves, the low-frequency vibrations from our own vocal chords conducted to our own ears by the bones make our speech sound more powerful and dynamic than the pure

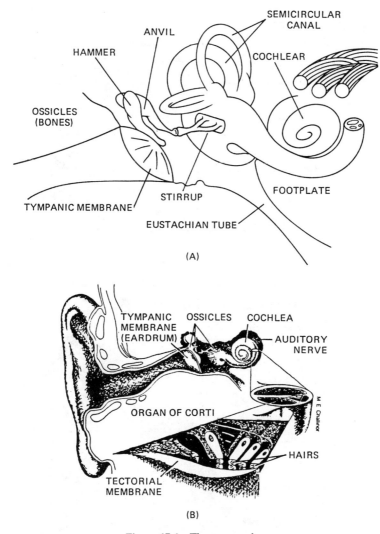

Figure 17-1 The ear canal.

sound waves heard by another person or via a recording system. (The comparative insensitivity of the ear at low frequencies is an obvious physical necessity because we would otherwise hear all the vibrations of our own bodies!)

The residual sound level that exists around the audience seat severely affects the intelligibility of speech at that location. This ambiance can mask parts of speech, causing garbled syllable perception. Since this level is seldom measured, almost all playback systems do not compensate for the closed-door, full-audience, and empty room differences.

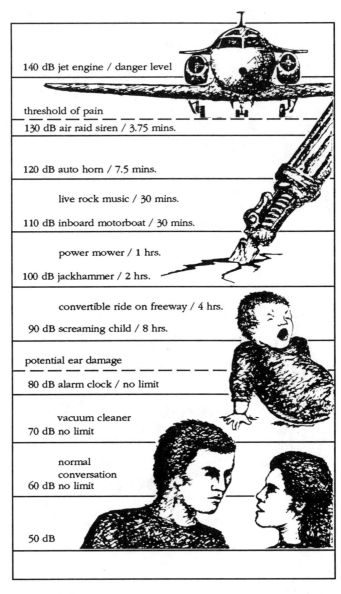

140 dB jet engine / danger level

threshold of pain

130 dB air raid siren / 3.75 mins.

120 dB auto horn / 7.5 mins.

live rock music / 30 mins.

110 dB inboard motorboat / 30 mins.

power mower / 1 hrs.

100 dB jackhammer / 2 hrs.

convertible ride on freeway / 4 hrs.

90 dB screaming child / 8 hrs.

potential ear damage

80 dB alarm clock / no limit

vacuum cleaner
70 dB no limit

normal
conversation
60 dB no limit

50 dB

Figure 17-2   The change in human hearing over time.

Fletcher-Munson Effect

The energy level of any sound is measurable as intensity, but the relationship between intensity and loudness is not linear. Loudness contour curves of the human ear exhibit the *Fletcher-Munson effect*. (See Figure 17-4.) Sound pres-

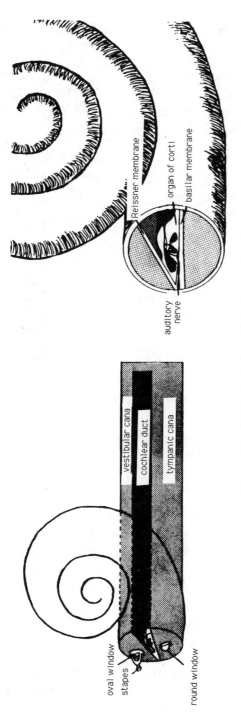

Reissner membrane

organ of corti

basilar membrane

auditory nerve

vestibular cana

cochlear duct

tympanic cana

oval window
stapes

round window

Figure 17-3 (A) Oval window; (B) basilar membrane.

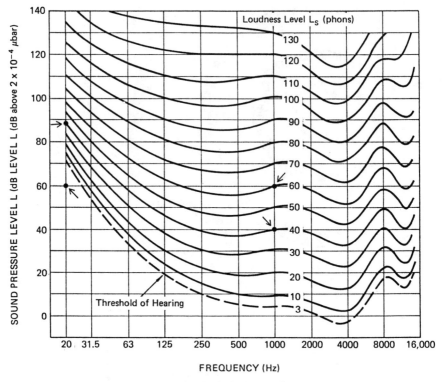

Figure 17-4 Fletcher-Munson Curve.

sure is the actual energy reaching the ear. Numbers on the curves are *phons* (perceived loudness), the sensation of loudness that registers with the brain. The graph, first published in 1933 by Fletcher and Munson, suggests the following:

- The ear is less sensitive at low frequencies.
- This insensitivity is more acute as pressure drops.
- A 50-dB tone sounds 30 dB louder at 50 Hz, and 10 dB louder at 10,000 Hz.
- The greatest sensitivity is around 3,500 Hz.
- The conversational level is at 60 dB (60 phons).
- The threshold of hearing is 20 dB at 125 Hz.

Dialogue for film is usually played back in the theatre at 5 or 10 dB louder than it was recorded on the set. The apparent change in the frequency curve seems to emphasize the low region of the frequency spectrum at the expense of the midrange. This is why, as an audio designer, you must listen to tracks at the highest possible level that you can stand when equalization takes place in the mix, because often more bass must be taken out in order to avoid tubbiness.

The other problem encountered is the generally low projection of the voice on the set, which must be compensated for by adding midrange energy via theatre equalization.

If music was recorded at full level (on a scoring stage) and you want to use it in the final film at a very low level, the opposite condition holds true. Notice the *loudness balance* on home hi-fi gear.

If the track is mixed at a low level and played back at a loud level, it sounds "bassy." Loudness contour circuits in some reproduction systems alter the frequency response in relation to volume according to the F&R curves.

Detecting Pitch

How does the ear detect the pitch of a pure tone? In the low-frequency range up to 60 Hz, the vibration of the basilar membrane in the ear produces the auditory nerve volleys, or *electric spikes*, synchronous with the rhythm of the sound. As sound pressure increases, the density of the spikes increases. The number and rhythm of the spikes are transmitted to the cortex. There, the variables alone convey the loudness and the pitch of the sound according to Georg Von Bekesy. Short waves, it has been found, act at the base of the spiral cochlea, and long waves (low frequencies) act at the apex of the cochlea. They stimulate hair cells causing impulses to pass up the cochlear nerve. The impulses are amplified by the *organ of Corti*, while neurons initiating the nerve impulses to the brain react among the hair cells of that organ.

Above 4,000 Hz, pitch is determined by the location of maximum amplitude along the membrane. This is an inhibitory system that suppresses less intense sounds and thus sharpens the sensation of the maximum amplitude. Without this auxiliary system, the *tone* would sound like a noise of a certain pitch but not like a pure tone.

The sound signal passes through vibrating bones. The signal is conveyed through the aqueous fluid of the inner ear into the spiral path of the cochlea (indicated as a plane divided by the organ of Corti). The cochlea differentiates between wavelengths, being sensitive to some and not to others at particular areas along the path. The sensations are clarified by the organ of Corti and converted to electrochemical information, which is passed along the auditory nerve to the cerebral cortex. This acoustic path between the sound source and the listener is called the *transfer function*, which contains both time and frequency data decoded by the brain into angular direction and distance.

Image localization is determined by adjusting the ratio of transfer functions, which in turn alter the *ratio* of sound pressure common to both ears and between the ears. Theoretically, this allows manipulation of the perceived location of a sound source.

Body placement in relation to the source, room acoustics, and head shape alter the perception of aural localization. The position of the head cannot move outside of approximately a 3-in radius to preserve the integrity of the apparent sound source. Considered also must be the fact that the distance between ears from the back of the head is different than that in the front of the head. Creative manipulation of phase relationships (time-delay) also account for accurate side-to-back localization. The outer ear produces a delay and time smear effect on signals reaching the ear drums, underscoring the significance of head shape and motion in accurate localization.

The following parameters are the key factors in creating the illusion of apparent sound source:

- Visual cues.
- Head motion.
- Head masking.
- Shape of the outer ear.
- Time differences between ears.

The Physiological Significance of the Sound Track

In the literature of psychoanalysis, notably in the work of Guy Rosolato and Didier Anzieu and in the theory and practice of pediatrician Dr. Frederick Leboyer, there is ample evidence to assert the primacy of musical sounds in providing a sense of security and even pleasure in the listener. Rosolato and Anzieu see auditory space as the primal "psychic space." As in birthing techniques that reflect a concern for the sensitivity of the infant (Leboyer's quiet birth), the "sonorous envelope created by the mother provides a sonorous "omnipotence" for the child; the infant's psychic and spacial limits have not yet been defined. The infant can hear and be heard (in the dark, as in the theatre); it can project its voice into space. Perceptions yield imaginary fantasies, an "oceanic feeling," as reported by some moviegoers during intense melodic moments—a melodic bath in which the voice of the mother is perceived as a "good object."

For the movie audience the effect of some musical sounds—their effect from without and within—can be traced to a preverbal, pre-Oedipal state "where self and other do not exist." Sound soothes the imaginary longing for bodily fusion with the mother. When the infant experiences quiet birth, the transition to life outside the sonorous envelope of the womb is without pain or stress. These babies smile and feel more secure with their new, multisensory environment. In the theatre, sound serves to reinforce this psychosonic regression into the pleasurable.

How Dolby Surround Works

The predominant sounds originate from and are associated with their on-screen sources. The surround channel conveys spatial information, adding depth by mimicking the ambiance and directional signals that occur in real life.

The Haas effect, a psychoacoustic phenomenon, defines the way in which Dolby surround provides time delay. The mind identifies the first place from which a sound is heard as that sound's origin (according to current theory), mentally ignoring or masking out other sources of the same sound arriving a fraction of a second later.

Time delay makes sound connected to screen action appear to come from the front speakers.

Effects of Humidity and Temperature on Acoustics

According to tests reported by Dennis Bohn (*Sound & Video Contractor*, April, 1988), within the range of 10 to 40% relative humidity in a given acoustic space, the increase in sound absorption in air is greatest. The same increase in absorption also causes a decrease in reverberation time in auditoria where surface absorption is low. The change in absorption at high frequencies can be the dominant factor in determining whether a concert (or a mix) is spectacular or dull. It is evident that severe changes in humidity and temperature in a mixing room from day to day alter the mixer's response to the day's work. This may account for some inconsistencies in the mixes that take months to complete. Obviously, the absorption phenomena has far-reaching implications in the theatre where the experience of the sound track may be very different, such as on rainy versus bright (dry) sunny days. (See Tables 17-1 and 17-2.)

The small percentage change is for every cycle undergone by the sound wave. Here's how humidity affects the sound wave: Moisture affects the density of air. Moist air is *less* dense than dry air, increasing the speed of sound in air, but moisture causes the specific heat ratio to decrease, which decreases the speed of sound in the air. Temperature changes cause density changes, which do not affect pressure, but changes in pressure affect density, but not vice versa. The speed of sound increases with the square root of absolute temperature. The effects of temperature and humidity differ for different frequencies. (See Table 17-3.)

Temperature and humidity changes affect the sound wave even in small amounts. Just a small change in temperature or even a slight humidity shift causes the waves to become shifted in phase—different from the originally transmitted wave. It will be different than when the room was equalized. In addition to phase, high-frequency levels change due to absorption.

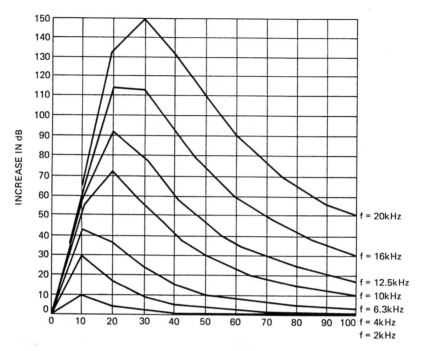

Figure 17-5 Graph of sound absorption increase in dB/1000 ft vs. relative humidity as a function of frequency at 20°C. (*Source: Sound & Video Contractor* [April 15, 1988])

TABLE 17-1 Velocity of sound in dry air vs. temperature

Temp °C	Temp °F	Velocity m/sec	Velocity ft/sec	Temp °C	Temp °F	Velocity m/sec	Velocity ft/sec
0	32.0	331.45	1087.42	21	69.8	343.96	1128.46
1	33.8	332.06	1089.42	22	71.6	344.54	1130.37
2	35.6	332.66	1091.39	23	73.4	345.12	1132.27
3	37.4	333.27	1093.39	24	75.2	345.71	1134.20
4	39.2	333.87	1095.36	25	77.0	346.29	1136.11
5	41.0	334.47	1097.33	26	78.8	346.87	1138.01
6	42.8	335.07	1099.30	27	80.6	347.45	1139.91
7	44.6	335.67	1101.26	28	82.4	348.02	1141.78
8	46.4	336.27	1103.23	29	84.2	348.60	1143.69
9	48.2	336.87	1105.20	30	86.0	349.18	1145.59
10	50.0	337.46	1107.14	31	87.8	349.75	1147.46
11	51.8	338.06	1109.11	32	89.6	350.33	1149.36
12	53.6	338.65	1111.04	33	91.4	350.90	1151.23
13	55.4	339.25	1113.01	34	93.2	351.48	1153.13
14	57.2	339.84	1114.95	35	95.0	352.05	1155.00
15	59.0	340.43	1116.88	36	96.8	352.62	1156.87
16	60.8	341.02	1118.82	37	98.6	353.19	1158.74
17	62.6	341.61	1120.75	38	100.4	353.76	1160.61
18	64.4	342.20	1122.69	39	102.2	354.32	1162.45
19	66.2	342.78	1124.59	40	104.0	354.89	1164.32
20	68.0	343.37	1126.53				

Source: Sound & Video Contractor (April 15, 1988).

TABLE 17-2   Total % increase in speed of sound (re 0°C) due to temperature and humidity combined

Temp °C	Relative humidity in %					
	0	30	40	50	80	100
5	0.91	.952	.966	.980	1.02	1.05
10	1.81	1.87	1.89	1.91	1.97	2.01
15	2.71	2.79	2.82	2.85	2.93	2.98
20	3.60	3.71	3.75	3.79	3.90	3.98
30	5.35	5.55	5.62	5.69	5.90	6.03
40	7.07	7.43	7.54	7.66	8.03	8.27

Source: Sound & Video Contractor (April 15, 1988).

TABLE 17-3   Percentage increase in speed of sound (re 0°C) due to moisture in air (only). Temperature effects not included except as they pertain to humidity

Temp °C	Relative humidity in %									
	10	20	30	40	50	60	70	80	90	100
5	.014	.028	.042	.056	.070	.083	.097	.111	.125	.139
10	.020	.039	.059	.078	.098	.118	.137	.157	.176	.196
15	.027	.054	.082	.109	.136	.163	.191	.218	.245	.273
20	.037	.075	.112	.149	.187	.224	.262	.299	.337	.375
30	.068	.135	.203	.272	.340	.408	.477	.546	.615	.684
40	.118	.236	.355	.474	.594	.714	.835	.957	1.08	1.20

Source: Sound & Video Contractor (April 15, 1988).

Appendix A

EXERCISES IN SINGLE AND DOUBLE SYSTEM SOUND RECORDING

Sound Synchronization

Refinements in technology, not directorial resensitizing, have changed the practice of location recording over the past ten years. Trouble-free wireless microphones, multitrack re-recording techniques, and MIDI/SMPTE interface, coupled with the need for fast, unsophisticated editing of video for news and cable markets, have taken sound recording back out into the streets.

Double-system film is still the most versatile format for the classic social documentary. Single-system video is sufficient for all news operations while the precision of double-system video (Betacam CCD plus Stereo Nagra) offers many creative options.

Most (80%) of production sound may be handled with two microphones for either mono or stereo broadcast. Motion picture production is utilizing multiple-microphone techniques for spacial and dramatic integrity. In practice, since the birth of the "talkies" sound synchronization is principally concerned with a descending order of priorities: music, natural effects, dialogue.

If sound cannot be recorded synchronously on location using one of the classic methods outlined herein, the emulation of sync is created in post-production with little effort. The historical development of sync sound recording thus follows this outline:

1. *Direct recording:* The signal is recorded optically or magnetically onto the *original* film emulsion along the edge. This single-system method was introduced initially in 35-mm studio work in which the camera exposed the picture and audio at the same time. However, the process required great care and precision since balance and level controls were minimal and there was little room for error.

   Television found single-system portable 16-mm cameras to be ideal for location work. However, film stock costs and the need for faster turn-around (the time from processing of the raw stock to an edited master set for broadcast) forced the move to single-system video in which sound and image are recorded on magnetic tape, first on 3/4-in and then on Beta format and 8-mm video.

   Both the magnetic stripe of film and the videotape oxide leave much to be desired in the way of sensitivity and fidelity. In addition, both recording systems require high-quality mixers and microphones to achieve anything more than mediocre results. Before the advent of higher-quality home receivers (component television with good speakers and processing gear), sound was not a factor in TV production. Stereo broadcasting, high-definition TV standardization, and home video entertainment hardware have necessitated a rethinking of the value of good audio.

2. *Double-system sound recording:* Employs portable cassette, 1/4-in reel-to-reel or 16/35-mm recorders (fullcoat magnetic film as the recording medium) linked to the camera via time code, crystal oscillators, or cable-linked sync generators (an archaic system still in use in some parts of the world) in camera and recorder. A sync pulse is a record of the camera speed recorded on the picture medium for a reference match in post.

In digital recording, this analog match is accomplished entirely in the digital domain. Double-system allows for a moving camera, greater control of the sound recording via sophisticated recorders and mixer/microphone combinations. The recording format has a quality bottom line with 35-mm magnetic film providing the most efficient recording medium. However, microphone choice and technique are more important than the limitations of the recording medium.

3. *Studio double-system (Hollywood studio technique):* Works on the basis of a perfect lock of camera and recorder motors, both of which are running from the same AC line current. Although the motors may come up to speed at different rates, once they reach 24 fps, an AC interlock provides the most trouble-free mode of synchronization. However, the system requires voltage regulators, are not portable, and are mostly used for fixed studio applications in a totally soundproofed space.

PRACTICUM

1. Techs are broken up into teams of three or four to work with a loaded Nagra recorder. They use a simple hand-held dynamic cardioid microphone like an Electro-Voice RE-10. They make several test recordings beginning at 2 ft from a voice source at a 45° angle to the source. Recordings are made at three speeds, with and without the *limiter*, with and without *filters*, and finally from double and half the original distance without changing *level* and then changing level to maintain full modulation or 0 db on the modulometer. They must properly *slate* the tape with *date, speed, production number* or *name, roll number,* and *location*. Machines are cleaned, the battery test is made, recordings are made while running on AC and then on DC as time allows. Playback is accomplished through an external speaker/amplifier at a high level to listen to the changes of background and noise to wanted signal (signal-to-noise ratio).

MOTOR TYPE	SYNCHRONOUS MOTOR	CONSTANT SPEED MOTOR	VARI-SPEED MOTOR
SPEED	24 fps EXACTLY	24 fps APPROX.	1 fps-6000fps
POWER USED	AC	DC	AC/DC
SYNC. PULSE	FROM 60-HZ AC SOURCE	Self-Generating cable, radio, crystal	None

POWER SOURCE	FREZZI POWER PACK	ATN-2	BATTERY
POWER GIVEN	AC (DC converter)	DC	DC
POWER NEEDED TO CHARGE	DC BATTERY from AC INVERTER	AC FROM WALL OR FREZZI	IF RE-CHARGABLE FROM AC INVERTER
SYNC MODE	60 HZ	Relay 60HZ from WALL or Frezzi	None

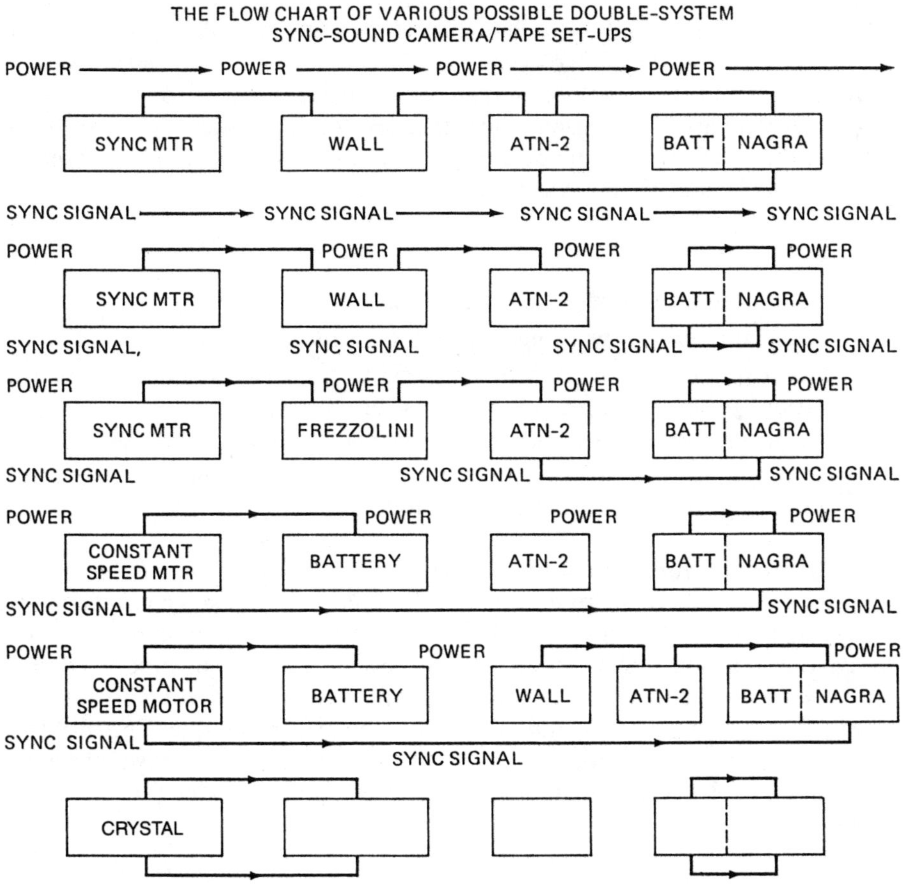

Figure A-1 Flow chart of various sync-sound set-ups.

GOAL:

Familiarity with mechanical adjustments of recorder.

Diagnose sources of noise.

Awareness of check points and maintenance.

Test inverse square law.

Discover affects of mike placement, subject to mike distances, filtering and limiting, off-axis conditions.

Ascertain fidelity as a function of speed of voice recording.

Determine proper level and distance for intelligibility of voice.

2. Techs are introduced to various types and classes of microphones in relation to pattern and powering. Each team records in a different location with as many of the varied mikes as time allows. They will have the opportunity of hearing the effect of each mike in each situation since the slating for this session includes type of mike and placement and level setting. Dynamic and condenser mikes are compared when used at identical levels and identical distances from subject. Mikes with different angles of acceptance or patterns are compared in similar situations at similar levels and distances.

GOAL:

Determine effects of pattern on subject.

Determine proper working ranges for a wide variety of mikes.

Learn proper test and setup according to powering function of mike—battery pack, preamps, transformers, proper inputs.

Ascertain best mike for each standard situation: close-up interview, radio drama, long shot, moving shots, interior, exterior, concealed or boom mounting, perspective, and intelligibility.

3. Previous functions are repeated but in multiple miking arrangements allowing the student to learn to use a mixer and/or multiple mike inputs on the recorder. Techs try to "ride-the-gain" on each mike duirng an interview situation and/or position mikes in order to achieve a level averaging all source levels without altering it during recording. Students attempt to *crossfade* between voices using the mid-level technique or the steep level technique. The problem of a moving shot is introduced and students must solve the coverage issue through mike placement, mike boom operation and the mixing function combined.

GOAL:

Simulate typical studio live recording session with complexity of set-up and movement. Introduce mixing techniques.

Enable the student to choose between two basic approaches to recording the multiple-miking situation: preset mixing or multiple perspective mixing by a kind of choreography and orchestration of mike booming and level adjustment.

Learn the need for rehearsal and planning.

Learn process of analyzing the coordinates of the shot.

4. The sound camera is introduced as yet another limiting issue. All previous functions are incorporated in an effort to achieve the proper coordination of the sound set-up vis-a-vis the framing of the shot. The issue of noise becomes more critical. Proper perspective and noise control problems are induced during a typical theatrical set-up in the studio. Another team deals with the same problem on location with a typical news gathering situation. Both exercises are accomplished with a stationary and moving camera.

GOAL:

Introduction to mechanics of sync-sound set-up without directorial controls.

Examination of limitations of mike placement in relation to frame and movement.

Learn coordination between sound and camera in studio in comparison with on-location documentary set-ups.

Demonstrate need for observation, awareness, coordination, analysis, discipline.

5. A tech is selected to design a sync-sound production to be shot in the studio. Three or four shots, planned to incorporate all that has been previously learned, are scripted: one moving shot, one close-up, one long shot, one multiple-miking situation. A different crew is called on to handle each shot-sound and camera, others observe solutions to the directorial challenge. Acting students or professionals are utilized for the session. A "director" coordinates the activity. Each director *calls* the shot, reciting commands methodically and lucidly so that all efforts are timed properly. Techs are particularly responsible for proper utilization of all equipment in terms of *technique, use of time, control of actors,* to produce a *noiseless, intelligible, intelligent sound track.*

GOAL:

Apply all previous experience to actual production situation.

Afford opportunity to observe mistakes and possible alternate solutions.

Develop sensitivity to requirements of each crew member, talent, and director.

Learn to work as a unit.

Begin to acquire an inventory of possile approaches to a specific sound recording problem.

Learn proper procedure for executing the sync-sound recording.

6. Projects are assigned to production teams to record in various live situations in the city and on the campus. Techs are responsible for specification of the location or studio recording rental package which is signed out, checked out, and then employed with the best professional attitude attainable at this level of experience. They may, for instance, interview construction workers during a lunch break on a downtown construction site. They plan and execute the session to the best of their current abilities.

GOAL:

Solid understanding of individual responsibilities.

Perform proper test of equipment.

Learn to anticipate possible location problems and needs by choosing an adaptable but portable equipment package.

Solve typical and atypical sound recording problems.

Analyze and evaluate efforts during an interlock session.

By setting a wide variety of microphones from proximate to distant positions, maintaining full modulation, the user determines the working range for each type: omnidirectional, unidirectional, hyperdirectional. The user also places each mike off-axis at varying distances. The same is accomplished without regard to level. This is done indoors and outdoors, in quiet spaces, and in hollow spaces with apparent noise sources. This affords the opportunity to listen to most of the possible conditions and most of the possible ways a particular mike reacts to similar conditions.

7. Two omnidirectional lavalier mikes are pinned to a performer. One is dynamic and one is condenser-powered. At the same position and level, a recording is made and characteristics analyzed. The mike is pulled off and pulled back until it no longer can pick up a signal. It is found that this occurs at about 5 or 6 ft for most omnidirectional mikes.

Various mikes are mounted on a fishpole. Without using a cueing device, boom man must follow movement as best he can with the particular isolation shockmount employed. It is determined that a mike with a cardioid pattern covers a greater area but has more of a chance of severe level losses trying to cover long trajectories. A hypercardioid (shotgun) seems to offer a greater range allowing the boom person to move back and assume a clean angle of approach to follow movement with much less movement of the boom. Every doubling of the subject to mike distance causes a 6-db drop. In practice the boom should never be moved more than 2 to 4 ft in any direction in an effort to maintain the consistent subject to mike distance required for normal recording levels. The wider the pattern and the closer the position of the mike to the subject at the start of the shot, the greater the chance of loosing coverage. The mixer must resort to *riding the gain* in order to compensate for inadequate position. Exact and quick responses must be made. This is quite difficult. A rehearsal aids in anticipating the degree and extent of compensation but the work is quite arbitrary and difficult to orchestrate.

Front-to-back response is tested by having someone recite and walk around the space until he or she is also directly behind the particular mike. The field of sensitivity is therefore determined at various levels and distances.

A hand-held omnidirectional is compared to a tie-tac electret condenser omnidirectional mike. Both are compared to a dynamic omnidirectional studio mike mounted on a boom supported over head. The users determine subjectively which they prefer in terms of presence, signal-to-noise ratio, intelligibility, and resonance characteristics.

After review of basic set-ups and various mike applications, students are asked to specify a typical sound rental package in an effort to arrive at the budget for an average daily rental.

Tapes are monitored in an effort to hear the effect on the signal of proximity, diffraction, impedance inefficiencies; the effect of high frequencies attenuated, high-pass filtration in the Nagra, in relation to flat recording of voice, at three speeds.

8. The performance of the location recorder depends on many elements working together as a system. Any deficiency in one element causes inefficiencies throughout. The following checkpoints are advisable.

Azimuth: Head alignment must be perfect and consistent from record to playback, according to the NAB standard. Heads are "trimmed up" with calipers and precision tools to effect maximum output while a test tape is played.

Bias: Due to limitations of the head and magnetic emulsion of the tape, a high-frequency current must be passed or applied to the record head. Its amplitude is much higher than the audio signal and is mixed with it just before the record head in the system. This sets the "operating point" of the magnetic system to the most linear part of its transfer curve. Ratings differ for each kind of head and tape emulsion. The Nagra 4.2L is presently biased for Scotch tape #208 and #206.

Equalizers: Used in record and playback amplifiers to make up for other deficiencies, equalizers are set after azimuth and bias to achieve flat frequency response.

Cue track: An audio track on cassette and multichannel recorders can be used for automated operation. Since valuable information may be deposited on the cue track and since it can "bleed" into other channels, become over modulated, etc., its performance should be tested through metering.

An oscilloscope may be hooked up to the head cables and the waveform monitored.

On-board metering: Use the test function of the recorder to determine battery level, pilot signal level, compression, etc.

9. Since it is not likely that a situation will be planned to fail due to some neglect in the way of equipment, the students are given a checklist of the small, hard-to-find items that help to either solve location problems or make life easier in general. An example is the shorting plug, a small 4-pin dime-shaped plug that fits into the right side Nagra XTAL input to complete the crystal circuit. If it is inadvertantly left out, the recorder cannot function as a sync system! (See the location inventory checklist on page 157.)

10. Sources of noise and interference in the line are noted and defined.

- An isolation transformer separates the house ground from your equipment ground. Make sure voltage capacity is overestimated, and of a constant voltage variety to safeguard against power drops.
- Some RF may come from power lines. Use a line filter.
- Ground all equipment with a 14 gauge wire from each to a common ground.
- Getting hum out of balanced and unbalanced combinations of lines. Ground each mike to a common.
- AC hum may be "induced" if mike cable runs parallel to an ac power cable. Cross all cables at 90 degrees.
- Ground loops are caused when shield is grounded at one end. If the line interconnects two systems decide where the ground will be and disconnect one of the two grounds.
- Do not use lines on which there are dimmers and flourescent lights.

See Figure A-2 for line repair technique.

11. Sensitivity to the use of the location mixer is developed by comparing two direct mike attachments into the Nagra recorder and setting each level independently for two diverse voices. The recordist has the choice of "riding the gain"—raising or lowering intensity of each input as voice level changes—or choosing an average setting without further manipulation. The alternative is to move the mike. The option is to change the kind of mike.

Goal: Determine the need for rehearsal. Practice obtaining balance between two kinds of voice. Sensitize to cumulative noise effect of two or more mikes. Determine the need for mixer.

12. For three or more microphones, the recordist is asked to connect a small portable location mixer into the single microphone input of the Nagra. If the mixer is *active,* it is supplying its own power and can be tested. To power a mixer from the Nagra, a cable must run into the Accessory input. The Mike or

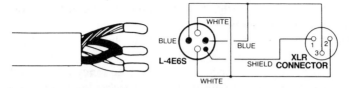

Full noise rejection depends upon proper paring of the inner conductors. Both blue leads should be connected together and inserted in the "low" pin of the XLR (3), and white leads should be inserted in the "high" pin (2); the shield goes to pin 1.

Because the shield density on Canare cable is very high, it is somewhat difficult to push back the braid and pull the inner conductors through. Instead, we strongly recommend unbraiding the shield by "combing" it out with a pointed tool, beginning at the end of the cable.

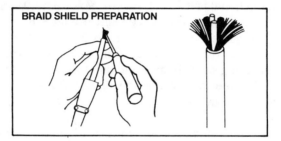

All Canare AT-style (fixed installation) cables utilize an **A**luminum **T**ape (foil shield). Cable prep is fast and efficient.

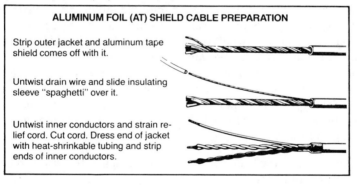

Figure A-2   How to prepare braided shielding for microphone cables. (Source: Canare)

Line potentiometer is set to the middle position. The first mike level is set according to the desired effect and full modulation, its position marked. The second, likewise set, is marked and turned down. The third is set. All are placed to marks and the recordists listens to the cumulative effect and level. Should a problem exist, the master control is reset; *then* each individual mixer pot. If the mixer battery runs down, increased hiss occurs. The goal is to achieve proper balance between voices; secondly, it is to avoid excessive amplification at the mixer input; third, reduce noise.

The quality of the successive recordings are judged according to factors that tell us if this can be transferred without adding more noise: intelligibility, fidelity, signal-to-noise ratio, spacial character, frequency range, and dispersion of energy over that range. In other words, we are seeking a fully modulated track with little background noise of a voice that sounds like the natural inflection but with a bit more emphasis of the highs since they tend to be mutilated later in the process.

In preparing for a voice recording in the studio, the recording crew is asked to use four microphones at about 1 to 2 ft from the voice. The microphones are as follows: an AKG ribbon-type dynamic cardioid, a TR-50 electret condenser omnidirectional lavalier, an Electro Voice RE-10 dynamic cardioid, a Sennheiser RF condenser ultra-directional cardioid 816 or MK470.

The TR-50 is pinned on (see Figure A-3), the others hand held to eliminate the possibility of vibration from mike stands. Levels are set in the same way. The recording space is large and quiet. After the four recordings, a subjective choice between them must be made. The same criteria obtain: Intelligibility, fidelity, signal-to-noise level, response, spacial considerations are not relevant.

Goal: To determine the appropriate class of mike for general narration recording with a consideration of the transfer process and the exhibition mode. We want to reduce low frequencies and capture all the highs.

13. The situation is repeated with multiple mikes in the mixer for three voices. The class that was previously determined as the best may now not be suitable. This is subjectively determined. All playback should be made at high levels through an external speaker/amplifier. Line output setting on the Nagra should be at 0 db. Monitor relation of that point to swing of the needle of the modulometer when Nagra function switch is in Playback/Loudspeaker.

These set-ups do not take into account other possible problems. A very good portable location mixer should have the following attributes in addition to being quiet and *small:*

- A black box at the monitor output that exaggerates *distortion* before it becomes problematic.

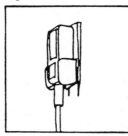 

Figure A-3   TRAM TR-50 hexan noiseless omni tie tac set in side lapel.

- A reversing polarity switch to accommodate Nagra and DIN standard phasing.
- Internal batteries.
- Equilization.
- Peak overload indicator.
- High-pass filters to eliminate wind noise and low-Hz rumble.
- Variable gain/attenuation controls to accommodate low-output ribbon and dynamic mikes, as well as high-output condensers.
- 1-kHz tone oscillator for transfer reference.
- Balanced and unbalanced outputs for tape or video recorder.
- Peak limiter.
- Good shielding.
- Monitor level control.
- Illuminated VU meter for night work.
- AB and simplex (phantom) power at all inputs.

Reference: CM-1 Cinetronics
            MX80 Coherent
            SELA 2880
            Sonosax

The recordist practices *crossfading* as a technique for masking the noise or sound of moving the pots on a mixer. Instead of moving each pot through the entire range from the proper setting to the bottom (down), one pot is dropped

Figure A-4 Crossfeeding with the Sonosax slip pan pots is easier than with knobs.

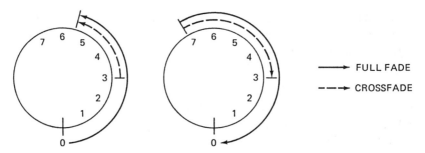

FULL FADE
CROSSFADE

Figure A-5   Level is kept at half-way position to facilitate the catch-up of crossfade manipulation.

down halfway as the other pot is moved from halfway up. At any one time, unused pots are at the halfway point so there is no noticeable change in signal-to-noise ratio *within* the shot.

14. A crew is sent out to shoot several wild and sync-sound shots. Back in the studio, the dailies are screened and a timing log is made shot by shot. Narration is written according to this time log. Spacial considerations are noted, the need for a certain "quality" of voice is analyzed (male-female, gruff, sweet, etc.).

A narrator sits before a mike in a comfortable setting. No projection is required. Each take is recorded directly onto 16-mm sprocketed fullcoat magnetic film and also onto 1/4-in tape with the Nagra.

The 1/4-in tape is transferred "flat" to 16-mm fullcoat, played back through theatre speakers, and compared to the playback of the direct recording.

Both recordings are then played against the projected film before editing.

GOAL:

Determine the quality changes between two methods of recording.

Afford experience in timing and preparation of narration for studio recording.

Ascertain need for postsynchronization of dialogue and effects.

Familiarize students with rigors of direct studio recording.

Figure A-6 PZM® 2½ boundary lexan plate rejects all sound at rear.

15. A pressure zone microphone (PZM) is used to record narration in the two manners cited above. It is placed on a podium, on the floor, and on the wall. (See Figure A-6.) The results are compared to each other and to the first set of recordings with conventional microphones.

GOAL:

Determine the suitability of PZM for voice recording.

Practice walking through the studio to determine the best listening vantage point, and therefore, the best position for the PZM.

16. Dailies are timed for preparation for narration. During projection, each shot is listed and measured with a stop watch. Some time is spent analyzing shot content for other possible roles for a narrative track as well as natural and special sound effects. A log is prepared for use in the narration recording session. Two methods are possible.

Using the Nagra ¼-in tape recorder, students use several kinds of microphones as close as possible to the narrator. The narrator does not hold the sheet of narration, does not hold the mike, but does assume a comfortable position.

A log is made of the recording. The roll is slated with the following information:

Roll number.	Recording speed.	Shot number.
Date.	Level.	Sound take number.

Should a bad recording be made, it is *tail slated* "N.G.," so that it is not transferred to the editing medium. Projection is not necessary.

The second method is a direct record to sprocket-driven recorder in the studio chain. A microphone is connected through the mix console to a synchronous fullcoat 35-mm recorder. Again, projection is not necessary, only the timing sheet. After rehearsal, a take is made on fullcoat magnetic film and played back in the studio to judge quality.

At this point, a PZM may be used. They may be mounted on various sized plates from 4-in to 4-ft square and mounted on the back wall. Generally, the larger the plate, the more lows can be captured.

17. A simulation of a "dubbing" session is set up using a segment of a shot sequence shot for the session.

After filming the short sequence, the tech prepares the film with leader at the head and tail and between the shots to be used for dialogue replacement. The lines to be re-recorded in the studio are transcribed from the scratch track. The scratch track is transferred to fullcoat and played back over and over to the person to recite the lines through headphones. As the narrator listens, the film is projected and the person at the control console also watches the footage counter, which corresponds to the measurements on a "Cue Sheet," which has both the timing and the dialogue. After rehearsals, a take is made, played back, and a determination made as to quality, level, intelligibility.

GOAL:

Learn coordination required for automatic dialogue replacement in the studio.

Ascertain appropriate microphone for dubbing of voice.

18. The same shots must be studied and a log made of required background sound effects, which must be recorded and added to the dialogue to all be postsynchronized and edited to preserve sound perspective consistency. The scratch track gives some of the necessary information, but the creative choices involve an understanding of what *could as well as should* constitute the background sound.

Goal: Sensitize techs to elements of background sound by offering the challenge to build up a background from scratch.

19. A team is asked to record a sync-sound sequence on location with the idea of maintaining high signal-to-noise levels from shot to shot without notions of spacial perspective. This should produce a consistent track with little discrimination as to size of shot or size of acoustic space.

Goal: Work under the assumption that background will be reconstituted in the mix should the information be lacking on the track. Concentration is on obtaining high level recordings for transfer and further processing utilizing one or two mikes at most.

20. This exercise includes the recording of natural sound effects, live music and synthesized sounds. Several so-called "stereo" microphone techniques are suggested. Narration is recorded utilizing three divergent systems and compared to mono (single-mike) recordings, judged according to efficiency of *separation* of key elements.

Techs are encouraged to try other approaches including the Nakamichi three-point technique for voice and instrument. (See Figure A-7.)

GOAL:

Differentiate between "stereo" sound and multitrack sound in terms of spacial localization.

Gain understanding of relationship of binaural hearing to stereo "effect." Determine a definition of stereo in terms of its function in the shot.

Analyze noise effects in multiple microphone set-ups.

Ascertain which class of microphone is more suitable for stereo and/or 2-track applications by experimentation with all patterns in combination and separately.

Develop a hybrid technique for video and film using PZM and wireless systems.

Develop a sense memory for appropriate microphone positions for specific vocal and instrumental renditions.

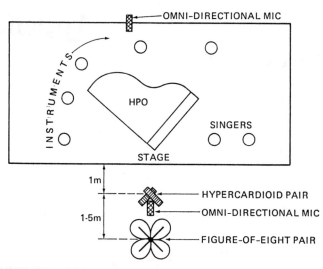

OMNI-DIRECTIONAL MIC

INSTRUMENTS

HPO

SINGERS

STAGE

1m

HYPERCARDIOID PAIR

OMNI-DIRECTIONAL MIC

1-5m

FIGURE-OF-EIGHT PAIR

MIC LAYOUT FOR BAROQUE SOLOISTS CONCERT (BOOMS USED TO RAISE ALL MICS TO A HEIGHT JUST ABOVE THAT OF THE PERFORMERS.)

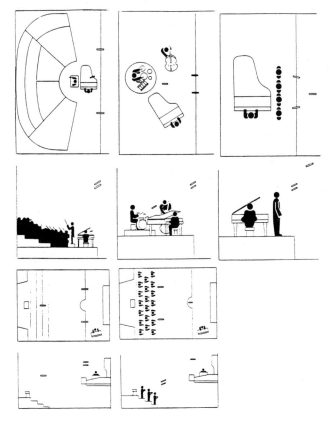

Figure A-7   The Nakamich: three-point enhanced stereo set-up requires a matched pair set against a blend mike of a different pattern.

GLOSSARY

Acoustics

Amplitude distortion: Nonlinear relation of input and output induced harmonics a function of voltage fluctuations, or power consumption.

Audible spectrum: When wave motion in air has a frequency that lies between 20 and 15,000 Hz, it produces a sensation of audibility transmitted through the ear by means of solids, gases, and liquids.

$$13,000 \text{ Hz} = 1 \text{ inch} \qquad 30 \text{ Hz} = 36 \text{ feet}$$

The minimum audible difference in sound level is about 3 dB. Differences in intensity in dB are calculated as $10 \log_{10}$. Thus, a tenfold increase in intensity (power) = 10 dB. Doubling the audible intensity is equivalent to a rise of 3 dB.

Directional characteristic: The variation in response for different angles of sound incidence.

Directivity: A rejection figure, stated in dB units, indicating the attenuation of sound inciding from an angle relative to the zero position. For supercardioid mikes the angle of best rejection is at 235, for cardioid at 180.

Directivity coefficient: To make a comparison between various microphones, this term was introduced to indicate the power output of a nondirectional mike in relation to a directional mike of equal sensitivity in a diffuse sound field. An ideal cardioid mike has a DC of 3. Since the intensity of sound decreases as the square of the distance, the cardiod mike may be used at a distance of 1.7 times farther than a nondirectional mike with the same amount of disturbing ambient noise.

Drift: Flutter occurring at random rates.

Dynamic distortion: Alteration of volume range of a program when it is transmitted.

Effective output level: The mike sensitivity rating defined as the ratio in dB of the power available from the mike relative to 0.001 W at a sound pressure level of 10 dynes/cm^2.

Equivalent noise: A mike in a completely silent room still generates some residual noise. This generated noise can be measured and is figured by taking a mike's sensitivity and relating it to the threshold value of hearing, 2×10^{-4} μBar. A more common method is stating the signal-to-noise ratio.

Frequency discrimination: Exaggeration or diminution of particular frequencies in relation to others usually a function of resonance frequency of the system.

Harmonic distortion: Acoustic distortion, unwanted changes resulting from nonlinear relation between input and output at a given frequency.

Inductance: The resistance of a coil of wire to rapidly fluctuating ac currents. The field built up by the current resists any change in the rate of flow of the current; and this resistance increases with frequency.

Intermodulation distortion: A kind of amplitude change in which *sum* and *difference* tones (harmonics of the original signal) are present in the recorded signal.

Level: The logarithm of the ratio of an acoustic quantity to a reference quantity. Measurement of amplitude in decibels relative to 1 atmosphere of pressure. 0 ± 2 db is a midpoint on the scale.

Matching: Arranging for the impedances presented by a load to be equal to the internal impedance of the generator; this is essential to avoid loss of power. In mikes, the loss results in poorer signal-to-noise ratio. Matching is done by means of a transformer. Where mike impedance is strongly capacitative; e.g., in electrostatic types the output voltage is fed to the grid of a valve and controls the current in an external circuit.

Microphone impedance: The nominal load impedance for a mike indicates the optimum matching load which utilizes the mike's characteristics to the fullest extent. Inpedance is a combination of dc resistance, inductance and capacitance, which act as resistances in ac circuits. An inductive impedance increases wth frequency; a capacitative impedance decreases with frequency. Either type introduces change in phase.

Phase distortion: Shifting of output voltage relative to input by an amount not proportional to frequencies present. Not detectable until it reaches a TV amplifier.

RMS (root-mean-square): The effective sound pressure taking into both positive and negative pressures in a system. The squares of the compression and the refraction of a wave are added and the average taken.

770 mi/hr Speed of sound in air.
Velocity of sound in the open is influenced by air temperature more than

by atmospheric pressure. At 21°C, speed is 344 m/sec (1,100 ft/sec); at 50°C, 360 4m/sec, or 42 ft/sec faster.

Scale distortion: Voice sounds too loud in the front seat of a threatre. Signal rendered higher or lower than is expected. Frequency distortion results since frequency response of the ear is different to different levels of volume.

Signal-to-noise ratio: Proportion of amplitudes (intensity) of the wanted signal to the unwanted noise in an electrical transmission system. It sets an upper limit to the dynamic range of the system.

SPL (sound pressure level): Sound pressure measurement in decibels.

Wow and flutter: Deviation of frequency resulting from irregular motion in the recording, from duplication or reproduction of a tone, or from deformation of the recording medium.

Postproduction

AGN (antiground noise): The noise reduction unit in an optical sound recorder.

Ambient noise: The total effect of reflected sound in a given space which is peculiar to that space (room tone).

Backing track: Prerecording of the accompaniment to a singer who then listens through headphones to a replay as he performs. The two signals are mixed to give the final recording.

Backtracking: Preliminary recording is done by the same performer and used as the accompaniment.

Bilateral sound track: A type of symmetrical variable area sound track recognizable by the fact that in the print the central axis and surrounding modulated area are transparent, whereas as in the duplex type they are opaque.

Binaural hearing: Utilizing two ears.

Binaural reproduction: Transmission and reproduction system utilizing two channels to duplicate conditions of binaural listening. Stereophonic systems actually represent systems of three or more channels.

Blooping: Any method of silencing the unwanted noise produced by the passage of a splice through a sound reproducer. A small opaque tape fixed over a splice is called a blooping patch. The "bloop" occurs because of the greater opacity of the splice or by the transparent line caused by scraping or scratching by the splicer blades. Blooping ink is sometimes used to mark areas for taping. The tape enables the recording or playback head to slide over the splice.

Capacitance: The ability of an electrical component (or components) to store electric charges. Charges present in a *conductor* attract opposite charges to nearby but not electrically connected conductors. A signal may therefore cross between one component and another, between which there is no direct path. Capacitors are used in systems for coupling, smoothing, and tuning purposes. In lines, capacitance is the reason for loss of signal; this varies with distance between plates or components. Stray capacitances from the mains are the cause of the *ac Hum,* which is transferred unintentionally from component to component.

Compression: The function of a compressor that transfers a wave motion from its input to its output and at the same time reduces the span of amplitudes of the wave motion.

Control track: An auxiliary sound track used to manipulate the volume of the main track according to some predetermined plan or to bring additional loudspeakers into play. Most commonly used to increase dynamic range or reproduced sound.

Control unit: Device in a sound recorder that varies the signal input of one or more mikes or dubbers (dummies).

Dead spot: In acoustics, a place at which a train of sound waves is cancelled by reflections arriving out of phase with the wanted signal thus creating an area of silence or poor audibility.

Direct positive playback: A sound film originally exposed and developed in a single bath. The resulting image is in positive form available for normal sound reproduction.

Dubber: A sound reproducer of high quality, the output of which is mixed in a console with outputs from other dubbers. They are loaded with fullcoat or stripecoat sprocketed magnetic film.

Dubbing: Synchronization with lip movements of an actor of a voice not originally recorded in sync with the picture. Loops, or short extracted sections of dialogue in composite form, are used to guide the actor or narrator. Used also to prepare foreign films for new markets.

Looping: A 9-ft continuous band of sound track runs repeatedly on a sync projector in interlock with dubbers as a guide for voice re-recording.

Mix: Combining electrically the signals from microphones, tape, and reproducers and other sources.

Phase shift: The displacement of a waveform in time. Some electrical components introduce phase shift into a signal, and the shift is of the same angle for all frequencies. This means that each frequency is displaced differently and distortion occurs. Electrical cancellation may occur when two equal signals are out of phase by 180°.

Reproducer: A playback system.

Recorder: A record system.

Sibilance: Exaggerated hissing in voice patterns.

Standing waves: Tubby sound in a small room of booth from low frequency and poor response—caused by long waves with short reflection pattern. Almost all sound present goes directly into the mike producing "unnatural" sound presence.

Exhibition

Coloration, reverberation: A moving coil dynamic mike makes use of resonances to render its frequency response flat. When a signal appears suddenly it takes time to move and when the signal disappears suddenly the resonator continues to produce a signal. The result is that the transient signal (a percussive sound) will be colored by the inherent resonances of the mike. This explains differences noted by the ear between mikes of identical characteristics.
In general condenser mikes, use resonators only in the high frequencies where coloration has little effect. Fidelity is excellent. Ribbon mikes can color low frequencies. Moving coil dynamics color greater ranges, but they can also improve voices and partially filter.

Crossfade: The gradual mix between sound sources accomplished through the simultaneous manipulation of two or more "open" faders. Both fade pots are preset at a ratio to each other rather than fading down one completely. By keeping both open, the fade movement cannot be detected and the transition is smooth and blended.

Crossover: The frequency at which a signal is split in order to feed separate parts of a loudspeaker. Crossover network is the filter that accomplishes this slitting.

Crosstalk: In stereo, the breakthrough between channels measured as separation (in decibels) between wanted and unwanted sound. Crosstalk in magnetic recording heads is caused by magnetic coupling and the transformer action between head coil windings. In reproducing heads the cause is due to leakage between windings and the fringing effect at low frequencies (induction).

Echo: A wave that has been reflected or otherwise returned with sufficient magnitude and delay to be perceived in some form as a wave distinct from that directly transmitted.

Frequency response: Represents the sensitivity of a system as a function of frequency. It is possible that the response will be different according to the direction from which the sound comes. Since mikes are designed to be more or less sensitive within special ranges, these differences form a mike's characteristic pattern that can be used to enhance or retard signals from given areas of a given space.

ME track: Music and effects tracks combined into one for use with foreign language re-recording.

Octave: The interval between two sounds having a basic frequency ratio of 2 to 1.

Optical Stereo: A film recording system replayed by scanning the tracks by means of a photo cell, lamp and scanning slit. The Dolby optical stereo system employs a 6-track 70-mm release optical print with noise reduction characteristics, less distortion, and greater frequency response; in place of conventional "stereo" speakers, five front, two side, and one rear "surround: speaker is employed.

Original sound negative: Negative that is exposed in a film recorder and after processing yields a negative sound image on the film.

Photographic sound: Sound signal in the form of a photographic image.

Pink noise: A sound signal that has an equal amount of energy per octave or fraction of an octave. Therefore, the amount of energy between 100 Hz and 200 Hz, a 100-cycle-wide segment, is the same as the energy between 10 kHz and 20 kHz.

Sensitivity: The measure of a microphone's sensitivity is an indication of efficiency. A classical dynamic mike may have a sensitivity of 0.2 mV/μBar from 200-Ωv internal impedance. A model giving 0.25 is considered sensitive and 0.1 is unsuitable for recording low frequencies.

Condenser mikes always have a preamplifier in the mike casing otherwise their high impedance would not allow the signal to be transmitted along a cable. It is difficult to produce a very low noise preamp (capable of receiving without overloading) a signal given by a condenser mike placed in a strong acoustical field. For this reason it is better to have special preamps for condenser mikes such as the preamps built into the Nagra.

Signal: The form of variation with time of a wave whereby information, message, or effect is conveyed in communication.

Signal-to-noise ratio: Background noise from the microphone and preamp is a function of electron movement or thermal activity, thermal noise. The ratio of the level of the wanted signal to the unwanted noise.

Slateboard: Scene identifier placed before the camera at beginning of a take.

Sound check print: Made from the sound release negative for the purpose of checking negative cutting, sound quality, etc.

Sound master positive: Sound print on special stock made from the sound release negative for producing duplicate negatives of the sound record for release printing.

Sound cut negative: Composed of sections of original sound negative spliced in sequence.

Sound daily print: First sound print made from the original sound negative for checking of sound quality.

Sound negative: A negative sound image on film obtained by exposure through a positive sound image; by direct recording or by the reversal process, from another sound image.

Sound print: Any positive obtained by printing from a sound negative, or direct positive recording, or by the reversal process from another sound positive.

Sound release negative: A photographic sound negative in the form required for final printing consisting of rerecorded negatives, intercut original sound negatives duplicate negatives of sound records.

Sound release dupe negative: A duplicate negative prepared printing the sound track of release prints.

Sound speed: 24 frames per second (fps, synchronous speed).

Sound work print: Intercut sound daily prints sound effects, music on the same or separate films, with synchronous constantly maintained with the corresponding picture work print.

Playback (reproducing): Technique of filming musical action first, playing music through loudspeakers while performers dance, etc. A silent camera is not necessary. The action is postsynched. The system may be used in poor acoustic locations.

Postsynchronization: The addition of speech or sound effects to synchronize with picture, which is already "in the can."

Pre- and postequalization: A system of complementary filtering at the recording and reproducing stages which serves to improve the overall signal-to-noise ratio and reduce breathing and other audible unpleasant consequences of location recording and noise reduction.

Prescoring: Recording of music or other sound prior to the shooting of the picture which is to accompany it (in predetermined synchronism. Used always in animated features.

Re-recorded negative: A re-recorded negative is exposed by re-recording and when processed yields a negative sound track on the film.

Re-recording print: Sound print used in re-recording to produce a re-recorded negative. May be from a sound cut negative, an intercut print or a combination of both.

Re-recorded print: A sound print from a re-recorded sound track negative.

Reverberation: The presence (persistence) of sound at a given point due to repeated reflections.

White noise: A signal having an equal amount of energy per hertz. Therefore the energy between 100 and 200 Hz is equal to that between 10,000 and 10,200 Hz.

Electricity

A-B test: Direct comparison of sound quality between hi-fi components accomplished by switching from one to another.

Alternating current: A continually fluctuating flow, at one instant positive, the next negative.

Ampere: The rate of flow of this charge. One ampere of current flows when one coulomb passes a given point in a second.

Baffle: The panel to which most speakers are mounted, usually the front panel of an enclosure.

Binaural sound: Two-channel sound in which each channel recorded is heard through only one ear.

Capacitance: The ability of an electrical component to store electric charges. Charges present in a conductor attract opposite charges to nearby, but not electrically connected conductors. A signal may therefore cross between one component and another between which there is no direct path. Capacitors are used in systems for coupling, smoothing and tuning purposes. In lines, capacitance is the reason for loss of signal; this varies with distance between plates or components. Stray capacitances from the mains is the cause of ac hum which is transferred unintentionally from component to component.

Cathode follower: The type of electronic circuit used in an output stage of a recorder to permit the use of longer interconnecting cables without the loss of high frequencies.

Coulomb: A unit of electrical charge; quantity of excess electrons.

Crosstalk: Signal leakage between two channels.

Direct current: Flow of electrons from a negatively charged body to a positively charged body.

Dual track recorder: Type of monophonic recorder which utilizes half of a standard 1/4-in tape in one direction and the other half in the opposite direction.

Farad: A unit of capacitance or electrical storage. A capacitor has a capacitance of 1 farad when 1 coulomb causes a charge of 1 V on the capacitor.

Frequency range: All microphones are supplied with a manufacturer's frequency range test report, which gives a visual reference for the particular microphone's sensitivity to a given range. Sensitivity to the higher frequencies is more significant than ideal flat response overall since much of the highs are lost in further sound processing.

Ground: A point in any electrical system that has zero voltage, usually the chassis of any electrical component.

Interference: Broken shielding, missing ground wire, corrosion, and fraying at the connector cable to the microphone can cause *electrostatic induction* yielding a stray magnetic field or voltage into the recording chain. The interference can be at an audio frequency or high frequency.

    All inputs must be shielded. Shielded transformers attenuate passage of interference. Symmetrical inputs in which the middle point is grounded and external filters protect against induction leaks.

    Magnetic induction is caused by use of microphones near motors, transformers, twisted power cables, or other elements like auto ignitions, refrigerators, lighting grids. This source of noise tends to record as low-frequency hum.

Ohm: A unit of resistance; the higher the temperature of a substance, the greater the resistance. Resistance depends upon length, area and material used in a wire. A copper wire 0.1 inch diameter and 1,000 ft long has a resistance of 1Ω.

Ohm's law: Current in ampere $(I) = \dfrac{\text{Voltage in volts } (E)}{\text{Resistance in ohms } (R)}$

$$I = E/R \qquad E = IR \qquad R = E/I$$

Phase shift: The displacement of a waveform in time. Some electrical components introduce phase shift into the signal, and the shift is of the same angle for all frequencies. This means that each frequency is displaced differently and distortion occurs.

Power: The rate of doing work in watts:
$$P = EI \qquad P = I^2R \qquad P = E^2R$$
$$P = \text{Watts} \qquad R = \text{Ohms} \qquad E = \text{Volts } I = \text{Amps}$$

Preamplifier: Device that boosts extremely weak signal voltages, such as those from microphones or mag heads, to a level that is usable by power amplifiers, and at the same time accomplishes the necessary equalization for industry standards.

Sound-on-sound: A method in which previously recorded material on one track may be re-recorded on another track while simultaneously adding new material.

Volt: The external force or "pressure" that tends to cause flow of current. A pressure of 1 V is required to maintain a 1-amp current through 1-5 L.

Wow: Repetitive slow variations in tape speed.

Wrap: The length of the tape's path along which tape and head are in intimate contact. Sometimes measured as the angle of arrival and departure of the tape with respect to the head.

Film Editing

A and B printing, AB printing, A and B roll printing: Printing from original film (usually positive) which has been conformed into two rolls, each having alternating shots and black opaque leader. A and B printing eliminates splice marks in release prints, and permits the printing of dissolves and supered titles.

A and B rolls, AB rolls: Arranged for duplication, two or more matching rolls of film having alternate scenes intercut with opaque leaders in such a way that, from a common starting point, Roll "A" presents picture to the duplicate being printed where Roll "B" presents opaque leader, and vice versa. This arrangement also permits double or multiple exposures in printing to obtain title or picture superimpositions, dissolves from one scene to another—provided appropriate scene length overlaps are taken into account and "checkerboarding" to eliminate the appearance of film splices on the screen. A third roll is called "C" roll, etc.

Acetone: An organic liquid chemical used in the manufacture of some types of film cement. Also used to clean film splicing equipment.

Action cutting: The cutting of film from one shot to another in a way yielding the impression to the audience that the action as seen on the screen is continuous and uninterrupted, even though changes of camera position have taken place. Usually achieved by overlapping the action on successive shots so that the beginning of shot "B" includes action appearing at the close of shot "A," but can also be achieved by running two or more cameras simultaneously. Thus a transfer from shot "A" to shot "B" can be made to appear to be continuing action. The principle is also applied in editing shots in which actors enter or leave the action field, and in shots in which an action starts or stops within the action field.

Assemble: In editing, to do the preliminary work of organizing and joining the shots of a film, as workprint, in approximately the sequence in which they will appear in the finished version.

Associational editing, relational editing, associative editing: The juxtaposition of shots in order to present contrast, comparisons, similarities, or ideas.

Asynchronous sound: Sound which is indigenous to the action, but is not precisely synchronized with the action. In some cases, the source of the sound may not be visible, but is assumed to be present.

Automatic slate, automatic slating: A camera attachment which, when actuated at the start of a shot, records on the film the shot and take numbers and a visible sync mark which corresponds to a tone fed to a tape recorder.

A-wind: An indication of the emulsion and perforation positions on rolls of single-perforation film. An A-wind roll, when held vertically, flat side toward the holder, with the end of the film coming off downward from the right side, has the emulsion in and the perforations on the edge nearer the person holding the roll.

Balance stripe: On magnetic-striped film stocks, the narrow band of magnetic coating applied to the edge opposite the magnetic sound track to make the film lie flat when it goes over magnetic heads. The balance stripe is sometimes used to carry additional audio or magnetic cueing information.

Bar sheets, lead sheets: A chart showing words of dialogue which have been recorded and the number of motion picture frames of duration for each syllable and pause in the dialogue; used chiefly in animation.

Base-to-emulsion: Term used to indicate a special winding of film to be placed in a printer when a filmmaker wishes to change the usual genealogy of his film. A base-to-emulsion print from an original would have its emulsion and sound track in B-wind position.

Base-to-base splice: A splice made with the base side of the end of one piece of film overlapping the base side of the piece to which it is being attached. Sometimes used in checkerboard cutting to eliminate the need for scraping emulsion.

Beep: A sound track tone of short duration aligned with a visual point of reference for precise synchronization in editing and printing.

Bilateral variable-area sound track, bilateral track: A variable area sound track in which the modulations are symmetrical about the longitudinal centerline of the track.

Bin, editing bin: A container, usually like a large wastebasket, lined with cloth, with a rack from which film can be hung, used in editing rooms for temporary storage of pieces of film.

Black leader, black opaque leader: Opaque leader, free of pinholes, used in conforming original film for A and B roll printing in order to black the printer light.

Blimping: Sound proofing material used in a blimp.

Blip tone: A sync pop.

Bloop: (1) The sound produced in an energized amplifier and speaker system when a film splice passes the photo cell scanning slit to which the amplifier is connected. (2) To opaque the track section of a positive film splice to reduce the sound of the bloop. In a negative, to punch a specially shaped hole in the track area for the same purpose. (3) To remove unwanted sound from a magnetic sound track by erasing it by hand with a small magnet. *Note:* Definitions 2 and 3 are also called *deblooping.*

Blooping ink: Ink used to make a triangle-shaped hole over a splice in a negative sound track.

Blooping tape: Tape used to cover unwanted portions of sound tracks.

Bulk eraser: A device which magnetically aligns all of the iron oxide molecules on a magnetic tape or film, thus eliminating any "sound" on them. A degausser.

Butt splice: A film splice in which the film ends come together without overlapping, usually held together by means of splicing tape.

Butt-weld splice: A film splice made by joining the two pieces of film end-on, without an overlapping portion, usually by applying both heat and pressure.

Buzz track: A test film soundtrack used for the adjustment of the lateral placement of the optical film in an optical sound reproduction system.

B-wind: An indication of the emulsion and perforation positions on rolls of single-perforation film. A B-wind roll, when held vertically, flat side toward the holder, with the end of the film coming off downward from the right side, has the emulsion in and the perforations on the edge away from the person holding the roll.

Cement splicer: A film splicer which provides for the overlapping of the film and holding the overlapped ends securely while liquid cement seals the overlap.

Center track: A standard position for the placement of the audio signal on double perforation magnetic film, in a narrow band centered between the two edges of the film.

Checkerboard cutting, checkerboarding: A technique of splicing AB rolls in order to eliminate the image of the film splice from the duplicates. The physically overlapped portion of the film is covered to the frame line in all cases by black leader, thus effectively preventing transfer of the splice image.

Cinch marks: Scratches on film caused by the presence of dust or other abrasive particles between successive coils. Longitudinal cinch marks may result if the center of a roll of film is rigidly held while the outside end is pulled tight.

Coded edge numbers, coding: Any system of marking two or more films with the same series of sequential numbers for the purpose of maintaining an established synchronous relationship. See *Edge number.*

Contrapuntal sound: Sound, especially music, which contrasts or conflicts with the action in a motion picture.

Crossmodulation tests: Tests used to determine the correct negative and print densities for a variable area optical sound track.

Cueing: (1) In voice-over or other postrecording situations, the marking of the cue-print in a way which will permit a signal to be given to the narrator to begin each portion of narration at the appropriate time. (2) Any system used by a second person to signal a narrator during narration recording.

Cue patch: A piece of self adhesive magnetic or metallic material placed on the edge of film as a means of actuating a printer light change or an automatic stop on a projector.

Dead sync: Editorial synchronism.

Degausser: Any of several devices used to erase recordings on magnetic tapes and films or to demagnetize magnetic recording heads.

Derived sound: Sound taken from two stereo tracks and played on a third, middle loudspeaker.

Dialogue track: A sound track which carries lip sync speech, or distinguished from sound tracks carrying music, sound effects, and commentary.

Differential rewind: A device designed to permit simultaneous winding of film on more than one reel at a time, even though the diameters of the rolls of film are unequal.

Edge track: A standard position for the placement of the audio on single perforation magnetic film, a narrow band along the edge opposite the perforations.

Edited music track: Background music or sound which is specifically edited to the action. See *Laid-in track.*

Environmental sound: General low-level sounds coming from the action field, either synchronous or nonsynchronous.

Equalization: The alteration of frequencies for a specific purpose. Equalization may be used to improve the quality of speech and may even involve removal of certain frequencies.

Exciter lamp: An incandescent lamp used to supply nonvarying luminous energy to a photoresponsive cell, such as the photocell in a motion picture projector. Interposition of a variable mask or matte, such as a sound track, in the optical path between the exciter lamp and the photocell then results in corresponding variations in the electrical response of the photocell.

Feed lines: To read lines of dialogue outside camera range for the benefit of an actor being filmed. The lines may be dialogue which the actor has forgotten, or they may be lines spoken by other actors, to which the actor being filmed reacts or speaks.

Fill leader: Leader used to fill in blanks in picture workprint, often where some of the film has been damaged, and in sound workprints between sound sections.

Film base: The flexible, usually transparent, support on which photographic emulsions and magnetic coatings are carried.

Film cement, cement: Common but erroneous term for the welding solvent used in splicing film.

Film handler's gloves: Thin cotton gloves worn during the process of cutting or handling of original films or duplicating intermediates in order to keep fingerprints from the film. Commonly worn only on the left hand, the right hand being kept free for operation of editing equipment.

Film notcher: A device used to punch out a small portion of the edge of a piece of film in order to permit electrical contacts on a printer to come together and thus activate light charges.

Flub: (1) To make an error in pronunciation or to make some other mistake in speaking lines or commentary. (2) An error in pronunciation.

Fluff: A mispronunciation or other mistake in oral delivery.

Flux: The amount of light present, measured in lumens.

Gamma: The tangent of the angle formed by the straight-line portion of the D log E curve and the log E axis. Gamma is thus related to the maximum gradient and serves as a measure of the extent of development.

Gang synchronizer: A synchronizing device having more than one sprocket wheel, used in setting up relationships between originals, workprints, and sound tracks.

Guillotine splicer: A device used for butt-splicing film with splicing tape. The splicer includes provision for cutting the film, for properly aligning the two strips to be spliced, and, usually, for perforating and trimming the splicing tape.

High-pass filter: An electronic filter used in audio circuits to attenuate all frequencies below a particular chosen frequency. Frequencies above the cutoff are passed without attenuation.

Hot splicer: A film splicing machine, usually of precision construction, in which the metallic members in contact with the overlapped portions of the film splice are warmed by means of an electrical resistance unit in order to hasten the action of the film cement.

Intercutting: Insertion into a series of related shots other shots for contrast or other effect.

Interlock projector: A projector used to reproduce the picture while synchronized sound is played back on an accompanying machine or device. The provision for sound playback may be a part of the projector, or it may be separate.

Internegative: A color negative duplicate made from a color positive. Internegatives are used for release printing as a means of protecting their source film.

Interpositive: Any positive duplicate of a film, used for further printing.

Invisible cut: A cut made during the movement of a performer, achieved either by overlapping the action or by using two cameras, then matching the action during editing. Such cuts make shifts of camera position less noticeable.

Jump-cut: An instantaneous advance in the action within a shot or between two shots due to removal of a portion of film, to poor pictorial continuity, or to intent.

Key numbers, latent-image edge numbers: Numbers placed by exposure on the edge of film by the manufacturer. On 16-mm film they occur every 20 frames (6 in), on 35-mm film every 16 frames (1 ft).

Kuleshov effect: Imputation by audiences of various meanings from shots depending upon their context or juxtaposition as determined through editing; based on experiments conducted by Lev Kuleshov in Russia during the 1920s.

Leader: (1) A length of blank film at head *(head leader)* or tail *(tail leader)* of a roll of film. (2) Any kind of nonimage film used for editing, threading, or identification purposes.

Library shot: A stock-footage shot.

Light-struck leader: Film, fully exposed to light, used as leader.

Lip-sync, lip synchronization: The relationship of sound and picture that exists when the movements of speech are perceived to coincide with the sounds of speech.

Low contrast original: An original reversal film which is designed to yield prints having good projection contrast.

Machine leader: Strong leader threaded through a film processing machine, used to pull film through the machine during its operation.

Magnetic film, mag film, full-coat: Standard width film coated with an iron oxide compound on which sound is recorded and from which sound is reproduced.

Match-action cut, match cut: A cut, made on action, between two shots in which the action has been overlapped either by repetition of the action or by the use of more than one camera.

Match dissolve: A dissolve linking images which have similar content or form.

Match-image cut: A cut from one shot to another shot having an image of the same general shape as the one in the processing shot.

Matching action: The process of aligning overlapped-action film in order to achieve a smooth action cut. See *overlap.*

Mercer clip: Trade name for a small plastic clip used to hold film ends together during assembly.

Mix cue sheet, cue sheet: A sheet having several columns for notations for footage, fades, volume levels, and equalizations, used in mixing sound tracks. Each column represents one track.

Montage: The assembly of shots, hence, editing, and especially the portrayal of action and creation of ideas through the use of many short shots. In the 1920s, the Russians formulated several kinds of montage styles. Later, in the United States, montage came to mean a series of shots, often with superimpositions and optical effects, showing a condensed series of events, e.g., a crime wave in a city.

Narrow-gauge film: Any size film less than 35 mm wide.

Negative: (1) Of a black-and-white image, having tonal values which are the opposite of those in the original subject. Of a color image, having color values which are the complementary of those in the original subject. (2) A film having negative images.

Negative scratch: A scratch on negative film. Also, such a scratch as it appears (white) on a print.

Negative splice: On 16-mm film, an overlap splice 1/16 inch wide.

Notch: A recess on the edge of a piece of film to be duplicated in a printer. The notch automatically triggers a mechanism effecting some modification of the duplication process, commonly a change of exposure light intensity, through a diaphragm control.

One-light print: A print made with a single printer light setting for all shots in the film being printed.

Opaque leader: Any strip of flexible, optically opaque material sized and perforated to match motion picture film standards. Used to space picture in AB roll cutting. A special type is available for threading film processing machines.

Overlapping and matching action: Repeating part of the action in one shot at the beginning of the next shot, or covering the action with two or more cameras, then matching the overlaps on the editing table for the purpose of making a smooth cut on action and also to avoid a jump cut.

Positive scratch: The black image on a print of a scratch on the positive from which the print was made.

Prism shutter, prism intermittent: A device used on many film viewers, editing machines, and some high-speed cameras, consisting of a rotating prism of four or more sides through which the viewer light passes as film is pulled continuously through it.

Projection-contrast original: An original reversal film which is designed to have normal contrast when projected.

Projection leader: A short length of film having standard markings on it, used to enable projectionists to make instant changeovers from one projector to another.

Punch: (1) *Synchronization:* A device for punching a hole in film leader to locate a starting point for editorial or printing synchronism. (2) *Anima-*

tion: A device for forming holes in the edge of a piece of animation or title card stock to fit the pegs on an animation stand or artist's easel. (3) *Blooping:* A device for silencing splices in prints from an optical sound negative by removal of a formed slug of the negative film at the intersection of the splice and the sound track.

Relational editing: Editing of shots for purposes of comparison or contrast of their content.

Release negative: A duplicate negative from which release prints are made.

Reversal film: A film that is normally processed in such a way as to produce a positive image after exposure to a subject. A reversal print of a negative would have a negative image, however. See *Reversal position process.*

Reversal intermediate: A second generation duplicate which is reversed to make it the same type, negative or positive, as the original, and used for printing in order to protect the original.

Reversal original: A reversal film designed to be exposed in a camera.

Reversal positive process, reversal process: The process by which film exposed in a camera or film printed from a positive are developed to be positives. The major steps are: first development, bleaching of the developed image, re-exposure, second development, fixation, washing, and drying.

Rough cut: A preliminary trial stage in the process of editing a film. Shots and sequences are laid out in approximate relationship, without detailed attention to the individual cutting points.

Slug: A strip of blank leader or image-bearing film used as leader.

Spacer: A hub placed between reels on rewinders to keep the reels in the proper position to feed into, or take up from, a synchronzier.

Splice: The act of joining two pieces of film by any of several methods—by cementing, butt-welding, taping, or, for processing, by staples or grommets. Also, the resulting lapped or joined portion of film.

Sync beep, sync tone: In double system shooting with certain cameras, a tone feed into a magnetic tape recorder at the same time that a light in the camera exposes a few frames of film. The fogged section is later aligned with the beep tone to achieve synchronism of sound a picture.

Synching dailies: Assembling, for synchronous interlock projection, the picture and sound workprints of a day's shooting.

Tail leader: Leader used at the finish end of a strip of film.

Time base signal: A signal recorded on the edge of film in a camera to match a signal recorded on a magnetic recording, used as a fast means of synchronizing film and sound workprints.

Veeder counter: Trade name for a mechanical counter actuated using rotary shaft movement, which can be calibrated in any system, e.g., feet and frames.

Workprint: Any positive duplicate picture, sound track print, or magnetic duplicate intended for use in the editing process to establish through a series of trial cuttings the finished version of a film. The purpose is to preserve the original intact and undamaged until the cutting points have been established.

Zero cut conforming and printing: A method of preparing A and B rolls for printing in which the original shots overlap several frames or more. The change from one roll to another to match the edited workprint is done automatically by the printer. Much of the original film can thus be preserved uncut. Also, image definition at the cut is better in the print because of the absence of a splice in the original at that point.

Appendix C

BIBLIOGRAPHIES

General Bibliography

ABBOTT, J. E., "Development of the Sound Film," *Journal of the SMPE* (June 1942), p. 541.

AIKEN, JOSEPH, "Technical Notes and Reminiscences on the Presentation of Tykociner's Sound Picture Contributions," *Journal of the SMPTE* (August 1958), p. 521.

ALKIN, L., *Sound Recording and Reproduction* (London, Focal, 1981).

ALTEN, STANLEY, *Audio in Media* (Belmont, CA: Wadsworth, 1981).

ARNHEIM, RUDOLPH, *Film* (London: Faber and Faber, 1933).

APPELMAN. *The Science of Vocal Pedagogy* (Bloomington, IN: Indiana University, 1986).

ATSUKA AND NAKAJIMA. *MIDI Basics* (New York: Amsco, 1987).

BAIRD. *Understanding MIDI* (New York: Amsco (Billboard), 1986).

BALIO, TINO (ed.), *The American Film Industry* (Madison: The University of Wisconsin Press, 1976).

BALLOU, LEN, *Handbook for Sound Engineers—the New Audio Cyclopedia* (Howard Sams, 1987), 1247p.

BARNOUW, ERIC, *The Magician and the Cinema* (New York, Oxford University Press, 1981), 128p.

BARRON AND TUCHMAN, *The Avant Garde in Russia 1910–30, New Perspectives* (Cambridge, M.I.T. Press, 1980), 288p.

BARTHES, ROLAND. *Image, Music, Text* (New York: Cambridge University Press, 1986).

BARTLETT, BRUCE, *Introduction to Professional Recording Techniques* (Indianapolis: Howard Sams, 1986), 300p.

BLAKE, LARRY. *Film Sound Today* (Hollywood: Reveille, 1984), 56p.

BEGUN, S. J., *Magnetic Recording* (New York: Murray Hill, 1949), 238p.

BELAZS, BELA, *Theory of Film* (New York: Dover, 1970).

BLAND, W. S., "The Development of the Sound Newsreel," *British Kinematography* (August 1950), p. 50.

BRIGGS. *Sound Reproduction* (Bradford: Wharfedale Wireless Works, 1949).

BURCH, NOEL, *Theory of Film Practice* (New York: Praeger, 1973), 172p.

CAGE, JOHN, *Silence* (Cambridge: M.I.T. Press, 1961), 276p.

CAMERON, EVAN WILLIAM, "On Mathematics, Music, and Film," *Cinema Studies, #3* (Spring 1970).

CAMERON, E. W. (ed.), *Sound and the Cinema: The Coming of Sound to the American Film* (Pleasantville, NY: Redgrave, 1980), pg. 117–135.

CAMERON, JAMES R., *Motion Pictures with Sound* (Manhattan Beach, NY: Cameron Publishing Co., 1929).

CAMERON, JAMES, *Sound Motion Pictures* (Coral Gables, Cameron Publishing, 1959), 994p.

CAMERON. *Sound and the Documentary Film* (London: Pitman, 1947), 157p.

CAPRA, FRANK, *The Name Above the Title* (New York: MacMillan Company, 1971).

CARLIN, FRED, AND WRIGHT, *On the Track* (New York: Schirmer, 1989).

CARR & HAYES. *Wide Screen Movies* (New York: McFarland, 1988), 502p.

CHA, T. H. K., *Apparatus* (New York: Tanam, 1980), 437p.

CHEW, V. K., *Talking Machines, 1877–1914* (London: Her Majesty's Stationery Office, 1967).

CLIFFORD, JOHN, *Microphones, How They Work* (Chicago, TAB, 1975).

COFFMAN, JOE, "Art and Science in Sound Film Production," *Transactions of the Society of Motion Picture Engineers,* #14 (February 1930), p. 176.

CONANT, MICHAEL, *Antitrust in the Motion Picture Industry* (Berkeley: University of California Press, 1960).

CRAWFORD, MERRIT, "Pioneering Experiments of Eugene Lauste in Recording Sound," *Journal of the SMPE* (October 1931), p. 632.

CURTIS, DANIEL, *Experimental Cinema* (New York: Delta, 1971), 205p.

DANIELIAN, N. R., *AT&T: The Story of Industrial Conquest* (New York: The Vanguard Press, 1939).

DAVIS, RON, AND DAVIS, PAM, *Sound System Engineering* (Indianapolis: Howard Sams, 1987), 730p.

DAVY, CHARLES (ed.), *Footnotes to the Film* (London: Oxford University Press, 1938, reprinted 1972, The Arno Press).

DE FOREST, LEE, "Pioneering in Talking Pictures," *Journal of the SMPE* (January 1941), p. 41.

DEUTSCH, D. *The Psychology of Music* (New York: Academic, 1982).

EISENSTEIN, SERGEI, *Film Form* (New York: Harcourt Brace, 1977), 280p.

EISENSTEIN, SERGEI, *Film Sense* (New York: Harcourt Brace, 1975), 288p.

EISENSTEIN, SERGEI. *Nonindifferent Nature* (Cambridge University Press, 1988).

FIELDING, RAYMOND, *Technological History of the Motion Picture* (Berkeley, University of California Press, 1967), 255p.

FRANKLIN, HAROLD B., *Sound Motion Pictures* (Garden City, N.Y.: Doubleday, Doran & Co., 1930).

FRATER, DOUGLAS, *Sound Recording for Motion Pictures* (London: Tantivy, 1979).

FRAYNE AND WOLFE, *Elements of Sound Recording* (New York: Wiley, 1949), 686p.

GAUMONT, LEON, "Gaumont Chronochrome Process Described by the Inventor," *Journal of the SMPTE* (January 1959), p. 29.

GILLE, B., *Engineers of the Renaissance* (Cambridge: MIT Press, 1968).

GEDULD, HARRY, *Birth of the Talkies* (Bloomington: Indiana University Press, 1975).

GILLINGS, TED, "The Color of the Music: an Interview with Bernard Herrmann," *Sight & Sound,* 41, #1 (Winter 1971/72), pp. 36–39.

GOETHE. *Color Theory,* in his *OPTICS.*

GOMERY, DOUGLAS, "The Coming of the Talkies: Invention, Innovation, and Diffusion," in Balio, *op. cit.,* pp. 193–211.

——, "The Coming of Sound to the German Cinema," *Purdue Film Studies Annual,* #1 (August 1976), pp. 136–143.

——, "Tri-Ergon, Tobis-Klangfilm, and the Coming of Sound," *Cinema Journal,* XVI, No. 1 (Fall 1976), pp. 51–61.

——, "Problems in Film History: How Fox Innovated Sound," *The Quarterly Review of Film Studies,* Vol. 1, #3 (August 1976), pp. 315–330.

GORBMAN, CLAUDIA, *Unheard Melodies* (Bloomington, Indiana University Press, 1987), 190p.

GORBMAN, CLAUDIA, "Annotated Bibliography on Sound in Film," in Weis and Belton (eds.), *Film Sound: Theory and Practice* (New York: Columbia University Press, 1985), pp. 427–225.

GRAHAM, F. LANIER, *The Rainbow Book* (New York: Vintage, 1979), 200p.

GREEN, FITZHUGH, *The Film Finds Its Tongue* (New York: G. P. Putnam's Sons, 1929).

HAMPTON, BENJAMIN B., *History of the American Film Industry from its Beginnings to 1931* (New York: Dover, 1970).

HAPPE, BERNARD, *Basic Motion Picture Technology* (New York: Hastings, 1971).

HAYS, WILL H., *See and Hear* (New York: Motion Picture Producers and Distributors of America, 1929).

HENDRICKS, GORDON, *The Kinetoscope* (New York: The Beginnings of the American Film, 1966).

HEUTTIG, MAE, *Economic Control of the Motion Picture Industry* (Philadelphia: University of Pennsylvania Press, 1944).

HUMPHREY AND TANNER, *Sound, Hearing, Resonance* (San Francisco: The Exploratorium, 1977).

HUNTLEY, JOHN AND ROGER MANVELL, *The Technique of the Film Music* (London: Focal Press, 1967).

HUBER, DAVID M., *Audio Production for Video* (Indianapolis: Howard Sams, 1986), 320p.

HUBER, D. M., *The Microphone Manual: Design and Application* (Indiana: Howard Sams, 1987), 336p.

IRWIN, ORVIS, "Infant Speech," *Scientific American* (September 1949).

JONES, G. F., *Sound-Film Reproduction* (London: Blackie and Son, Ltd., 1936).

JONES, L. A., "A Historical Summary of Standardization in the Society of Motion Picture Engineers," *Journal of the SMPE* (October 1933), p. 280.

KANDINSKY, WASSILY, *Point and Line To Plane* (New York: Dover, 1986).

KEENE, SHERMAN, *Practical Techniques for the Recording Engineer* (Los Angeles: Keene Publishing, 1981), 390p.

KELLOGG, EDWARD W., "The Development of 16mm Sound Motion Pictures," *Journal of the SMPE* (January 1935), p. 63.

—— "History of Sound Motion Pictures," *Journal of the SMPTE* (June 1955), p. 291; (July 1955), p. 356; (August 1955), p. 422.

KELLOGG, EDWARD W., *The ABC of Photographic Sound Recording* (New York: SMPTE, 1945), 44p.

KRACAUER, SIEGFRIED. *Theory of Film: The Redemption of Physical Reality* (New York: Oxford University Press, 1965).

KRACAUER, SEIGFRIED, *Caligari to Hitler, A Psychological History of the German Cinema* (Princeton, NJ: Princeton University Press, 1966), 361p.

KROWS, ARTHUR, *The Talkies* (New York: Henry Holt & Company, 1930).

KRYTER, KARL, *The Effects of Noise on Man* (New York: Academic Press).

LARSON, RANDALL D., *Musique Fantastique: A Survey of Film Music in the Fantastic Cinema* (New York: 1985), 602p.

LAWDER, STANDISH, *Cubist Cinema* (New York: New York University Press, 1975), 265p.

LEGRICE, MALCOLM, *Abstract Film & Beyond* (Cambridge, M.I.T. Press, 1977), 160p.

LEVIN, GAIL, *Synchronism and American Color Abstraction 1910–25* (New York: Braziller, 1978), 144p.

LEYDA, JAY. *Eisenstein At Work* (new York: Pantheon/Museum of Modern Art, 1984).

LEYDA, JAY, *Kino: A History of Russian and Soviet Film* (New York: Collier, 1973), 501p.

LICHTE AND NARATH, *Physik und Technik des Tonfilms* (Leipsig: Edwards Bros., 1943), 411p.

LUSTIG, MILTON, *Music Editing for Motion Pictures* (New York: Hastings, 1980), 181p.

MCCULLOUGH, JOHN B., "Joseph T. Tykociner: Pioneer in Sound Recording," *Journal of the SMPTE* (August 1958), p. 520.

————, "Work of Lee De Forest," *Journal of the SMPE* (December 1940), p. 542.

MANKOVSKY, V. S., *Acoustics of Studio and Auditoria* (London: Hastings), 416p.

MONTAGU, IVOR, *Film World.* (London: Penguin, 1964.)

MORITZ, WILLIAM, "Abstract Film and Color Music," in *The Spiritual in Art: Abstract Painting 1890–1985* (Los Angeles: Abbeville, 1986).

MUELLER, W. A., AND M. RETTINGER, "Anecdotal History of Sound Recording.

MUNSTERBERG, HUGO, *The Film: A Psychological Study* (New York: Dover, 1970), 100p.

NARATH, ALBERT, "Oskar Messter and His Work," *Journal of the SMPTE* (October 1960), p. 726.

NESBITT, A., *The Use of Microphones* (New York: Hastings, 1974).

OLSEN, HARRY, *Acoustical Engineering* (New York: Van Nostrand, 1957).

PASQUELLA, GEORGE DONALD, "An Investigation in the Use of Sound in American Motion Picture Exhibition, 1908–1919" (unpublished Master's Thesis, University of Iowa, 1968).

PASOLINI, PIER PAOLO, *Heretical Empiricism* (Bloomington: Indiana University Press, 1988).

POHLMANN, KEN, *Principles of Digital Audio* (Indianapolis: Howard Sams, 1987), 288p.

PRENDERGAST, ROY M., *Film Music a Neglected Art* (New York: 1977), 268p.

PUDOVKIN, V. I., *Film Technique and Film Acting* (New York: Vision, Memorial Edition 1968), 388p.

QUIGLEY, MARTIN, *Magic Shadows* (New York: Biblo & Tannen, 1969), 191p.

RAMSAYE, TERRY, "Early History of Sound Pictures," *Journal of the SMPE* (September 1928), p. 597.

RAYLEIGH, *Theory of Sound*. Paper, Royal Academy of Sciences, London, circa 1895.

REISZ, KAREL, AND GAVIN MILLAR, *The Technique of Film Editing* (New York: Hastings House, 1968).

RETTINGER, MICHAEL, *Acoustic Design and Noise Control* (New York: Chemical, 1973).

ROSSI, NICK, *The Realm of Music* (Boston: Crescendo, 1974), 159p.

RUSSETT, ROBERT AND STARR, CECILE, *Experimental Animation* (New York: Van Nostrand, 1976).

SADOUL, GEORGES, *L'Invention du Cinema*. (1912) pp. 48–75 covers years 1832–1897.

SCHRADER, JOHN, *Introduction to Electroacoustic Music* (Englewood Cliffs, NJ: Prentice-Hall, 1985).

SHANET, *Learn to Read Music* (New York: Simon & Schuster, 1956).

SILKE, JAMES R. (ed.), *Rouben Mamoulian: "Style Is The Man"* (Washington, D.C.: The American Film Institute, 1971).

SHARFF, STEFAN, *Elements of Cinema* (New York: Columbia University Press, 1982), 187p.

SILVERMAN, KAJA, *The Acoustic Mirror* (Bloomington: Indiana University Press, 1988).

SITNEY, P. ADAMS, *Visionary Film* (New York: Oxford University Press, 1974), 452p.

SMILES, S., *Lives of the Engineers* (Cambridge: MIT Press).

SPONABLE, EARL I., "Historical Development of Sound Films," *Journal of the SMPE* (April, 1947), p. 275; (May 1947), p. 407.

SPOTTESWOODE, ROGER. *Film and Its Technique* (Berkeley, CA: University of California Press, 1951), 516p.

STANLEY, ROBERT, *The Celluloid Empire* (New York: Hastings House, 1978).

STAUFFACHER, A., *Art in Cinema* (New York: Arno, 1969). Reprint San Francisco Museum of Art 1947; see "My Statements are in my Work"—Fischinger.

STEWART, JAMES G., "The Rerecording Process," *Audio Engineering Society Preprint #719* (New York: Audio Engineering Society, 1970).

STRONG AND PLITNIK, *Music, Speech, Hi Fidelity* (Los Angeles: Soundprint 1983), 377p.

SWENSON, JOEL, "The Entrepreneur's Role in Introducing the Sound Motion Picture," *Political Science Quarterly* (September 1948).

THEISEN, W. E., "Pioneering in the Talking Picture," *Journal of the SMPE* (April 1941), p. 415.

TYLER, PARKER, *The Hollywood Hallucination*. (New York: Simon & Schuster, 1970).

WARREN, R. M. AND ROSLYN, "Auditory Illusions & Confusions," *Scientific American* (December 1970), pp. 2–11.

WEIS, ELIZABETH, AND JOHN BELTON, *Film Sound: Theory & Practice* (New York: 1985), 462p.

WEIS, ELIZABETH, *The Silent Scream* (New Jersey: Associated University Press, 1982).

WELLS, *Technique of Electronic Music* (New York: Schirmer, 1987).

WINCKEL, *Music, Sound and Sensation* (New York: Dover, 1967).

WENTE, FREDERICK, MACKENZIE, STOLLER, SCRIVEN, AND SANTEE, "Synchronized Reproduction of Sound and Scene," a monograph reprinted from *Bell Telephone Record* (November 1928).

WEYNAND, DIANA, *Computerized Videotape Editing* (Weynand, 1987).

WOLLEN, PETER, *Signs and Meaning in the Cinema* (Bloomington: Indiana University, 1969).

WYSOTSKY, MICHAEL, *Widescreen Cinema and Stereophonic Sound* (New York: Focal, 1971), 282p.

Microphones

BARNETT, S., "Techniques for Preserving Sound Perspective in Film Production Recording," *Recording Eng./Prod.* (August 1980), pp. 54–61.

——, *Hearing and Listening* (San Francisco: The Exploratorium, 1976).

BOBROW, ANDREW C., "The Art of the Soundman: An Interview with Chris Newman," *Filmmakers Newsletter,* Vol. 7, #7 (May 1974).

GINSBURG, FRED, "Roundtable on Wireless Microphones," *Video Systems* (January 1984), pp. 34–46.

HERROLD, R., "Realities of Surface Mounted Microphones," *Sound and Video Contractor* (February 1988), pp. 78–90.

HUFKER, B., "Re-inventing the Microphone," *db* (January 1980), pp. 50–53.

LAZARUS, A., "FRAP Point Source Microphones," *db* (December 1979), pp. 47–52.

LONG, J., "Layman's Guide to Microphone Specifications," *Audio* (August 1969).

MIKEMEMO, Notes on PZM Microphone Applications—Crown International, Box 1000, Elkhart, Ind. 46515.

MILLER, P., "Audio Cable the Neglected Component," *db* (December 1978), pp. 39–43.

RETTINGER, MICHAEL, "Microphone Sensitivity & Microphone Signal-to-Noise Ratio," *Recording Eng./Prod.,* pp. 64–76.

SCOTT, DALE, "Zen and the Art of Using Wireless Microphones," *Recording Eng./Prod.* (April 1981), pp. 62–73.

WORAM, JOHN, "A Backward Glance at Cardioid Microphones," *db* (August 1978), pp. 37–40.

Acoustics

CONTACT. Sound Systems Installation Notes issued by University Sound, 600 Cecil Street, Buchanan, MI 49107.

DALTON, D., "Creating Synthetic Sound for Star Trek," *db* (March 1980), pp. 44–47. Pamphlet.

EHLE, R., "Operation of the Moog Synthesizer Modules," *db* (August 1975), pp. 25–29. Pamphlet.

FOREMAN, C., "Math for Sound Systems," *Recording Eng./Prod.*, pp. 83–104.

KRAUSE, LOTHAR, "And Now a Word about Ground Problems," *Modern Recording* (May 1978). Pamphlet.

MANTEL, J., "Advanced Room Acoustics," *Audio Engineering Society,* Preprint #1312 (March 1978).

SILVER, S. L., "VU Meters vs. P.E.P. Meters," *db* (January 1980), pp. 46–50.

Post-Production

CARR, R., "Recording String Sections," *Recording Eng./Prod.* (October 1983), pp. 68–78.

JOY, KEN, "The Unsung Heroes," *Millimeter* (May 1988), pp. 193–205.

LANIER, ROBIN, "Millions of Sharp Ears are Rating Your Sound," *Millimeter* (November 1983), pp. 83–118.

LETOURNEAU, T., "Sweetening: A Sound Technique," *Video Systems* (July 1981), pp. 22–24.

NORTH, JOHN, "Stating the Art of Audio Post Production," *Millimeter* (November 1983), pp. 121–136.

NORTH, JOHN, "Variations on a Theme," *Millimeter* (May 1988), pp. 175–188.

SCHUBIN, MARK, "Audio for Video Revolution," *Videography* (November 1981), pp. 29–36.

SPINA, LILLIAN, "TV Audio: How Sweet It Is," *Millimeter* (November 1981), pp. 127–39.

SWETLAND, G., "How Synchronizers Sweeten Audio for Video," *Video Systems* (March 1984), pp. 60–66.

Video Post

BLAKE, LARRY, "Return of the Jedi—Sound Design for the Star Wars Trilogy by Ben Burtt," *Recording Eng./Prod.* (October 1983), pp. 150–158.

———, Part II: "The Final Dubbing Process," *Re/p* (December 1983), pp. 72–87.

FOX, JORDAN, "Walter Murch, Sound Design," *Cinefx* (1977), pp. 43–56.

GOLDBERG, M., "The Art of Tape Editing," *db* (December 1976), pp. 36–41.

JACOBSON, LINDA, "Sound Effects for Video Post Production," *Mix* (April 1988), pp. 29–40.

JONES, TILSLEY, ROCHE, "An Advanced Computer-Assisted Sound Mix System for Film and Video Post Production," *SMPTE Journal* (October 1982), pp. 931–933.

LEHMAN, PAUL, "High Quality Audio for Video Post Production," *Recording Eng./ Prod.* (October 1983), pp. 55–73.

SANGER, G., "Sounds for the Eye," *Millimeter* (May 1983), pp. 97–107.

SCHWARTZ, HOWARD, "Audio for Video, ADR and the Magic of Foley," *Video Systems* (August 1988), pp. 22–44.

SERAFINE, FRANK, "New Motion Picture Sound," *American Cinematographer* (August 1980), pp. 796–846.

Playback

ALLEN, IOAN, "Dolby Sound System for Recording Star Wars," *American Cinematographer* (July 1977).

ALLEN, JOHN, "Upgrading your Sound: A System from the Ground Up," *Boxoffice* (February 1981), pp. 48–54.

ALLEN, JOHN, "How Much Power Does Your Stereo System Need?" *Boxoffice* (February 1983), pp. 34–35.

BARNETT, S., "Let's Spend the Night Together," *Recording Engineer/Producer* (December 1982 & February 1983).

BERGER, I., "Those Monster Power Amps—Not Louder but Better," *Popular Mechanics* (April 1974).

BERARU, DAVID, "Star Wars Times Two," unpublished paper for Cinema 09 LACC—1980).

BOHN, D., "The Speed of Sound," *Sound and Video Contractor* (April 1988), pp. 176–185.

SIMONE AND CARR, "Concert Sound Grounding Problems," *Recording Eng./Prod.* (February 1980), pp. 43–55.

CASHIN, JACK, "Evaluating Stereo Sound Systems," *Boxoffice* (January 1983), p. 24.

CROWHURST, N., "How Loudspeakers Work," *db* (September 1977).

CLAWSON, J., "Upgrade Your Motion Picture Sound," *Boxoffice* (February 1983), pp. 34–35.

CZERWINSKI, "Sensurround Sound," *American Cinematographer* (June 1976), pp. 577–581.

EARGLE, JOHN, "Motion Picture Sound Systems," *db* (March 1980), pp. 37–40.

ENGEBRETSON, MARK, "Theatre Sound-Looking Toward the Future," *Boxoffice* (January 1984), pp. 17–26.

FELDMAN, L., "Making Sense of Crossover Networks," *Audio Times* (September 1982), pp. 22–24.

FINNEGAN, P., "Crosstalk," *db* (April 1978).

FORMAN, C., "Evaluating Loudspeaker Specifications," *Recording Eng./Prod.*, pp. 30–45.

GEIL, F., "Experiments with Binaural Recording," *db* (June 1979), pp. 30–36.

HODGES, R., "Do You Need Super Power?" *Popular Electronics* (May 1974).

HODGES, RALPH, "Sound for Cinema," *db* (March 1980), pp. 30–35.

HOLMAN, TOM, "THX Sound System Installation Instructions," Lucasfilm Ltd., 1983.

KEEN, DAN, "Understanding Maximum Power Transfer," *db* (March 1978).

KLAPHOLZ, JESSE, "History of Sound System Design," *Sound & Video Contractor* (February 1986), pp. 14–16.

LOND, H., "Motion Picture Sound: A Technological Update," *Boxoffice* (January 1981), pp. 38–44.

MEAD, W., "A New Dimension in Cinema Sound," *Sound & Video Contractor* (June 1985), pp. 112–116.

OLSON, HARRY, "Monitor Loudspeakers," *db* (December 1967).

RETTINGER, MICHAEL, "Sound Transmission Through Perforated Screens," *SMPTE Journal* (December 1982), pp. 1171–1159.

STUMPF, RICHARD, "Hitchcock Theatre: A Lesson for Exhibitors," *Boxoffice* (January 1981), pp. 45–48.

UZZLE, TED, "Surround Loudspeakers in the Theatre," *Tan Notes 3A,* Altec Lansing.

UZZLE, TED, "Motion Picture Theatre Sound," *Sound & Video Contractor* (June 1985), pp. 14–26.

WELLS, R., "Distortion Balance Tests for Motion Picture Sound Tracks," *SMPTE Journal* (September 1977), Vol. 86.

Appendix D
THE NAGRA SYNC RECORDER

Location production has evolved to the point where very few manufacturers are interested in competing in a market that already has a more or less ideal portable location reel-to-reel recorder. The economics dictate only a handful of reliable options (Stellavox, Sandor, and some Sony cassettes) that have the following features important to film/video applications:

- A highly efficient erase head.
- Modulometer—peak-reading level control.
- Low-impedance balanced microphone inputs.
- Capacity for time code or crystal sync operation.
- Low-noise drive system (capstan DC servo drive).
- Efficient wide-range monitoring during recording.
- Capacity for microphone preamps and multiple powering sources.
- AC/DC operation with long running times.
- A full-track recording head, which defines track width as equal to tape width.
- Reel displacement compensation of tension across the heads.

The Nagra fulfills these expectations and is the principal system in use. We will limit our discussion of recorders (analog) to the basic Nagra and its low-budget alternatives, the Super 8 Sound recorder and various crystal sync audio cassette recorders.

Description of the Nagra Front Panel

- Principal Selector Switch: In *test* position amplifiers are on but motor is inoperative.
- Battery Reserve Switch: Needle should fall to the right—indicating full voltage for AC operation.
- Modulometer: A direct-reading peak program meter in *record* function and *level* position full modulation is indicated as *MAX,* but optimum results are achieved between 0 and +2 dB. (See Figure D-1.)
- Auto/Manual Switch: Controls recording level. In manual position, the #1 microphone pot controls modulation (sensitivity).

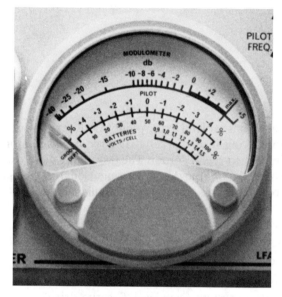

Figure D-1   Modulometer.

- Tape/Direct Switch: In *tape,* reads signal after amplification on tape; in *direct,* reads signal at micro input.
- Pinch Wheel: A tape guide controls-disengages the transport mechanism and drive belt for rewind, principal function selector must be in *playback* mode. Automatically disengaged when *PFS* is in *stop.*
- Line Output: PFS in *playback* only—listen to recording on an external speaker. Loudspeaker signal should not be allowed to feed a microphone which would cause acoustic feedback (Larsen effect, a howling noise).
- Power Selector: To avoid accidental discharge of battery switch to *external* when in storage. Use 12 1.5-V D cells. Batteries must deflect test needle toward middle ground on meter. Volt/compression ratio test should be near 1.2 V. *Nicad* batteries should only be charged with the *PAR* accessory and *ATN* transformer in tandem. Avoid memory problems by fully discharging before recharging.
- Line Inputs: Two-pin banana socket impedance is 100K Ω, maximum voltage 150 V—exceeding 10 V may cause *crosstalk.* When pot is fully clockwise, accessory connector is fed by current 3.73 ARMS modulating tape to 0 dB. This is the input for any *mixer* via a *QCB* adapter.
- Limiter: Prevents saturation of tape when *in.*
- LF Low Frequency Roll-Off Attenuator: When should filtering in the Nagra be done?
  When using a ribbon mike very close.

When trying to duplicate a voice recording in a similar but different room.

In dubbing sessions.

To clean up playback for simple quality evaluation.

To reduce modulation noise.

To improve intelligibility.

To reestablish linearity.

To create a sense of unreality.

- Compressor (Noise Reducer): In cinema, the dynamic range depends upon the intended audience. Genre tends to dictate level changes. Comedy provoking laughter requires increased levels following the joke, suspense requires softness for dialogue effects. The Nagra's wide dynamic range allows the fortissimi to be recorded at a level below the maximum, hence avoiding accidental distortion due to intermittent or sudden bursts of sound. Very often, background noise from microphones and their preamps dominates tape hiss. Since microsensitivity cannot be increased, higher levels create higher noise levels which can be reduced through compression.

- QGX Time Sync Generator: Supplies a precise 60-Hz signal to the Nagra Neopilot system allowing for cableless sync with a camera equipped with a crystal-controlled motor.

- QRT Radio Slate: Camera start activates transmitter whose code is received by Nagra QRR internal module. Slate is inaudible but can be read with a QDAN reader, which furnishes "take" numbers in transfer. These are representative units in the modular design system of the Nagra.

Short Schnops Tech Tips

In practice, SPL below 80 dB on the pot scales are seldom required. This point varies with the sensitivity of the tape, battery voltage output and microphone impedance characteristic.

The American NAB standard requires greater preemphasis than the European CCIR. In Europe it is normal to slightly overbias the tape giving a better signal-to-noise ratio, but this reduces the recording level at high frequencies, which is critical.

The responsibility of the recordist is to obtain a linear signal at a sufficiently strong level (0 dB to $+/-1$ dB) without having to extend the range of the microphone pot outside of the normal operating area between 75–85 dB. The 1 dB incremental indexes allow for precise, repeatable settings. This is the low-noise, high-fidelity range which makes optimum use of the recorder's good specs.

The range of levels throughout a fully recorded tape should not have great

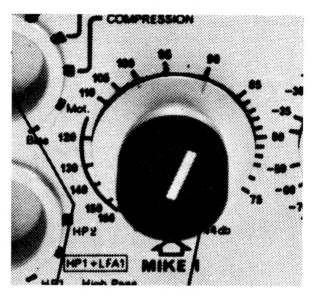

Figure D-2   Potentiometer.

differences in intensity if microphone is used as close as possible, rarely moved outside of a 4-ft operating range, and the operator avoids excessive reliance on riding the gain (turning the pot during source level changes).

Earphones must be as sensitive as the rest of the system. Listening to full frequency range at high levels is necessary to analyze noise, linearity, intelligibility and to determine placement, filtering, amplification.

Make notations on each tape box indicating the microphone potentiometer setting, meter level, recording speed, date, type of microphone, location, (filter, if any). This information may come in handy if problems occur in postproduction.

Monitoring During Recording

In *test* position, the level may be set with earphones position in either *direct* or *tape.*

- In *direct:* Allows for instant change in modulation.
  Allows ease in listening, no delay.
  Evaluates signal from microphone to recorder chain.
- In *tape:* Detects dropouts on tape emulsion.
  Discovers overmodulation.
  Controls level by *line* pot during playback.

When the meter position (toggle switch) is pressed in, the instantaneous peak level is displayed during recording.

The direct signal is a combination of the microphone, line and mixer-amplifier-filter signals.

The tape signal is the composite of playback with amplifier and equalization. The modulometer measures the level of the direct signal only. During playback, line pot controls output level, the meter reads the output level, not the level of sound on the tape. So chances are they will be different. The recordist should monitor during recording on *Tape* position once they become accustomed to the slight delay in audio, as the signal passes the record head. (See Figures D-3, D-4, D-5.)

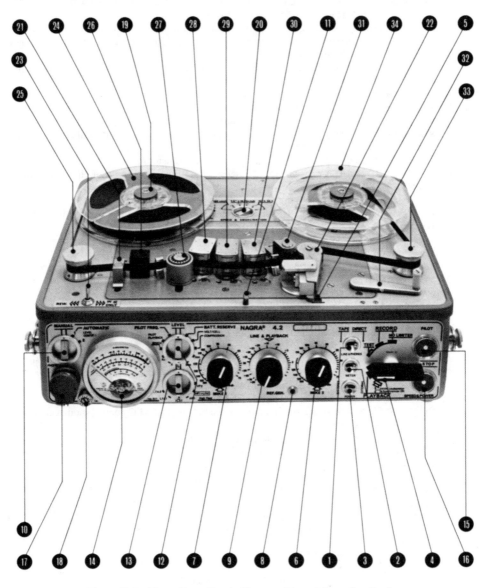

Figure D-3   Nagra Front Panel. (Source: Nagra Magnetics, Inc.)

1. **TAPE/DIRECT, LINE & PHONES:** switching of the playback signal or of the direct signal on the line output, headphones and loudspeaker; switch inactive on TEST
2. **TAPE/DIRECT, METER:** switching of the playback signal or of the direct signal on the circuit of meter 14; this switch cannot be locked on TAPE
3. **POWER:** power selector switch, i.e., built-in batteries or accumulators (BATTERIES) or external power supply (EXTERNAL) connected to plug 48
4. **Main function selector:**
   STOP: recorder at a standstill
   TEST: power supplied to all circuits, except record and erase
   RECORD: power supplied to all circuits and the motor; erase and record with limiter
   RECORD NO LIMITER: as RECORD, but without limiter
   PLAYBACK: the recorded signal can be heard on the headphones and is fed to line output 45. If switch 1 is on DIRECT the signal is reintroduced into the direct chain, passing through potentiometer 9 and filter 13
   PLAYBACK with Loudspeaker and Synchronizer ON: playback of tape as above, but using loudspeaker and with internal synchronizer switched on (optional circuit)
5. **Pinch-wheel position stop**
6. **MIKE 2:** potentiometer for microphone input no. 2
7. **MIKE 1:** potentiometer for microphone input no. 1
8. **REF. GEN:** switched on when the button is pressed, the reference generator supplies a -8 dB signal to the direct amplifier after the potentiometers
9. **LINE & PLAYBACK:** line input and playback potentiometer
10. **MANUAL/AUTOMATIC:** switch for the sensitivity adjustment mode of the microphone inputs:
    MANUAL: adjustment by potentiometers 6 and 7
    ALC: automatic level control, 1 for microphone input 1 and 2 for microphone input 2
11. **Lid catch**
12. **Selector switch for meter 14,** 11 positions:
    X = position not used
    Rx = level of the RF signal picked up by the antenna of the QRR receiver
    SYNCH = phase shift between the playback pilot signal and a reference signal; synchronism is obtained when the needle is stationary
    PILOT PLAYBACK = playback pilot signal level
    PILOT FREQ. = on the $+4$ to -4% scale, frequency shift as determined by the built-in QFM frequency indicator, between the pilot signal recorded or played back on the pilot track and a 50 to 60 Hz internal reference
    LEVEL = modulometer showing on the decibel scale the level of the direct or recorded signal
    BATT. RESERVE = on the lower scale, the bold line shows the supply voltage reserve; the lower limit at the extreme left of the bold line = 11 V
    VOLT/CELL = battery check on the V/CELL scale, voltage indicated per cell
    COMPRESSION = compression reading in decibels on the ALC compression scale when switch 10 is on AUTOMATIC
    Mot. = motor current, maximum deviation = 250 mA
    Bias = bias level on record, indicated on the V/CELL scale
13. **Filter selector:**
    LFA 2: low frequency attenuation, -8 dB at 50 Hz
    LFA 1: low frequency attenuation, -4 dB at 50 Hz
    FLAT: linear response
    HP 1: high-pass filter, -10 dB at 50 Hz
    HP 1 + LFA 1: combination high-pass and low frequency attenuation, -14 dB at 50 Hz and -3 dB at 400 Hz
    HP 2: high-pass filter, -20 dB at 50 Hz

Figure D-3   (continued)

14. **Measuring instrument:** modulometer and checking functions according to the position of selector switch 12
15. **PILOT:** indicator which shows a white segment when the conditions for recording or using the pilot signal are fulfilled
16. **SPEED & POWER:** indicator which shows a white segment when the following three conditions are fulfilled:
    —power supply voltage higher than the minimum admissible value
    —motor regulation within the correct operating range
    —tachometric speed fluctuations not exceeding the maximum value
17. **PHONES:** connector for headphones, impedance 50 to 600 Ω
18. **Phones Level:** adjustment of the headphones volume
19. Tape reel fixing nut
20. **SPEED & EQUALIZATION:** tape speed and type selector switch
    $3^3/4''$ = 9.525 cm/s ⎫
    $7^1/2''$ = 19.05 cm/s ⎬ STD = standard tape
    $15''$ = 38.1 cm/s ⎭ LN = low-noise tape
21. **Mobile guide**
22. **Pinch-wheel**
23. **Fast wind switch**

    REW. ◀◀◀   rewind with main switch 4 in any position except STOP, lever 32 in
    disengage position

    ▶▶▶ IN ◻ ONLY   fast wind when main switch 4 on PLAYBACK with Loudspeaker

24. **Supply reel**
25. **Tension roller of the supply reel**
26. **Erase head**
27. **Stabilizer roller** with 50 or 60 Hz stroboscope
28. **Recording head**
29. **Pilot head**
30. **Playback head**
31. **Capstan**
32. **Three-position lever** controlling the pinch-wheel and tape guides:
    —lever pulled to the left: for threading the tape, rewind possible
    —level at 45° to the edge of the tape-deck: motor running, but tape not moving
    —lever pushed backwards: tape running
33. **Tension roller** of the take-up reel
34. **Take-up reel**
35. **Refer to Figure D-4 on page 440.**
36. **MIKES, RIGHT:** Microphone input, channel 2 (right)

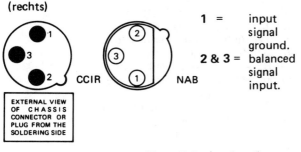

(rechts)

1 = input signal ground.
2 & 3 = balanced signal input.

CCIR   NAB

EXTERNAL VIEW OF CHASSIS CONNECTOR OR PLUG FROM THE SOLDERING SIDE

Figure D-3 (continued)

37. **MIKES, LEFT:** Microphone input, channel 1 (left) identical to 36.

38. **Six-position microphone type selector, channel 2** (right)

    DYN 50 = dynamic microphone, impedance 50 Ω, 0.1 mV/μbar sensitivity.

    DYN 200 = dynamic microphone, impedance 200 Ω, 0.1 mV/ = bar sensitivity.

    +12 = condenser microphone, 1 mV/μbar sensitivity, +12 V phantom powering.

    +48 = condenser microphone, 1 mV/μbar sensitivity, +48 V phantom powering.

    −12 = condenser microphone, 1 mV/μbar sensitivity, −12 V phantom powering.

    T = condenser microphone, 3 mV/μbar sensitivity, +12 V T-powering (Ton-aderspeisung).

39. **Six position microphone type selector, channel 1** (left), identical to 38.

40. **MIKES, PHASE:** phase inverter for channel 1 (left) microphone input.

41. **INPUTS:** line input connector

    EXTERNAL VIEW OF CHASSIS CONNECTOR OR PLUG FROM THE SOLDERING SIDE

    1 = **Channel 2 (right) input:** impedance variable from 0 to 5 kΩ (0 to 10 kΩ when switch 11 is on ST. HS), current drive with minimum source impedance 47 kΩ; current to obtain 0 dB at max. sensitivity 7.8 μA.

    2 = **−10G:** −10 V stabilized voltage output; maximum current 100 mA for all −10 V terminals.

    3 = **Channel 1 (left) input.** Identical to 1.

    7 = **Ground** for input signals.

42. **EXT. NRS (external noise reduction system):** connector

    EXTERNAL VIEW OF CHASSIS CONNECTOR OR PLUG FROM THE SOLDERING SIDE

    for connecting an external NRS, output and input voltage 560 mV for 0 dB.

    1 = **Ext. NRS output,** channel 2 (right).

    2 = **−10G:** −10 V stabilized voltage output. I_{max} Total = 100 mA.

    3 = **Ext. NRS output,** channel 1 (left).

    5 = **Ext. NRS input,** channel 1 (left), minimum impedance 47 kΩ.

    6 = **Ext. NRS input,** channel 2 (right), minimum impedance 47 kΩ.

    7 = **Ground** (common)

43. **OUTPUTS:** line output connector

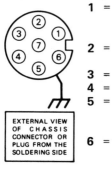

    EXTERNAL VIEW OF CHASSIS CONNECTOR OR PLUG FROM THE SOLDERING SIDE

    1 = **Channel 2 (right) output:** output voltage 1 V at 0 dB, minimum impedance load 500 Ω.

    2 = **−10G:** −10 V stabilized voltage output. I_{max} Total = 100 mA.

    3 = channel 1 (left) output: identical to 1.

    4 = V_{unstab}: unstab. power supply voltage.

    5 = **−10R:** −10 V stabilized voltage output available on record only, I_{max} Total = 100 mA.

    6 = **STOP:** input for the motor stop control (connect to −10 V to stop).

    7 = **Ground**

Figure D-3 *(continued)*

44. PILOT: pilot signal input for the pilot track

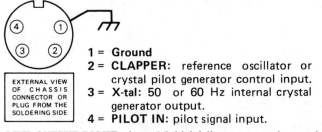

EXTERNAL VIEW OF CHASSIS CONNECTOR OR PLUG FROM THE SOLDERING SIDE

1 = **Ground**
2 = **CLAPPER:** reference oscillator or crystal pilot generator control input.
3 = **X-tal:** 50 or 60 Hz internal crystal generator output.
4 = **PILOT IN:** pilot signal input.

45. LINE OUTPUT RIGHT: channel 2 (right) line output on banana jacks
46. LINE OUTPUT LEFT: channel 1 (left) line output on banana jacks
47. CUE: multiple connector for recording and playback on the pilot track

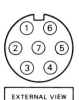

EXTERNAL VIEW OF CHASSIS CONNECTOR OR PLUG FROM THE SOLDERING SIDE

1 = **CUE IN:** modulation signal input.
2 = **−10V:** −10 V stabilized voltage output, maximum current 100 mA for all −10 V terminals.
3 = **PILOT OUT:** pilot signal output.
4 = **SPEED CORRECTION:** tape speed correction signal input.
5 = **−10 V FM:** voltage terminal to activate the FM modulator.
6 = **CUE OUT:** signal output (direct or recorded).
7 = **Ground**

48. POWER PACK: multiple connector for external power supply

EXTERNAL VIEW OF CHASSIS CONNECTOR OR PLUG FROM THE SOLDERING SIDE

1 = **−BATT:** negative pole of the battery box.
2 = **+BATT:** positive pole of the battery box.
3 = **STOP:** motor stop control terminal (connect to −10 V to stop).
4 = **SPEED CORRECTION:** tape speed correction signal input.
5 = **EXTERNAL −12 TO −30 V:** input for 12 to 30 V external power supply, negative pole.
6 = **−10G:** −10 V stabilized voltage output, maximum current 100 mA for all −10 V terminals.

Figure D-3 (*continued*)

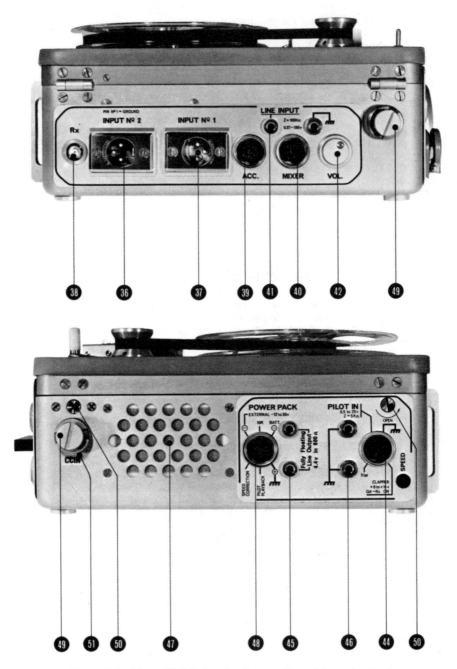

Figure D-4   Nagra IV Side Panels. (Source: Nagra Magnetics, Inc.)

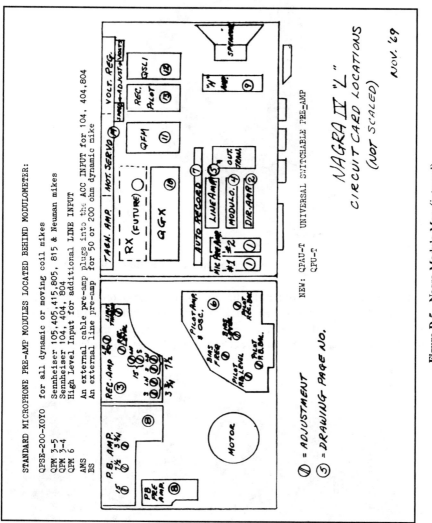

Figure D-5 Nagra Module Map (internal).

Monitoring During Recording

Figure D-6   Beyer DT 48 Headphones. (Source: Beyer Dynamic.)

Listening is the most important function of the audio recordist. Since it is imperative that the production track be as clean and free of problems as possible, headsets with sensitivity equal to the recorder must be used. (See Figure D-7.) The Nagra has a direct/tape switch that controls monitoring:

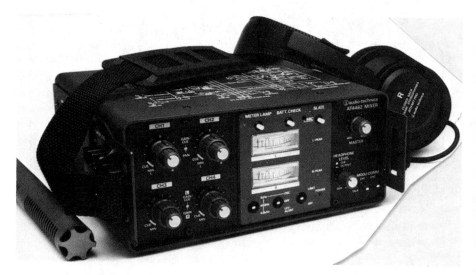

Figure D-7   AT4462 Stereo Field Mixer by Audio-Technica. (Source: Audio Technica.)

When the principal function selector is in *test* position, level may be set with earphones' position in either *direct* or *tape*.

- In *Direct:* Allows for instant change in modulation allows ease in listening, no delay in trouble-shooting signal as it passes from microphone to record chain.
- In *Tape:* Can detect dropouts on tape emulsion after recording. Discover any overmodulation. Line pot controls level during playback.

The direct signal is a combination of microphone, line, and mixer/amplifier/filter mixed signal.

The tape signal is the composite of playback with amplifier and equalization.

The modulometer measures the level of the direct signal. During playback, line potentiometer controls output level, while the meter reads output level not the tape level (as recorded) so chances are that they will be different. Generally, then, the recordist should monitor during recording on *tape* position once they become accustomed to the slight delay in audio.

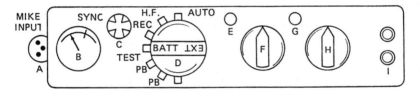

Figure D-8   Nagra III front panel.

Nagra III Front Panel

The Nagra III is still used worldwide for field production and deserves a basic operational outline. (See Figures D-9 and D-10.)

1. The *ATN* provides 18 V, a 60-Hz pulse independently of each other.
2. The automatic level record is a compressor and works independently of volume control.
3. *Hi fi playback* indicates level on meter, and signal is fed to pins on the side of the recorder, not to the internal speaker. If the playback mode is set on zero, a fully modulated signal should read zero on the meter.
4. Rewind function made operative by switching *PFS* into *playback* position and placing tape transport control fully counterclockwise.

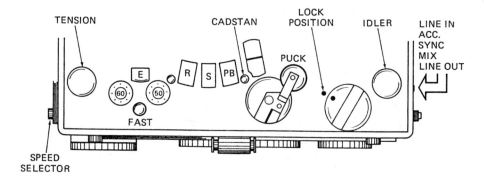

Figure D-9 Nagra III top view.

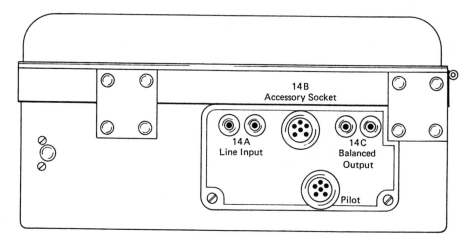

Figure D-10 Side panels, Nagra III.

5. Fast-forward activated by pushing button on panel top while tape is either in *run* or *test* position. In *playback* forward spooling is accomplished.

Nagra III "Short Schnop" Hints

1. When not in use, align dots on PFS to release belt tension.
2. When using batteries, test voltage should not fall below the lower scale limit displayed in *playback/hi fi* position.
3. After threading tape, turn transport control to *on* position pressing the

roller up against the capstan fully. Set *PFS* to *test;* choose level that does not peak over 0 dB.

4. Turn switch to *hi fi record.* Deposit a beep tone reference by depressing button (E). Then slate the take, record while listening to signal supplied from tape after the recording. To monitor signal before it reaches the record head, depress monitor select button on front panel (BA).

5. Rotate the *PFS* to *external* when using the *atn* for AC power.

6. In the *playback* and *meter* position, meter indicates battery voltage and internal speaker is connected, volume is controlled by knob (C).

7. *Hi fi playback* indicates signal level on meter, and this signal is fed to pins on the side.

8. *Sync check*—if a sync signal is being fed or present on the tape, the white geneva cross is up in the view window.

QSEF	Preamplifier for 2 balanced inputs, 80 mV - 8.8 V
QSHZ	Preamplifier for 2 high impedance inputs, 80 MΩ, 10 mV - 2 V
QSNES	Accessory for inserting an external system (e.g. DOLBY, compressor, etc.) in the recording chain
QSQC	Accessory for connecting the direct chains of 2 to 4 recorders in parallel
QSCM	Commentary microphone for the pilot track
QSGX2	Quartz controlled generator for pilot signal
QFMS	Pilot signal frequency metering circuit
QAA	End-of-tape stop device
QSSF	External preamplifier for balanced outputs 1.55 V into 600 Ω
QCA	Start-stop remote control
QSV2	Manual speed varier, ±12% range
SLO	Synchronizer to control playback speed in order to phase lock the speed control signal on the pilot track with internal, external or mains reference frequency, with cathode ray tube display and plug-in SLQ quartz-controlled generator; built-in recorder power supply
QCLS	Adapter for connecting the SLO to the recorder
QSLS	Synchronizer to control playback speed in order to phase lock the speed control signal on the pilot track with an internal or external reference frequency
QSSC	Synchronizer to control with recorded pulses a slide projector
QDAN	Decoder with digital display for the location of recorded sequences and preselection for automatic stop
QRT	VHF transmitter of the radio slating system from camera to recorder, for pilot signal, clapper and take identification signals
QSRR	VHF receiver of the signals transmitted by the QRT
ATN2	Mains power supply 110–250 V with pilot signal output
PAR	Charger with current regulator for rechangeable cells
PPD	Multiple connector for the Power-Pack input
QRAC	Tape cleaning blade
MAG	Electronically controlled demagnetizer
QHT	Standard black leather carrying case
QHTP	Carrying case with pocket
QSET	Cover for 7″ reels

Figure D-11 Modules available for the field Nagra.

9. *Internal faults to check*—mechanical friction, dirty commutator, misalignment of the axis of commutation.

10. *Noise sources* on microphone preamps, record amplifier, external crystal, semiconductor noise-flicker noise, electrostatic discharge, parasitic noise from the motor, magnetic induction, electrical coupling at low frequencies, spindle loss of ground.

> **1.** TAPE/DIRECT, LINE & PHONE: switching of the playback signal or of the direct signal on the line outputs, headphones and loudspeaker; switch inactive on TEST.
>
> **2.** TAPE/DIRECT, METER: switching of the playback signal (TAPE) or of the direct signal (DIRECT) on the circuit of meter 14; this switch cannot be locked on TAPE.
>
> **3.** POWER: power selector switch, i.e. built-in batteries or accumulators (Batt.) or external power supply (External) connected to plug 48.
>
> **4.** Main function selector
>
> | | |
> |---|---|
> | **STOP** = | recorder at a standstill. |
> | **TEST** = | power supplied to all circuits, except record and erase. |
> | **RECORD** = | power supplied to all circuits and the motor; erase on all three tracks and record with limiter. |
> | **RECORD NO LIMITER** = | as RECORD, but without limiter. |
> | **PLAYBACK** = | the recorded signal can be heard on the headphones and is fed to line outputs 43, 45 and 46. If switch 1 is on DIRECT, the signal is reintroduced into the direct chain, passing through potentiometer 6 and 7, mono-stereo switch 11 and filter 13. |
> | **PLAYBACK with Loud-speaker** = | playback of tape as above, but using loudspeaker. |
>
> **5.** LIGHT: meter 14 lights up momentarily; remains illuminated when the button is turned to the right.
>
> **6.** Potentiometer CHANNEL 2 (right), lower track; *graduated in dB* in relation to a 0 dB reference, which corresponds to a sound pressure of $2 \cdot 10^{-4}$ µbar (20 µN/m^2), picked up by a 200 Ω dynamic microphone with 0.2 mV/µbar sensitivity; when the potentiometer has been adjusted to give a modulometer reading of 0 dB the *pointer* of the potentiometer directly indicates the sound pressure. The arrow at 120 dB = 200 µbar shows the level at which the microphone preamplifier begins to be overloaded using the above-mentioned microphone.
>
> **7.** Potentiometer CHANNEL 1 (left), upper track, identical to potentiometer 6. The button is fitted with a lever for coupling the shafts of the two potentiometers 6 and 7 mechanically.

Figure D-12 Stereo Nagra details. (Source: Nagra Magnetics, Inc.)

1. Six-position meter function selector switch:

M = current through the motor

P = groove depth of a record made from recorded signals in accordance with *NAB* standards.

Pilot Frequency: Green needle shows channel with greatest amplitude.
Red needle shows frequency shift.

Level—red = channel one

green = channel two

2. Potentiometers may be coupled, thereby allowing precise duplication of fading and gain control.

3. Filter selector channel 1 and 2:

Flat	linear response curve
Music	high pass filter inserted – 3dB at 40Hz
M = LFA	music and low frequency attenuation
Speech	high-pass speech filter − 3dB at 80Hz gets rid of sibilance.
S = LFA	speech and low frequency attenuation − 7.5dB at 80Hz & − 3dB at 40Hz
Roll-off	− 10dB at 100Hz, − 3dB at 400Hz choice.

4. NRS/Normal Switch: Inserts internal noise reduction system.

5. XLR Connectors: Microphone inputs with phantom powering switch.

INDEX

by Tatiana A. Zaza